CN00685744

LEGITIMACY IN INTE

Legitimacy in International Society

IAN CLARK

OXFORD

UNIVERSITY PRESS

OXFORD

UNIVERSITY PRESS

Great Clarendon Street, Oxford OX2 6DP

Oxford University Press is a department of the University of Oxford.
It furthers the University's objective of excellence in research, scholarship,
and education by publishing worldwide in

Oxford New York

Auckland   Cape Town Dar es Salaam Hong Kong Karachi
Kuala Lumpur Madrid Melbourne Mexico City   Nairobi
New Delhi Shanghai Taipei Toronto
With offices in
Argentina Austria Brazil Chile Czech Republic France Greece
Guatemala Hungary Italy Japan South Korea Poland Portugal
Singapore Switzerland Thailand Turkey Ukraine Vietnam

Oxford is a registered trade mark of Oxford University Press
in the UK and in certain other countries

Published in the United States
by Oxford University Press Inc., New York

ISBN 978-0-19-921919-3

Printed in the United Kingdom by
Lightning Source UK Ltd., Milton Keynes

For Danny, Hamish, Riley, and Lachlan

Preface

I ostensibly started work on this project three years ago. In fact, on re-reading the conclusion of my previous book, *The Post-Cold War Order* (2001), it becomes clear that my engagement with legitimacy had already begun well before this. Additionally, the theme of legitimacy recurs in my even earlier work on globalization, and in particular in *Globalization and International Relations Theory* (1999). I have obviously been working on legitimacy much longer than I had been aware. For that reason, the thanks due undoubtedly extend beyond those mentioned below.

Above all, I must express my deepest gratitude to the Leverhulme Trust. Its award to me of a Major Research Fellowship in 2001 provided the time to undertake the principal researching and writing of this book. It was an enormous privilege to have this extended period for research and, without it, the book would have taken much longer to complete. Thanks are due also to the University of Wales Aberystwyth, and to the Department of International Politics, for releasing me during this period. I was very fortunate to have Dr James Vaughan cover for my teaching, and I now look forward to working with him on a more permanent basis.

During 2003, I was the delighted recipient of a Rockefeller academic residence at its study centre, the Villa Serbelloni at Bellagio. This is a magical place that generates a wonderfully creative atmosphere. I was able to write more in that month than during any comparable period in my life. The time spent there was a highlight of my professional career, and I wish to thank the Foundation, the villa staff, and all fellow residents for this most stimulating experience. During July–October 2003, I was a Visiting Fellow at the Department of International Relations, Australian National University, Canberra. This provided a very congenial platform to try out some of my ideas, as well as giving me the space and excellent resources to continue with my writing. I enjoyed many fruitful exchanges whilst there, and heartily thank the entire Department for hosting me so amiably and constructively. I would like to thank, in particular, Paul Keal, Cindy O'Hagan, Len Seabrooke, Greg Fry, and Shogo Suzuki.

Parts of the argument have been worked out in various seminars. These have included presentations at the University of Queensland (thanks to Marianne Hanson), the Australian National University (thanks to Pauline Kerr), Cambridge University (thanks to Mike Sewell), the London School of Economics (thanks to Mick Cox), ASERI, Milan (thanks to Vittorio Parsi), as well as at Aberystwyth (thanks to Andrew Linklater). Comments and exchanges during these seminars, as always, have proved invaluable.

I owe special debts to many individuals who have directly contributed to this work. Adriana Sinclair and Wolfango Piccoli both served as highly efficient and imaginative researchers. Many people have read drafts of parts of the work, and have provided insightful comments. These include Andrew Linklater, Will Bain, Peter Jackson, Mike Williams, Gerry Hughes, Alex Bellamy, as well as OUP's own readers. The book benefited considerably from their various suggestions. Justin Morris appeared in Aberystwyth at a fortuitous moment, and I am grateful for his numerous comments and recommendations of specific sources that proved helpful.

I wish to single out three individuals for special mention. Nick Wheeler and I enjoyed a writing partnership in the 1980s, and have now been departmental colleagues for several years. Nick is very much exercised by the concerns of this book, and he has generously read extensive drafts of it. The book has profited enormously from his challenging questions, and I am delighted to acknowledge this deep personal and intellectual debt. When Tim Dunne left this Department, he could have been forgiven for thinking that he was leaving behind the chore of honorary commentator on my drafts. Exeter, however, has not proved distant enough, and Tim read an entire draft as one of OUP's readers, but gave additional feedback over and above. I very much appreciate the time and energy he devoted to this task. I enjoyed some very productive exchanges with Chris Reus-Smit while I was in Canberra. This has continued, and Chris has offered weighty comments on my arguments, and forced me to sharpen some conceptual definitions. I am deeply grateful to him.

At OUP, my thanks go to my editors Dominic Byatt and Claire Croft for their encouragement and support throughout this project.

As always, Janice has patiently put up with the distractions imposed by the writing of any book, including in this case some lengthy absences on my part. I once again record my deepest appreciation. Legitimacy is not a matter of passing consequence. It counts for the long term, and speaks across the generations, as the historical perspective of this book will hopefully demonstrate. In that spirit, I wish to dedicate this book to my delightful grandsons, spread across two hemispheres: so close, and yet so far apart.

IC
Aberystwyth

Contents

Introduction

This is a book about legitimacy in international relations, and within the specific setting of what is commonly called an international society. It is not, strictly speaking, a history of the *idea* of international legitimacy, although, to be sure, it draws upon many ideas held on this subject. More precisely, it is a study of the international *practice* of legitimacy. That is to say that its principal concern is how notions of legitimacy have been presented, debated, and applied in the context of particular events in international history, and how such practices might now be evolving in contemporary international society. Its expository device, of necessity, is therefore both historical and theoretical.

There has, in recent years, been much legitimacy talk about international relations. Those participating in it have been official practitioners, as well as diverse publics. This is striking enough in itself. Even more so is the adoption of this language in particular. What is noteworthy is not merely the injection of evaluative statements into the field, but the self-conscious resort to this word, in preference to alternatives. There might just as well be talk of international legality, or morality, or justice—and to some degree this has been present as well. Nonetheless the language of legitimacy has been dominant and recurrent.

Here is some small foretaste of it. Hard on the heels of its military seizure of Kuwait in August 1990, the Iraqi government was reported to have undertaken a diplomatic offensive 'to convince the world of the legitimacy of its move into Kuwait' (*The Times*, 28 August 1990). Shortly thereafter, commentators congratulated the United States for dealing with the ensuing crisis 'within the boundaries of UN legitimacy' (*The Times*, 5 September 1990). As the tragedy unfolded in Yugoslavia, Shlomo Avineri, former director-general of the Israeli Foreign Ministry, pointed to its outcome as a critical test for the UN, and remarked that 'if Bosnia cannot be saved, never again will anyone believe in the efficacy and legitimacy of this organization' (*Jerusalem Post*, 10 August 1992: 6).

The UN became the centre of much of this legitimacy talk during most of the next decade. On the occasion of the first anniversary of the attacks of 11 September 2001, Secretary-General Kofi Annan insisted that, in the war against terrorism, 'it is only the [UN Security] council that can provide the unique legitimacy that one needs to be able to act' (*BBC News*, 11 September 2002). As the crisis over Iraq deepened in early 2003, French President, Jacques Chirac, warned that 'only the Security Council can legitimize the use of force' (*Times of India*, 18 March 2003). Such talk reached its crescendo in the spring of 2003. Annan pressed for a UN role in post-war Iraq. 'Above all the UN involvement does bring legitimacy', he advised, 'which is necessary for the country, for the region and for the peoples around the world' (*The Times*, 8 April 2003). French Foreign Minister, Dominique de Villepin, echoed that sentiment. A UN role in Iraqi reconstruction was a 'question of legitimacy. . . This legitimacy cannot exist outside the United Nations' (*Asahi Shimbun*, 14 April 2003). Malaysian Foreign Minister, Datuk Seri Syed Hamid Albar, opined that 'there had been no legitimacy for the invasion of Iraq, but consequently there should be legitimacy in its reconstruction' (*New Straits Times*, 10 April 2003: 2). Russian Foreign Minister, Igor Ivanov, had earlier warned the United States of its war in Iraq that 'we will not, of course, give legitimacy to this action in the Security Council' (*Moscow Times*, 24 March 2003).

And so it rumbled on. The central importance of legitimacy for the future of world politics has been lent additional support from a perhaps unlikely quarter. Summing up the situation in the aftermath of the Iraq war of 2003, Robert Kagan adjudged that 'the struggle to define and obtain international legitimacy in this new era may prove to be among the critical contests of our time, in some ways as significant in determining the future of the international system and America's place in it as any purely material measure of power and influence' (*New York Times*, 24 January 2004). Legitimacy is much the most favoured word in the practitioner's lexicon, but one that remains widely ignored in the academic discipline of international relations. This book seeks to rectify that imbalance by investigating the nature of legitimacy as an historical international practice, and by inquiring into its status in contemporary international society. It makes the case for legitimacy as a key concept in the study of international relations, and as a distinctive feature of its practice.

WHY LEGITIMACY?

Legitimacy has been fundamental to the conduct of international relations, even if many standard texts make no mention of it whatsoever (e.g. Waltz 1979). The core principles of legitimacy express rudimentary social agreement about who is entitled to participate in international relations, and also about appropriate forms in their conduct. As we shall see shortly, this represents the very essence of what is meant by an international society: *legitimacy thus denotes the existence of international society*. Legitimacy, in this sense, is attached to society as the subject. Separately, the actors within international society are engaged in endless strategies of *legitimation*, in order to present certain activities or actions as *legitimate*. These are then properties attached to the actors and their actions as the predicate. The realm of legitimation draws upon core principles, and also from a discrete set of other international norms. At the point where legitimacy and legitimation overlap is a political terrain— the meeting ground of norms, distributions of power, and the search for consensus—that denotes what will be called *the practices of legitimacy*. We thus have three interacting realms: international society's core principles of legitimacy; its practices of legitimacy; and its actors' strategies of legitimation. The full significance of this scheme for the overall argument will be elaborated in Chapter 1.

The book deals with two sets of practical problems: substantive and procedural. The substantive refers to values and which, or which combinations, are to be privileged at any one moment. Under this heading, from time to time, international society has expressly adhered to the principle that it is itself the ultimate sanction of acceptable change; that it is in its own best interests to maintain a balance of power amongst its members; or that it is charged with responsibility for securing fundamental human rights, and so on. This will be one major theme in the unfolding historical narrative.

The other concerns the procedural dimension. How are these priorities amongst values to be determined, and their clashes reconciled? How are general principles to be applied to particular cases, given the inevitable diversity of interpretation? Here, it will be suggested, the procedural face of legitimacy reveals itself as a quest for *what can reasonably be accepted by international society as a tolerable consensus on which to take action*. What is thought reasonably acceptable, and what amounts to a tolerable consensus, have both undergone continual historical transformation. As we shall see, this issue runs through such key areas as: the format of peace settlements, and who participates within them, especially as regards the defeated enemy; what are the rights and responsibilities of the great powers, relative to those of the small; how are such concerns to be implemented in practice, in such things as voting systems and powers of veto; are these procedural forms designed to work on an assumption of a consensus already in being, or is it their task to create such a consensus where none might otherwise exist?

It will become apparent in the following assessment that this notion of consensus is crucial, but highly problematic. What exactly is the relationship between legitimacy and consensus? For instance, we might start out with the assumption that principles of legitimacy pertain only when a prior value consensus is in existence to support them: this more basic consensus makes possible a sense of legitimacy. Otherwise construed, it could as easily be participation in shared notions of legitimacy that makes consensus possible: legitimacy spawns consensus, not the other way around. Each of these is initially plausible, and the book will need to untangle as best it can what is potentially a very confusing relationship, both conceptually and in practice.

Why do some ideas achieve consensual status? One reason might be that they appear inherently persuasive, and thus states are convinced to subscribe to them. If so, what are the normative foundations on which the appeal to legitimacy is based? As we shall see, apart from its grounding in consensus, the practice of legitimacy draws heavily upon a number of other norms. Foremost amongst these are the norms of legality, morality, and constitutionality. These will be discussed in Chapter 1 and again in Chapter 11, but provide a recurrent set of reference points for the ongoing discussion. Substantially, they contribute also an important content to the unfolding argument. In the development of international society's core legitimacy principles, each of these norms has been more or less influential at various historical junctures. But these norms operate principally in the realm of legitimation, and translate as legitimacy principles only through the filtering process of contested politics. For this important reason, legitimacy is not to be thought of as a norm co-equal with those other three, and with its own substantial content: there is no independent legitimacy scale of values. Instead, legitimacy—to the extent that it is normatively grounded—draws upon the values found under these other three headings. It is, however, separated from them by a dense field of politics, and this makes all the difference to how each is understood, and to their respective degrees of influence at any one moment. Between the principles of legitimacy, on the one hand, and the strategies of legitimation, on the other, is to be found the practice of legitimacy where these norms are interpreted, developed, reconciled, transcribed, and consensually mediated.

The other reason that consensus might emerge has less to do with these normative appeals directly, albeit that they remain always present in the contest for legitimation. It is produced also as part of a process of political calculation and contingency, and as a result of negotiation and diplomatic pressure in which power differentials, material as well as ideational, most certainly matter. If it is the case that dominant conceptions of legitimacy, especially those expressed at the end of great wars, tend to reflect the views of victorious and powerful states, we are compelled to acknowledge the existence of an important relationship between power and legitimacy (Bukovansky 2002). From a critical perspective, it might then be concluded, 'what is true or right is entirely contingent on the play of power and domination' (Dunne 2001: 88). If so, does this make the study of legitimacy any less important, or less interesting?

This book stakes out an important middle position. Legitimacy constrains power, but also enables it; power suffuses legitimacy, but does not empty it of normative content. The book's focus on principles and practices develops the perspective of legitimacy as a contested political process, drawing upon both norms and material power, and thereby captures some key characteristics of international behaviour.

As regards the evolution of the core principles of legitimacy, this study adopts one central categorization. The structure of international society, Donnelly (2002:15) tells us, is a composite of several elements, amongst which he includes 'principles and practices of international legitimacy', as well as a distinct category of 'principles and practices of domestic legitimacy'. This is close to Dunne's rendition in which the structure of international society embodies 'rules for identifying who gets to count as a member', as well as rules about 'what conduct is appropriate' (Dunne 2001: 89). These two faces of legitimacy will be traced as that of rightful membership and that of rightful conduct, respectively.

It makes perfectly good sense to conceive of legitimacy in this dual fashion, and hence as possessing both an inward and an outward dimension. This will emerge in all the historical cases considered in this book. 'Domestic' legitimacy has always contained an essentially international aspect, not least because it gives rise to collective acts of recognition. At the same time, it has frequently been the case that 'international' legitimacy has done much to bolster the 'domestic' legitimacy of individual regimes.

It is the rightful conduct aspect that has been least successfully developed in the existing literature. A number of studies have focused sharply on the evolution of legitimacy with respect to shifts in ideas about legitimate statehood (Reus-Smit 1999; Bobbitt 2002). They have said relatively less about the facet of rightful conduct, and much of the ensuing historical narrative will be devoted to issues that arise under this heading. At core, they revolve around the complex relationship between legitimacy and international consensus.

While, for analytical purposes, the analysis will disentangle the 'rightful membership' side of legitimacy from its 'rightful conduct' counterpart, these are far from wholly separate narrative strands. On the contrary, a major part of the argument concerns the relationship between these two dimensions. Indeed, in terms of historical evolution, one of the most striking trends is precisely the intensification of this relationship. Increasingly, the two faces of legitimacy have come to operate in tandem, such that 'rightful membership' is presented as the key instrument for generating 'rightful conduct'.

WHY INTERNATIONAL SOCIETY?

This book develops its understanding of legitimacy within the particular perspective of international society. It is self-consciously entitled legitimacy *in* international society, and this stipulates both the core of the argument, as well as the boundaries of the discussion. It is not an attempt to probe, from the outside, the justice of the international order, or of any actions to which it gives rise. It is rather an exploration of the principles and practices that, historically, manifest international society's own evolving account of legitimacy. There are basically two reasons for insisting upon this robust association between legitimacy and international society. First, society makes sense of the concept of legitimacy. Second, and more controversially, legitimacy lies at the very heart of what is meant by an international society.

As to the first, it is hardly possible to make any plausible argument about the place of legitimacy in international life without nesting it in a concept of international society, or near equivalent. Only within such a social setting can legitimacy have real resonance, and only on that basis can a historical survey of this kind be adequately mounted. 'Community', it has been roundly affirmed, 'must be present for legitimacy to have content' (Franck 1995: 26). Questions of legitimacy thus arise only in a situation in which 'individuals are sufficiently integrated into a given community, so that they identify with it and are aware of their rights and duties' (Coicaud 2002: 205). Legitimacy, in this sense, and employing Franck's own analogy, is tantamount to acceptance of Greenwich Mean Longitude—a social fact meaningful only to those members of the community who accept it (Franck 1990: 204–5). It is quite beside the point for any non-member to dissent from such a convention. In short, for there to be principles and practices of legitimacy, there needs to be a community/society.

Second, and central to the argument of this book, its core principles of legitimacy *constitute international society*. This is a bold assertion, and will be justified in the remainder of this work. However, by way of brief overview, the essence of the theoretical case can be outlined at this stage. We need a more parsimonious theory of international society than is currently available, and legitimacy provides the key to such a theory. If legitimacy defines both rightful membership and rightful conduct, it specifies the key requirements for international society.

An international society is thought to have existed for several centuries, at least since the sixteenth or seventeenth (Keene 2002: 13). One of the luminaries of this approach had stated categorically that 'international society is, prima facie, a political and social fact' (Wight 1991: 30). Although the terminology varies, this central idea has been constantly appealed to by theorists, as well as practitioners. One famous eighteenth-century analyst of diplomacy typically held that 'all the states of Europe have necessary ties and commerces one with another, which makes them to be looked upon as members of one and the same Commonwealth' (Callières 1983: 68).

This theme has been most extensively developed by English school theorists: it is their 'flagship' idea (Buzan 2004: 1). Foremost amongst them, Bull (1977: 13) famously defined an international society as 'a group of states' which is 'conscious of certain common interests and common values', and which accordingly sees itself as 'bound by a common set of rules', and as sharing in the 'working of common institutions'. The elements of this definition recur, slightly reordered, in a later formulation with Watson. According to this, states have 'established by dialogue and common consent rules and institutions for the conduct of their relations' and, it was added, they also 'recognize their common interest in maintaining these arrangements' (Bull and Watson 1984*b*: 1). This poses an immediate set of questions for this study. In terms of such a conception of international society, what role does legitimacy play? Is it an expression of common values? Is it a common set of rules? Is it a common institution?

Most accounts of international society, following Wight and Bull, ground it in interests, values, rules, and institutions, or in some combination (Armstrong 1993: 12; Reus-Smit 1997; T. Dunne 1998: 188; 2003: 305; Keal 2000: 61). All such formulations remain problematic, and have been questioned (Bellamy 2004; Buzan 2004). Generally, the problem is that analysts of international society have hesitated uncertainly between what *constitutes* international society, and what it is that international society, in turn, *institutes*. It is common-place for English school theorists to designate international society in terms of its own unique institutions, such as the balance of power, war, international law, and the role of the great powers (Bull 1977). However, it is never fully clear what exactly the relationship then is between international society and any one institution in particular.

Given the unsatisfactory nature of existing accounts, it is better to separate values and institutions from our essential conception of international society. This is not to imply their unimportance; it is to assert that such values and institutions have purchase only given a prior commitment to pursue them by social means. Accordingly, instead of as specific values (like sover-eignty) or institutions (like international law), we can think of international society as a set of historically changing principles of legitimacy. These extend beyond international law. They are not necessarily expressed in institu-tions. And they are often too informal to be classed as rules. In their most rudimentary form, they posit an international society as the conditioned acceptance of mutual obligations to which the principles of legitimacy give rise.

The *fact* of the existence of this sense of obligation can be treated separately from its specific normative *source* (Reus-Smit 2003). The principles will, of course, be justified by appeal to particular norms, but these represent political accommodations amongst competing value systems. The location of legitimacy at the core of the international societal project distances it from any specific institution, and separates it from the realization of particular values. Legitimacy is more than the sum of the total of the norms of legality, morality, and constitutionality as recognized at any one moment. For this reason, the argument dissents from the notion that, literally, 'international society is a moral and legal framework' (Jackson 2000: 39). As will be demonstrated, international society is a political framework: its commitment is to a consen-sually mediated application of these norms, and that makes a qualitative difference to our understanding of it. Legitimacy draws substance from such norms, but is distinct from them. These norms operate as evaluative denomin-ators for international acts and performances, understood as objects. In con-trast, legitimacy refers to international society as the subject: it denotes the condition of international society, not the condition of its individual actors and actions.

This formulation privileges a particular conception of the *political* at the heart of international society. If this is accepted, legitimacy does the theoretical work of the complex array of values, rules, and institutions found in existing English school accounts. Core principles of legitimacy offer the possibility of a more parsimonious theory of international society.

WHY INTERNATIONAL HISTORY?

But how are we to trace the practice of legitimacy? What is its empirical evidence? In common with a number of other studies (Holsti 1991; Osiander 1994; Ikenberry 2001; Bobbitt 2002; Lesaffer 2004), the device will be a set of focused analyses of the major international peace settlements of the modern period. In the deliberations of the peacemakers about the terms of the peace, and about the key principles of the future international order, we can glean the best evidence available of how international society has attempted to put legitimacy into practice. This involves reflecting upon the key principles of legitimacy at any one moment, and how these were translated from the politically contested and consensually mediated norms currently available. Who was to be represented in the settlement, and were all participants to count as equals? Was the defeated state to take part, and upon what grounds? Were some states to be assigned special responsibilities and entitlements, and if so why? What were to be the overarching principles of the settlement? In those historical gatherings, we encounter a rich body of evidence as to international society's shifting frameworks of international legitimacy. We discover also how they were acted upon in the specific political conditions of the period.

To be sure, the articulation of core principles of legitimacy is ongoing—not confined to moments of peacemaking alone—but the tendency to reformulate them is highest at those great moments of international reordering (Osiander 1994; Knutsen 1999: 64). These are important conjunctures for the practice of legitimacy for two reasons. On the one hand, at these periods the impetus for general speculation is strongest, and appeal to broad principles most likely. On the other, the spirit of pragmatism is equally prominent when the international order has collapsed, and the imperative is to rebuild consensus, usually in the most inauspicious of circumstances. The historical workings of this process will be recorded, to see the forms this practice of legitimacy has taken, and the degree to which its objectives have been realized.

Indeed, one analyst has kindly supplied us with a score card for legitimacy in these past settlements. According to this table, legitimacy was achieved at Westphalia in 1648, Vienna in 1815, and San Francisco in 1945. It failed to be realized at Utrecht in 1713 and at Paris in 1919 (Holsti 1991: 340). The problematic issue this poses is what to conclude from such verdicts, even if acceptable. If there is an existential relationship between an international society and its principles of legitimacy, what do these failures signify? Do they mean that at those moments, say in 1713–14 and again in 1919, international society actually broke down and ceased to exist? Or do they mean only that international society persisted during those years but was unable, for whatever reasons, to secure a settlement that adequately conformed to its preferred principles?

These are complex matters, and they go the very heart of the argument. On the basis of the distinctions already presented, we can fairly ask historical questions about whether there is sufficient commitment to core legitimacy principles to warrant a judgement that an international society is actually in being. As a separate matter, important questions can be asked also about the degrees of success in legitimizing particular actions, or the international order as a whole. These strategies make appeal both to the core principles, as well as to the other norms from which they derive. The measure of success in these strategies is the extent to which an action or an order is deemed to be legitimate in the eyes of its participants. However, any assessment that an international order was illegitimate—say, after Versailles—certainly does not imply the eclipse of international society at that point. On the contrary, the expression of the judgement in these terms makes sense only on the assumption of its continuation.

As regards the historical aspect of this study, there are four principal evolutionary questions that need to be asked. Each is concerned to trace one historical trajectory in particular:

1. How has the scope of international society—the legitimacy constituency—been conceived, and how inclusive or exclusive has it been at various historical periods?
2. Can we make judgements about the varying degrees to which international society has succeeded in legitimating its actions, and—in that sense alone—have some international orders been more legitimate than others?
3. In what ways has the content of international legitimacy—as regards its 'rightful membership' face—shifted over time?
4. In what ways has the content of international legitimacy—as regards its 'rightful conduct' face—transformed across the period?

Before embarking on this historical account, the book needs first to develop its distinctive approach to legitimacy in greater detail. Why should legitimacy be taken seriously by students of international relations and why, thus far, has it never been regarded as one of the discipline's key concepts? How is legitimacy practised in international relations, and what perspective will this book adopt to gain greater insight into it? These preliminary reflections will assist in validating the broader claim that legitimacy lies at the heart of what is meant by an international society.

1

International Legitimacy

Does the concept of legitimacy apply in the context of the international, and if so, why and how should we study it? This chapter fleshes out the approach to legitimacy deployed throughout the subsequent historical and theoretical investigations. At its core lies the need to vindicate its concentration upon the study of legitimacy *in* international society.

In the discussion of international relations, the idea of legitimacy has not always proved a popular term of reference, and has more often been self-consciously eschewed. Metternich, it is reported, announced that 'I have struck out from my customary diplomatic vocabulary the use of the words *legitimacy* and *divine right*' (de Sauvigny 1962: 36–7). The last generation of international relations scholars appears to have followed his example, with the result that discussion of legitimacy has been 'neglected', 'ignored', 'fallen out of favor', or remains yet 'in its infancy' (Vincent and Wilson 1993: 129; Williams 1996: 40; Barnett 1997: 529; Coicaud 2001a: 260). The reason for this consistent marginalization has not been disciplinary oversight, but rather a positive rejection of a concept widely considered inappropriate to an international setting. If, both in the history of political thought, and in more recent developments within political science, the idea of legitimacy has come to be focused upon 'the right to rule', then it was deemed radically irrelevant to a political sphere characterized by the absence of government (J. Williams 1998: 2). Lurking beneath this formal argument, derived from the supposed anarchy of the international system, was the additional problem that the 'international' appeared to lack a sufficiently highly developed community of values to make any shared sense of legitimacy sustainable. The international system, we are commonly told, displays a marked 'normative indeterminacy' that can support, at best, 'different legitimacies' (Coicaud 2001b: 538). For example, it has been suggested that the embryonic International Criminal Court (ICC) will not enjoy anything more than selective regional support, since the attainment of a genuinely global legitimacy 'could only come from a wider sense of community than exists at the moment' (Brown 2002: 222). Recently, some political theorists have succumbed to their own scepticism, and have recommended that, for the time being at least, the word should be 'put in storage' (Barker 2001: 25).

These are scarcely auspicious opening notes for this study. But there is a less despondent perspective. As noted in the Introduction, there has been a veritable renaissance of international legitimacy talk over the past decade or more. At the same time, the ideational turn within the international relations discipline has made it more receptive: once again, after decades of structural orthodoxy, ideas are thought to matter (Finnemore 1996; Philpott 2001; Gelpi 2003), and the idea of legitimacy possibly more than most. Important instances of state behaviour, such as humanitarian intervention, are now argued to have been encouraged, or restrained, by prevailing codes of legitimacy (Wheeler 2000: 4). Despite the erstwhile neglect, taking legitimacy seriously in international relations now enjoys much greater potential support: it is an idea whose time has come.

This mood is best captured in those recent writings that have turned traditional objections on their head. The supposed anarchy of international society becomes, from this perspective, the very reason for taking international legitimacy seriously, rather than the prima facie case for its neglect. Since a key evidence of legitimacy is thought to be compliance that is not coercive (Hurd 1999), then international society provides the ideal laboratory. As Franck (1988: 710) had argued, 'the operation of the noncoercive element, or specifically, *legitimacy*, becomes easier to isolate and study in the interstate system than in societies of persons, where the coercive sovereign always lurks in the background'. It is this very lack of effective enforcement of international law, as he later amplified, that makes the widespread tendency to comply with it 'so extraordinary and invites an examination of the legitimacy factor' (Franck 1990: 29). This is a judgement shared by writers such as Richard Falk, however otherwise critical his general reading of international relations. 'The role of legitimacy in achieving policy objectives is of particular importance in international society', he avers, exactly because of 'the absence of centralized and important third-party procedures of interpretation and enforcement' (Falk 1999: 87). In this same spirit, the present volume takes the idea of international legitimacy seriously. Why then is legitimacy relevant to the conduct of international relations, and to our reasons for studying it?

WHY LEGITIMACY MATTERS

We can begin by proposing three key justifications for this type of enquiry. First, we should study international legitimacy because this offers a fundamentally important way of presenting an account of international history. Second, we need to concern ourselves with legitimacy because this emphasizes the role of norms within international society, and this is what, it is claimed, both shapes and constrains actual state conduct. Third, the degree of legitimacy present in any particular international order, so a profusion of scholars tells us, is directly related to the stability of that order. We have, therefore, a compelling practical interest in analysing the nature of that legitimacy, and the conditions which appear to give rise to it.

Legitimacy as International History

> Principles of legitimacy are born, grow up, age, and die; sometimes they come into collision and clash. Their life cycles and their clashes are the invisible foundations of history. (Ferrero 1942: 49)

This first perspective proceeds from the contention that principles of legitimacy evolve historically: they are not fixed. This claim is scarcely controversial, and there is an abundance of evidence to support it at the international level. Much of it will be presented in the course of this book. Typically, the literature is in broad agreement that principles of legitimacy are 'not static' (Hall 1999: 41); instead, 'fashions in legitimization change from time to time' (Claude 1966: 369), and it 'means different things at different times' (J. Williams 1998: 2–3). Accordingly, legitimacy should not be approached as a set of absolute principles, standing apart from time and place, but should be understood simply as 'the norms of a specific cultural system at any given time' (Bukovansky 2002: 24).

From this agreement about the evolving nature of the principles of legitimacy, one important conclusion for the study of international relations can be drawn. It is that a survey of the changing content of legitimacy provides one key insight into the critical stages in the evolution of international society itself: it offers the foundations upon which such a history may be developed. In such a vein, it has been declared by one writer that 'I define systemic change as a transformation of the parameters of political legitimacy' (Bukovansky 2002: 50). The full import of this suggestion deserves extended reflection. It means no less than that the major (if rare) international systemic shifts actually take place around the axis of prevailing legitimacy principles. If such is the case, we can trace those shifts by close scrutiny of the successive layers of legitimacy that have been deposited over time. In short, legitimacy provides the key evidence about the important historical shifts that have actually taken place. If the concept can play such a potentially central role in our historical understanding, its relative neglect and marginalization in the discipline to date becomes that much more puzzling.

Bukovansky (2002: 39–40) defines hegemonic wars—as against the realist conception typified, for instance, in Gilpin (1981)—as ones involving a 'legitimacy contest'. This again vindicates the major historical device to be employed in this book, namely that of concentrating upon the peace settlements at the end of major, and possibly hegemonic, wars. What happens at the end of these wars is that the settlements devise 'new sets of principles, procedures, or territorial distributions' (Holsti 1991: 21–2) for post-war relations and, in that sense, might be thought to issue in a *new constitution for the states system* (Randle 1973: 317). At the same time, those settlements remain unavoidably political devices, and it is within this realm that the peacemakers must operate. As Vattel

(1916: 350) once pointed out to his readers, 'a treaty of peace can be nothing more than a compromise', and is not attainable by application of 'principles of strict and rigorous justice'. If so, it is also the essentially political nature of the practice of legitimacy that is the source of much of its historical interest: the way in which general principles are applied to particular cases tells us much about legitimacy as an actual practice, not simply as an abstract idea.

Legitimacy and State Conduct

State interests are defined in the context of internationally held norms and understandings about what is good and appropriate . . . The normative context also changes over time, and as internationally held norms and values change, they create coordinated shifts in state interests and behavior across the system. (Finnemore 1996: 2–3)

This study of legitimacy is, secondly, situated more broadly within one of the most prominent of recent debates within international relations. It is concerned with the sources of state conduct: are these to be understood as essentially material or structural, on the one hand, or as ideational, and socially constructed, on the other? While a historical survey of various legitimacy formations might hold its own interest, it would stand at one remove from 'real' international life unless it could be persuasively demonstrated also that these changing ideas do affect behaviour. international relations theory has, by now, been engaged in an extended discussion of this very issue for a number of years.

This is the *general* context of the discussion. It cannot here be reviewed in any great detail. There are four stages in the argument that have a bearing upon legitimacy. The first is to assert that those accounts of international relations that dwell exclusively upon material and material–structural influences are unbalanced (Reus-Smit 2002: 121). This is not necessarily to dismiss structural approaches as such, but to insist that ideational factors need to be imported into the relevant structure (Ruggie 1998: 33). Indeed, it has been famously asserted that 'constructivists are structuralists' (Wendt 1995: 72–3), in a more deep-seated way than are neorealists. That this is so reveals the second claim, namely that ideational structure shapes not rational calculations alone, but the very identities and preferences that underlie them (Wendt 1999; Jervis 2002: 174). That is why some express the wish to reinstate legitimacy within the structural principle of anarchy, in order to 'capture this missing dimension of legitimacy standards', which tends otherwise to get left out of neorealist accounts (Nau 2002: 180). It is because of this impact upon identity and preferences that ideas have the capacity, thirdly, to modify behaviour. Shifts in norms socialize states to want different things, and to behave differently in order to attain them (Finnemore 1996: 23; Gelpi 2003). They enable states to change their own rules of interstate conduct. Ruggie (1998: 25) cites as examples the end of colonialism, and of the slave trade, where normative drift has resulted in a new 'collective intentionality' that, in turn 'can "will" the rules of the game to change'. Fourthly, however, whilst international relations theory has indeed taken some ideas seriously, it has tended to become fixated by a few, and particularly by that of sovereignty. Since that idea has been broadly in place since the seventeenth century, it does not seem sufficiently robust to account for all the behavioural variation that has been demonstrated across the period since (Reus-Smit 2002: 135). In any case, ideas about sovereignty depend upon more fundamental norms, and legitimacy should be considered in this way. This, in a nutshell, is why legitimacy matters, and how it can contribute to this ongoing theoretical debate.

There is also a more *specific* context to the consideration of state conduct, and this has been provided by policy developments from the 1990s onwards. The most interesting instances have been those of humanitarian intervention, and other cognate operations performed by various 'coalitions of the willing'. What has been the underlying condition that has given rise to this development? Was it merely that the West after the cold war found itself liberated by its now unconstrained (material) power, and hence able to impose its will on others as it saw fit? Or was it rather (or in addition), that its conduct was increasingly shaped by emerging ideas and new norms? Accordingly, some analysts became interested in how far the norms of international society had shifted to permit humanitarian interventions (Wheeler 2000: 6). Such actions, so it could be argued, became possible only in so far as the normative context had changed to permit them. As a case in point, it has been said that 'it may not be too fanciful to see the Kosovo coalition as the agent of a new conception of international society based on a substantive understanding of the requirements of humanitarianism' (Brown 2001: 97). This does not necessarily mean that humanitarian action had somehow become 'right', in any absolute sense, but that it was increasingly possible to act on such principles because 'some international actors have become convinced of their rightness and validity' (Murphy 2000: 797). What proves to be legitimate at any time offers us an insight into historical evolution, but, just as importantly, it provides an essential explanation of state conduct.

Legitimacy and Stability

When legitimacy standards converge, all other things being equal, the level of threat among states is reduced. States, despite power disparities, may be able to establish a legitimate international order comparable, though not identical, to legitimate domestic order. (Nau 2002: 180)

A third reason for taking legitimacy seriously is the equally practical concern with a possible connection between international legitimacy and the greater international stability that results from it. It has long been suggested by political theorists (not to mention practitioners) that a legitimate system of rule is more efficient (certainly less costly) than one reliant on coercion alone. Additionally, it has frequently been pointed out that such systems of rule, by their very nature, are more stable (less prone to conflict about the fundamentals of the system). This was certainly the view held by Max Weber, one of the earliest and most influential theorists of legitimacy. In his ranking of the stability of various types of social system, he thought one based on expediency to be weaker than one based on custom. In turn, however, he judged the latter to be less stable than 'an order which enjoys the prestige of being considered binding, or, as it may be expressed of "legitimacy" ' (Weber 1968a: vol. II, 31). Contemporary writers tend to follow this logic in ascribing enhanced stability to 'a legitimate system of power' (Beetham 1991: 33). The central theme is that such stability derives from an order that is not coercive (Barnett 1997: 548; Reus-Smit 1999: 93), and a legitimate order is to be contrasted with one that is coercive precisely on account of the stability that it displays as a result.

The essentials of this argument, while usually applied to a single political system or regime, have since been steadily imported into international relations. The prime exponent of this transposition was Henry Kissinger in his elaboration of the nature of the post-Napoleonic settlement. 'Stability', he famously pronounced, 'has commonly resulted not from a quest for peace but from a generally accepted legitimacy' (Kissinger 1977: 1). What did he mean by this? His core definition followed: 'An order whose structure is accepted by all major powers is "legitimate" ' (1977: 145). The emphasis here is upon the existence of consensus, inasmuch as an order needs to be acceptable to all the great powers (but to them alone). The order 'must not seem oppressive or unacceptable to any major actor' because, if it does, that actor will pursue a 'revolutionary' course instead (Hoffmann 1978: 37–8). In this version, legitimacy pertains to the diplomatic conventions devised by the great powers, and is present whenever these are deemed acceptable to all concerned. It is the absence of such agreement that creates tension and instability in the system *because*, as this argument would have it, the order is then illegitimate. This is explicitly set out in Kissinger's suggestion that, after 1815, 'the period of stability which ensued was the best proof that a "legitimate" order had been constructed, an order accepted by all the major powers' (Kissinger 1977: 5).

Kissinger's was not, however, an isolated voice. Although his contribution was to be less sustained, Raymond Aron (1966) drew attention to the same underlying relationship in his classic contribution to international relations. He did so in the context of distinguishing between what he called homogeneous and heterogeneous systems (Sadeniemi 1995: 109). Aron's general argument was that state behaviour is not a function of power alone, but reflects also 'ideas and emotions'. The distinction he then drew was as follows:

I call homogeneous systems those in which the states belong to the same type, obeying the same conception of policy. I call heterogeneous, on the other hand, those systems in which the states are organized according to different principles and appeal to contradictory values. (Aron 1966: 99–100)

For Aron, the European state system had remained essentially homogeneous until the First World War, but this quality was lost with the Russian Revolution of 1917, and issued thereafter in what he called a 'heterogeneity of the principle of legitimacy' (Aron 1966: 102–3). Tellingly for the present discussion, he concluded that 'homogeneous systems afford, on first analysis, greater stability' (1966: 99–100). Once again, the link between legitimacy and stability is explicitly made. The principal difference between them is that, for Kissinger, legitimacy is a matter of policy consensus amongst the leaders of the great powers, whereas for Aron it depends upon a more deep-seated commonality of cultural and value systems. It is clear also that, for Aron, legitimacy concerned the principles on which the states were themselves organized, more so than it did their behaviour towards each other. This is exactly the reverse of the point that Kissinger was making about the post-1815 period.

More recently, claims about stability are to be found in the writings of a number of international historians and political scientists. Paul Schroeder has followed Kissinger in his attribution of the more stable era after 1815 to the emergence of a style of international relations in which there was 'acceptance of mutual rules and restraints, common responsibility to certain standards of conduct' (Schroeder 1994: 802). Osiander, likewise, has argued that stability is not a matter of material equilibrium (balance of power), but rather of 'the degree of congruence of the principal assumptions on which the system is founded', and in particular of 'adherence to a consensus agenda' (Osiander 1994: 5, 10). Holsti (1991: 337–9) included legitimacy in his list of factors that potentially contributed to a stable order, and Watson (1992: 315), in his study of the evolution of international society, concludes that legitimacy is 'one of the factors determining the stability of a system at a given time'. Altogether, this forms a weighty body of opinion, suggesting that international relations should take legitimacy seriously because this is where the key to stability is to be found.

Each of these arguments makes a strong claim on behalf of the centrality of legitimacy. If these are conceded, it is then necessary to look more closely at its nature. What is it, and how should we study it? We can begin with some reflections on the concept, before moving on to a discussion of what this means for legitimacy as an actual historical practice.

LEGITIMACY IN THEORY

No attempt need be made to provide a comprehensive intellectual history of the term. Authoritative discussions tell us that, in the Roman form, *legitimus* meant simply 'lawful, according to law', whereas by the medieval period this had transmuted into 'what conforms to ancient custom and to customary procedure' (Sternberg 1968: 245). As a matter of explicit political theorizing, it is equally asserted that the concept came into common usage only after the French revolution. It had not been a part of earlier Enlightenment discourse (Kitromilides 1986: 60–1). This post-1789 usage, as we shall see, was to be distinctive.

The towering figure in the modern social theory of legitimacy was, of course, Weber, and it is fair to say that ever since theorists have found themselves unable to live comfortably either with, or wholly without, this concept. It is commonplace to distinguish between the so-called normative theories of legitimacy (those that set out general criteria in terms of which the right to rule can be appraised), and the so-called empirical theories (which instead take as their focus the belief systems of those subject to government) (Habermas 1976; Connolly 1984*b*; Barker 1990: 47; Sadeniemi 1995: 8; Beetham and Lord 1998: 1; Applbaum 2000: 324–5). This follows from Weber's discussion. He had described a form of social action that 'may be oriented by the actors to a *belief* in the existence of a "legitimate order" ' (Weber 1968*b*: 11). Elsewhere, he based the prestige of modern states on 'the belief, held by their members, in a specific consecration: the "legitimacy" of that social action which is ordered and regulated by them' (Weber 1968*a*: vol. I, 903–4). In his version, rule is legitimate when its subjects believe it to be so (Grafstein 1981: 456). This Weberian approach leaves to political philosophy the task of developing exogenous schemes for adjudging the legitimacy of any political system, and concentrates instead on the quality of the endogenous political relationship itself. The test for political legitimacy is then taken to be 'not the truth of the philosopher, but the belief of the people' (Schabert 1986: 102).

A second recurrent analytical classification that pervades the legitimacy literature is between procedural and substantive conceptions of legitimacy (Applbaum 2000: 326). Typically, legitimacy is thought to be intrinsically bound up with adherence to established rules. In turn, these rules may be deemed appropriate either because they emanate from a 'rightful source of authority' (procedural), or because they embody 'proper ends and standards' (substantive) (Beetham and Lord 1998: 3). This central distinction has been elaborated as between

a legitimacy of formal rationality (legal rational norms and authority) in which laws and authority are accepted because of the formal legality attached to them . . . and a legitimacy of substantive rationality (absolute value norms and value rational authority) in which laws and authority are accepted because of their congruence with fundamental extra-legal values. (Spencer 1970: 133)

In terms of this particular distinction, Franck—at least in his earlier work—is a good example of a 'procedural' legitimacy theorist in the context of international relations. It is central to his understanding that fairness has two elements, namely legitimacy and distributive justice. He depicts legitimacy as being 'primarily procedural', in contrast to distributive justice which is 'primarily moral' (Franck 1995: 7–9). He explicitly adopts some key elements of the Weberian position. In his widely cited definition of international legitimacy, Franck maintained that it has two principal components. First, legitimacy is to be understood as '*a property of a rule or rule-making institution which itself exerts a pull towards compliance on those addressed normatively*' (Franck

1990: 16). Note that it is not any kind of compliance that counts, but normative compliance, rather than any based on coercion or self-interest. However, he then adds a second dimension to this definition: '*the perception of those addressed by a rule or a rule-making institution that the rule or institution has come into being and operates in accordance with generally accepted principles of right process*' (Franck 1990: 19). The pertinent fact here is the perception of those addressed, rather than some immanent reality. It brings out also that the pull to compliance is essentially procedural, rather than substantive.

The best way to bring this procedural/substantive distinction into the present analysis is to juxtapose legitimacy to some other cognate concepts. The discussion so far derives legitimacy, either from the formal idea of rule or law rationality (legality), on the one hand, or from substantial value rationality (morality/justice), on the other. As will become apparent, the public international discourse about legitimacy has traditionally drawn freely upon both these elements—legality and morality. But is it distinct from them? Is legitimacy no more than a conflation of these two ideas (and if so in what proportions), or does it have a meaning separate from them? Crucially, where does legitimacy stand if legality and morality pull apart?

In addition to those constraints of legality and morality, state conduct is often measured against notions of constitutionality. These arise where there are expectations created about forms of political conduct, often within political institutions that are more or less 'sticky'. Critically, in this case, the norm is based—not upon legal nor moral notions—but upon a sense of what is politically appropriate, rooted in expectations rather than in rules. This is the essence of Ikenberry's (2001) notion of a 'constitutional' order, as one that constrains what can be done by both strong and weak alike. Even if these institutions have their origins in the exercise of power by the strong, the paradox is that they remain 'constitutional' even for those leading powers that politically crafted them in the first place. In that sense, we can include a third normative concept—that of constitutionality—in our discussion of legitimacy. This idea will be further elaborated in Chapter 11. Precisely how legitimacy relates to those other norms will be explored in the next section.

LEGITIMACY AND INTERNATIONAL SOCIETY

This section clarifies three critical sets of relationships: between legitimacy and those other international norms; between legitimacy and power; and between legitimacy and international society. Each forms an interlocking stage in the argument overall.

First, what role do other norms play in the shaping of legitimacy? Three cognate concepts—legality, morality, and constitutionality—mark out the terrain within which the practice of legitimacy tends to take place. While these norms appear fixed at any one moment, one effect of legitimacy talk is to move them over time. Normatively, legitimacy can most helpfully be thought of as that political space marked out by the boundaries of legality, morality, and constitutionality. At any one point in time, it is constrained by prevailing conceptions drawn from these three areas. However, since these often 'pull' normatively in incompatible directions, there needs to be an accommodation struck amongst them. The practice of legitimacy describes this process, as the actors reach for a tolerable consensus on how these various norms are to be reconciled and applied in any particular case. However, this sphere of legitimacy is not a wholly passive one, determined by unchanging 'ideational structures'. Over time, this practice helps to reconfigure the legal, moral, and constitutional landscape. The practice of legitimacy, in this way, describes the process of normative shift in international relations. It is helpful to think of it as the political brokerage that leads to this normative adjustment. We can then agree with Claude's verdict that 'the process of legitimization is ultimately a political phenomenon, a crystallization of judgement that may be influenced but is unlikely to be wholly determined by legal norms and moral principles' (Claude 1966: 369). Legitimacy is no absolute standard, however much appeal might be made to putative absolute standards in the quest to reach agreement about it.

Second, legitimacy cannot be divorced from power. Legitimacy constrains power, while also being an important element of it. Power also impacts upon the practice of legitimacy, and contributes to the substance of the principles of legitimacy that come to be accepted. It is, in any case, only within the context of power relations that legitimacy becomes relevant at all. Accordingly, a decision to ignore legitimacy is not an option for the student of political behaviour, internationally as elsewhere. It has, for instance, been asserted that, to realists, 'legitimacy has no place in the study of world politics' (Gelpi 2003: 12). This suggestion is very wide of the mark as far as any number of realists— Morgenthau, Kissinger, and Aron, for example—are concerned: realists are as likely to take legitimacy seriously as anyone else. However, the precise conceptualization of this relationship is extremely difficult, and the spectrum of opinion ranges from some absolute opposition between power and legitimacy at the one end (whereby the generation of legitimacy is autonomous from the power relations that it 'legitimizes'), to the opposite end where legitimacy is reduced to the preferences of those hegemonic forces that are thought to manufacture it in the first place. As stated, this study is located in the middle, assuming a degree of autonomy for both material power and norms. These interact in the practice of legitimacy.

Beetham takes us to the heart of this general issue. 'It is because it does not recognize any causal influence at all between power and the process of its legitimation', he insists, 'that the so-called "consensus" model of society falls down'. Its deficiency is its mistaken assumption that consensus 'is somehow established and maintained by processes that are completely independent of the existing relations of power within the society' (Beetham 1991: 104). This describes the problem in a nutshell. We imagine that the whole point of legitimacy is to ratify, and thereby restrain, power relations. At the same time, we are asked to accept that this ratification exists, not apart from, but actually arising out of, those same power relations. What sense can we make of legitimacy as poacher and gamekeeper? It is effectively both, and that is the reason to take it seriously, not the justification for its neglect. This ambivalence is characteristic of the practice of legitimacy, operating in the indeterminate terrain between society's avowed principles, and its actors needs to attach them to its specific performances.

Finally, then, we must return to this relationship between legitimacy and international society, briefly sketched in the Introduction. As noted there, current usage on the nature of international society remains confusing and inconsistent. It is also unwieldy. This is so with regard to both institutions and values: which institutions, and which values, make international society what it is?

Granted that international society develops its own institutions, does this mean that international society *is* no more than their sum (Brown 1998; Charvet 1998)? Or are some institutions more fundamental to its existence? We are told that a number of theorists (Holsti, James, and Jackson) regard sovereignty as its most basic institution, whereas others (Mayall, Kratochwil, and Nardin) consider this to be international law (Buzan 2004: 175). By extension, are rules central to international society, or should they be regarded simply as a subset of its institutions, broadly comparable with international law? Buzan highlights this central problem for the English school in his discussion of the so-called *primary* institutions (Buzan 2004: 167*ff*, 184). This idea acknowledges the similarity with other cognate conceptions, such as constitutional structure in Reus-Smit (1999), as also with the distinction between regulative and constitutive rules in Ruggie (1998). All share the implication that primary, constitutional, or constitutive rules (or institutions) make international society what it is in some fundamental way. However, Buzan's own list of primary institutions runs to eight (Buzan 2004: table 2, 184). This may be appropriate for describing international society at any point, but is overly cumbersome for any essentialist definition: since the institutions of international society are evidently changeable (Buzan 2004: 169), one wonders why there is a need to identify international society per se with any one institution in particular. Instead, we should identify a more fundamental property of which these institutions are an expression. What this is will be returned to shortly.

In any case, it is seldom clear in English school discussions what role institutions play. For example, both in Bull and in Wight, the great powers collectively are described as one important institution of international society. Yet elsewhere, Wight makes a different claim. According to proponents of realist thought, the great powers—far from being just one institution amongst several—'constitute what international society there is' (Wight 1991: 32). Without a recognized and leading role on the part of the great powers, it follows that there could be no international society. How are these two positions to be reconciled?

This ambivalence is starkest in the case of international law, yet another of international society's purported institutions. John Westlake had gone beyond any such claim: 'When we assert that there is such a thing as international law, we assert that there is a society of states: when we recognize that there is a society of states, we recognize that there is international law' (quoted in Koskenniemi 2002: 49). This sets out what was to become the legal positivist assertion that 'international society is not merely regulated by international law but *constituted* by it' (Nardin 1998: 20; Arend 1999). 'Defenders of international society', acknowledges Tim Dunne (2003: 314), 'argue that the existence of international legal rules is the best indicator of the presence of society'. But why should this be so? Wight had already retorted to the legal positivists that theirs 'is pretty little of a society', as they did not even manage to explain 'in what sense international law is binding at all' (Wight 1991: 36). For these reasons, we are well advised to dismiss international law's claim to being the 'definitive foundation of international society' (Reus-Smit 2004*d*: 276).

This general ambivalence within the international-society perspective applies specifically to the notion of legitimacy as well, where the confusion is best captured in its treatment by Watson. In one essay, Watson (1984: 24–5) had specified the four institutions of international society as the balance of power, international law, the practice of congresses, and diplomatic dialogue. There was no mention of legitimacy in this scheme. However, by the time of his subsequent book on international society, Watson's framework had undergone change. We find there that, by the eighteenth century, international society embraced four institutions: international law, legitimacy, diplomatic dialogue, and use of force (limited war) (Watson 1992: 202–8). His elaboration suggests that the institution of legitimacy emerged around the Peace of Utrecht in the early eighteenth century since when 'legitimation by the international society of sovereigns was now required' (Watson 1992: 204).

Elsewhere, Watson appears to give a substantially different account in his remarks upon developments during the seventeenth century, and in particular at Westphalia in 1648. According to this interpretation, various international trends during the Thirty Years War came to be formalized as rules at Westphalia and, in turn, 'were then developed by *ad hoc* practice into the *constituent legitimacy of the European society of states*' (Watson 1992: 195). This is a much more ambitious claim. Its historical basis will be examined later (Chapter 3), but its theoretical import needs to be confronted immediately. The suggestion here is evidently that the emergence of a practice of legitimacy at this historical conjuncture was, in some basic sense, constitutive of European international society itself. But how could it be that, at one and the same time, legitimacy both constituted international society in 1648, and was subsequently introduced as one of its institutions in 1713? Can legitimacy be constitutive of international society, and also one institution within it?

Equally problematic has been the topic of values. If international society is defined as its shared values, this gives rise to a debate about what these are. In turn, this leads directly to the traditional bifurcation between pluralist and solidarist accounts (Wheeler 1992; Wheeler and Dunne 1996; Mapel and Nardin 1998; Buzan 2004: ch. 5). Elsewhere, the similar distinction is drawn between the so-called practical and purposive societies (Nardin 1993; Keal 2000: 69; Brown 2001: 92). These differ on the degree to which values are actually shared and whether, on that basis, international society can pursue agreed substantial 'purposes', beyond the rudimentary tasks of peaceful coexistence. If we are so uncertain about the nature of the shared values, this may erode confidence in the concept itself: instead of making the case for the existence of international society more secure, the appeal to shared values often appears to weaken it further (Alderson and Hurrell 2000*b*: 6; Bellamy 2004).

The alternative position urged here is that international society is essentially neither pluralist nor solidarist: it is essentially legitimist (cf. T. Dunne 2001). Legitimacy, as international principle and practice, can comfortably straddle divisions between pluralists and solidarists, as well as those between practical and purposeful conceptions of international society. As a procedural device for establishing some form of consensus, it is broadly in line with the pluralist/ practical perspective. Equally, however, in dealing with issues of rightful membership, it has frequently pursued a substantive agenda; at these moments, it encompasses the solidarist/purposeful conception. International society potentially embraces both systems of values. If we think of legitimacy as consensually mediated, instead of as a set of values as such, the problems caused by these normative divisions begin to disappear. They can instead be regarded, as Buzan would wish, as forming a spectrum, rather than as existing in fundamental contradiction (Buzan 2004: 49).

Accordingly, the different approach recommended here is to detach international society from any one institution, or from any one set of values, in particular. To accomplish this, we then need to anchor international society in some other property. This is where the concept of legitimacy is so central. When the English school discussions of international society are examined closely, what emerges—despite the prominence of institutions and values in the foreground—is the more important emphasis actually placed upon something else in the background. In Bull's discussion of common interests, values, rules, and institutions, his recurring subtext is the sense of being *bound* (Bull 1977: 13). Similarly, Wight (1991: 7) had written of a concept of international society, as one imposing 'certain moral and psychological and possibly even legal ... obligations'. It is, in fact, this notion of obligation that lies at the heart of international society (Armstrong 1993: 12; Dunne 1998: 98–9; Wheeler 2000: 24–5). Accordingly, this is as much as is needed to vindicate the concept: where there is a *belief* in being bound, there is an international society. The belief, in turn, is revealed in the practices that follow from it. Moreover, we can appropriately distinguish between the historical fact of the existence of such belief, and the various possible sources giving rise to it.

In sum, to describe the social bond as a sense of obligation—a recognition of being bound—is another way of referring to the presence of core principles of legitimacy. These reveal the existence of a bond, regardless of the specific reason for it. This is the essentialist—albeit minimalist—notion of international society. Core principles of legitimacy articulate a willingness to be bound, both to certain conceptions of rightful membership of society, and to certain conceptions of rightful conduct within it. This is what defines international society, rather than its expression in any specific institutions or values—all of which are historically variable. The point can be otherwise made by reference to first-order and second-order rules of international society. The former specify what is necessary for an international society to exist at all, and the latter what that society will thereafter permit. Legitimacy needs to be understood as a first-order category, and should be distinguished from the norms that apply directly to its second-order activities. When specific actions, classes of activity, or constellations of order as a whole are presented for legitimation, they succumb to international society's political practice where norms must confront other political imperatives. The continued existence of international society is not dependent upon the successful *claim* to legitimacy, on the part of any one particular institution or norm.

This entails a refinement of Wheeler's position. He held that 'states form a society of states constituted by rules of sovereignty, non-intervention, and non-use of force', and, accordingly, his subject of investigation was how far states '*have recognized humanitarian intervention as a legitimate exception to the rules*' (Wheeler 2000: 2, 6). By tying international society to practices of sovereignty and non-intervention, he starts at the wrong place. Once international society is claimed to be existentially linked to specific norms (sovereignty, etc.), then there is indeed little room for argument, except by the route of the 'legitimate exception'. The problem is that if humanitarian intervention successfully registered its claim to be considered legitimate, it would no longer be an *exception*, as the practice would have already changed. Instead, we should acknowledge that international society is constituted by its changing principles of legitimacy (first-order), which express its commitment to be bound: we can then trace its evolving (second-order) rules, revealed in its practices with regard to sovereignty, non-intervention, and non-use of force. Only in this way, as will be seen later, can the historical argument be made that behaviour at Westphalia reflected a belief in an international society, even if it expressed no clear principle of sovereignty.

Why does such a conceptual reorientation matter so much? It does so critically for a number of related reasons. First, it anchors legitimacy in international society, and makes principles of legitimacy the necessary attribute of it: when we study legitimacy, we are studying the behaviour of that society. Its principles of legitimacy express an obligation: this is to the project of a viable international society, rather to any one norm in particular. Second, this allows us to distinguish between what is necessary for international society to exist, and what its practices subsequently permit. This additional concentration on the practice of legitimacy emphasizes its political dimension, rather than any straightforward application of specific norms. Although appeal is indeed made to individual norms, their application is politically contested and consensually mediated. Third, this matters because, while taking norms seriously, it acknowledges also the play of political power in all its many guises. By locating the practice of legitimacy in social behaviour, and emphasizing its political aspect, we open the door to a sensible engagement between norms and power. This is, after all, the meaningful distinction between a normative and an empirical theory of legitimacy. By concentrating upon the practice of legitimacy, we are led to recognize the full array of forces that condition states of belief and temper the possibilities for consensus. This assuredly does not rule power out, but it rules more than this in. Finally, this approach permits us to distinguish between legitimacy as a property of international society, and the condition of being legitimate as a property of any of its actions. The former is qualitative, and exists or not; the latter is quantitative, and is a matter of degree. The distinction is sharp, but much of the historical practice of legitimacy has served to blur it.

LEGITIMACY AS PRACTICE

Accordingly, the practice of legitimacy is located in a complex field of forces. It is contingent upon conceptions of consensus that have themselves displayed considerable historical variation. It is adjacent to—but not the same as—such other international norms as those of legality, morality, and constitutionality. This whole mixture is influenced, but not crudely determined, by deployments of power and its distribution. These themes will be prominent throughout the historical survey in Part I, and form the explicit organizational structure for the analysis of contemporary international society in Part II.

So how has international society practised legitimacy? At this point, we must return to the essential *duality* inherent in international society's conception of legitimacy. Historically, this has revealed a simultaneous regard for an 'inward-looking' notion of legitimacy—as a specification of the credentials for membership of international society—and also an 'outward-looking' set of ideas—about how the members of international society should conduct themselves in relation to each other. The core principles of international society have already been identified as those of rightful membership, and rightful conduct, and this duality is widely recognized in the literature (T. Dunne 2003: 310; Buzan 2004: 167). They need now to be considered in greater detail. They will henceforward be discussed, however, not as abstract principles, but as practices of legitimacy, denoting the ground where norms have confronted the political domain, with all the accommodations, reconciliations, and imposition that this might imply.

Rightful Membership

The prime exponent of this first position was Wight. 'By international legitimacy', he wrote in a famous essay, 'I mean the collective judgment of international society about rightful membership of the family of nations' (Wight 1977: 153). Similarly, Philpott draws attention to the interplay between legitimacy, membership, and the constitution of international society when he remarks that 'international constitutions prescribe the legitimate polities of an international society. A legitimate polity is simply one that the members of a society recognize as properly participating in the society' (Philpott 2001: 15). When theorists have drawn attention to the historically dynamic character of legitimacy, it is most often in this sense that the evolution is traced. Thus we have been presented in the literature with a rich array of schemes, each mapping the evolution of the legitimacy principle from various territorial and dynastic forms, through national and popular states, towards liberal constitutional forms, and eventually into welfare, trading, virtual, and other global types (Hall 1999; Reus-Smit 1999; Shaw 2000; Philpott 2001; Bobbitt 2002; Bukovansky 2002; Rosecrance 2002). The 'distinct fashions' (Moulakis 1986*b*: 4–5) of legitimacy are starkly recorded in this evolutionary story.

It is, of course, misleading to regard these 'domestic' principles of legitimacy as purely internal. Issues about membership finally come down to questions about 'who has a right to have rights?' (Coicaud 2002: 234), and this is a decision on which the society acts collectively. While, to be sure, it expresses itself as a (changing) set of principles about the desirable character of statehood, it counts also as a statement about international legitimacy. The latter dimension is brought out graphically by its appeal to *recognition* by international society (Wight 1977: 158). The principle may stipulate the elements of domestic constitutional organization, but the recognition of that as an entitlement to membership is an international practice of the society of states. As Wight had made clear about the idea of sovereignty in particular, it is not something that each state simply claimed for itself, but something that it logically had to bestow upon the others as well. This 'reciprocity' was inherent in the concept, and as such was also revealing of the very nature of international society (Wight 1977: 135; Dunne 2001: 75). The same is the case with rightful membership.

How, more specifically, are we to understand the nature of these acts of recognition? There is a widespread view that, given its pluralist basis, international society's policy of recognition is a purely formal one. Any state possessing the minimum attributes of statehood is acceptable for membership, and these come down to 'clear evidence of the existence of territorial sovereignty' (Armstrong 1993: 36). Thus Mayall (2000: 62–3) suggests that international society 'precluded making the internal political arrangements of states a legitimate concern of their neighbours'.

This claim is dubious at best. In international legal theory, it raises complex issues about whether recognition should be seen as merely declaratory, or as constitutive (Onuf 1998: 187). The latter, with its emphasis on the act of acknowledgement, arguably allows more scope for discretion than is present in any simple recognition of the 'facts'. In this regard, international society may have come to act in a more solidarist way than many of its adherents are prepared to admit. Even Wight (1972: 27) was to imply as much when he drew attention to a 'dislike for the variety and complexity of international society, and a belief that improved rules of legitimacy would lead to a greater uniformity'. Any such practice is manifestly not innocent of internal arrangements, nor disposed towards tolerance on the grounds of pluralism (Buchanan 1999). That international society has actively discriminated against other types of would-be international actors, so as to marginalize their importance, is widely accepted. For instance, the Hansa were not admitted as legitimate and equal participants at Westphalia (Spruyt 1994: 16). It is quite another matter to say that international society has actively discriminated in favour of, or against, certain *types of state*. And yet that is exactly the direction in which the logic of legitimacy has pressed at various times. 'It has never been enough merely to have the corporate identity of a state', but always necessary also 'to conform to type identity criteria which define only certain *forms* of state as legitimate' (Wendt 1999: 292–3). For purposes of this discussion, however, we will distinguish between formal legal or diplomatic recognition, on the one hand, and more subtle and informal criteria of 'full' membership, on the other. The interest of this book is in practices that fall within the latter category.

There are various historical instantiations of this practice, and they will be reviewed in greater detail in the historical chapters to follow. The application of the 'standard of civilization', as a test for fit membership, was a clear instance in the nineteenth century (Gong 1984*a*, 1984*b*: 172; Donnelly 1998: 14). More recently, of course, other overt tests for membership have been applied. Since the end of the cold war, the insistence has been increasingly upon good governance, and adherence to human rights norms, as the 'conditionality' for enjoying certain of international society's privileges (Williams 1996: 52; Armstrong 1999: 560–1; Beetham and Lord 1998: 8; Dunne 2001: 76). The demarcation of a separate category of 'rogue' states, and the active pursuit of 'regime change' within them, simply demonstrates some logical conclusions of these tendencies. Thus Donnelly (1998: 21) comments upon human rights that they are part of the idea that 'international legitimacy and full membership in international society must rest in part on standards of just, humane or civilized behaviour'. When it has engaged in this particular practice, international society can be regarded as a powerful source of state 'socialization' (Armstrong 1998), and has taken on a 'constabulary role' (Keal 2000: 69). The important thing to note, however, is that this preference for greater 'uniformity' has usually been considered not as an end in itself, but as a means to fostering greater international consensus. The underlying belief has been the conventional liberal internationalist one that, the more alike in type and value system, the more likely are states to discover a harmony of interests, and, in consequence, to live in greater peace and economic prosperity. States deemed individually legitimate in the eyes of international society will collectively, so it has been supposed, prove more likely to sustain legitimate patterns of conduct.

That there is an intimate connection between the two is nicely revealed in Wendt's discussion of the 'Lockean culture'. The Lockean membership criteria he believes to be more stringent than the Hobbesian, but he notes also that the 'Lockean culture pays for its relative tranquillity with a less open membership policy' (Wendt 1999: 292). The comment is astute, and reveals how the two forms of international legitimacy can act together in mutually reinforcing ways.

Rightful Conduct

When the international relations literature on legitimacy is not concerned with membership, its focus turns instead to the second, 'outward-looking' dimension—that of rightful conduct. Legitimacy then tends to be seen as a set of prescriptions about how international society should conduct itself. At its core are a number of complex questions about consensus, how this is produced, and what consequent effects its attainment has upon international society.

The first issue is what this consensus is about, and returns us to a distinction already made. Is the consensus only on procedural forms, or must it embrace substantive values as well? The debates since the end of the cold war—about humanitarian interventions, and about the wars fought, for example, in Kosovo and Iraq—have served to bring out these issues powerfully (Bellamy 2003; Holzgrefe and Keohane 2003; Smith 2003). For instance, is action by the UN to be assessed solely in terms of a consensus about adherence to its procedural rules (Security Council resolutions, majority voting, and putative or actual vetoes), or is it rather about the ultimate purposes and values which this body was created to serve? Proponents of the latter position are prone to appeal to such values, as a way of trumping any absence of procedural sanction for taking or thwarting specific courses of action. Some of the most acrimonious disputes to date have been driven essentially by a lack of consensus over this deep-seated issue.

Such matters inevitably arise when any institution is required to operate on the basis of consensus (Murphy 1994: 261). At one level, it seems straightforward that the relevant judgements we make of a body like the Security Council pertain to its adherence to the rules. This, however, is to set aside important expectations about the substantive role that body is to play. 'Even if an organization acts in accordance with its rules', one analyst of the Security Council has remarked, 'it nonetheless may be viewed as illegitimate against some broader frame of reference' (Caron 1993: 559; Murphy 1994: 259). In the case of this body managing to reach unanimity, one is still compelled to enquire about the nature and source of any consensus that is present. Murphy contended that agreement within the Security Council in the early 1990s reflected 'broad-based support', and not just 'some states imposing their will on others'. At the same time, he recognized the existence of diplomatic pressure, and conceded that the Council, unlike a Court, 'is supposed to operate in a political environment' (Murphy 1994: 252). It then becomes analytically difficult to locate the source of any consensus: does the broad-based support come from general endorsement of certain values, or is it produced by diplomatic pressure and arm-twisting? Does international consensus act to mitigate the distribution of power, or serve merely to reflect it?

This question can be placed in the related context of the relationship, introduced above, between legitimacy and stability. The discussion by Kissinger provides a good example of how consensus is supposed to stabilize international society. His contention was that an order enjoying legitimacy is distinct from one reliant upon power alone. Although he is clear that it is the very legitimacy of an order that is the key to its stability, and hence to its durability (as after 1815), his understanding of that relationship remains complex. This emerges in his various descriptions of the order established after the Vienna settlement:

Thus the new international order came to be created with a sufficient awareness of the connection between power and morality; between security and legitimacy. No attempt was made to found it entirely on submission to a legitimizing principle ... Rather, there was created a balance of forces which, because it conferred a relative security, came to be generally accepted. (Kissinger 1977: 318)

Elsewhere, and more succinctly, he sees the post-Vienna order as predicated on 'not only a physical equilibrium but a moral one' (Kissinger 1995: 79). What this seems to suggest is that a physical balance of power is necessary, but not sufficient, for a stable order to exist. What is additionally needed is a 'moral balance' which, given what is said elsewhere, can express itself only through consensus.

CONCLUSION

This chapter has sketched an ambitious agenda, both theoretically and historically. We are faced with the twin tasks of making sense of legitimacy within the framework of international society, as well as providing historical substance to its various instantiations across the centuries. Has the foregoing review provided any clear guidelines for this survey?

Legitimacy can be conceived as a *political space, but not an unbounded or normatively autonomous one.* While the collateral values of legality, morality, and constitutionality do shift over time, at any one point they take on the appearance of semi-permanent structures. The practice of legitimacy describes the political negotiation amongst the members of international society as they seek out an accommodation between those seemingly absolute values, and attempt to reconcile them with a working consensus to which all can feel bound.

It is crucial to emphasize again that this process is not wholly unbounded. Legitimacy is, to a degree, what states make of it, but not entirely so. International society is constrained by shifting normative pulls, even as it helps to push these in new directions by its own political projects. It is in this respect that the claim can be asserted that the states system, historically, has 'been embedded within a normative framework that appeals to standards of justice and legitimacy above and beyond the consent and practice of states' (Donnelly 1998: 22–3). In their pragmatic responses to these putative standards, states remake them, but not in the manner or the time of their own choosing.

Accordingly, the conceptualization of legitimacy advanced in these pages is essentially twofold. First, there are the core principles of legitimacy that define the presence of international society, and are the key property of it. The second—the practice of legitimacy—dwells upon the pursuit of consensus within international society, considered as a political process constrained by existing, if shifting, norms. This shares the general perspective on legitimation, described 'as an active, contested political process, rather than legitimacy as an abstract political resource. Since it is an activity, not a property, it involves creation, modification, innovation, and transformation' (Barker 2001: 28). Even more succinctly, and greatly to the point, we should conceive of the practice of legitimacy as 'a process of consensual empowerment' (Minchev 2000: 5).

These reflections present the analysis in highly abstract terms. We turn now to a historical survey of the principles of legitimacy, and their partial embodiment in actual international practice. To begin, the crucial questions to be faced were whether any international society existed and, if so, what its scope was. An important stage in answering such questions was reached with the so-called 'discovery' of the New World at the end of the fifteenth century. This prompted an unprecedented degree of self-consciousness about the nature and possible scope of international society, as it reflected on how Europe related to these newly discovered territories. In turn, this provoked thought about how the European states should conduct themselves in relation to each other. The unifying themes that emerged in these deliberations were rightful membership of international society, and what this implied for rightful conduct. How should the states of Europe behave towards those on the outside, and what might this mean for their behaviour towards fellow insiders? Here was a practical matter that posed important questions about international legitimacy, and also about the very possibility of international society.

Part I

Historical International Society

2

Europe and the Scope of International Society

The immediately following chapters of this historical survey will concentrate largely upon developments within the European system of states. Initially, some comments need to be made about the geographical scope of this emerging international society, and the role that was played by legitimacy in its formation. This issue arises with regard to what might be seen as its specifically European origins, followed by its later 'expansion' to incorporate the remainder of the globe. It is superficially attractive to see these as two discrete stages, but it has become decreasingly persuasive to do so. The misdirected implication of this view is that the European international society formed itself in isolation, in advance of its subsequent encounter with the rest of the world. Thus two observers have drawn our attention to the development within European legal thinking of 'the somewhat misleading image of a Eurocentric international society into which non-European states were progressively admitted' (Kingsbury and Roberts 1990: 49).

INTERNATIONAL SOCIETY: THE EXPANSION OF THE EUROPEAN?

To prepare the ground for an important argument, it is necessary to discuss two interconnected issues about the historical trajectory of international society. First, in terms of its *character*, did it start out essentially European, and then change in fundamental ways to become increasingly, and genuinely, multicultural? Second, in terms of its *scope*, has its historical course been one of constant and continuous expansion in the sense that it started from a narrow geographical base, and ever since has become progressively, and consistently, broader?

As to the character of this international society, there are competing interpretive frameworks that might suggest themselves. The first possibility—the two-stage evolution noted above—is that it developed originally on an exclusively European basis, and then later transmuted into something qualitatively different. A second alternative has it that, python-like, European international society steadily swallowed other geographical regions. In the short term, the shape of these other societies remained visible, but once fully digested, the European/Western python resumed its original shape: international society became all-embracing in composition, but it nonetheless continued to reflect distinctive, and limited, cultural values. A third perspective is that European and non-European societies have been in continual dialogue, and the encounter between them helped to create the nature of European international society from the outset, just as it has continued to influence the character of the ensuing wider international society ever since. Each of these assessments provides a distinctive perspective upon the evolution of international society, and of the role of legitimacy within this development. The following analysis will subscribe to a version of this last framework. While there can be no denying that, for much of the period after 1500, European—and later Western—states had unique power to forge an international society in their own image, what needs to be challenged is the notion of the autonomy of that image. Europe certainly held sway, but its self-image was to emerge in direct encounters with other parts of the world, and this immediately introduces a reflexive element into international society's beginnings. This is critical for our understanding of its concept of legitimacy.

On the second connected issue—that of its scope—there is a more compelling alternative account, and this will be set out below. This is that there has been no single and consistent expansion of international society, but rather a more complex and variable recurrence of different trends: the theoretical frameworks that accounted for an international society were originally broadly conceived, then contracted, then expanded again, and may well be undergoing yet another new phase of contraction at present. The full import of this interpretation will be set out shortly.

Character

There are complex issues at stake in this discussion, and a clear appreciation of them is vital to understanding how an international society increasingly coalesced around a core set of legitimacy principles. Most teasing of all is the nature of the correlation between the development of legitimacy principles within Europe, and the elaboration of rules for dealing with the rest of the world. So striking is this correlation that it invites the suggestion that they were causally related. Even so, this could have worked in either, or both, of two directions. First, the more conscious Europe became of its own social identity, the more it was drawn to distinguish itself from those thought to be beyond the pale, and hence to elaborate different codes of conduct to operate in these respective spheres. Second, and in reverse, the more conscious Europe became of the rest of the world through its various 'encounters' with it, the more necessary and possible it became for Europe to identify itself. In the first case, a hierarchy of legitimacy principles—different ones being thought applicable in different domains—was the natural consequence of the development of a distinctively European international society. In the second case, the invention of European international society can be regarded as the necessary accompaniment to its dealings with those others. It is this second account that is the more compelling, with regard to both international society's origins and its subsequent development.

The discovery of a 'New World', as well as the increasingly intense practical encounters with much of the 'non-European' world elsewhere, compelled Europeans to relate other peoples to themselves, and more formally to specify the rules of engagement with them. In the process of doing so, Europeans also discovered the necessity to elaborate more fully the basis of their own mutual relations: as they sought to legitimize their own activities elsewhere, they were driven to articulate the principles of legitimacy that operated within the intra-European domain as well. In this profound sense, elaboration of doctrines of international legitimacy already possessed a global dimension from the sixteenth century onwards, even if this was to be implemented as actual state practice from a dominantly European perspective. The earliest beginnings of a modern conception of international legitimacy can thus be traced to the imperial projects of this period. As the expanding European powers began to work out the doctrinal grounds on which they were entitled to their new dominions, and to regulate their mutual competition in the quest for them, they were forced back into discussions of first principles about what it was that Europe stood for, and hence of the codes of practice to operate within its own embryonic interstate society. 'The New World came, in this way,' one historian attests, 'to be incorporated during the course of the seventeenth century into the legalistic framework devised for a Europe of sovereign states' (Elliott 1970: 101–2). As we shall see shortly, the more this took the form of specifying a principle of differentiation, the more it was drawn to set out what it was about Europe that made it so different. The two processes were intimately related, and as this differentiation occurred, 'European states refashioned their own identity as a cultural whole and were better able to create the rules and institutions distinctive to their own interstate game' (Neumann and Welsh 1991: 329–30). Concepts of international legitimacy were to be central to both of these processes, and this relationship recurs at various key phases from the sixteenth to nineteenth centuries. If it was to be the case that the later codification of the standard of civilization 'helped to define more clearly the customs of European international society' (Gong 1984*a*: 3–4; Neumann and Welsh 1991: 343–4), then equally the attempted expounding of the basis on which Europe might have legal title to the New World during the sixteenth century can be seen to have produced similar effects within the limits of Europe. For cognate reasons, one legal historian has contended that the early development of trade contacts with the East Indies, and its regulation in international treaties, undermines the 'traditional view that the law of nations grew up exclusively in the confines of Christian Europe' (Alexandrowicz 1967: v).

In these various ways, the study of legitimacy in international society should be considered part of that wider, and still ongoing, revisionist historiography that seeks to emphasize not just the impact on the rest of the world of Europe's expansion, but equally the impact of that expansion on Europe itself. This can be understood both in the narrow sense of the significance of the discovery of the New World—which, as Elliott (1970: 7) long since argued, 'helped to shape and transform an Old World'—but also in the more generic sense of the transformational impacts of the imperial experience as a whole upon the European centres, not simply upon the colonial peripheries (Daunton and Halpern 1999; Drayton 2000). The first awareness of the existence of a new continent induced not only a cultural re-examination within Europe, but also shook the basis of hitherto dominating political assumptions. If some legal publicists in the sixteenth and seventeenth centuries, such as Vitoria and Grotius, were to go on to insist that there could be no 'lord of all the world', then the ground for this denial had been provided by the recent explorations. 'In the period after 1492', as Pagden (1995: 38) neatly points out, 'the discovery that there existed an entire continent of which the Ancients had been wholly ignorant effectively excluded the possibility that any ancient emperor could have been literally a world ruler'. This was to have a direct, and enduring, impact on the style of contemporary political argumentation.

It is this general issue of the European character of early international society that lies at the heart of some recent criticisms levelled against the English school. Its deficiency, supposedly, has been that it turned its attention to the extra-European world only from the late nineteenth century, and became interested in European/extra-European relations only 'when the latter's entry into the society of states came on to the agenda' (Keene 2002: 26). Elsewhere, the same author admonishes 'orthodox theorists' for their starting assumption that 'the modern world was organized as a society of states that was originally confined only to European members', and hence for thinking 'of the construction of a global political and legal order solely in terms of the expansion of the European society of states' (Keene 2002: 122). This is scarcely fair. It ignores the explicit statement to the contrary made by the two key exponents of this perspective. 'The evolution of the European system of interstate relations and the expansion of Europe across the globe were simultaneous processes', they declared, '*which influenced and affected each other*. Both began at the end of the fifteenth century' (Bull and Watson 1984*b*: 6–7, emphasis added). It was not then the case, according to this expression of English school thinking, of a fully formed European international society subsequently encountering the rest. Instead, this perspective already acknowledges what has become such a powerful theme in the recent historiography of the West, namely the importance of the discovery of the New World to its own self-image: the West was to be shaped as much by this encounter as was the New World itself (Pagden 1995).

How does all this have a bearing on the role of legitimacy? The question can be answered by an adaptation of Keene's provocative critique. His main claim is that, as international society evolved, it came to internalize two alternative, and inconsistent, sets of values. At its (European) core, it became committed to promotion of the value of toleration, reflecting its essentially pluralist stance as a practical association. In its dealings with the remainder, it sought to propagate instead the value of civilization (Keene 2002: xi, 148). Keene goes on to conclude of this notion of civilization that it performed two roles. First, 'it defined the border between the two patterns of modern international order', and second, 'it described the ultimate purposes that the extra-European order was for'. This contributed to the perception of a 'bifurcated world' (Keene 2002: 6–7).

There is much of value in this general account, and it raises an intriguing point for the present discussion. What appears to be claimed in these words is that international society was, at one and the same time, both pluralist/practical at its core, and solidarist/purposive in its relationship with the periphery. Otherwise considered, this then would suggest a further important role for legitimacy within international society. While, thus far, we have drawn attention to the domestic and international facets of international legitimacy, there may be yet a third dimension that is still to be uncovered. The question that is posed is whether Europe's relations with the non-European world were considered *ultra vires* as far as emerging concepts of legitimacy were concerned, or—more formatively—whether agreements about how to proceed outside European international society became a *necessary part* of the identity of European international society. This opens up a third sphere of analysis. Just as there is an interrelationship between rightful membership and rightful conduct, so is there also an intimate connection between Europe's vision of appropriate interstate conduct and its own understanding of Europe's place in international society as a whole. From that perspective, the legitimacy of what could be done in European international society came itself to be defined by Europe's encounter with the greater social whole. One might even suggest that there was a functional relationship between the two: in order to act purposively outside, European international society was compelled to become more tolerant, and practical, inside.

Accordingly, it is precisely in this encounter between what was to be done within Europe, and what was to be done elsewhere, that legitimacy principles came first to be developed and subsequently transformed. A similar association can be drawn from the apparently different account devised by one international lawyer (Rölling 1990). He distinguishes three separate phases in the expansion of international society: 1648–1856 (Christian nations); 1856–1945 (Civilized nations); and 1945 onwards (Peace-loving states). Each of these phases was shaped by the core value that it sought to promote, and around that value was the definition of legitimate statehood to be established (Rölling 1990: 291–3). However, the critical point to emerge from such a scheme (whether convincing or not in its particulars) is that this key internal value—be it Christianity, civilization, or a commitment to peace—adopted by the core sector of international society both defined its purpose in relation to the remainder, and also was constructed as part of its encounter with it. Legitimacy *in* European international society in its early beginnings is, to this extent, comprehensible only as an aspect of the debate about the nature of the international social whole, and about Europe's place in that wider sphere.

Scope

This second issue concerns the degree of inclusiveness within international society, and whether or not there has been a straightforward trajectory towards an ever widening scope from the outset. It deals with Martin Wight's question, 'how far does international society extend?' (Wight 1991: 49; Keal 2003: 186). As suggested, the argument to be presented here dissents from any notion of a continuously broadening membership. It holds instead that, in the original conceptions, international society could be defined in potentially universal and inclusive terms. Subsequently, the theoretical and legal frameworks within which it came to be discussed resulted in a substantial contraction of membership during the course of the eighteenth and nineteenth centuries. It was to expand again during the twentieth, but arguably is experiencing a bout of further contraction at present. What is the evidence for claiming such a cyclical, rather than linear, history?

It begins with the proposition that international society was originally conceived in very broad, almost universal, terms. This can be demonstrated in the work of one international legal theorist, Alexandrowicz (1967), himself a prime expositor of the encounter between European law and the outside world. According to one summary of his argument, non-European states had once belonged to the 'universal family of nations' during the early modern period. However, under the impact of subsequent positivist thought, the size of that family 'shrank', 'effectively evicting non-Europeans from membership, and forcing them to apply for readmission on less favourable terms' (Keene 2002: 26). This notion has been challenged, it seems mistakenly, by Gong (1984a: 9–10), when he appears to dispute the central element advanced by Alexandrowicz (1967). Gong presents his own book as a refutation of this notion that 'a universal Family of Nations existed prior to the nineteenth century' (1984a: 9–10). The grounds for his critique are that a range of extra-European states newly entered international society only at that point, and after passing the test imposed by the standard of civilization. But these two positions are not necessarily as inconsistent as Gong appears to think.

The key argument here is that there existed already in the sixteenth century an intellectual framework, heir to the wider natural law tradition, that focused on a universal society to which all peoples belonged. This reasoning was powerfully demonstrated at the time in Vitoria's analysis which maintained that rationality, not Christianity, was 'the criterion of civility', and that this was demonstrated in a capacity to live in society. The American Indians 'by showing their capacity for such existence, had vindicated their right to membership of the club'. It followed that all rational men were citizens of 'the whole world, which in a certain way constitutes a single republic' (Elliott 1970: 45–6; Victoria 1918). Vitoria specifically argued that the American Indians enjoyed the same entitlements as the Christian states of Europe (Scott 1934: 282–3). Much the same sentiment was to be expressed by Francis I to Pope Paul III in 1535:

If nations are divided among themselves, it is not nature which separates them but tradition and usages...It would have evil effects if the ties of blood and nationhood would estrange particular societies from the *universal* society of nations...differences of religion and cultural tradition cannot destroy the natural association of mankind. (quoted in Alexandrowicz 1967: 236)

Similar conclusions were equally to be reached by an alternative route. Medieval Christian thought itself posited its own version of universalism, not least as a principle that would justify the incorporation of other peoples within it. 'The Christian world order...had always', remarks Pagden (1995: 30–1), 'been thought of as identical *de jure* with the world...and thus potentially as a cultural, moral and finally political order with no natural frontiers'.

Such ideas were not, of course, subscribed to by all—as the intense controversies about the American conquests were amply to reveal. But neither was there any clear majority position on the other side. There are, of course, important distinctions that need to be made to appreciate the nuances of the positions that were put forward at the time. Arguably, Vitoria's position was one couched in natural, not juridic, rights (Keal 2003: 89), and thus shaded off into moral/philosophical discourse, rather than as a statement of legality. By way of clarification, Wight (1991: 73) was to comment that Vitoria had confused natural law with the *jus gentium*. Nonetheless, in this highly fluid intellectual atmosphere, there was at least the potential for the emergence of a different view of the scope of international society from that which was, in fact, to prevail. That this was so is further demonstrated in Alexandrowicz's account of actual state practice in the sixteenth to eighteenth centuries in relation to the Indies. European states found no difficulty in shaping legal instruments for their activities in this area. Indeed, the necessity for development of a treaty apparatus with peoples of different religions and cultures contributed, he maintains, 'to the *secularization* of treaty law as such' (Alexandrowicz 1967: 231). On these various grounds, he advances his general thesis that 'to consider the European nucleus of States as the founder group of the family of nations to the exclusion of Asian Sovereigns in the East Indies was to view the origin and development of that family in the light of positivist conceptions which were only born at the turn of the eighteenth and nineteenth centuries' (Alexandrowicz 1967: 11). In this way can be justified the assertion that the original conception of international society was, indeed, broad and inclusive.

It was not long so to remain. Wight (1991: 72) concedes that while Grotius himself adhered to 'a society of mankind' (although not exclusively to that alone), thereafter it increasingly 'proved impossible to persist in this generous view'. What replaced it, in Wight's account, was a framework that depicted the emerging three concentric circles. The state formed the innermost circle. It was bounded by a second that was 'international society, subject to a volitional, positive law of nations'. Beyond that again was a third, and this was 'mankind, subject to natural law' (Wight 1991: 73). This presented an increasingly differentiated scope of various possible human societies, and each of these entailed distinctive obligations. By the late eighteenth century, the intellectual apparatus was already in place (Butler 1978), and by the nineteenth century it had been further codified, to bring about a 'correction' in the actual composition of international society, in conformity with this theoretical justification. This generated a contraction of international society, with the consequential invitation to those expelled to reapply on specifically European terms. The idea that took hold, and the state practice that emerged from it, was that of 'a distinction between the civilized world of the society of states and the uncivilized world beyond' (Keene 2002: 101). This shrinkage in the scope of international society occurred *pari passu* with the new tenour of positive international law. In consequence, 'European egocentricity left the Sovereigns of the East Indies ... outside the confines of "civilization" and international law shrank to regional dimensions' (Alexandrowicz 1967: 2). This contributed to the paradox, noted by Keal (2003: 107), that 'as the expansion of Europe proceeded, international law became simultaneously more universal and exclusionary'.

The next turning point began with the First World War, although its full effects were largely delayed until after the Second. If, until 1914, Europe felt self-confident enough about its own 'civilization' to make this the test for admission to international society by others, then the Great War did much to shake this self-belief (Bull 1984b: 219). The conjunction of the principle of national self-determination (although initially envisaged as applicable only to the European successor states), along with a return to a more formal test for recognition of new states, ensured a dramatic expansion in the scope of international society, one that persisted throughout the twentieth century. Numerically, this expansion accelerated after the end of the cold war, with a yet new wave of successor states emerging from the old Soviet Union, and from other disintegrating states and federations. At the same time, it is not too far-fetched to see, at this stage, the explicit re-emergence of 'civilizational' tests, once more being imposed by the inner core of international society. This took the form of greater emphasis upon democratic good governance, respect for human rights, and amenability to the requirements of the global economy. It was part of the 'double movement' by which a set of particularistic values had once again come to dominate the conception of an appropriate international society, and to protect this core society and its values from the encroachments resulting from the much greater pluralism to which formal numerical expansion had thus far contributed. Nervous about the full implications of toleration, the core states retreated behind a new civilizational barricade as the expression of the true purpose of international society (Clark 2001*b*). From this perspective, the late twentieth and early twenty-first centuries represent a new turning point. This, like the nineteenth, seems set to introduce new tests for, and categories of, membership of international society (Bain 2003*a*). If not formally (in terms of diplomatic recognition), then at least substantively, the effective membership of international society is once more undergoing shrinkage. In its 'dignified' aspects, international society remains universal; in its 'efficient' aspects, it more clearly reveals its exclusionary face. Its notions of international legitimacy have been central to these cyclical transformations.

LEGITIMACY AND NEW WORLD ENCOUNTERS

As noted, the starting point for this analysis is the effect that the discovery of the New World was to have upon Europe itself. This reorientation of the debate—away from an exclusive concentration upon the impact on the New World—has continued apace since the 1970s, and has resulted in the widely shared conclusion that 'in discovering America Europe had discovered itself' (Elliott 1970: 53; Pagden 1993: 89). Otherwise expressed, it suggests that 'it is in fact the conquest of America that heralds and establishes our present identity' (Todorov 1984: 5). More recently, and more generally, the point is made that 'Europe did not simply expand overseas; it made itself through that expansion' (quoted in Pagden 2002*b*: 13–14). Methodologically, these arguments tend to be grounded in notions of European identity, and how discovery and expansion contributed to its construction in distinctive ways: Europe was not an autonomous creation. In turn, more general claims of this nature become directly relevant to the specific points under discussion. Just how exclusively 'European' was early European thinking about international legitimacy when it was already being formed by encounters with the non-European world? This is the heart of the claim, *contra* any notion of a static European international society eventually incorporating the rest, that 'it was not the case that the values of a constant European core simply expanded to cover new areas. Rather, the very idea of what Europe was was from the beginning defined partly in terms of what it was *not*' (Neumann and Welsh 1991: 329).

One critical dimension of this relationship was the felt need to legitimize the conquest of the New World, and the reciprocal effect that this had upon the need to articulate adjacent principles of legitimacy to operate within Europe as well. Both developed in tandem. It has been coyly observed that the age of discovery 'coincided' with 'the need for a Law of Nations to regulate relations between the independent states of Europe' (Keal 2003: 112). But was this mere 'coincidence', or was there not a more important causality at work in this conjunction? Wight is closer to the mark in his robust assessment of the situation. He remained convinced that it was this 'great debate' about the Spanish conquest that 'laid the foundations for modern international law'. In amplification, he sets forth his own challenging thesis:

It was not the development of the diplomatic system in Europe, nor war in Europe, nor the disintegration of Christendom and the need for its reunion that provided the occasion for international law; it was the problem of the barbarians. (Wight 1991: 69–70)

If this was so for international law, the same might be said for emerging notions of international legitimacy more generally. If Wight is correct, then these need to be understood, not simply as an outgrowth of purely European developments, but precisely as issuing from the interstices of Europe's encounter with the New World.

'The great official concern about the legitimacy of the conquest of the Americas and about the rights of the Indians who lived there', remarks one leading scholar, 'provided a dominant theme for Spanish intellectuals in the sixteenth century' (Muldoon 1994: 4–5). Its effects necessarily spread beyond this narrow constituency, as the arguments impinged upon much of the old world, just as they did upon the new. Elliott is thus adamant that, a century after discovery, 'no real progress had been made in incorporating the New World into a fixed framework of international relations'. However, he acknowledges that the loss of the Spanish dominance came to be reflected in the international instruments of the time. Spain, he asserts, was unable to sustain its claim to exclusive dominance, based on papal assignment, and had to settle instead for '*de facto* acceptance of effective occupation as sufficient title to overseas possession'. Importantly, he stresses that this recognition was implicit in the Münster Treaty of 30 January 1648 that settled the Spanish conflict with the Dutch (Elliott 1970: 100–1). This observation forcefully makes the point under discussion: in thrashing out its principles for dealing with the New World, the Old World was compelled to thrash out principles for dealing with itself.

How was this so? Issues about the title to the Americas pertained directly to intra-European state relations, and Spanish decline contributed to a reconfiguration of those claims. Article V of the terms of peace between the king of Spain and the Netherlands affirmed now, in 1648, that the possession of overseas territories would henceforth be in accordance with the existing facts on the ground, rather than on the basis of some overarching prescriptive principle:

And both the aforesaid Lords, the King and the States respectively, shall continue in possession of such lordships, cities, castles, towns, fortresses, countries and commerce in the East and West-Indies, as also in Brazil, upon the coasts of Asia, Africa, and America respectively, as the said Lords, the King and the States respectively hold and possess, comprehending therein particularly the places and forts which the Portuguese have taken from the Lords and States since the year 1641, and also the forts and places which the said Lords and States shall chance to acquire and possess after this. (Grewe 1988: 421; French text in Parry 1969: vol. 1, 74)

A number of things had hitherto been at stake. Clearly, the debate about the legitimacy of the conquest, and the nature of the title to possession, drew upon existing European systems of thought. This was particularly so in the connection of this debate to traditional just war theory (Donelan 1984: 78). As Pagden notes, the legitimacy of the occupation depended on whether the war fought against the American Indian had been a just one (1995: 94), and thus explicitly drew upon the existing frameworks of this discussion. It also raised questions about the basis of legitimate entitlement to possession of the new territories by the Castilian crown. Vitoria had dismissed any claim based on mere discovery as unconvincing. Discovery, he adduced sardonically, 'of itself provides no support for possession of those lands, any more than it would if they had discovered us' (Pagden 1995: 80). The core issue that was to run through the ensuing debate was the nature of the rights of the Indians, and in particular whether they enjoyed a right of possession of the lands they inhabited (Victoria 1918; Hanke 1965; Muldoon 1994; Keal 2003). As already noted, the discovery had challenged concepts of ancient 'lordship of all the world', and it followed from this that many publicists, including Vitoria, objected to the derivation of any valid title to possession from the papal bulls of 1493. The logic was simply that since the pope 'was not in fact lord of the whole world, he was in no position to hand over a portion of it to the Spanish Crown' (Elliott 1970: 81–2).

This issue was then to become increasingly controversial as the political dimension of imperial rivalry amongst the European powers, driven by attempts to get in on the act by others—some protestant—became such a prominent feature of the new situation. In this respect also, we can see how the articulation of principles to govern the emerging relationship between Europe and the Americas became intimately tied up with the articulation of principles to govern the old relationships within Europe itself. Those who had been excluded by the papal bulls from enjoyment of the fruits of the New World had a vested interest in denigrating the validity of this particular title, whereas arguably the Portuguese and the Castilians both benefited from a title couched in these terms: a title based on conquest or actual occupation would serve only to throw the business open to everyone else. Inescapably, the debate about what rights the Old World enjoyed in the New became bound up with the rights that were to be distributed amongst the members of the Old World itself. 'Arguments for the next three hundred years', it has been observed, 'therefore turned as much upon justifications for dispossessing the native peoples as they did upon asserting positive rights of ownership against other European states' (Armitage 1998: xxii).

Increasingly, and certainly by the time of Grotius in the seventeenth century, two sets of factors were impinging upon these issues, each pushing the debate in broadly similar directions. First, as noted, there was the intensifying competition from other European quarters. Second, the expansion was taking materially different forms on the ground. In the Spanish case, there was a need for a set of principles that could be seen to legitimize actual possession of territories, and in a case where there evidently existed indigenous inhabitants: in some form, Spanish possession had to be rooted in indigenous dispossession. Arguably, Grotius's treatment was to deal with a discrete set of international problems. Clearly, he had no vested interest in supporting exclusive Spanish claims. Equally, from the Dutch perspective, the interest lay in establishing sound trading relations with stable existing societies: actual possession of territories—and hence a theory of dispossession—was not for him the concern of the rudimentary international law of this period, as it had been for the Spanish (Muldoon 1994: 23). Moreover, while appeal to papal fiat retained some force in a Europe still united around one religion, this inevitably lost much of its force in post-Reformation circumstances. What seemed odd to some emerging settler colonies was the very idea that the legitimacy of Spanish claims could rest on pre-existing papal authority, and hence title to have been 'established even before they had come into existence' (Pagden 1995: 73). To this extent, the shaping of legitimacy principles within Europe, and beyond, was being pushed and pulled by a number of major new social and ideological forces: discovery, imperial rivalry, and the religious divisions of the age. Thus, it is claimed, when Grotius wrote his *Mare liberum*, he was seeking both to invalidate Spanish titles that rested on papal authority to dispose of the New World, and conjointly to attest to the rights that the American Indians continued to enjoy (Muldoon 1994: 29). He was also concerned with establishing the legal basis for trade, not occupation. In that sense, it has been suggested that his theory fitted the case of the East Indies, but was wholly inapplicable to that of the Americas (Muldoon 1994: 174). Clearly, by the mid-seventeenth century, the terms of Europe's encounter with the rest of the world were being set in ways that differed from a century earlier, and this reflected the course of events also within Europe. For all these reasons, it can be said that the newly discovered Americas were to serve as an important source of debate about legitimacy *in* international society, even if those peoples were considered by some not fully a part *of* that international society.

SOCIETY, CHRISTENDOM, AND CIVILIZATION

The terms of that encounter continued to shift over the next two centuries. The idea of Christendom, as a point of identity within Europe, and the basis of its claim to constitute effective international society, remained robust for much of that period. To that extent, emerging principles of legitimacy were predominantly influenced by conceptions of a shared morality, rooted in religion. It expressed what Europe enjoyed in common, even more so in the aftermath of the confessional conflicts that had plagued the sixteenth century, and contributed to the Thirty Years War of the seventeenth. It also increasingly marked the opposition between Europe and much of the remainder of the world. However, Christendom also became an increasingly problematic framework within which to conceptualize the nature and extent of international society itself. Accordingly, during the seventeenth century, the normative source of legitimacy came more commonly to be defined in terms of subscription to a common legality—albeit that the source of obligation to that legality remained essentially 'sacral' (Reus-Smit 2003). What we then witness is the emergence of a notion of civilization, initially as an adjunct of Christendom, but finally as a displacement of the latter as the operative basis of international society. This, as noted above, was to work in tandem with that narrowing down of the concept of international society that proceeded from the late eighteenth century onwards. In practice, and as Gong (1984a) points out, this shift to a civilizational concept took place as part of the physical expansion of international society in the late nineteenth century. However, this expansion must be set in the context of the theoretical contraction that had already taken place, and which amounted now to new tests for readmission.

Shared Christianity was fundamental to early European thinking about international society, despite—or even because of—the religious disunity that occurred during the sixteenth century. It was formative because it overlapped with the beginnings of expansion and, as a result, 'Europe's first modern overseas empires came into being at the moment when a series of predominantly civil wars had divided it along confessional lines' (Pagden 2002b: 13). For this reason, the settlement of the religious schisms became embedded in the wider issue of how to deal with the empires as well, as also in the emerging principles of international relations. If, as Pagden (2002b: 14) maintains, Westphalia was a critical juncture in what became the dominance of the secular state in an emerging international society, this was the price that had to be paid to overcome the debilitating internal religious strife to which Europe had been subjected. It signalled also, for the much longer term, how problematic a preoccupation with Christendom could become for an increasingly diverse and potentially greatly expanded international society. For this reason, there was mounting pressure to relax that 'domestic' principle of international legitimacy that expressed itself in an insistence upon a religious test for inclusion, just as that issue had already been confronted in the meeting with the non-Christian societies of the Americas. However, it remained clear that European society was unwilling to relinquish its constabulary role altogether. Instead, the terms in which it was to be expressed gradually transmuted from an emphasis upon Christendom and a common religion, to an emphasis upon due regard for appropriate standards of civilization. It was this that came to define the parameters of international society, and 'underscored international society's need for a universally acceptable identity' (Gong 1984a: 4–5). This could no longer adequately be provided within the framework of religion. But a shift in the terms of recognition certainly did not mean an abandonment of tests for rightful membership altogether. This was far from being the case.

The standard of civilization presents a highly ambivalent face towards the concept of international legitimacy. In the first, and most obvious, sense it is redolent of international power differentials, and of cultural imposition. It smacks too much of the unacceptable face of cultural interaction. And yet, paradoxically, it also evinces support from the most unlikely quarters as an expression of a mollifying, and potentially progressive, force in international relations. Most interestingly, Donnelly offers a positive interpretation. He is convinced that the standard had a less 'sinister' side, and should be seen as an appeal to 'universal moral values' that were not just a 'cover for the pursuit of self-interest' (Donnelly 1998: 6; 1999). He makes the equation between the standard, in the nineteenth century, and that of human rights today. Both, on this accounting, appear firmly entitled to be considered as fundamental legitimacy principles of their respective phases of international society. Does this argument stack up? What is the standing of the standard of civilization in terms of the encounter between the European and non-European world, and what might this tell us about the evolving nature of international society across this period?

The key elements of the standard have been definitively set out by Gong (1984a: 14–15). Succinctly expressed, they required guarantees of 'life, liberty and property of foreign nationals', viable governmental organization, adherence to diplomatic practice, and respect for international law (Gong 1984b: 179). This fits classically into Wight's tests for rightful membership of international society, and provided international society with a legal basis for its tutelage of the constitution of its members, or would-be members. This is exemplified in the instances of extraterritoriality introduced for the 'protection' of expatriate European nationals resident, for example, in China and Japan.

As state practice, this had already begun to reveal itself in a slightly different context in Europe's dealings with the Ottoman Empire. The Ottoman Empire had been 'recognized' de facto as a diplomatic 'reality' by Europe for centuries, but not fully accepted as part of European international society as such. The act of admission to it, formally, took place in the Peace of Paris of 1856 at the end of the Crimean War. The signatories, according to the treaty, 'déclarent la Sublime Porte admise à participer aux avantages du droit public et du concert Européens' (Parry 1969: vol. 114, 414). This admission to full membership came with a preceding undertaking on the part of the Sultan, in a firman issued by him, which, it was said in the treaty, testified that the Sultan 'sans distinction de religion ni de race, consacre ses généreuses intentions envers les populations Chrétiens de son Empire'. It was, however, added that this undertaking gave no right to the Powers 'de s'immiscer, soit collectivement, soit séparément, dans les rapports de Sa Majesté le Sultan avec ses sujets' (Parry 1969: vol. 114, 414). The fig-leaf was that this was a voluntary undertaking, not an imposition, but the connection between the admission to European society, and the promise of good treatment for the Sultan's Christian subjects, was none the less apparent for that.

The standard, in some respects, was to operate also within Europe, especially as regards new states. This confirms the verdict that the standard did not operate outwards alone, but also 'was making significant inroads into the European society of states itself' (Keene 2002: 123). Such reciprocity became abundantly clear at the Congress of Berlin in 1878, and this is again highly revealing of the interactions between relations within Europe, and those between Europe and the outside. Independence for new states in the Balkans was agreed at Berlin, but was contingent on acceptance of codes of minority protection for religious and national groups. Such instruments were imposed on Serbia, Montenegro, Romania, and Bulgaria, and form the linear predecessors of the protection system to be instituted after 1919 (Philpott 2001: 38–9). In this sense, 'national minority undertakings ... were externally dictated preconditions for the new nation-states' membership in international society' (Preece 1998: 62). This applied in the Balkans after 1878, in the same way that the principle was to operate in Central and Eastern Europe after 1919. Although the standard, as it were, faced outwards, its gaze was increasingly to be turned inwards as well. This was so, even in so far as the motives for applying such protection were in part instrumental, in seeking to avoid instabilities that might draw into conflict the great powers themselves (Preece 1998: 62).

The shift of emphasis from a Europe depicted as Christendom to one depicted in civilizational terms occurred gradually, and was certainly well under way by the Enlightenment. Eighteenth-century historians, we are told, dated this benighted condition of civility from the Peace of Utrecht which had demonstrated Europe's emergence from 'barbarism, fanaticism, and conquest' into a new international society, bound together by treaties 'and by a common system of civilized manners communicated everywhere by commerce' (Pocock 2002: 64–5). However, the translation of this vision of civility into an actual legal practice that would regulate international behaviour was largely an accomplishment of the late nineteenth century. This invites the obvious question as to why such a concept of international legitimacy was to be formulated at that historical juncture in particular. Two principal forces may be thought to have shaped this development, and they underscore the interaction between the ideological debate about intra-European relations, and its connection to the outside world. The relevant intra-European dimension was most obviously the increasingly competitive mood of imperial rivalry in the closing third of the nineteenth century. The arrival of new participants such as Germany, combined with a sense that this was now a zero-sum game which would determine the balance of power within Europe as much as it did that outside it—in effect obliterating this distinction—helped generate this distinctive atmosphere. It played itself out in the African partitions, and the scrambles in China. The other, and related, phenomenon was the shift from 'the imperialism of free trade' to more formal empire. The net result of this, it has been recalled, was that 'the end of informal empire meant that European public institutions—in particular, European sovereignty—needed to be projected into colonial territory' (Koskenniemi 2002: 121). The full force of the reciprocal causality needs to be brought out in this context, since it demonstrates the continuing mutuality that this chapter has sought to uncover. The precise reason that the standard of civilization became so formalized at this time was that it served the dual purpose of regulating both intra-European competition, and also the form of Europe's imperial provenance elsewhere: the one was a logical adjunct of the other. Thus Koskenniemi explains the rise of international law at this time from the need 'to deal with conflicts of jurisdiction between European powers', and simultaneously of the need 'to determine the rules applicable in the relations between the colonizing power and the indigenous population' (2002: 121). We have here an exact reprise of the reciprocity demonstrated in the sixteenth and seventeenth centuries with regard to the New World. The rise of the standard of civilization should be understood as one particular manifestation of this general tendency within international law during this period.

We end up back at Keene's claims about the duality of international order, concerned as it has been about toleration within the core, but at the same time intent upon fostering civilization at the periphery. The standard of civilization provides a good demonstration of this twin aspect. Attention has been drawn already to the two dimensions of international legitimacy, namely those of 'rightful membership', and that of 'rightful conduct'. As soon as we begin to unpack the notion of the standard of civilization, we discover that it represents a conflation of both of those themes. Demonstrably, it deals head on with the issue of membership. But equally it is concerned with defining rightful behaviour, and with distinguishing between different codes of conduct appropriate to different sectors of international society, as well as the relationship between those who wholly belong and those who do not. Keene (2002: 117) is therefore correct to insist of this idea that it acted 'not merely as a standard for regulating the entry of new states in international society, but also for validating the entirely different set of legal rules and political institutions in its own right'. To the extent that European international society was the bearer of this standard, and sought to situate others in relation to it, this code both articulated the principles upon which European society might expand to embrace others, while at the same time providing a deepening appreciation of the kind of rules that might already be thought to apply within the existing (European) international society. In these ways, the formation of international society has drawn upon reciprocal interactions between its European and other dimensions across the whole period from the sixteenth to nineteenth centuries. The central strand of this reciprocity has been concerned with simultaneously defining the legitimacy principles that were to apply within each geographical area; the development of relations between Europe and the outside world has been a continuously key feature in the evolution of European international society as well.

CONCLUSION

This survey has made two critical references to the events of 1648. The first amounted to claims that the settlement of Westphalia was instrumental in fostering the concept of an international society composed of secular states: it was a key phase in the secularization of the notion of international society. This can be traced in the shifting basis of legitimacy from a predominantly moral/theological one to one rooted in conceptions of legality. Second, the connection was made also between European developments and the conquest of the New World in the shape of Elliott's (1970) contention that the Spanish Treaty with the Netherlands documented the decline of Spanish hegemony by the tacit recognition in the Münster Treaty that it had lost the international argument about legitimate title. Henceforth, it was acknowledged, such title would depend on actual occupation (as the emerging contenders had claimed), and no longer on the papal gift of 1493 (as Spanish apologists had persisted in asserting).

Elliott's contention that a resolution of the issue of overseas expansion is 'implicit' in the Münster Treaty has a wider resonance in the context of the events of 1648 as a whole. The very manner of the territorial and religious settlement decreed at Westphalia, and the political competencies implied by these, were an abomination to the papacy, and the treaties were roundly so denounced as a result. In that sense, the Westphalian Treaties of October confirmed more generally what the Münster Treaty had specifically acknowledged with regard to the 'open door' in the Americas, namely its challenge to the powers of the papacy to authorize restrictive titles to possession. Most momentously of all, we can see in this the substantive nature of that challenge, and the reasons why the papacy was to find the Westphalia proceedings so execrable. Pope Innocent X complained that the Emperor had ceded Church lands and the treaties violated canon law (Bonney 1991: 68–9). The objection, no doubt, was in part to a religious settlement that recognized the status quo on the ground, and hence provided no final restitution of the papal patrimony as a whole. Equally, the objection was to the manner of this doing. What, in fact, was implicit in Westphalia was the competence of a duly constituted international society to authorize its own territorial and religious settlements. Henceforth, titles would be bestowed by that international society, and not by the papacy. It was this revolutionary assertion of a new source of international legitimacy that spurred the papal denunciation.

Having established the general point that the international development of notions of legitimacy was grounded in a real debate about the nature and scope of international society, sparked off by the age of discovery, we are now in a position to trace the emergence of the consequent theory and practice of legitimacy within the nascent European international society itself. This can appropriately begin, as do so many historical accounts of the modern state system, with those very Westphalian Treaties. In this case, the reasons for doing so are appreciably different from those traditionally adduced.

3

Westphalia: The Origins of International Legitimacy?

The peace settlement struck at Westphalia in 1648, combining the Münster Treaties (the Empire and France) and Osnabrück (the Empire and Sweden), has long enjoyed iconic status in the study of international relations. It is the eponymous characterization of the international order that is taken to have emerged at that point, to have persisted until at least the twentieth century, but that is now thought to be unravelling as its key principles fail to cope with the new conditions and challenges (Lyons and Mastanduno 1995; Zacher 1992). This status rests upon the putative emergence in 1648 of the modern state system, and above all of its key principle of sovereignty.

There are many reasons to be suspicious of these claims. However, before Westphalia's reputation is wholly discarded, we should review it instead from the perspective of international legitimacy. Could it be that the widespread sense amongst international relations scholars of Westphalia's significance is erroneously attributed to its implementation of a concept of sovereignty, and much more justifiably based on its development of a sense of international society, grounded in shared concepts of international legitimacy? This chapter will focus upon the notion of society as constituted by mutual recognition, and on a procedural principle of international consensus. Many of the terms of the treaties touched upon these issues of rightful membership and rightful conduct. More fundamentally, what was at stake in Westphalia was the capacity of an international forum, acting for an embryonic international society, to stake out a position on these matters at all. This chapter will investigate the evidence in support of such an interpretation.

THE SETTLEMENT AND ITS BACKGROUND

The Thirty Years War was not fought over a single issue. Rather it became a vortex that sucked in a number of disparate conflicts, and in so doing experienced a number of distinct phases. Its beginnings lay in the Bohemian revolt against the Empire, and this was overlaid with the post-Reformation distribution of confessional divisions within the Empire, a conflict that persisted throughout much of the war. The Edict of Restitution of 1629 and the Peace of Prague of 1635 were earlier, but failed, attempts to settle this matter. Onto this was grafted the more general political need of the Empire to resist both its own centrifugal forces, as well as the ambitions of its various predatory neighbours. In turn, Denmark (encouraged by England), Sweden, and France (the latter two in alliance) were to be drawn into the Empire's turmoil, both to shape the religious settlement therein, as well as in pursuit of their wider power political objectives. The net effect was to 'draw in the whole of western Europe' (Bonney 1991: 188). What this finally left behind in its troubled wake for Westphalia to settle were both the religious-constitutional provisions of the Empire, and the politico-territorial terms between the Empire and its two major protagonists, Sweden and France, respectively.

Westphalia drew to a conclusion one of the most destructive phases of modern European history. 'There is no doubt', one student of the period reminds us, ' that . . . the disintegrations of the Thirty Years War . . . the unprecedented slaughter, and the lawlessness of international relations, seemed to have brought Europe to the edge of the abyss' (Rabb 1975: 119). If it is the case that legitimacy is a concept 'associated with the politics of crisis' (Kitromilides 1986: 61), then the period at the end of this war certainly qualifies as such. Having peered over that perilous edge, the rulers of Europe tentatively sought agreement on some underpinning principle of legitimacy, to prevent the impending tumble over it. Europe, sliding into a 'nadir of helplessness' (Rabb 1975: 76), sought salvation instead.

The two treaties were negotiated, slowly, over a period of several years, culminating in their coordinated signings on 14 October 1648. At any first glance, they scarcely appear to bear the heavy weight of expectation that international relations scholarship has placed upon them. Collectively, they detail the constitutional, religious, and territorial dispositions in the Holy Roman Empire, and also the Empire's terms with France and Sweden. Compared with many other peace treaties, their overall territorial provisions were relatively modest. Moreover, Krasner (1993) is certainly correct to protest that, for documents that are held so dear by *international* scholars, they are, in terms of the number of articles within them, predominantly concerned with matters *internal* to the Empire. 'It is to the empire, not to the European system at large,' Osiander sternly reminds us, 'that the Peace of Westphalia is devoted' (Osiander 2001: 269). Even more disconcerting for the student of international relations, making a pilgrimage to this hallowed shrine, is the discovery that any articulation of the great principles of international order, if there at all, is pretty hard to glean from texts that are much more concerned with specifics than with generalities. One wonders whether, without prior knowledge of the posited historic importance of Westphalia, any judicious reading of the texts alone would support the weighty claims made on their behalf. If we cannot read quite as much as we might expect *out* of the actual treaties, is there not a danger that we are then reading too much *into* them?

It could not be the case that Westphalia was by itself an origin, arising from nowhere. The background to the peace reflected many important tendencies already under way. Philpott (2001), for example, chooses to locate Westphalia in the context of the intellectual revolution wrought by the Reformation. Other influences would seem to have been just as important. Westphalia was far from being the beginning of either moral or legal theorizing about international relations. There was an already well-established tradition of just war reflection. To this had been added after 1492, as discussed above, the ethical and legal issues that emanated from the acquisition and settlement of the New World during the course of the sixteenth century. Under the impetus of the Spanish school, the study of international legal frameworks had blossomed during that period, and was given even greater prominence by the publication of Grotius's major work *De Jure Belli ac Pacis* in 1625 (Grotius 1918). Running through all these intellectual endeavours was the quest to establish secure foundations for human reasoning in the face of the new challenges to the old orthodoxies. These remained, during the seventeenth century, a complex compound based on human nature (and its natural law), human reason (and its capacity to discern the law), and divine will. As far as concerned international relations, the key issue was to be the establishment of a viable foundation for legal intercourse, and this expressed itself in the attempt to make the step from the traditional *ius gentium* to the emerging *ius inter gentes* (Mattingly 1955: 284; Kingsbury and Roberts 1990: 28). At the same time, and arising out of the religious struggles and the Thirty Years War specifically, was the genesis of a new concept of the political, with its increasingly secularized basis. It was the fundamental agreement upon the need for this new mode of politics, as Schilling (1998: 16–17, 19) has powerfully argued, that made possible the stabilization of post-1648 Europe, but also the reaching of the 1648 settlement in the first place. Others too acknowledge the importance of this 'secularization that had recently taken place in European politics' (Parker 1987: 219). If Westphalia could ring the changes, then that was in part because of the changes already underway.

The peace has many claims to importance, not least that it resulted in new distributions of power amongst the major powers. In particular, it confirmed the secular decline of Spain, and the incipient emergence of France as the rising power (Doran 1971: 70). It was important also because of its scale. According to the best estimates, there were some 150 representatives in attendance at the two venues, the principal absentees being those of England, Russia, Poland, and Turkey (Mowat 1928: 108; Giry-Deloison 2000: 401; Croxton and Tischer 2002: xix). Others put the figures even higher, there being some '176 plenipotentiaries ... who acted for 194 European rulers, great and small' (Parker 1987: 178). Given the size of the proceedings, part of the difficulty in organizing it lay in the absence of any clear and relevant precedents (Sturdy 2002: 70). The most notable thing that the settlement did not achieve was peace between France and Spain. These two continued to fight each other for another eleven years, until the Pyrenees Treaty, like two 'punch-drunk boxers, clinging to each other in a state of near-exhaustion' (Kennedy 1988: 58–9).

In present-day format, both treaties run to approximately forty pages. Westphalia was called upon to establish both an Imperial and an international peace (Steiger 1998: 438; Sturdy 2002: 68–9). That the root cause of the war was to be found in the former, which had then spilled over into an international conflagration, is neatly set out in the succinct description of the war included, for instance, in the Münster text: 'That for many Years past, Discords and Civil Divisions being stir'd up in the Roman Empire, which increas'd to such a degree, that not only all Germany, but also the neighbouring Kingdoms, and France particularly, have been involv'd in the Disorders of a long and cruel War' (Avalon 1996–: 1).

If this was the accepted causal sequence, it reflected also the order of priorities for the peacemakers and, to be sure, establishing the 'peace of the land' occupied the lion's share of the successive articles of the treaties (Schmidt 1998: 447). Since the provisions devoted to the Empire were the bedrock of both treaties, they were essentially repeated in the two texts. These covered mainly the religious settlement, which now abandoned the Augsburg principle that had hitherto allowed the ruler to determine the religion (Osiander 2001: 272). Instead, it settled for the base year of 1624, and the religion of each territory was assigned on the basis of what had then prevailed, as did the divisions of ecclesiastical territories and properties. Importantly, this agreement embraced the Calvinists, not just Lutherans. These new religious arrangements were to be incorporated also into Imperial institutions (Bonney 1991: 201). At the same time, other aspects of the Empire's constitution were 'clarified' (Osiander 2001: 270; Bonney 1991: 200), with some disagreement as to whether this brought about any significant changes or not. It is the presence of the imperial princes at the negotiations, as of right and as full participants, that has attracted most comment. Even if it was not Westphalia that started this process of princely autonomy, the treaties 'provided a powerful stimulus to an existing dynamic' (Sturdy 2002: 72). But, as is equally clear, the ability of the princes to play this role, as Krasner (1993: 240) insisted, reflected also the military facts on the ground (Croxton and Tischer 2002: xvi), not just some doctrinal innovation. They were encouraged to play this role because France and Sweden wanted them to, and in order to diminish Habsburg power (Croxton 1999a). The Swedes, amongst others, were adamant that international peace required an imperial peace, and that this gave those outside an entitlement to a voice about its form.

In the remainder, Münster specified the territorial recompense to be given to France, while Osnabrück dealt with the territorial and financial settlement with Sweden. In the case of France, its acquisitions took the form of outright transfers of sovereignty. In the Münster Treaty, Article LXXI stipulated that the 'chief Dominion, Right of Sovereignty, and all other Rights upon the Bishopricks of Metz, Toul, and Verdun... shall for the future appertain to the Crown of France' (Avalon 1996–: 20). This is important because, unlike the transfers to Sweden, international law, and not the feudal institutions of the Empire, was the chosen instrument for its execution (Steiger 1998: 440). In the case of Sweden, as Krasner had objected, territories were made over 'not in full sovereignty but as fiefs of the Holy Roman Empire' (Krasner 1993: 241; Steiger 1998: 439). Sweden gained Bremen, Verden, and parts of Pomerania and, as duke of Bremen, its monarch gained voting rights in the Imperial Diet (Teschke 2003: 239).

There is one intriguing element that is present in most accounts of the peace settlement. However much conscious or not of the novelty of the work on which they were embarked, the peacemakers operated within a guiding principle that, far from *establishing* some new order, assumed they were *reinstating* an already existing architecture of rights. The negotiators at Westphalia were not operating with schemes of abstract thought, but sought a peace 'through the restoration of legal principles which, they believed, had been undermined by thirty years of warfare' (Sturdy 2002: 74; Teschke 2003: 239)). If such was the case, we need to get to the bottom of what this signified for the international society of the middle of the seventeenth century. It is only in relatively recent years that this topic has generated such a lively debate within international relations.

THE DEBATE ABOUT WESTPHALIA

If Westphalia was the great turning point, it is by no means clear that the peacemakers had any sense of their historic mission. They did not see 'themselves as innovators' (Osiander 1994: 44), nor as being 'present at the creation', preoccupied as they were with resolving the very specific problems that had given rise to the devastations of the Thirty Years War. Nor, for that matter, is it evident that historians, retrospectively, have always and consistently assigned Westphalia such a seminal role. Like most traditions, this is one that has been invented, and reinvented, to suit subsequent contexts and agendas. There had been earlier debates about the historical stature of Westphalia. For example, post-revolutionary writing in France, particularly that of Koch, may have had a very specific purpose in so elevating Westphalia, as part of its own counter-revolutionary project (Keene 2002: 20–1). Likewise, in a book published in 1800, the Comte d'Hauterive recorded the collective judgement that Westphalia had founded 'the public law of modern times'. This, however, had been contemptuously dismissed by 'the secretary of Europe', F. Gentz, on the grounds that it neither included 'all the nations even then important', nor did it 'embrace all the relations of the states which it did include' (Haslam 2002: 109–10). Writing immediately after the Second World War, Leo Gross, in a much-cited article, equally had his mind on contemporary order-building developments when he offered his own assessment of the great symbolic importance of the Peace. The Peace stood for 'the end of an epoch and the opening of another', and represented 'the majestic portal which leads from the old into the new world' (Gross 1948: 28)). Gross was writing with one eye firmly fixed on the dislocations of the post-war period, the incipient cold war, and the quest to translate the UN Charter into a meaningful part of the international order.

Thereafter, the orthodox position within the international relations literature has been that Westphalia marks a clear turning point in European international relations, and stands out as an historical watershed. It has been widely regarded as establishing a 'new diplomatic arrangement—an order created by states, for states' (Holsti 1991: 25). In this respect, it is the 'crucial demarcation between an era still dominated by competing claims to religious universalism and hierarchical authority', and the onset of a new period of 'autonomous political communities' (Walker 1993: 90). It is reputed to have served as 'opening the modern era of international relations' (McKay and Scott 1983: 3) generally, and, more specifically, to have been 'une étape importante dans la série des grandes réorganizations européennes' (Bély 2000: 611–12). Even those who are otherwise sceptical have conceded that it did mark significant changes, not least in undermining 'the hierarchical geopolitical structure centred on the Holy Roman Empire' (Rosenberg 1994: 136).

Recently, the status of Westphalia has been challenged by various revisionist schools, and it is now commonplace to dismiss the 'myth' of Westphalia as a fabrication of naive international relations theorists, largely innocent of the historical facts of the matter (Croxton 1999b; Osiander 2001). The assault has come from three distinct quarters, ranged across the international relations discipline's theoretical spectrum. First, it has been subjected to the general critique of postmodernism, and its suspicion of anything that purports to be a foundational 'origin'. Second, it has fallen foul of the historical materialists, who reject any notion of Westphalia as the inception of 'modern' international relations, since the states involved were both absolutist and not yet capitalist. According to Teschke (2003:3, 217), '1648, far from signaling a breakthrough to modern inter-state relations, was the culmination of the epoch of absolutist state formation', and was rooted in 'pre-capitalist social property relations' (Rosenberg 1994). Westphalia 'was more of an end than a beginning' (Teschke 2003: 245). Over the past decade or so, the orthodox interpretation has also been subjected to serious revisionist challenge from a realist direction. Most prominently, Krasner has denied that the settlement amounted to a 'decisive break with the past' (Krasner 1993: 246; 1995/6; 2001). The orthodox position 'that the Peace of Westphalia of 1648 marks a turning point', he asserted bluntly, 'is wrong' (Krasner 1993: 235). Moreover, the guiding force of the peace lay in the short-term interests of the victorious powers, namely France and Sweden, and not in 'some overarching conceptualization of how the international system should be ordered' (Krasner 1993: 246). Central to Krasner's argument was that the present-day reader would not find in Westphalia a 'modern' notion of sovereignty at all. Indeed, given the restrictions which it imposed upon the ruler's right to impose a preferred religion upon his/her subjects, it was 'less consistent with modern notions of sovereignty than Augsburg' (Krasner 1993: 244; Wyduckel 1998: 77). Indeed, some scholars would characterize Westphalia as a restriction on sovereignty, and as part of the story of 'minority rights' protection (Preece 1998: 56–7; Croxton and Tischer 2002: xix). Krasner's general critique was, in some respects, endorsed in Osiander's (1994) detailed study. 'That the Peace of Westphalia was a milestone on the road to a states system built around the concept of sovereignty is a popular view, especially with students of international relations', he chided, 'but it is a myth' (Osiander 1994: 78).

It should be remembered, however, that there had been yet earlier dissenters from the notion that Westphalia had single-handedly given rise to modern international relations. Wight (1997: 147) himself had placed Westphalia in the context of a lineage of settlements (Lodi, Madrid, Cambrai), and his perspective was the more modest one that Westphalia 'is singular only as the basic diplomatic arrangement that has had the longest run in European history'. From his point of view, it was the durability and persistence of Westphalia that was to be important, more so than the revolutionary quality of any of its principles.

In the wake of this widespread revisionism, we now have the possibility for some kind of post-revisionist synthesis, heralded by the contribution of Philpott (2001). While acknowledging the appropriate qualifications, he has nonetheless sought to restore the reputation of Westphalia as a key episode in modern international relations. *Contra* Krasner, he has insisted that Westphalia is 'a fulcrum, not just an incremental milemarker' (Philpott 2001: 83). He refutes the central challenge of the revisionist case, as having failed to 'dethrone the conventional wisdom', and concludes by restating the claim that Westphalia can properly be regarded as the 'origin of a European system of sovereign states' (Philpott 2001: 89–90).

There is a sensible post-revisionist position to be staked out on this issue. To do so, the precise grounds on which the various claims to Westphalia's status have been both asserted, and refuted, will now be set out with greater precision. This will clear the way for a statement of the present argument. Those most favoured accounts of Westphalia's historical stature—that emphasize the doctrine of sovereignty—are, indeed, ill-founded. This, however, does not amount to an across-the-board vindication of the revisionist position.

WESTPHALIA: THE ORIGIN OF WHAT?

The orthodox account makes the case for Westphalia as the major turning point in the history of modern international relations within Europe. If it was such an important beginning, of what exactly was it the origin? The sundry claims can be recounted as follows: the origins of the state system; the consolidation of the principle of sovereignty; the inception of a distinctive international legal order; and the emergence of an international society. Many of these claims are indeed interconnected, and overlap. However, they do not all amount to exactly the same thing.

For some, the historic significance of Westphalia is to be found in the very beginnings of the European state system *tout court*: it was such a system that was established by the peace settlement. International historians thus report that the 'Westphalian settlement is frequently seen as the beginning of the modern state system' (Black 2002: 74). Holsti (1991: 26) is typical of this genre in his conclusion that Westphalia 'paved the way for a system of states to replace a hierarchical system'. Although not subscribing to it, Wight acknowledged this point of view as an alternative 'starting-point' to his own preference for 1494 as the year of origin. His refinement of the argument was to aver that at 'Westphalia the states-system does not come into existence: it comes of age' (Wight 1977: 152), while at the same time conceding that Westphalia appeared to become the 'legal basis of the states-system' (1977: 113). This is not the moment to rehearse this debate in detail. Some, following Wight, evidently see the origins preceding Westphalia (Anderson 1998), whereas others, such as Hinsley (1967: 164), defer the commencement of a fully articulated legal and political state system until the eighteenth century. Yet others again prefer the nineteenth century, for the reasons that in the seventeenth there was not yet any clear concept of territoriality, and the actors were private rather than public (Teschke 2003: 230–8). Of the many claims made on its behalf, the wholly unqualified assertion that Westphalia gave birth to the state system is the least persuasive.

Even those who do endorse this claim make clear that the state system, to the extent that it became manifest after 1648, did not yet enjoy all the appurtenances of the system as it would eventually develop. For instance, there is no suggestion at Westphalia, or in the intellectual context of the period, of a legally or politically distinct category of great powers, enjoying special rights and responsibilities (Suganami 1990: 226–7; Osiander 1994: 323). Nor, for that matter, was there as yet any clear articulation of equilibrist thinking as a formal aspect of the peace settlement (Osiander 1994: 80), however much influence it exercised de facto over the balance of power (Bolingbroke 1932: 17–18; Bull 1990: 76). Bull (1990: 90) had suggested that, in Grotius's time generally, there was little conscious development of balance of power thinking. This is untenable. It is belied by the inclusion in a Treaty between France and Denmark in 1645 of a statement explicitly endorsing the principle (Anderson 1993: 154). Elsewhere, Count Salvius, the Swedish plenipotentiary at Osnabrück, reported back that 'people are beginning to see the power of Sweden as dangerous to the "balance of power" ... When one begins to become powerful ... the others place themselves, through unions or alliances, into the opposite balance in order to maintain the equipoise' (Parker 1987: 184). Nonetheless, Osiander is correct to insist that balance of power, as such, is nowhere mentioned in the actual treaties (Osiander 2001: 266).

The second basis for the claim that Westphalia was a turning point rests upon the notion of sovereignty, rather than the state system as such. This may appear counter-intuitive, inasmuch as the latter might be thought to already comprehend the former: what makes the state system a system is the separation of the units into sovereign entities. However, this does not strictly follow. Without sovereignty, a state system would assuredly not be the one with which we have actually become familiar, but it is equally plausible to imagine a system with other attributes, while remaining essentially a system of states. If anything, it is upon the more specific notion of sovereignty that the claim in support of Westphalia tends more commonly to be advanced. 'Sovereignty', we are instructed, '...became the fundamental principle of the European order' after Westphalia (Steiger 1998: 440). Such formulations are legion in the literature. Holsti's (1991: 39) rendition is that Westphalia 'legitimized the ideas of sovereignty and dynastic autonomy'. Jackson (2000: 165) traces to it the emergence of a *societas* 'based on the pluralist norms of state sovereignty'. In Watson's words, the Westphalian settlement 'legitimized a *commonwealth of sovereign states*' (Watson 1992: 186). For Bobbit (2002: 508), Westphalia is important because it gave birth to a 'new society of states characterized by their sovereign equality'. In so doing, it initiated a powerful and complex normative structure, embracing 'sovereignty, sovereign equality, territorial integrity, political independence and non-intervention' (Williams 1996: 43). And so on.

There is no doubt that much of this is seriously misleading, if thought to result from the specific provisions of the Westphalian Treaties, as Osiander (2001) and Croxton (1999*b*) so trenchantly make clear. Krasner is correct to point out that, in so far as Westphalia deals with sovereignty at all, it is within the specific context of the Empire that it does so. Commentators tend to cite the famous provisions LXIV and LXV in the Münster Treaty, that specify the rights of the princes ('Rights, Prerogatives, Libertys, Privileges, free exercise of Territorial Right, as well Ecclesiastick, as Politick'), including the right to form alliances (Israel 1967; Grewe 1988; Avalon 1996–: 18) and the similar VIII in the Osnabrück version (Parry 1969: vol. 1, 241). These are reinforced by the very explicit reminder in the preamble to Münster that the treaty had been devised and agreed 'with the consent of' all the princes (who, implicitly, might equally have withheld it) (Avalon 1996–: 2). It may well be true, as Heeren (1834: 160) was later to put it, that 'the princes were in the fullest sense rulers of their respective states', or that the princes acquired, by their participation, 'a sacrosanct quality of sovereignty' (Watson 1992: 196). These judgements remain problematic, however, because this part of the settlement is essentially about the imperial constitution, and it is hazardous to extend the argument from this to a set of principles about the nature of the international order more generally. In any case, it is far from convincing that what was being articulated within the Empire amounted to the subsequent doctrine of sovereignty (Croxton 1999*b*: 574).

Outside the context of the Empire, the claim remains more contentious still. Osiander (2001: 251) suggests that it derives from a backwards reading of history, and 'is really a product of the nineteenth-and twentieth-century fixation on the concept of sovereignty'. Since this is where history was seen then to culminate, there has been a tendency to read this evolution back into the Westphalian arrangements in a completely anachronistic way. Even if compelling ideas about sovereignty were to develop in the decades after Westphalia, these may just as well have emerged as contingent aspects of then current political practices, rather than as direct linear descendants of a philosophical principle expounded at Westphalia. In particular, it has been plausibly asserted that subsequent developments occurred as an adjunct of the visible strengthening of state structures in the last third of the seventeenth century (Kaiser 1990: 139). It was to be these financial, political, and military reorganizations of that later period that gave real content to the concept of sovereignty. Under the force of these, and especially with the creation of standing armies, states began to make 'real their claim to monopolize violence' (Hall 1996: 53). There can be many convincing reasons, apart from the Westphalian settlement, for the post-1648 development of sovereignty.

The third basis of novelty that is commonly attributed to Westphalia is that it gave rise to a qualitatively new international legal order. This was once presented as a simplistic morality tale, according to which, after 1648 'the rule of international law...began' (Mowat 1928: 59). But it endures in much more sophisticated accounts of the present day that continue to assign Westphalia 'a general meaning for the European order of the following century' (Steiger 1998: 437). This was to be found, essentially, in its establishment of a 'droit public de l'Europe', understood as a 'self-created, contractual legal order built on consensus' (Steiger 1998: 445), and as laying the 'first foundations of the international law of treaties' (Steiger 1998: 440). It matters not that this did not then take the form of a fully developed concept of international law, as we might now understand it. What was important was the perceived linkage between scrupulous adherence to a body of legal entitlements, and an anticipated pacification of international politics. This operated on the belief that, as Osiander puts it, 'provided the rights of each of the participating actors could be established definitively, no source of conflict would remain'. In turn, this belief was derived from 'the status of legality as a consensus principle' (Osiander 1994: 48). In short, as will be shown below, this notion of an international consensus was to become critical, and it was around the sanctity of the legal order that it was first able to express itself.

It is interesting to contrast these claims with the negative appraisal provided by Leo Gross who was to criticize the aftermath of Westphalia from exactly such an international legal point of view. The fulminations he directed at the conduct of international relations thereafter presented Westphalia as a step backwards, not forwards, for the international community:

It led to the era of absolutist states, jealous of their territorial sovereignty to a point where the idea of an international community became an almost empty phrase and where international law came to depend upon the will of states more concerned with the preservation and expansion of their power than with the establishment of a rule of law. (Gross 1948: 38)

However much Gross might have been justified in condemning the wars of absolutism in the late seventeenth and early eighteenth centuries, he scarcely had reason to do so on the basis of the content of the Westphalian Treaties. The idea of a 'public law of Europe', based on general consent, finds explicit endorsement in some of their articles. Notably, with regard to the transfer of territories from the Empire, these 'Cessions and Alienations' were taken to override all 'Decrees, Constitutions, Statutes and Customs of their Predecessors' (Avalon 1996–: LXXXI, 22). They could never be reclaimed on any of these titles, which were now trumped by the international legal basis of the treaty, 'as having been legally transfer'd to another's Dominion, with the common Consent of the States, for the benefit of the publick Tranquillity' (Avalon 1996–: LXXXII, 23).

This argument about the nature of the post-Westphalian legal order slides into, and may properly be considered part of, a fourth position about the settlement's contribution to a developing international society. If, in Wight's version, the state system developed much earlier, what did he mean by his claim that in 1648 it had come of age? What new quality did it acquire at that point? A variety of writers would respond that, for the first time, it came to possess the demonstrable quality of a working international society. Perhaps unsurprisingly, it is Bull who asserts this line most boldly. Having determined that Grotius was important precisely because of his contribution to the development of the idea of an international society, Bull then concluded that 'the Westphalian treaties demonstrated in practice, just as Grotius had done in theory, that the independence or sovereignty of states was not incompatible with their subjection to law or their recognition of the common bonds of society' (Bull 1990: 77, 93). Elsewhere, he describes Westphalia succinctly as 'a kind of constitutional foundation of international society' (Bull 1990: 76).

This view has been challenged on historical grounds by those, for example, who would see earlier treaties, such as that of Augsburg in 1555, as 'the first constitution of the European society of states' (Bobbitt 2002: 506). It is dismissed also by Gross, for the very reasons given above, that Westphalia inaugurated a phase of 'anti-social' behaviour by absolutist monarchs 'instead of creating a society of states' (Gross 1948: 39). In the broader picture, these rebuttals remain unconvincing. It is within this framework of an emerging international society that the significance of Westphalia is best to be appreciated. Key to its development was to be a set of practices made possible by acceptance of principles of legitimacy at its core.

WESTPHALIA, LEGITIMACY, AND INTERNATIONAL SOCIETY

The importance of Westphalia is best conceived in terms of the necessary linkage between the formation of an international society and the development of its shared principles of legitimacy: the existence of the society makes possible practices of legitimacy, while the incipient standard of legitimacy, in turn, bears witness to the emerging reality of that society. Having a notion of legitimacy is what, in shorthand, we mean by an international society. For this reason, any argument that Westphalia is bound up with the articulation of a principle of legitimacy is inescapably also a claim about its importance for the development of an international society. This chapter then seeks to extend the argument set out by Armstrong that Westphalia can be seen as 'the symbolic origin of the society of states', in part for its articulation of a general principle of legitimacy (Armstrong 1993: 33*ff*).

More concisely, Westphalia stands as a historical fulcrum, not because of its endorsement of sovereignty, but because of its more fundamental articulation of a notion of legitimacy as a constitutive act of this new international society. That sovereignty was, indeed, to suffuse the principles of legitimacy in the centuries after Westphalia is not in any doubt. However, we should not confuse principles of legitimacy, as a necessary part of a functioning international society, with its historically variable instantiations—of which sovereignty is one. It is in this respect that the case for Westphalia's importance can most securely be made. Thus far, the debate about Westphalia has become unhelpfully fixated on the specific principle of sovereignty. This has been at the expense of appreciating the prior movement towards a consensual principle of legitimacy at all, and of which sovereignty was to be but one of its many possible incarnations. At the time of Westphalia, the consensus was around an agreed concept of legality, not sovereignty. It is all the more urgent to make this separation since the historical case for associating the Westphalian provisions with sovereignty is itself so very weak.

It is thus upon those arguments that regard Westphalia as the seminal stage in the development of an international society that this analysis must build. 'The conception of international society as a whole acting as a source of legitimacy', it has been observed, 'was one that was to have a lingering influence in later versions of international society' (Armstrong 1993: 23). If that was so in a theoretical sense, it was equally in the practical, and Westphalia was a tangible demonstration of exactly such a project. This argument will be outlined in general, and then supported with reference to a number of specific aspects and characteristics of the Westphalian settlement. These represent the evidence for a practice of legitimacy at Westphalia, conducted in the shadow of its emerging principles.

Heeren's assessment, reached early in the nineteenth century, is a good point of departure. He conceded that Westphalia had not settled 'all the great political relations'. Nonetheless, he maintained that it became 'the foundation of the subsequent policy of Europe', by 'settling the leading political maxims' (Heeren 1834: 161–2). He does not spell out in detail what is meant by this. In context, however, given his notion of a European polity, the maxims can be understood as the very principles which gave meaning and reality to that polity as a consciously shared enterprise. There could be a European international society only if it could express itself in such shared maxims, and it was the willingness both to generate and to subscribe to them (rather than their specific content) which makes Westphalia important to a more general appreciation of the nature of international legitimacy. At a fundamental level, what the peace-makers had reached was the realization that goals (such as an effective peace) could no longer be attained unilaterally, or in small groups, but only by a universal consent. Hence, an affirmation that international society would now operate on the basis of consensus (however that was to be made manifest) became the meaningful expression of its acceptance of a principle of legitimacy. Divine will, as will be seen, remained important, but what that actually entailed had to be discovered principally by reference to what was acceptable to the society of rulers. Here also, in embryonic form, was the normative principle of constitutionality, albeit for the moment overshadowed by those of morality (Christendom) and legality.

The historical novelty of Westphalia, it has thus been asserted, rests on the specific instruments of its peacemaking but also, and more importantly, on the 'claims to legitimacy' that these involved (Gerhardt 1998: 486). This is the heart of the matter. These can be found in both of the areas that constitute the framework of international legitimacy: an operative practice of consensus and rules of recognition for membership of international society (both of which have been implemented on a variety of changing historical principles over time). Westphalia was to be of major significance in both of these domains. It formulated essential dimensions of international legitimacy that have preoccupied international society ever since.

As to the first, it revealed itself particularly in the unstated assumptions that lent validity to the settlement as a whole. The belief was that states would comply with it because it was an instrument of their collective will. 'This requirement of consensus', it has been suggested, is what brought about 'the constitutional achievement of Westphalia' (Bobbitt 2002: 504). That such a consensus existed is, from this point of view, of far greater historical importance than the precise matters around which that consensus was able to express itself. It drew a map of Europe 'that defined the bounds of legitimacy' (Holsti 1991: 43), thereby contributing to the new identity of Europe as a 'really existing' international society. It expressed itself also in the refusal to operate on the basis of a straightforward right of conquest. This was rejected because, by its nature, it would violate the consensus that the settlement was designed to signify. 'The consensus agenda was bound up with the desire for a degree of stability', Osiander (1994: 50) concludes, and for that reason, 'the right of conquest therefore could not be part of it'.

This principle of consensus spilled over into the second area, the rights to membership. What comes through so powerfully in the settlement is the goal of constructing an international society, as a deliberate choice and as a work of artifice. It could no longer be thought of as some gift of nature, or of God alone. What entitled any political unit to participation was the social act of its recognition by the others. This was to become the only real test of legitimate membership.

This point is usually illustrated with specific reference to the examples of Swiss and Dutch independence. Neither is straightforward. A strong case has been made that the relevant clause in the treaties dealing with the Swiss had a much narrower, and specific, import than any general grant of independence from the Empire. It was prompted by the anomalous situation of Basel (Osiander 2001: 267). Swiss 'autonomy' was thereby reconfirmed, not granted *de novo*. As to the Dutch, it is true that that the treaties 'do not even deal with them' (Croxton 1999*b*: 576; Osiander 2001: 267). Dutch independence had been already acknowledged by Spain in the Münster Treaty of January 1648, not in the two October treaties. The force of that point, however, may be somewhat diminished by the extent to which some historians see all three treaties as interlinked, and the former to be incorporated in the latter (Petrie 1949: 149; Parker 1987: 179). As with the Imperial constitution more generally, what was important was less the degree of innovation, and more the extent of the felt need for codification: the messenger counted as much as the message.

There is a broader claim at stake. Despite his denials that Westphalia granted sovereignty to the Swiss and the Dutch, Osiander draws a very illuminating parallel between the nature of the Imperial system and the European system more generally. The point he makes encapsulates much of the present argument:

With the military strength of most estates of the empire negligible or indeed nonexistent, evidently their actorhood was exclusively ascriptive: based on rules, not power. They, as well as the collective entity they made up, existed exclusively because of collective and mutual empowerment, which in turn was based on a shared, rather elaborate code of structural and procedural legitimacy... As well as a system of empowerment, the empire was therefore also a system of collective restraint. *It actually shared this double quality with the European system of which it was part.* (Osiander 2001: 279, emphasis added)

This is the point exactly. It was for international society to dispose, and in this disposition existed also a form of restraint. What was important about any new act of admission hereafter was that the 'congress (and thus the new international society) found it acceptable' (Bobbitt 2002: 120). Hence, what indicated 'at least a nascent society of states' by 1648 was the fact that 'states were not just created by their own efforts, but were to gain international recognition by the acts of the collectivity' (Holsti 1991: 36). The precise sense in which Swiss autonomy was confirmed may be now obscure, but confirmed it was. Dutch independence was recognized in a treaty that fell within the subsequent ambit of Westphalia. It was not the mere status of the member states that was to be crucial, but the legitimacy attached to that status by the society itself. In Philpott's precise words, what Westphalia represented was a system that 'was codified into legitimacy' (2001: 97). Scholars of international relations have been so preoccupied with understanding this in terms of sovereignty—which in any case is not soundly based—that they have lost sight of this dimension of legitimacy. In this way, international society came better to recognize itself, and its own existence. It might have said, 'I legitimize, therefore I am'. And having undergone the beginnings of this fundamental self-realization, it remained for that society to develop henceforth the specific, and historically changing, rules upon which its subsequent grants of recognition would be made, or withheld.

If this is the central claim, predicated upon a greater self-consciousness of a principle of legitimacy in international society, it can be substantiated by appeal to two further practices that were present in various parts of the Westphalian Treaties: these will be called its implicit *comprehensiveness*, and its express intention to stand in *perpetuity*.

That Westphalia was implicitly comprehensive is true in a very particular sense. It certainly is not to be understood as a claim that Westphalia sought to regulate all matters of concern to the states of Europe. In fact, its direct ambit was relatively narrow, if thought of in territorial terms, and hence Osiander (2001: 266) has dismissed any pretension that it was 'a pan-European charter'. Procedurally and instrumentally, however, there was a self-conscious adoption of mechanisms that implied that this was a settlement, not *of* all Europe, but *for* all Europe. Even if the treaties themselves were essentially bilateral affairs, the congress was genuinely multilateral (Croxton 1999*b*). It thus fully merits its attribution as the 'first peace conference of modern times' (Parker 1987: 177). What was being settled, in a groping and tentative way, was as much the nature and scope of international society, as the various particulars on the ground. This is widely recognized and accepted in the historical literature. Typically, its very logic is specified as being the creation of a peace 'that will prevail all over Europe' (Gerhardt 1998: 488). It was not 'an *ad hoc* agreement', amongst a select few, but very deliberately 'a once-and-for-settlement, agreed to by *all* the major powers' (Rabb 1975: 78), one designed to be 'comprehensive, governing all Europe' (Philpott 2001: 82). This reflected the full impact of the war itself which had given European society an awareness 'of its existence and its essential unity' (Polisensky 1971: 257). The expression of this unity was, naturally enough, to be through the instrument of a comprehensive European congress, and the first of its kind (Gerhardt 1998: 485; Steiger 1998: 443–4). It has been portrayed as a 'veritable Estates-General of Europe' (Holsti 1991: 25–6), and this was to be the telling precedent. 'What was it not deemed possible to effect after this by congresses', Heeren (1834: 172–3) speculated rhetorically, and evidently in some awe at the prospect which it opened up.

Symbolic of this general view of the comprehensive nature of the settlement is an important characteristic of the two treaties themselves. While all students of the subject are at least dimly aware of the separate negotiations at Münster and Osnabrück, what is normally not realized is the great effort expended on precise coordination of the two texts. Given the vagaries of the two protracted sets of negotiations, and the slowness of the communications between the two towns, it may seem curious indeed that such a nicety was actually observed at all:

The texts of both treaties developed over a long period of time. They also had to be closely coordinated. Substantial sections concerning the general peace as well as the Imperial internal peace had to be identical in the texts. *Both treaties formed a treaty system.* (Steiger 1998: 444–5, emphasis added)

What this careful, if time consuming, procedure underlines is the symbolic importance of presenting this as an integrated peace for Europe, regardless of the specificities of the individual signatories, or of the details under agreement. The project was greater than the sum of its two parts, since it was actually about agreement to create a European international society, crafted around an agreed standard of legitimacy.

This was made that much more possible precisely because it was able to draw upon traditional conceptions of unity, based upon continuing notions of Christendom, just as can be found in the work of Grotius (Bull 1990: 87). While the idea of an international society is often counter-posed to that of Christendom, there were also significant connections between the two, and Westphalia certainly did not see the latter wholly eclipsed (Osiander 1994: 27). Hinsley (1967: 156) was adamant that the idea of Christendom remained powerful for the remainder of the seventeenth century. Fittingly, the Münster Treaty acknowledged this idea in the standard treaty language of the age, declaring that it would establish 'a Christian and Universal Peace' (Avalon: I, 2). Schilling interprets this as a 'bridge' whereby the 'secularisation of the political'—and away from the 'sacral' (Reus-Smit 2003)—was both 'legitimated and made acceptable' (Schilling 1998: 19).

The other key dimension of the peace was to be its consciousness of its validity in perpetuity (Burkhardt 1998: 58). This was a peace that was to be 'frozen forever' (Holsti 1991: 40), one deemed to be 'definitive and final' (Osiander 1994: 43). It was not a settlement convenient for the moment, until a better one should come along. It was understood both then, and subsequently, to have provided the benchmark of acceptability against which later orderings of Europe would be measured. In short, it was about establishing the bases of a new international society, and thereby inhibit subsequent actions in violation of them.

There are again a number of specific characteristics that can be called upon to support this interpretation. The first was the clear appreciation that this needed to be a peace in perpetuity, and offered the prospect of being so, exactly because it had received the formal approbation of international society as a whole. This gave it a standing above other treaties, and enabled it to legitimate the treaties that followed in its wake. Procedurally, this was a common enough device within the developing area of international treaty law, as Callières, the noted commentator on diplomacy, was later to point out. 'New treaties of peace have almost always a great conformity to the former treaties...' (Callières 1983:

155). As for the international lawyers, in the eighteenth century Vattel (1916: 351) was to acknowledge as a matter of principle that mention of any earlier treaty, in a new one, was tantamount to incorporating it 'word for word'. But the point here goes beyond that formal and legal one. In the case of Westphalia, it was specifically seen to enjoy a special status: 'each new peace agreement between contracting parties to either of the treaties of Münster and Osnabrück was based on the latter as a *norma* or *norme* or *fundamentum* or base', it is reported (Steiger 1998: 445; see also McKay and Scott 1983: 6). This is corroborated in the long list of important treaties thereafter, which, when they alluded to earlier treaties, always *began* with Westphalia. Examples, can be found in the Ryswick Treaty (1697), Utrecht (1713), Baden (1714), and Paris (1763) (Parry 1969: vol. 22, 82; vol. 27, 489; vol. 29, 177; vol. 42, 323). It was this legal lineage, with Westphalia standing at the head of it, that had so impressed Koch, and led him to draw attention to the settlement's historical significance (Keene 2002: 20).

Second, the hope and expectation of perpetuity was reinforced by the 'guarantees' to be embedded in the peace. The sense that the treaties enjoyed permanent validity was intimately connected with the explicit provisions to 'guarantee' such an outcome (Croxton 1999b: 584). This should not be overstated. Treaties in the past had utilized a long list of measures to ensure durable compliance, such as oaths, the good offices of guarantors, and the placement of various sureties, be it of property or persons. In that general sense, Westphalia was no different in wishing to see that its terms were both executed in the short term and also honoured in the longer. What was different was the manner in which it sought to ensure such outcomes.

There is a complex pre-history to the articles that finally found their way into the treaties. In the period 1637–41, Cardinal Richelieu, French chief minister under Louis XIII, had developed his own ideas about a stable peace—a 'bonne paix de la chrétienté'. This was not to be simply the conclusion of a war, but instead 'l'établissement et la garantié d'un état de paix permanente' (Malettke 2000: 57). He had issued an instruction in January 1637 to the effect that, as part of any future peace, there must be created two leagues—proto-collective security mechanisms—that would protect and defend the peace against any attempts to violate it (Malettke 2000: 57). Similar schemes continued to be studied under Mazarin, Louis XIV's chief minister (Croxton 1999a). In the event, the treaties contained only the pale shadow of these proposals, too many objections having been raised against them along the way. The specific suggestion for the two leagues was not to be realized. More modestly, however, elements of the guarantee of perpetuity were to survive. They operated in two stages. In Article CXXIII of Münster, 'all Partys in this Transaction shall be oblig'd to defend and protect all and every Article of this Peace against any one' (Avalon 1996–: 33). If the threatened violation could not be resolved over a period of three years, Article CXXIV enjoined that 'all and every one of those concern'd in this Transaction shall be oblig'd to join the injur'd Party, and assist him with Counsel and Force to repel the Injury' (Avalon 1996–: 34). Such a secular guarantee, calling upon the signatories to act in unison, as an international society of enforcement, was to replace earlier forms of guarantee 'which relied on linking the affirmation of the oaths by the parties to the treaty and their submission to the papal power to bind and annul' (Steiger 1998: 443). Holsti (1991: 36) is no doubt correct to point out that, as a system of 'collective security', this was defective, since there was no body to determine that an 'injury' had been committed. But this is to miss the greater truth that, since the treaty was to be considered an act of international society, that society was now made responsible for future compliance with it (Gross 1948: 24). For good measure, Article CXXVIII provided that there could be no walking away from the terms of the treaty, simply by a refusal to ratify: 'all and every one of the other States who shall abstain from signing and ratifying the present Treaty, shall be no less oblig'd to maintain and observe what is contain'd in this present Treaty of Pacification, than if they had subscrib'd and ratify'd it' (Avalon 1996–: 35). Such was to be its binding force.

Finally, one can see elements of the perpetual validity of the treaty, somewhat paradoxically, in its retrospective focus. Westphalia looked backwards to ensure the permanence of its solution for the future. The emphasis throughout was on pacification by means of restoration of an earlier enjoyment of rights. Even in what is conventionally, if mistakenly, seen to be its most 'revolutionary' undertakings, namely the recognition of considerable degrees of autonomy, if not formal sovereignty, for the states of the Empire, this was clearly the case. As has been said, the treaties sought to 'reestablish' the ancient rights of the princes of the Empire (Philpott 2001: 85). Having no abstract conception of what a peaceful international society should look like, the peacemakers looked to the past to guarantee the stability of the future. In Osiander's (1994: 73) words, 'the only way to achieve a stable settlement was to leave things at least roughly as they had been ... to remodel the system in accordance with what they saw as its own tradition'. Thus was it that the future could be linked seamlessly to the past and, in so doing, the future itself would be endowed with a seemingly timeless quality.

CONCLUSION

In sum, the Peace of Westphalia has rightly been assigned an important historical status in international relations, but usually for the wrong reasons. Its reputation as the origin of the state system is dubious, to say the least. Nor, for that matter, is the claim that Westphalia deserves recognition because it expounded the principle of sovereignty, or put that principle in practice, any more soundly based. In this regard, Westphalia was a pastiche of old and new conceptions, as exemplified in the differing instruments for the territorial dispositions to France and Sweden, respectively. It was also primarily within the context of the constitutional settlement in the Empire—and not as a clear expression of a universal doctrine for the European state system—that such a concept of autonomy was mentioned at all.

There is further irony. Given that the orthodox position places such great weight on the emergence of sovereignty, two of the major elements of the treaties are more impressive as instruments of international regulation than as statements of individual state autonomy. The first of these is with reference to the religious settlement. This ditched the prerogative of the ruler to determine the religion in favour of an internationally-sanctioned standard (1624) which thus replaced the jurisdiction of the ruler over that matter. Teschke (2003: 241) is right to be impressed that this amounted to 'nothing less than an international prescription of the territorial distribution of different confessions'. Likewise, the placing of the imperial constitution in an international legal framework meant a degree of 'internationalization of German politics' (Croxton 1999*b*: 583; Teschke 2003: 243). In both these areas, sovereignty is scarcely embraced, but the entitlement of international society to pronounce is very much to the forefront.

It is in this more self-confident assertion of an international society that the most convincing case can be made on Westphalia's behalf. In coalescing around a notion of legitimacy as the central precept of international society, the peacemakers drew upon existing religious and legal schemes of thought, but with a new sense of purpose. The awareness of unity which this required derived from earlier ideas, and was powerfully reinforced also by the calamities of the long period of warfare. To be sure, there were fewer substantive innovations contained in the settlement than many have supposed. At the same time, there was a procedural novelty in the many codifications, clarifications, and reformulations of which the treaties consisted. These were now beginning to be expressed on a different basis, as the purposeful statements of an increasingly self-conscious international society. Only when it had taken the first faltering steps towards producing these ideas could European international society feel some confidence in its own existence. What lay at the heart of this historic breakthrough was the very idea of international legitimacy itself.

If legitimacy is what, historically speaking, Westphalia's reputation is all about, how are we to explain the contrary judgement that Westphalia failed to construct a legitimate order? As already encountered, Kissinger's account would have it that a legitimate order is one acceptable to all the great powers. On that basis, Westphalia fails the test, since it is clear that Spain was not reconciled to it (Doran 1971: 87). Kissinger (1995: 27) was also to dismiss Westphalia explicitly, and in company with Versailles, for such a failure. This picks up on supposed parallels between Westphalia and Versailles, inasmuch as Westphalia was essentially a permit allowing France to keep Germany down (Teschke 2003: 244). In this respect, Kissinger's critique is based on the somewhat different ground that Westphalia did not achieve a proper balance between security and justice.

Neither assessment is convincing. The narrower conception of a legitimate order as one agreeable to all the great powers was one that was to develop much later, early in the nineteenth century. It could have little part in the thinking in 1648, if for no other reason than that there was not then any theoretical notion of the great powers as a separate category. To condemn Westphalia as illegitimate, on these grounds, is wholly anachronistic. As to the second point, it is difficult to know what this might mean. Whose sense of security, and which standard of justice, is the pertinent one for the discussion? It is clear here that Kissinger, standing on the outside, is judging the settlement by some abstract standard of legitimacy that is his own.

At the very least, it is not one shared by most other historians of the period. If stability is the practical test for the attainment of legitimacy, Westphalia can be argued to have achieved more than Kissinger admits. With regard to the affairs of Germany, and the Austrian Habsburgs, the settlement has been claimed to have produced 'solid and lasting achievements', with no future major conflict about these issues (Parker 1987: 217). More generally, it succeeded in further defusing religion as a source of international conflict (Rabb 1975: 80; Parker 1987: 218; Elliott 1998: 39). Rousseau was later to provide its most extravagant endorsement: 'The peace of Westphalia may well remain the foundation of our political system for ever' (Parker 1987: 216).

Historians can reasonably quarrel about such verdicts. For present purposes, the relevant issue is not about the legitimacy *of* Westphalia, assessed exogenously, but rather about the emergence of a concept of legitimacy *in* Westphalia, endogenously developed. Westphalia provides strong evidence of the emergence of principles of international legitimacy, whether or not successful claims to legitimation were made on behalf of all aspects of its terms. There is, from this point of view, every reason to acknowledge the Westphalian proceedings as an important formative stage in the history of legitimacy in international society.

4

Utrecht: Consensus, Balance of Power, and Legitimacy

The Utrecht settlement refers to the complex of treaties, signed in the period 1713–14, which brought an end to the wars of Spanish Succession. Like its Westphalian precursor, this was a treaty *system*, in which various provisions were repeated in separate bilateral treaties, and understood to be common and interlocking to them all. These treaties were devoted principally to the conditions on which the members of the Grand Alliance secured future peace with Louis XIV's France, and separately, to the effective partition of the Spanish territories.

This chapter has a tripartite agenda. It will seek to explain what the settlement was about, why it has been regarded as significant by various historians and international relations scholars, and, emerging from these debates, how it relates to the developing practices of legitimacy within international society. It will demonstrate how a traditionally dominant conception of rightful membership—through the principle of legitimate succession—was now challenged and subordinated to international regulation, and in particular to a governing principle of the balance of power. It will explore also the elaboration of various aspects of rightful conduct as manifested in the modalities of treaty-making, the articulation of a basic notion of consensus, and the self-conscious promotion of a societal norm of equilibrium. Finally, it will reflect on the complex interrelationship between the extent of the consensus around the treaty and the then prevailing balance of power. Was it the consensus that made possible the commitment to the principle of the balance of power, or was it the particular configurations of the balance then in existence that made possible the consensus?

THE SETTLEMENT AND ITS CONTEXT

In addition to ending the drawn-out campaigns of the Spanish Succession, Utrecht served more generally to bring to a close the even longer period of international turbulence associated with the reign of Louis XIV. The treaties stand out as a prominent landmark, if not some absolute turning point, in the landscape of modern international history. According to one felicitous description, the settlement 'did mark a comma, if not a full stop' in the international events of the period (McKay and Scott 1983: 97; see also Roberts 1947; Doyle 1978; Parrott 2001).

At first glance, it seems uncontroversial that both the war and the peace testified to the continuing centrality of dynastic concerns. If this episode relates to legitimacy, then it must surely be because it underlined how questions about the legitimacy of dynastic inheritance still dominated the international agenda. How could it be otherwise since the war had been sparked, as its name tells us, by concerns about *succession* to the Spanish throne? While this is true, it tells us only half of the truth. As will be demonstrated below, Utrecht was to be as important for what it revealed about the incipient constraints upon legitimate succession, as it was for reinforcing the centrality of this traditional dimension of statecraft.

The future of the Spanish crown was to cast a shadow over the closing years of the seventeenth century, given the incumbent Charles II's frail and childless condition, and the sensitivity of its becoming enmeshed in French Bourbon, or Austrian Habsburg, designs. To pre-empt another round of international conflict, the initiative had been taken by Louis XIV of France and William III of Britain to settle the matter by partition of the Spanish patrimony, and provisional agreements to this effect were reached in 1698 and 1699 (Kamen 1969: 3; Anderson 1976: 270; Black 1990: 47). These, in addition to possibly preserving the peace, had the useful advantage for Louis of detaching William from his erstwhile Allies, as the British monarch was only too fully aware. He wrote at the time that if he went along with partition, in agreement with the French, 'he could no longer count on past alliances, that there would no longer be any question of Austrian support and that he would only be able to count on a French alliance' (Black 1990: 46–7). William's prospective recompense for running this risk was that it would make him the key interlocutor with France, and position England well to maximize its benefits in any overall settlement. The manner of this pre-war *démarche* was later to be replicated in the Anglo-French dialogue that developed, after 1710, and that was to become the instrument for thrashing out the key provisions of the Utrecht settlement.

Charles II died in November 1700. In his final will, he left the Spanish crown, and all its possessions, to Philip of Anjou, the French king's second grandson. While other powers shared an interest in reaching some accommodation by means of partition, the Spanish voiced their own firm preference for the empire to be preserved intact (Shennan 1995: 13–14). Even though the will precluded the unity of the French and Spanish kingdoms, the Bourbon family connection would be significant nonetheless, and the fate of Europe stood at a crossroads (Hargreaves-Mawdsley 1979: 16). All depended upon the reaction of Louis XIV himself. Famously, he consented to Philip's accession, not on the basis of the will, but instead because this was the 'legitimate' order of succession in any event. His knowledge that a Bourbon refusal would have been swiftly followed by a Habsburg acceptance no doubt added further weight to his need to act in such a 'principled' way.

War broke out in 1702, as England—further alienated by Louis's recognition of James III, on the death of his exiled father—and the United Provinces made common cause with Austria against this seeming extension of Bourbon power across Europe. The turning point that finally made the beginnings of a settlement possible was not reached until 1710–11, when two important developments occurred. The first was the change of government in Britain, the Tories replacing the Whigs, the erstwhile supporters of the war. The logic of this new political situation was further reinforced in 1711 by the death of Joseph I of Austria. Archduke Charles—whose Spanish cause the Grand Alliance was supporting—thereby became Emperor Charles VI, and the prospective reunification of the Spanish and Austrian Habsburg patrimonies, à la Charles V, seemed just as distasteful an outcome to the other powers as any similar extension of Bourbon power (Wolf 1962: 88; Hargreaves-Mawdsley 1979: 36–7; Shennan 1995: 16). Both developments encouraged Britain to defect from the alliance, and laid the basis for its 'separate' peace with France. In turn, this dialogue was to prepare the way for Utrecht. The features of this negotiation between Britain and France will be reviewed in detail below, but the need to reach an accord was given yet further edge with a number of salient, but untimely, deaths in the French royal family in early 1712. These intensified the concern that the French crown might indeed yet fall to Philip V of Spain, and thus raised the stakes about the French succession, hard on the heels of the contested Spanish.

In April 1713, the main treaties with France were signed by Britain, the Dutch, and others. The Empire held out, and did not agree terms with France until the Rastatt Treaty in the following year. In a treaty of 30 January 1713 the Dutch secured their Barrier. On 13 July 1713, Britain treated separately with Spain (Pitt 1971: 470). The treaties were the culmination of a variety of negotiations and peace feelers that extended back to 1706. On matters of the succession, the treaties sought to ensure the Protestant succession in Britain and the separation of the French and Spanish crowns (Shennan 1995: 24). They resulted also in the partition of the Spanish empire, with the Italian territories, and the Spanish Netherlands, being handed to the Austrian Habsburgs. The Dutch barrier was reinforced. Britain acquired territories in North America (Hudson's Bay, Nova Scotia, and Newfoundland), and in the Mediterranean (Gibraltar and Minorca), as well as the commercially symbolic Asiento (Symcox 1974: 288–98).

UTRECHT: ITS HISTORICAL SIGNIFICANCE?

Given these relatively modest-seeming provisions, it does not immediately appear that Utrecht was of such great moment in the history of international relations. And yet, the treaties of 1713–14 are regularly included amongst the great milestones in the evolution of the international system. On what grounds has their reputation been based? It will be suggested initially that historians have fastened upon four aspects of the settlement: its material impact upon the balance of power; its ideational importance in articulating the primacy of balance of power as a principle; its attempted inception of a rudimentary system of collective security; and as a stage in the development of some other key principles of a working state system. When these various positions have been mapped out, we will be in a position to connect them to the analysis of international legitimacy in particular.

The first perspective draws attention to the material impact that Utrecht was to have upon the European, and wider global, balance of power. In this regard, two features in particular are commonly highlighted: a shift in the balance of power that was to inaugurate the long-term growth of British influence, and a corresponding transition from the highly structured 'bipolar' balance of the last two centuries (Habsburg versus Valois/Bourbon), towards a more fluid distribution involving several broadly equal states. Although the settlement was not punitive towards France, in retrospect it did mark the onset of its secular decline from the pre-eminence that it had recently enjoyed. This coincided with the laying of the commercial and imperial bases of future British power (McKay and Scott 1983: 93), relative to which the Dutch now became very much the secondary maritime power. Indeed, many historians regard Britain as the principal beneficiary of the peace (Hargreaves-Mawdsley 1979: 37; Kennedy 1988: 105). Given the maritime nature of its interests, however, this did not represent a direct challenge to the other continental European powers. At the same time, it did contribute to that other development, namely the emergence of a more diffuse balance. Hinsley stressed this dimension when he drew attention to 'the condition of near-equality between several states' which, in the eighteenth century, was to take the place of the previously 'long-standing situation in which Europe had been dominated by two conflicting leading states' (Hinsley 1967: 176; McKay and Scott 1983: 212). The outcome of the seventeenth-century wars, and of the development of state power with which they had been associated, was to contribute to a more self-conscious awareness of power internationally, demonstrated, in one example, by the 'unifying' trends manifest amongst Europe's 'composite' monarchies (Austria, Spain, and Britain) during this critical period of 1707–16 (Elliott 1992: 67).

A second, and presumably related, characteristic was to be the high-profile articulation of balance of power concepts in the framing of the peace settlement. As is acknowledged by virtually all historians, Utrecht was the first such peace explicitly to state that its provisions had been reached in order to advance this particular international principle (Hinsley 1967: 171; McKay and Scott 1983: 211; Anderson 1993: 164; Rosenberg 1994: 39; Haslam 2002: 102–3). There are two pertinent references to the concept in the texts of the treaties. The treaty between France and Great Britain of 11 April 1713 stated that the war 'arose chiefly from thence, that the security and liberties of Europe could by no means bear the union of the kingdoms of France and Spain under one and the same king' (Grewe 1988: vol. 2, 221; French text, Parry 1969: vol. 27, 482). Even more explicitly, the text of the Treaty of Peace and Friendship between Great Britain and Spain of 13 July 1713 justified the renunciations, that would prevent any future merging of the French and Spanish crowns on the same head, in the following terms: 'But whereas the war [arose] . . . from the too close conjunction of the kingdoms of Spain and France. And whereas, to take away all uneasiness and suspicion, concerning such conjunction, out of the minds of the people, and to settle and establish the peace and tranquillity of Christendom, by an equal balance of power (which is the best and most solid foundation of a mutual friendship, and of a concord which will be lasting on all sides) . . . have consented, that care should be taken by sufficient precautions, that the kingdoms of Spain and France should never come and be united under the same dominion' (Parry 1969: vol. 28, 325–6; Grewe 1988: vol. 2, 232). It is on the basis of such explicit proclamations that commentators have seen fit to suggest that the Utrecht settlement 'took a stage further the anti-hegemonial assumptions of Westphalia', and that it was at Utrecht that 'the balance-of-power principle started its two-hundred-year reign in the European states system' (Watson 1992: 198; Osiander 1994: 133). That said, it should not be imagined that all the business at Utrecht was self-consciously conducted on this principle, nor on this principle alone. Other influences continued to be exerted on the peacemakers, such that 'honour and compensation were more important', in some of the provisions reached, 'than any attempt to create a balance of power on a logical basis' (Black 2002: 134).

Third, Utrecht has been singled out as a significant milestone in the attempted implementation of a scheme for collective security. This interpretation has been developed with reference, respectively, to the diplomacy preceding the outbreak of the Spanish war, to the Utrecht peace itself, and, finally, to the diplomacy that was designed to preserve the peace settlement in the longer term. The origins of this effort have been traced back to the early partition plans of 1698–1700. The motives of William III and Louis XIV for this undertaking, it has been suggested, were that they might 'enforce a settlement, and thereby preserve Europe from renewed warfare', an approach described, if somewhat loosely, as 'the beginning of the idea of collective security whereby the great powers would seek to impose solutions' (Shennan 1995: 11–12). Emerging subsequently out of the Utrecht peace, there was also a more general scheme for underwriting the settlement. The inclusion of the Empire, in what became the Quadruple alliance of 1718, issued in what has since been described as an 'early collective security agreement' (McKay and Scott 1983: 111, 115), or as a 'series of mutual guarantees which together offered a form of collective security' (Shennan 1995: 25). The language of collective security has been used, in referring to these arrangements, for the specific reason that the form of these interlocking guarantees implied 'the use of *community* power to enforce the settlement' (Holsti 1991: 79). So entrenched in the literature is this version of events that Utrecht has been credited with 'animating a constitutional structure for collective security itself' (Bobbitt 2002: 523). The precise language of collective security might appear inappropriate to refer to these developments, but the emphasis upon the self-consciousness of a community responsibility is certainly noteworthy.

Fourth, and more generally, Utrecht has been regarded as an important stage in the development of some other key principles that were to become characteristic of the state system: the idea of a system itself, and its cognate notions of state autonomy and equality. A less consistent picture emerges from these disparate reflections. According to Osiander, the prime importance of Utrecht lies in its unequivocal assertion of a notional equality of states. 'The triumph of equality', he points out, 'is evident from the fact that, at Utrecht, the idea of a hierarchy of actors was discarded' (Osiander 1994: 121). In turn, this more vigorous acceptance of formal equality was seen to derive logically from the autonomy of states (Osiander 1994: 87). And yet all such claims about the formal equality of states have to be assessed against the contrary practice of great-power primacy. This much had already emerged in the very directing role of the major powers that underpinned the aspirant form of collective security, discussed above. It is additionally confirmed by the general observation that Utrecht 'marked a further advance in the principle that the establishment of international stability justified the setting aside—by force if necessary—of the preferences of small states and their rulers' (Shennan 1995: 27). In that sense, formal recognition of equality stood in sharp contrast to the emerging practical reality of the period, a key trend of which 'increased the distinction between major and minor powers' (Black 1990: 58), even if this was not yet to be formalized in ways that were to develop in the following century.

In the final section, these sundry claims need to be connected explicitly to emerging practices of international legitimacy. To the extent that any or all of those claims holds true, what might they indicate about the evolving nature of legitimacy as then understood?

UTRECHT AND LEGITIMACY

How do these claims relate to the issue of legitimacy? The key dimensions of this topic can be approached again under the twin headings of rightful membership and rightful conduct. Under rightful membership, it will review the contemporary debate about legitimate succession. The section on rightful conduct will consider the manner in which the treaty was negotiated; secondly, this leads directly into the cognate issue of the extent of the consensus on which it was based, and whether, in Kissinger's terms, a legitimate order was thereby achieved; thirdly, the case needs to be made more fully for the significance of the adoption of the balance of power as a social principle; and, finally, the settlement needs to be placed in the context of the actual balance of power that gave rise to it.

Legitimacy and Rightful Membership

What was remarkable about the settlement was the successful reaching of an accord, in spite of the wide gulf that had separated the protagonists at the outset over the issue of what constituted legitimate succession. Within an essentially dynastic concept of international relations, succession was the very heart of the matter, and rules governing it could be said to be the most fundamental legitimacy principles of all. It was the existing understandings that the settlement was directly to challenge. Sharp divisions were already manifest in the early exchanges between Bolingbroke and Torcy, the respective foreign ministers of Britain and France, during the spring and summer of 1712. Louis had bid Torcy to write to the British that any renunciation of the French throne, as was being suggested, would prove futile, as 'tout engagement contraire a ses Loix ne serait jamais solide' (Torcy 1757: vol. 3, 179). Bolingbroke had responded, acknowledging the French belief that 'God alone can abolish the law upon which your right of succession is founded', but adding pointedly that, in Britain, 'a prince can relinquish his right by a voluntary cession, and that he, in favour of whom this renunciation is made, may be justly supported in his pretension by the powers who become guarantors of the treaty' (Torcy 1757: vol. 3, 184–5; Black 1990: 55; Osiander 1994: 128). The stark contrast therein drawn was of succession, devised purely in terms of national laws (reflecting divine will), as against succession regulated, and alterable, by the explicit sanction of international society. Moreover, Bolingbroke conveyed Queen Anne's insistence that Philip V's renunciation of the French throne was of such importance that 'elle ne peut consentir a continuer la négociation de la paix, à-moins qu'un accepte l'expédient qu'elle a proposé, ou un autre que soit également solide' (Torcy 1757: vol. 3, 184–5). Even in the act of issuing such an ultimatum, however, the bitter pill was then sweetened by the qualification that, although there could be no compromise over the end, there was still scope for creative accommodation as to the means for bringing it about. British negotiators were to be instructed 'de chercher réciproquement, & de travailler de concert à trouver... quelqu'autre expédient...' (Torcy 1757: vol. 3, 186). Since Philip could not be allowed to inherit the French crown, while remaining king of Spain, he might still exercise his choice of which of the two was to be renounced. That choice was referred to Philip, but significantly Louis 'renouvella sa parole à la Reine d'Angleterre, de faire la paix sous l'une ou l'autre des deux conditions alternatives qu'elle avait proposées' (Torcy 1757: vol. 3, 189). Thereby, Louis undertook to respect the outcome, even if one of the choices would signify a clear breach of French law. Philip, in the event, chose to abjure his French birthright. In standing by this decision, Louis was indirectly violating the very principle that he had initially declared to be sacrosanct. What made this seemingly more palatable was the acquiescence of all in the diplomatic procedure that had brought it about: it was a triumph of form over substance. The terms of the renunciation, included in the Anglo-French Treaty, stated as follows:

At no time whatever either the Catholic King himself, or any one of his lineage, shall seek to obtain the crown of France, or ascend the throne thereof; and by reciprocal renunciations on the part of France, and by settlements of the hereditary succession there, tending to the same purpose, the crown of France and Spain are so divided and separated from each other, that the aforesaid renunciations ... being truly and faithfully observed, they can never be joined in one. (Grewe 1988: vol. 2, 222)

It was not the French succession alone that was to be so governed. Included also in the various treaties was an undertaking, on the part of other members of international society, to respect the Protestant succession in Britain. In the Anglo-French Treaty, Louis was obliged to honour this succession, including 'the limitation thereof by the laws of Great Britain', whatever might be his personal feelings about the divine origins of the monarch. He undertook also to give no succour, within France, to the Jacobite pretender (Grewe 1988: vol. 2, 219–20).

Louis XIV had initially approached all such questions in terms of strict legal entitlement, immune to the preferences of the individuals or the states concerned, and certainly of international society as a whole. By the end, however, all the Utrecht participants had acceded, whether enthusiastically or not, to a set of instruments that guaranteed certain successions (e.g. the Protestant in Britain), and guaranteed against certain others (e.g. the Spanish and French crowns being held by the same individual). In this narrow sense, then, it could be said that Utrecht was responsible for the violation of the established interpretations of legitimacy, conceived as a matter of dynastic succession, and did so long before the French revolution was to present its dramatic challenge to it.

The Format of the Negotiation

The format of the settlement was to become a very prominent issue in the later Vienna and Versailles negotiations. Was the Congress to be the collective forum for the negotiation of all the issues, or was its task confined to endorsement of the key arrangements already worked out bilaterally by the major protagonists? From this perspective, Utrecht offered the perfect model of an exclusive arrangement, negotiated largely between Britain and France, and which was then submitted to the multilateral Congress for its approval. The bases of the peace were largely in place in the preliminary articles, agreed by October 1711, and the Utrecht proceedings proper began only after January 1712 (Pitt 1971: 460–1). What were the implications of this modality for current perceptions of legitimacy?

On the face of it, there are considerable problems with the view that Utrecht expressed some kind of immanent consensus amongst the majority of the key players. Indeed, the format of the negotiations was determined exactly by the high level of divergence then in existence. The first stage of the negotiations had been conducted 'in secret, without any consultation with the allies' (Jones 1980: 170). According to the comment of one editor of the pertinent British documents, Britain 'entered upon negotiations for a separate peace contrary to the terms of the Grand Alliance'. To make matters worse, he adds, 'we feathered our nest at their expense' (Legg 1925: xx–xxi). Moreover, while the settlement was a multilateral one by the end, negotiated as it was at the Congress, in its beginning it had been an exclusively bilateral affair, involving Britain and France alone, who settled the 'real terms' (McKay and Scott 1983: 65). The opening of the Utrecht Congress, we are told, revealed 'for all to see that Britain and France were acting together, virtually as partners, in trying to impose on Europe their previously agreed version of the peace' (Jones 1980: 172–3). For his part, the French Foreign Minister, Torcy, had his own self-interested motives for approaching the British in 1710, through his agent in London, the Abbé Gaultier (Pitt 1971: 458). Apart from initiating the search for a desired peace, this secret opening invited the additional bonus, if successful, of leaving the Grand Alliance in disarray (Rule 1976: 281). For these reasons, and on first inspection, it is hard to see what role legitimacy was playing in the determining of the peace.

Did the ends justify the means? Central to any assessment of the treaty is whether the secrecy, and the betrayal of Allies, was in some sense necessary to securing a stable peace. A number of historians believe so. 'Bolingbroke's negotiations with Torcy and the subsequent betrayal of England's allies', is one such conclusion, 'were probably unavoidable if peace was to be secured in 1713' (Wolf 1962: 88). On this reasoning, the harsh reality was the divergence of allied goals by the end of the war. There simply was not a consensus on the terms of peace. To the extent that Dutch and Austrian goals were unrealistic— or attainable only at the expense of a stable peace with France—they were expendable to secure the greater good. Refraining from 'wounding French pride' was of greater long-term importance for the European equilibrium than the propriety of a clandestine negotiation (Legg 1925: xx–xxi). Bolingbroke is thus exonerated for his conduct because what he did was 'not to make a separate peace, but to secure a lasting settlement for Europe', even if incidentally acquiring also 'a series of exclusive advantages for Britain' (Pitt 1971: 471). The Anglo-French secret dialogue thus did not disrupt an extant consensus, but was the instrument for creating one that was otherwise unattainable.

Consensus and a Legitimate Order?

In the first instance, it might appear that Utrecht passes the Kissinger test as a settlement that inaugurated a legitimate order. 'When compared with

Westphalia or the treaties of the Congress of Vienna', one overall assessment hazarded, 'the Utrecht peace was mild indeed' (Doran 1971: 137). Given that its key provisions had been thrashed out by British and French negotiators, this may hardly seem surprising, at least in so far as it was mild in its treatment of France. France's Foreign Minister and chief negotiator, Torcy, played a clever game (not unlike Talleyrand was to do at Vienna a century later), to ensure such moderate treatment. On the British side, the new Tory government was eager to bring the war to an end, and was willing to exercise its restraining influence on the other Allies to achieve this purpose.

However, such a judgement scarcely seems appropriate when the different perspective of the treatment of Spain is adopted. To be sure, Philip V was confirmed in his tenure of the Spanish crown. Beyond that, however, it could hardly be pretended that this was a settlement with which Spain was satisfied. On this, historians speak with a uniform voice. 'The terms of settlement imposed on Spain prevented rather than encouraged assimilation of the defeated power', is one such frank accounting. 'The settlement thus lacked legitimacy and immediately gave rise to plans for a war...' (Holsti 1991: 80). Spanish discontent was most acute with regard to the loss of its Netherlands and its Italian domains, and for that reason Philip V could not accept the terms of the Rastatt Treaty. Instead, 'the desire to redress the loss of Italy led to a new aggressive policy in the Mediterranean' (Kamen 1969: 24), and there was a rapid succession of wars in that region (Black 2002: 138). Thus, from the Spanish point of view, Utrecht did not create the semblance of a legitimate order, but left in its wake a series of 'new ambitions and grievances' (Anderson 1976: 268). Spain's problem, unfortunately, was that it was isolated in harbouring these grievances, and this undercut any prospect of securing assistance from others in overturning the settlement (Osiander 1994: 165). What was presented above as an incipient system of collective security could just as readily be understood, from the Spanish perspective, as a system for perpetuating its dissatisfaction with the settlement. The Quadruple Alliance, it has been suggested pointedly, 'was used for coercion, to enforce the Utrecht settlement' (Holsti 1991: 78). If so, then the Utrecht order falls far short of any kind of legitimate order in which all the major powers could find some satisfaction. Where the treaty was most successful was in its lenient treatment of France, and in its binding of that power to the resultant system.

THE LEGITIMACY OF THE BALANCE OF POWER

At this point, several of the threads of the preceding discussion need to be pulled together. What was to be the reason for disallowing 'prescribed' successions in particular circumstances? The answer was to be found in the wider needs of international society. What was at stake was the extent to which hereditary lineages might be checked by other international considerations. Thus, it has been asserted of Utrecht, 'the notion that a country's succession was a matter of international concern and needed to be subject to international guarantees was central to the whole treaty' (McKay and Scott 1983: 65–6; Luard 1992: 169). The new reality of international relations in the eighteenth century was that now 'dynastic considerations were challenged by require-ments of national and international security' (Shennan 1995: 2).

What was the significance for international society of its pronouncements on the balance of power, its efforts to establish an embryonic form of collective security, and its proactive stance in managing the course of dynastic succession? Our interest in Utrecht lies, not simply in its impact on the prevail-ing balance of power, nor even in its formulation of a doctrine about the need for a balance of power, but more specifically in its espousal of the notion that maintaining a balance of power was a legitimate principle of international society, and one that should take precedence over other competing norms. This lay at the core of the settlement. 'It was this consensus on the necessity and legitimacy of a balance of power', Osiander (1994: 125) has concluded, 'that enabled the peacemakers to overcome the objections of their opponents'. It was at Utrecht that, for the first time, the '*the balance-of-power principle emerged as an intersocietal legitimacy principle*' (Hall 1999: 66). Be it noted, however, that the emphasis here is not upon the sudden emergence of the principle of the balance of power as such, but upon its acceptance as a legit-imacy principle by the international society of the period. Bolingbroke, Brit-ain's principal architect of the treaty, indeed saw this as the 'great article' on which 'the whole settlement hinged' (Osiander 1994: 125–6). In short, the balance of power now enjoyed a normative status 'as something with a moral value and justification of its own' (Anderson 1976: 211–12). It was because of this acceptance that appeal could be made to the balance of power to override other competing claims (Reus-Smit 2003: 619). In the words of one eighteenth-century commentator, even 'the most legitimate rulers must sometimes re-nounce their rights in order to maintain the balance' (quoted in Anderson 1976: 211–12).

Consensus and the Balance of Power

But what precisely was the relationship between balance of power, consensus, and legitimacy in this context? As we have already seen, Spain was demon-strably not a party to the consensus (about territorial partition of the empire), and the diplomatic instruments of the post-Utrecht period were turned against it to ensure otherwise unwilling compliance. To this extent, it might equally be said that consensus was no more than a function of the balance of power, and legitimacy little more than the dictates of the most powerful negotiators. Matters were not, however, quite so straightforward. Fully to appreciate the nature of the consensus that operated at Utrecht, and to understand what this meant for legitimacy, we need to look even more closely at the detailed negotiation of that settlement.

What clearly emerges from the surveys of the Utrecht negotiations was the willingness on the part of key negotiators to moderate demands in order to reach a satisfactory compromise. Such a diplomatic procedure is, of course, necessary to allow any consensus to emerge. The French plenipotentiaries had been instructed to 'meet the legitimate security requirements and frontiers, as well as the freedom of commerce, of all the parties to the conflict' (Holsti 1991: 73). The British, we are informed, acted to keep the 'demands of their allies within bounds', and favoured a policy of 'moderation' (Legg 1925: vol. II, xix). Black attributes this mood to the general experience of the recent war, and the consequent realization that 'pretensions, however strongly held, had to be moderated' (Black 1990: 45).

Osiander's assessment provides one succinct statement of the possible link between consensus, legitimacy, and the stability of the Utrecht settlement:

The success of the Utrecht settlement in preserving and strengthening the international system of eighteenth-century Europe was undoubtedly due mainly to this reliance on consensus notions. Because it was so legitimate, the settlement proved lasting—especially with respect to the successful integration of the French monarchy into the system. I would suggest that this is the most important, and, at the same time, the least acknowledged, aspect of the Utrecht peace. (Osiander 1994: 156)

Such an analysis, while certainly revealing of an important attribute of Utrecht, creates as many problems as it solves. The key questions that it fails to address are what made possible in the first place this coalescing around certain consensus notions, and whether this possibility might itself, in turn, have been related to the balance of power. Did the consensus emerge because a concomitance of interests propelled the British and the French to do a deal, and most of the remaining states (except Spain) then found it convenient to fall into line with it? And why were the British and the French able to strike this deal at all, given the seemingly insurmountable gulf of principle which separated their initial negotiating positions? Is much of this to be explained by other contingent factors impinging on foreign policies at the time—such as the general equilibrium, post-war fiscal indebtedness, and concerns about the succession in the cases of Britain, Austria, and France? (McKay and Scott 1983: 101). Osiander's own version of the argument becomes more complex elsewhere: 'This shows that the balance-of-power principle may operate as a vehicle of international consensus, and thereby as a safeguard for international stability, quite independently of the actual distribution of forces ... It is only necessary that the existing distribution of forces is not regarded as illegitimate' (Osiander 1994: 138). What this appears to say is that, as regards the future stability of any international order, the pertinent factor is not the distribution of power as such, but rather the degree of consensus about its acceptability. This suggests a clear distinction between the two motivating conditions—the distribution of power and its acceptability. Unhappily, what this leaves out of account is that the acceptability of the distribution may itself be shaped by its actuality. What states find tolerable, or not, is conditional upon the material prospects for changing that situation. If so, the consensus does not stand outside, and independent of, the balance—in the way that Osiander's argument might imply—and this has noteworthy implications for the nature of the legitimacy that operates in such a context.

So why did accommodation prove possible in those most inauspicious of circumstances? Osiander's answer is interesting, if ultimately ambivalent. 'The British argument—the balance of power—was a consensus principle', he maintains, whereas 'Torcy's counter-case—whether based on divine law, dynastic right, or whatever—did not have the same quality' (Osiander 1994: 132). That the British case, bolstered by appeal to the balance of power, did indeed become the consensus position is not in any doubt. What is less clear is whether it became so because it had the better of the intellectual argument, or simply because the French, when the chips were down, would have been too isolated to resist the logic of superior power which sustained it, short of a resumption of war. However, if it was that latter consideration that carried the day, it cannot simultaneously be claimed that the *acceptability* of the resultant distribution of power was a separate circumstance from the *existing* balance of power: consensus was possible because the French saw little choice but to subscribe to it. At the same time, the British had facilitated this acceptance by offering France a graceful means for doing so, and by ensuring that France lost less by this acceptance than she would otherwise have done.

In short, it is no part of the present argument to pretend that the application of legitimacy principles at Utrecht represented some kind of complete abandonment of self-interested power politics. It did, nonetheless, help put into practice a particular conception of these interests by incorporating a degree of toleration for the interests of others, as best serving the interests of all. Procedurally, this could be realized only by striving for such areas of agreement as might be found possible, but, above all, in open acknowledgement of the preference for conducting business in this way. It was the consensus about proceeding on the *basis of consensus* that was the interesting feature of the Utrecht settlement, however much qualified, both in theory and practice, such a statement has to be.

CONCLUSION

Historians return mixed verdicts upon Utrecht. On the positive side, it is hailed as having 'established a framework for international politics that lasted in its essential features until the 1790s' (Jones 1980: 177). Its achievement lay in having 'prevented a disruption of the balance of Europe', and having 'restored the principle of flexibility' (Pitt 1971: 479). On the negative side, the sceptics stress the alienation of Spain, the failure to prevent a new round of conflicts, and its inability to resolve even those very uncertainties around the British and French successions that lay at its core (Shennan 1995: 17). Holsti (1991: 77) adjudges it less successful than Westphalia, resulting in 'only partial compliance and legitimacy'.

Without question, both Britain and France sought their own specific advantages from the settlement which they had initiated. We should not, however, ignore the other fact that important ground was yielded in order to make this peace possible at all. The final achievement is all the more striking, given the seemingly incompatible respective sets of demands at the outset. Were we to focus upon the pursuit of narrow self-interest alone, the deal reached at Utrecht would remain largely incomprehensible. What made peace possible was the willingness—whether born of war, other political pressures, or partisan advantages—to give reasonable ground to others. Osiander is therefore correct to point out that what Bolingbroke sought was 'reciprocal moderation'. He did not want 'a peace that needed to be enforced', but preferred instead a peace 'that France would freely consent to' (Osiander 1994: 152). France's 'freedom' to consent was relative, rather than absolute, but the point stands even with that qualification. With the exception of Spain, most other parties to the settlement were prepared to negotiate on the bases that had already been laid out. This resulted in significant British commercial gains, enhancements of Dutch security, and an expanded Austrian patrimony in Italy, while also securing Philip on the Spanish throne. It issued also in a settlement that, while certainly disturbing to French principle, made it sacrifice less territory in practice than Louis or Torcy had original cause to fear. It was much less than a perfect peace, as the challenges to it—from Spain if not from France—were soon to testify.

For all that, it was a peace that succeeded in reasonable measure in establishing a benchmark for appropriate diplomatic conduct within a maturing international society. Now more conscious of itself, and of the primacy of certain public over private goods (Osiander 1994: 111)—foremost amongst which was a public balance of power to which private dynastic claims must henceforth be subject—the international society of the early eighteenth century felt confident in expressing the notion that sociability was intimately connected with a diplomacy of 'reciprocal moderation', and the need to search for shared interests wherever these might be found. As such, its working notion of legitimacy was not of some absolute standard, but was inherently pragmatic and political. It was a concept of international legitimacy with these characteristics that was coming to be embraced.

5

Revolutionary and Legitimate Orders: Revolution, War, and the Vienna Settlement

The last quarter of the eighteenth century witnessed the fermentation of radical ideas that were translated, however much transmuted in practice, into the American and French revolutions. In turn, these were succeeded by the protracted phase of revolutionary and Napoleonic warfare that engulfed Europe, and other parts of the world, from the early 1790s until 1815. Vienna had to pacify a system that had been exposed to these twin challenges of revolutionary upheaval and violent international conflict. Because the assault on the system had been twofold, the settlement had to calibrate carefully both the internal and the international requirements for future international order. Unsurprisingly, this then entailed the devotion of much energy to questions of rightful membership—the internal aspect of legitimacy. In fact, it gave birth to new formulations of prescriptive legitimacy that, at least superficially, seemed to amount to a retreat from the position staked out at Utrecht, whereby strict dynastic succession was to be curtailed in the interests of international balance. Of the various dimensions of rightful conduct, Vienna stands out for its contributions on four principal issues: the format of the negotiations themselves; its construction of a putative legitimate order; its development of thinking about consensus, as expressed through a concert; and its attempted transcription of ideas about a balance of power into a more specific formulation called a 'just equilibrium'. In these many ways, Vienna was possibly one of the more innovative, and certainly consequential, international settlements of the modern period.

THE SETTLEMENT AND ITS CONTEXT

Some novel ideas do not become embodied immediately in new international practices, but instead have a much longer-term impact on behaviour. This can certainly be said of the 'age of revolution' in the last quarter of the eighteenth century. Far from marking a watershed in international norms in the short term, this period evoked a partial conservative backlash in the 1815 settlement. Nonetheless, the continuing development throughout the eighteenth century of political ideas about individualism, rights, and social contract was eventually to leave its profound imprint upon international practice, progressively so from the mid-nineteenth century onwards.

Without question, one of the major implications of the revolutions was the increasingly important interconnections between the domestic and international dimensions of legitimacy, a feature that was to continue equally throughout the 'counter-revolutionary' phase from 1815 onwards. If it is true that there has always been an ambiguity about whether the norms of international society 'are wholly about relations between states . . . or whether they also encompass the inner workings of states' (Halliday 1999: 297–8), then this was to be especially so during this revolutionary period. '[T]he linkages between international and domestic politics became much tighter', Bukovansky insists of the late eighteenth century, 'precisely because of the emergence of democratic legitimacy' (2002: 163). Not least was this so because the revolutions created a new ideological divide within international relations. The existing largely homogeneous European system was now replaced by one displaying a marked degree of heterogeneity, and this was to have a pronounced destabilizing effect (Aron 1966: 148).

So what did the 'age of revolution' impart to the norms of international society? The rich symbolism of the American colonial revolt, and its democratic ethos, had conspicuous effects. In Bukovansky's words, 'bringing more of "the people" into politics on the basis of republican principles, now interpreted in increasingly democratic ways, linked domestic legitimacy and foreign policy more closely together' (2002: 114). What the American revolution had inaugurated, the French continued and mightily reinforced. This was to be a revolution, not just in principle, but also in its momentous practical implications: it was at once revolutionary and regicidal, revolutionary and internationalist. It was always unlikely that international society could emerge unaltered from this encounter.

It presented basically two alternatives for policy in the revolutionary aftermath. If revolution yielded an international society that was less stable—because more heterogeneous—then one solution lay in a restoration of its former homogeneity. This pointed to a policy of conservative interventionism, with the intention of eliminating its revolutionary elements. The other option was to accept the reality of this new heterogeneity, and to search instead for the means to cope with it. This issued in the experiment with congress diplomacy, and in explicit attempts to create a consensually based management of the international system. However, these two alternative strategies for dealing with the revolutionary implications were in deep-seated conflict with each other: interventionism placed too much strain on consensualism. The hidden tensions were to become apparent during the period of Vienna peacemaking, but even more explicitly during the ensuing brief spell of congress diplomacy.

The Congress of Vienna culminated in June 1815 after many months of negotiations. It was situated between the two Treaties of Paris of May 1814 and November 1815 (made necessary by Napoleon's hundred days), and formally ended that very protracted period of warfare originating after the French Revolution but enduring through the long years of Napoleon. This gave rise to a large and complex agenda. 'The history of the political system of Europe', noted one contemporary observer, 'can present no congress—not excepting even the congress of Westphalia—where so many and so great interests, comprehending those of all Europe, were to be adjusted' (Heeren 1834: 350).

The victorious allied powers emerged from the final stages of the war with a highly developed sense of their 'corporate responsibility for the peace of Europe' (Palmer 1983: 6). This had already become visible in the Chaumont Treaty of 1814 which bound them together to protect the future peace for at least another twenty years (Webster 1931: 227). At the Congress of Vienna, there was created simultaneously, but separately, what has been called elsewhere a distributive and a regulative peace (Clark 2001a). The first concerned the traditional agenda of territorial distribution, military occupation, and financial provisions. The second concerned the assertion of the role of the great powers, and the cognate development of the principles of a concert. In short, the distributive peace settled the division of the spoils, while the regulative peace devised the instruments to safeguard the arrangements that had been so agreed. The settlement as a whole thereby issued in a subtle combination of 'the old European logic of balance', combined with 'new legal-institutional arrangements meant to manage and restrain power' (Ikenberry 2001: 114).

The peace arrangements came in discrete stages. We tend to think of the Congress of Vienna as being the forum at which the fate of France was determined but, in fact, the Congress was sandwiched between the two Treaties of Paris, where the main terms of the peace with France were actually set. Vienna was mostly concerned with the wider territorial settlement, since the outline agreement of conditions for France was already in place (Dakin 1979). This sequence served to enhance the role of France during the Congress. 'By immediately determining what terms France was to get', he notes, 'the treaty gave France a certain freedom of action later on; this freedom came before the allies had been able to agree on the European settlement, and it enabled Talleyrand to influence their later agreements' (Gulick 1967: 177).

Notably, the first treaty was lenient towards France. It set France's borders at those of 1792, thus allowing it some actual gains relative to the pre-war situation (Dakin 1979: 25). There was to be no indemnity, nor occupation. Bizarrely, France was to retain even the great works of art looted during Napoleon's campaigns.

In the months between November 1814 and June 1815, the Congress of Vienna had little need to concern itself directly with France, apart from Napoleon's brief excursus: '...there was no French problem since peace had been restored with France' (Albrecht-Carrié 1965: 11). The Congress cast its net more widely to settle the affairs of Europe and, as it turned out, its energies were to be devoted largely to the fates of Poland and Saxony, and the extent to which these should be sacrificed to the expansion of Russia and Prussia respectively. Before the Congress could publish its Final Act, Napoleon made his escape from Elba and embarked on his hundred days' campaign. His final defeat at Waterloo necessitated a further peace with France, reached at the second Paris Treaty.

In the words of the peacemakers, this treaty now needed to provide both 'proper indemnities for the past', as well as 'solid guarantees for the future' (Hertslet 1875: 343). The recent recrudescence of the Napoleonic threat had left many demanding that future checks on French power be even more robust than those included in the original Paris terms. The sharp divisions about this new settlement are indicated by the fact that the second Paris negotiation lasted fully five months, whereas the first had been completed in only two (Webster 1931: 457). This new treaty now imposed marginally more severe terms (Dakin 1979: 29–30). France's borders were more stringently withdrawn to those of 1790, there was to be an army of occupation for up to five years, and an indemnity of 700 million francs was to be exacted by way of compensation. Works of art were, this time, to be returned. The occupation could be reviewed and terminated at the end of three years if, as the treaty specified, there was sufficient progress in France 'in the re-establishment of order and tranquillity' to satisfy the Allied Sovereigns that 'the motives which led them to that measure had ceased to exist' (Hertslet 1875: 347–8).

The British representatives had strongly counselled in favour of a temporary occupation, instead of permanent cession of French territory. The Duke of Wellington, then serving as British ambassador in Paris, urged this on his government in August on the grounds that any such cession would simply provoke France to seek in the future 'an opportunity of endeavouring to regain what she had lost' (Webster 1921: 357–9). Foreign secretary Castlereagh concurred, but in a memorandum of 12 August added the further consideration in favour of occupation, namely 'that it necessarily preserves Europe in a continued state of alliance for the surveillance of France by imposing upon the Allied Powers as a common duty the occupation and defence of what is ceded for a fixed period to all' (Webster 1921: 361). In short, this arrangement would be better for France, but would be good also for the unity of the Allies, and promote their sense of shared responsibility for the peace.

The Congress, additionally, had to settle affairs beyond France. Important changes were made along the French border. Holland was united with Belgium. Prussia was strengthened on the Rhineland and in Saxony. Swiss neutrality was guaranteed by the powers. The Habsburgs were entrenched in Northern

Italy. All this was of a piece with the future containment of France. Elsewhere, the two powers on the flanks consolidated their positions. Russian predominance in Poland was assured. Britain strengthened her hold in the Mediterranean by the acquisition of Malta, and also extended her holdings in the Caribbean.

Not only was a peace to be put in place, but measures had to be taken to keep it. Leniency in the distributive settlement was itself part of this wider design, the expectation being that moderation would encourage a consensual order. But the task of preserving the peace went beyond this. As early as 1813, Castlereagh had been determined to plan for the post-war situation, and had inserted in his diplomatic Instructions the requirement that the 'Treaty of Alliance is not to terminate with the war' (Webster 1945: 17). There would be no point in a peace settlement, if it could be speedily dismantled thereafter (Holbraad 1970: 137). Although an explicit great-power guarantee of the entire settlement could not finally be achieved, what was restated in the famous Article VI, of the reaffirmed Quadruple Alliance of November 1815, was the intention to manage the existing settlement through regular meetings of the powers. In that article, they agreed

To renew at fixed intervals...meetings for the purpose of consulting upon their common interests, and for the examination of the measures which at each of these epochs shall be considered most salutary for the repose and prosperity of the Nations and for the maintenance of the peace of Europe. (Hinsley 1967: 194–5)

It was this provision that was to give rise to the concert as the key mechanism for preserving the post-war peace (Nichols 1971).

VIENNA'S HISTORICAL REPUTATION

Such was the scope of the settlement that there was, at the time, considerable pessimism about its prospects. The secretary of the Congress, Friedrich Gentz, voiced fears in October 1814 that 'it will be a miracle almost as great as that which produced the downfall of Napoleon if one can bring about the condition of complete and lasting peace in Europe as a result of it' (Cecil 1923: 123). And yet, writing again in 1818, and against the then general mood of despondency about the tenability of the diplomatic system set in place in 1815, Gentz now felt disposed to the view that the 'European federation . . . is not threatened with immediate ruin' (Mann 1946; Walker 1968: 73).

The historical reputation of the Vienna Congress thereafter enjoyed mixed fortunes (Broers 1996: 1–2). For much of the nineteenth and early twentieth centuries, Vienna was indicted by the progressive Whig interpretation of history for its violation of liberal and national values. It was depicted as the epitome of repression, attempting Canute-like to hold back the rising forces of the age, in defiance of the seeming logic of history. A later generation of liberals looked back upon Vienna as a 'politically suspect settlement', and were to be equally dismissive of the conservative international legal commentaries, such as those by Von Martens and Klüber, to which it had given rise (Koskeniemmi 2002: 21–3).

In contrast, in the aftermath of the seeming failure of Versailles, the relative standing of Vienna increased considerably. Comparatively, whatever its shortcomings, it appeared to have established a viable and durable international order. This reputation has, if anything, been further enhanced by the most recent scholarship which presents Vienna as pivotal in the 'transformation' of international politics, and in its 'governing rules, norms, and practices', as between the eighteenth and nineteenth centuries. The concrete evidence of this was 'a dramatic decline in the incidence, scope, length and violence of wars' (Schroeder 1994: vii). As the pre-eminent scholar of the period, Schroeder has showered a number of such tributes on the diplomacy of the Vienna period. His overall assessment is that Vienna emerges with 'a remarkably positive balance sheet'. So confident is he in this judgement, that he feels entitled to assert that Vienna alone 'genuinely established peace', and that 'no other general peace settlement in European history. . . comes anywhere close to this record' (Schroeder 1994: 576–7).

The notion of legitimacy is now firmly embedded in Vienna's historical reputation in two distinctive ways. First, there is the argument that during the peacemaking a principle of legitimacy, understood as rightful entitlement or possession, came to be articulated, and that this was to be the key principle, if not the fundamental determinant, of the treaty provisions. Secondly, there is the somewhat different, but equally widespread, view that Vienna gave birth to a legitimate international order in so far as it managed to satisfy all the major powers, and possibly some of the minor as well. This was the secret ingredient that lay at the heart of the settlement's success.

This confronts us once more with the duality of legitimacy, inasmuch as it has both an inward-looking and an outward-facing aspect. Inwardly, legitimacy can be translated as a set of principles about the proper composition and constitution of individual states, so as to befit them for membership of international society. Outwardly, it manifests itself as a set of principles about the proper conduct of relations between states, in order to sustain a working international society. In much contemporary thought, the two were, of course, to be closely interconnected. This emerges, for example, in the various innovative schemes adumbrated by Russia's Tsar Alexander I, within which 'the fixing of the relations of states to each other by more precise rules' was considered no more nor less important than the 'attaching of the nations to their governments by making them incapable of acting save in the greatest interest of the peoples subject to them' (Philipps 1914: 117; Holsti 1991: 122; Bobbitt 2002: 555). To pursue this further, let us examine these two dimensions of legitimacy—domestic and international—separately, and in greater detail.

VIENNA AND LEGITIMACY

Rightful Membership

It is the widespread judgement that 'the French Revolution accelerated the shift in the European states system from the dynastic territorial state to the nation-state as the dominant model of political legitimacy' (Bukovansky 2002: 165). The precise nomenclature varies, but the essential claim remains broadly constant. Collectively, albeit in the longer term, the popular revolutions within states amounted to a revolution in international society itself by marking a watershed in its fundamental principle of membership, from 'dynastic' to 'popular' (Wight 1972: 6; Mayall 1990: 27; Armstrong 1993: 85 *ff*), from 'territorial-sovereignty' to 'national-sovereignty' (Hall 1999: 7, 142), or from 'territorial-state' to 'state-nation' (Bobbitt 2002: 346–7).

The whole point about the French revolution, and of the responses to it, was precisely the widespread perception that such changes in the domestic realm must inevitably have wider international repercussions. This focused attention on the issue of rightful membership of international society. The reason that the French revolution challenged the existing legitimacy principle was, as Wight put it, not simply because it overthrew dynasticism, but more specifically because 'dynasticism was rooted in custom', and was 'bound up with the principle of prescription' (Wight 1972: 3). It was this specific aspect of legitimacy that was to be violated by the revolution.

The revolution also had more tangible international implications. 'The lesson that popular sovereignty could enhance state power and military performance', Bukovansky is surely correct to remind us, 'was not lost on contemporaries' (2002: 168). Neither was the fact that France could now choose to ignore 'princely' treaties including, for example, the restrictions on navigation in the Scheldt that had been imposed at Westphalia, as no longer having a legitimate basis in popular will. This left a question mark, potentially, over the validity of all treaties (Bukovansky 2002: 202).

But just as the revolutionaries were to draw their own *international* conclusions from domestic change, so indeed did their opponents. Edmund Burke emerged as the great counter-revolutionary publicist of the age. He, famously, made the connection that the sanctity of prescription, as the basis of domestic political arrangements, entailed the additional international obligation, as a member of international society, that 'no member... had an unrestricted right to revolutionise itself' (Wight 1972: 3). The Burkean rhetorical counterblast was based on full recognition of the profundity of the challenge. Burke's starting point appears to be that of a domestic concept of legitimacy, an '*intra*-national' conception (Welsh 1996: 176). But this notion has a prior grounding in a wider notion of international society, or Commonwealth of Europe, as he frequently described it. From this more basic point of theoretical departure, he would conclude that 'the unity of the whole preceded the separateness of the parts' (Vincent 1984*a*: 210). In turn, this translated into an explicit principle of international conduct, namely one of *qualified* sovereignty. Since international order was itself predicated upon the stability of social and political institutions within individual states, there was then a need for a balance to be struck between 'international society as a whole against the absolute liberty and independence of its individual members' (Welsh 1996: 182). From the internal legitimacy of prescriptive institutions could be adduced the equally compelling international principle of the international tutelage of the affairs of individual states. Far from being a violation of international order, such intervention was a prerequisite for it. Burke championed this principle of intervention, as an antidote to any dangerous pursuit of the abstract 'rights of man'.

In the face of these currents, what was to be done? Since the fundamental challenge had been to prescriptive modes of domestic political legitimacy, then a doctrine had to be formulated to resurrect it. To be clear, however, in doing this, a tradition was being invented, and not simply restored: an 'ideological commitment to dynasticism was a product of nineteenth-century *programmatic* conservatism' (Osiander 1994: 76). The prescriptive entitlement of extant dynasties may well have been treated as a political reality during most of the eighteenth century (but certainly not the exclusive one, as had been displayed at Utrecht), but after the revolutions this came to be formulated as an explicit doctrine. In the words of one historian, 'there were no legitimists before the Revolution', and, more pointedly, 'the principle of legitimacy...was a new idea' (Holmes 1982: 166). Once affirmed as a doctrine denoting domestic constitutional propriety, however, there was a need for the international ramifications to be codified as well. Burke, as we have seen, set out the case in principled terms. The peacemakers at Vienna, and the practitioners of the early European concert, tried to translate their own versions of these principles into working diplomatic practices.

Understood with reference to the domestic constitutions of states, the principle of legitimacy is forever associated with the name of Talleyrand, the then French Foreign Minister, and key negotiator of the Paris and Vienna provisions. In his own account, he made an emotive appeal to the plenipotentiaries of the allied powers on their very first meeting:

The presence of a minister of Louis XVIII consecrates here the principle on which rests the entire social order. The first need of Europe is to ban forever the opinion that right can be acquired by conquest, and to revive the sacred principle of legitimacy, from whence come order and stability. (Cameron 1971: 6–7)

On this basis, as the story would have it, Talleyrand—despite speaking for the defeated power—became the presiding voice in the Congress and, according to one biographer, 'forced the other ministers to accept public law and legitimate sovereignty as the basis for the settlement of all questions before the congress'

(Bernard 1973: 383). 'The legitimacy of Kings, or rather of governments', he said, 'is the safeguard of nations; the legitimacy of a government is the effect of long possession, as prescription is a title to private property' (Talleyrand 1891: vol. 2, 159–60; Philipps 1914: 93–4; Talleyrand 1996: 292–3). In all cases, governments were lawful only in so far as their 'existence, form, and mode of action, have been consolidated and consecrated by a long succession of years' (Osiander 1994: 211–12; Talleyrand 1996: 292–3). That Talleyrand understood legitimacy as largely a domestic attribute becomes clear in his discussion of its relationship to the principle of equilibrium. In Gulick's version of his argument, 'equilibrium must be the general policy for Europe as a whole'. In contrast, Talleyrand considered that 'legitimacy must be used as a device to render stable the units within the equilibrium' (Gulick 1967: 227–8). In amplification, he adds, 'one was an external condition of a state and the other internal' (Gulick 1967: 229–30).

The view that Vienna was to be governed by this prevailing conception of legitimacy has been challenged by historians from two overlapping perspectives. The first is that legitimacy was mere window-dressing, not the guiding spirit, either because Talleyrand himself had 'no moral principles or scruples...no doctrines' (Namier 1958: 9), or, as Metternich was to put it, 'on ne peut que séparer en M. de Talleyrand l'homme moral de l'homme politique' (Metternich 1881: vol. 2, 234). His appeal to this version of legitimacy was undoubtedly self-serving (Philipps 1914: 97). It was deployed as a means to avoid a harsh peace, since any intemperance towards France would serve only to undermine the standing of the restored house of Bourbon (Holmes 1982: 178). In any case, the principle was to be so inconsistently applied. Pragmatism reigned at Vienna and the peacemakers 'restored old rulers only where it suited them to do so' (Dakin 1979: 14). Other factors influenced the outcomes, and spokesmen of the powers paid little more than 'lip-service' to legitimacy (Sked 1979*b*: 1). Schroeder's authoritative conclusion on the matter is that 'the doctrine of legitimacy was often restricted, twisted, manipulated, and shunted aside at Vienna, not least by Talleyrand himself' (Schroeder 1994: 529).

The second perspective, in part accounting for the former, is that decisions at Vienna were driven above all by concerns about the balance of power, and legitimacy was simply the handmaiden of this dominant purpose. Even French policy, in the estimation of a Gentz memorandum of 12 February 1815, was shaped by the wish 'to re-establish a political equilibrium' (Cameron 1971: 3). In a letter of 19 December 1814 to Metternich, the Austrian chancellor, Talleyrand was to lament that proposals over Saxony amounted to a compromise of the two principles of both legitimacy and equilibrium (Metternich 1881: vol. 2, 511–12), Gulick insists that Talleyrand's concern was more about the latter than the former. 'His own testimony indicated a primary concern with balance of power', he wrote of Talleyrand, 'and only a supplementary interest in legitimacy' (Gulick 1967: 229–30).

'[T]he Congress of Vienna was not the first such convention to define the legitimate constitutional form of government for member states', it has been claimed, 'but it was by far the most intrusive' (Bobbitt 2002: 553). This was certainly so in the case of France. The nature of the French constitution was, in effect, placed under licence from the international community, and this brought with it detailed surveillance of French domestic developments. During 1815–18, the great powers' 'interference... was indeed far reaching' (Schenk 1947: 127) in French internal affairs.

Legitimacy as a principle of domestic constitutionality became important, of course, precisely because it could be translated into a principle of international action: intervention. It was in this respect that it was to become celebrated, and controversial, during the short life of the congress system. The Quadruple Alliance had attested to the perceived link between legitimacy at home and stability abroad, in declaring 'the repose of Europe' to be 'essentially inter-woven with the confirmation of the order of things founded on the maintenance of the Royal Authority and of the Constitutional Charter' in France (Hertslet 1875: 372). It was arguably a simple extension of the selfsame logic (albeit that Castlereagh did not share it) that, by the time of the Laibach Congress of 1821, the three powers of Austria, Russia, and Prussia felt able to assert that 'in respecting the rights and independence of all legitimate power, they regarded as legally null, and as disavowed by the principles which constitute the public right of Europe, all pretended reform operated by revolt and open hostility' (Kertesz 1968: 24–5). Importantly, therefore, there was a measure of inter-national agreement about the impermissibility of such revolutionary domestic change. Even more striking, however, was to be the corollary of this doctrine. In Metternich's Preliminary Protocol, submitted to the Troppau Congress the year before, it had been declared that 'states which have undergone a change of Government due to revolution, the results of which threaten other states, *ipso facto* cease to be members of the European Alliance' (Walker 1968: 127). What is so noteworthy about this formulation is that the loss of domestic legitimacy would thereby entail, equally, a loss of full membership of international society.

Castlereagh became increasingly restive with these developments. British objections were manifestly not to the principle of intervention per se. 'It should be clearly understood that no Government can be more prepared than the British Government is', said Castlereagh in a Circular Despatch of 19 January 1821, 'to uphold the right of any State or States to interfere, where their own immediate security or essential interests are seriously endangered by the in-ternal transactions of another State'. Interference was fully acceptable in any such conditions. What the British government dissented from was the 'general and indiscriminate application to all Revolutionary Movements' that the Trop-pau Protocol seemed to portend (Hertslet 1875: 666). The final disruption of the congress system then resulted from this attempt to apply a general principle of domestic legitimacy as the basis for international action. Be it noted, how-ever, that the effort to establish the legitimacy of collective intervention against revolution was abandoned, not because it was resented and resisted by the smaller powers, but because the great powers themselves were to fall out over the issue: legitimacy was hostage to the faltering consensus amongst the great powers, not to any concept that a consensus should appropriately extend beyond them.

One key point remains to be clarified. Did Vienna represent a reversal of Utrecht's insistence that otherwise legitimate succession could be overridden in the greater interests of international society? This was plainly not the case, and it reinforces the claim that even Talleyrand's concept of legitimacy was rooted in the requirements of international society. According to Harold Nicolson's portrait of the Congress, there were to be two *competing* versions of legitimacy at play in its proceedings: one derived from prescriptive entitlement, while the other framed legitimacy in terms of what the great powers decreed. He is adamant that Talleyrand epitomized the former, as he had questioned, with regard to Saxony, 'what right had the Powers to defy the principle of legitimacy' (Nicolson 1946: 157). On closer scrutiny, this account is based on a serious misconception, since Talleyrand subscribed to both of these versions. What was absolutely critical for his notion of legitimacy, whatever the rhetorical garb in which it was dressed, was not merely the implementation of prescriptive rights but rather their *recognition* by international society. Thus understood, legitimacy was not simply the restoration of a former dynastic principle, but represented instead the securing of this principle in an acceptable societal basis. This was set out explicitly in the French diplomatic Instructions which Talleyrand had masterminded for Vienna:

'No title of sovereignty...has any reality for other states unless they recognize it'. In other words, if the sovereignty of a regime is to be *real* as well as *legitimate*, its legitimacy must be agreed upon and recognized by the other states of Europe. The only way to attain that agreement and recognition is for *all* Europe, not only the victorious allies, to decide upon the legitimacy of a regime: 'This can be done only by the sanction of Europe'...In the Instructions, Europe was made into what it had never been before, an almost metaphysical union of states which had the power, when acting together, to create and recognize the right of sovereignty. (Bernard 1973: 360-1; Talleyrand 1996: 317)

This is critical, and needs to be emphasized accordingly. What Talleyrand was intent upon was not the privileging of the domestic version of legitimacy against the international, but precisely the embedding of the one within the other. His purpose, in the words of one historian, was to 'make dynastic legitimacy legitimate' (Holmes 1982: 178), and there is a world of difference encapsulated in that simple repetition. The outcome was that 'after 1815, the legitimacy of states, especially new ones, rested not on patrimonial divine right, but on the treaty system and its guarantees, backed by the consent of Europe' (Schroeder 1994: 578). Legitimacy was dead; long live legitimacy. The important implication of this is that the idea of a purely domestic principle of legitimacy, in contradistinction to an international one, was no longer tenable. The one had slid seamlessly into the other. Domestic legitimacy had become itself a function of international legitimacy. So what then were to be the key elements of the latter?

The Format of the Negotiations

The negotiation of the peace was to give rise to several intense disputes about procedure. The key issues concerned the number of states to be involved in the Congress decision-making, the relationship between the victor powers and the Congress, the status of France specifically, and, more generally, the relative standing of the great and small powers.

Much of this originated in the mixed parentage of the Congress. It was not clear whether its authority derived directly from, and its form should replicate, the four-power Chaumont Treaty. Alternatively, was the formal management of the Congress to be based upon the Paris Treaty, signed as it was by eight powers, including France, Spain, Portugal, and Sweden, in addition to the four Chaumont powers (Philipps 1914: 92)? Even if the latter model prevailed, it needed to be borne in mind that a secret article of that treaty had provided for the disposition of territories at the Congress to be regulated 'upon the principles determined upon by the Allied Powers among themselves' (Hertslet 1875: 18). Initially, the Committee of Eight was given some standing, but from January 1815 this was effectively displaced by the Committee of Four (plus France).

What gave France its opportunity to insert itself was the emergence of the Saxon issue. When this was assigned to the Committee of Four for review, Castlereagh and Metternich, the Austrian Chancellor, argued that France also should be involved. In consequence, the new Committee of Five now 'became the real directing Committee of the Congress' (Webster 1945: 73–4). Talleyrand had successfully played upon, and intermingled, the twin issues of the standing of France, as well as the more general source of the authority for the four Allies to act independently. He had challenged their arrogation, initially in the name of the rest of international society, and particularly of the smaller powers. His objective, of course, was to ensure that France's voice was heard, and in this he was largely successful. As for the rest, Talleyrand was quite content to abandon the smaller powers, as soon as France's recognition as a participating great power became secure.

Talleyrand repeatedly played this procedural card, not least to serve his own ends (Talleyrand 1891: vol. 2, 315). Protesting at Allied proposals that would allow them to direct the Congress, he wrote that 'a commission can only be appointed by consent of the Congress, which if it is to accept the decisions, should also delegate the power of making them'. He continued to his compelling conclusion that 'business will not be expedited by passing resolutions of which the legitimacy will be disputed' (Philipps 1914: 102). The key point was that any committee that was seen to be the creature of the four Allied Powers alone would be tainted in the eyes of all others. Not only would business not be expedited, it would almost certainly also be short-lived in its effects.

This point was not lost on Castlereagh, who offered his own subtle proposal as to how best to proceed. It goes without saying that Castlereagh was by no means averse to safeguarding the prerogatives, and main interests, of the Allies. At the same time, however, he was demonstrably sensitive to the presentational issues that this involved. While he did not oppose the end, he yet felt it necessary to be circumspect about the means. If the great-power directorate were too blatantly imposed upon the remainder, the moral high ground would be lost. He resisted any such blunt imposition because, intriguingly, 'it too broadly and ostensibly assumed the right to do what may be generally acqui-esced in if not offensively announced, but which the Secondary Powers may protest against, if recorded to their humiliation in the face of Europe' (Webster 1945: 63). In another statement of his position, Castlereagh again pronounced himself in favour of notional concessions towards a wider circle of decision-making. He felt this desirable in order to treat the other plenipotentiaries with 'early and becoming respect'. More to the point, the benefit of so doing was that 'you obtain a sort of sanction from them for what you are determined at all events to do' (Nicolson 1946: 139), offering a glimpse, perhaps, into the realist face of his quest for legitimacy. Legitimacy, from this point of view, was substantially a function of the scope of the relevant consensus (and, to a point, he favoured inclusiveness), but also a function of the delicacy with which the matter of competence could be presented to the rest of international society. In the realm of legitimacy, appearances mattered, and were understood to do so.

It is clear from a number of commentaries that this procedural wrangle was important in crystallizing the general concept of the great powers. Both Web-ster and Nicolson insist that the distinction between the Great and the Small was effectively born at meetings held in the second half of September 1814. These gave rise to the 'first expression of the idea of the Great Powers, with rights as such, distinct from any derived from treaties' (Webster 1945: 61; Nicolson 1946: 137). If so, this is important for the general argument, as it marks a shift away from legitimacy as rooted in the 'public right' of Europe, and towards an explicitly consensual notion whereby legitimacy is to be thought of as marking the explicit bounds of great-power agreement. Instead of from a norm of legality, legitimacy was increasingly thought derivable from a norm of constitutionality.

This poses the question of the acceptability of such a great-power role in the eyes of the remainder of international society, and here the existing historical assessments remain contradictory. Evidently, it makes considerable difference to our understanding of the evolving concept of legitimacy just how extensive was the degree of support, or tolerance, for such a restrictive diplomatic procedure. Webster was in no doubt on the matter. His verdict was that 'the Smaller Powers resented the European Alliance', and 'always regarded it with great suspicion' (Webster 1929: 9). Others convey a more benign judgement. Recent interpretations are that the leadership role of the great powers, both at Vienna and beyond, was 'acknowledged as legitimate by the other actors' (Osiander 1994: 245), and that the great powers 'acted with the wider consent of the lesser states' (Broers 1996: 10–11). These assessments tend to echo Gentz's contemporary appreciation that 'the states of the second, third, and fourth rank submit tacitly, though nothing has ever been stipulated in this regard, to the decisions made in common by the preponderant Powers' (Walker 1968: 71–2).

Much was therefore at stake in this procedural agenda. Nicolson's summary of the outcome may be overdrawn, but it does nonetheless highlight an important theme of these discussions:

There was a real danger that the four victorious Allies ... would seek to impose their will upon the whole Congress. ... By exposing the legal and moral fallacies of such a contention, by asserting the principles of legitimacy and public law, Talleyrand did more than win a point of procedure for his own advantage; he established and changed the principles upon which the deliberations of the Congress were thereafter conducted. (Nicolson 1946: 144)

Such a procedural resolution was largely driven, in turn, by the unfolding of the substantive agenda. As noted, France was to be drawn into the Saxon committee, at the behest of Britain and Austria, to help check Russian and Prussian demands. The British case for so doing was that France 'might not feel excluded from the consideration of a question in which she had professed to take so strong an interest' (Philipps 1914: 112–13). In reality, the admission fulfilled the hope that Talleyrand had expressed 'qu'il aurait entre les puissances quelque divergences d'opinion', since 'ce genre de lutte ... m'offrait bien peu de chance de pénétrer dans les affaires' (Talleyrand 1996: 332; Talleyrand 1891: vol. 2, 276–7).

Famously, at the beginning of 1815, matters reached their head. In the face of what was regarded as virtually an ultimatum by Prussia, a defensive alliance between France, Britain, and Austria was signed on 3 January (Nicolson 1946: 177). Castlereagh explained this action by the need for a 'precautionary corrective', in response to 'such a domineering dictum' (Webster 1921: 277–8). Historians remain largely convinced that there was considerable posturing on both sides, and that this step was little more than 'a bluff to call a bluff' (Palmer 1983: 16). The British Prime Minister, Liverpool, certainly had misgivings about any kind of brinksmanship that might result in a premature war, as he had already communicated to his Foreign Secretary (Webster 1921: 244–5). The situation was nonetheless defused as a result, and Castlereagh was able to reflect cheerfully on the 'good consequences' of the Defensive Treaty, and especially upon the unexpectedly 'good humour' with which the territorial arrangements for Poland and Saxony were finally resolved (Webster 1921: 303–5). We need to remember, however, the basis on which the Saxon settlement was actually reached. Despite Talleyrand's vocal protestations up to this point, 'legitimacy and the rule of law' had not been saved. The bottom line was that the King of Saxony's rights 'were compromised, if not destroyed'. Even more to the point, we should not fail to notice that Talleyrand 'went along with the compromise' (Schroeder 1994: 536).

The Integration of France and a Legitimate Order

The classical expression of this argument—namely, that Vienna's significance lies in its construction of a legitimate international order—is to be found in Kissinger's discussion of the post-1815 period: 'An order whose structure is accepted by all major powers is "legitimate" ' (Kissinger 1977: 145). The emphasis here is upon the existence of consensus inasmuch as, for it to be legitimate, the order needs to be acceptable to all the great powers (but to them alone). In this version, legitimacy is attached to the conventions of international behaviour devised by the great powers, and is present whenever these are agreeable to all concerned. It is the absence of such agreement that creates tension and instability in the system *because* the order, as a result, is illegitimate. This is explicitly set out in his suggestion that, after 1815, 'the period of stability which ensued was the best proof that a "legitimate" order had been constructed, an order accepted by all the major powers' (Kissinger 1977: 5).

From this second perspective, the reason Vienna is associated with legitimacy is not because of its respect for rightful entitlement and succession domestically, but instead because of the international norms pursued by the major powers. What was important about Vienna was the successful modulation of the terms of peace so as to satisfy the minimum requirements for security of the victors, while not causing unnecessary resentment on the part of the vanquished. As most historians are prepared to acknowledge, Vienna 'left no major state, not even defeated France, nursing an irreconcilable grievance' (Anderson 1972: 1). This is not to say that in France there were no voices raised against particular aspects of the treaties. Indeed, there were many (Bullen 1979: 122–5; Towle 1997: 47). Despite these complaints, the clear intent of the victors was not to damage French standing in the long term, but rather to reincorporate France into the family of major powers as soon as possible. What was so striking about Vienna was this 'resuscitative policy toward the defeated power' (Kegley and Raymond 1999: 112–13), and it is in this respect that legitimacy was important in the overall peace settlement. If the first Paris Treaty operated on the assumption of the four allied powers making the key decisions, and presenting them to France as a *fait accompli*, then as early as the summer of 1814 things were already beginning to change with respect to the wider settlement. The contacts between France and Britain had become potentially so close that Wellington felt it necessary to warn Castlereagh, in a communication of 18 August 1814, of the dangers of the two becoming overly intimate (Webster 1921: 191). While ostensibly still the outsider, France was already acting in ways that suggested that it was one of the insiders.

Broadly speaking, there are three main factors that help to explain why a moderate settlement with France—the key criterion of legitimacy in this second sense—proved both possible and necessary. They revolve around the protective role of Russia, the logic of the 'legitimate' restoration of the Bourbons, and the accommodating mediation of Britain, and of its Foreign Secretary Castlereagh in particular.

That the role of Russia was important had been acknowledged by observers at the time. Indeed, Gentz felt this to be the 'deciding factor', in part because of Russia's remoteness, and consequent ability to play an objective role (Kraehe 1983: 12). Tellingly, this assessment was shared by Castlereagh, as he confided to his Prime Minister, Lord Liverpool, on 24 July 1815. As against those central powers who were pressing for more severe terms to be imposed on France, Castlereagh wrote that 'Russia, on the contrary, being remote, rather inclines to protect France' (Webster 1921: 350–1). There had, of course, been an early and practical demonstration of Tsar Alexander's position (as also of his tendency towards unilateral and emotive displays) when, on his triumphal entry into Paris, he had issued his famous proclamation of 1 April 1814. In this, he assured the French people that the terms of peace 'will become more lenient when France, by returning to a wiser government, will itself offer security for peace'. Moreover, he had insisted, it was also fundamental to Europe's general welfare that 'France remain large and strong' (Bernard 1973: 326–7).

The second factor reveals yet again the intimate connection between the first and second dimensions of legitimacy, the internal and the external. 'Legitimate' treatment of France, internationally, was itself logically predetermined by the legitimacy of the Bourbon return to the French throne. 'Louis XVIII could not be restored to his "legitimate" inheritance', one historian shrewdly comments of this chain of reasoning, 'if he were at the same time to be deprived of any part of it' (Albrecht-Carrié 1965: 12). In short, restoration made a lenient peace *possible*, because the peace could now be directed at the incumbent ruler, not his predecessor. The first Paris Treaty had explicitly made this point. The Allies were stated therein to be 'unwilling to require of France, now that, replaced under the paternal Government of Her Kings, she offers the assurance of security and stability to Europe, the conditions and guarantees which they had with regret demanded from her former Government' (Hertslet 1875: 2–3). The war had been with Napoleon, not with the Bourbons, nor the French people. But the restoration, additionally, made a moderate peace *necessary*. Otherwise, what was the point of a return of the Bourbons, as a hoped-for stabilizing force, if they were only to be undermined at the outset? Castlereagh pressed this logic repeatedly upon Liverpool, after Napoleon's hundred days. 'I doubt...the possibility of the King's holding his ground in France', he urged strenuously on 24 July 1815, 'if, after holding himself out to the nation as a means of appeasing the Allies, they disavow him so far'. The next month, he warned again that 'if ... we push things now to an extremity, we leave the King no resource in the eyes of his own people but to disavow us' (Schenk 1947: 46). The necessary implication of domestic legitimacy, embodied in the restoration, was a peace that would be tolerable to France, and to the reputation of its monarch. Thus would it issue in an equally legitimate international order.

Finally, the moderation of the peace was in no small measure a reflection of the particular objectives sought by the British representatives. Castlereagh resolutely opposed demands for a tougher peace, especially in the run up to the second Peace of Paris. He even had to work hard to carry his Cabinet colleagues with him, let alone the House of Commons. His role has, in this regard, been compared to that of Bolingbroke at Utrecht a century earlier (Osiander 1994: 199).

Whatever the precise balance between these various dispositional factors, there can be no doubting that, by the end, the Allies felt that they had reached a settlement with which all could live. It was legitimate, in Kissinger's terms, because, being acceptable to France, it held out the welcome prospect of being self-enforcing. After such a period of warfare, no power was eager for any early return to the fray. Accordingly, the great virtue of a settlement that was tolerable to France was that France would develop an interest in itself maintaining it. It would not have to be *enforced* by explicit allied action from the outside, beyond the limited terms of the arrangements for military occupation. On the date of the second Paris Treaty, the allied ministers candidly spelled out to the French Prime Minister, the Duke de Richelieu, those advantages that would accrue from a tempered peace with France. Better than any other statement, it reveals the logic of a legitimate peace. The restored monarchy held out the prospect, they explained, of

Public Repose ... while it will relieve the Allied Powers ... from the painful necessity of recurring to the adoption of means, which, in the event of renewed disorder, would be imperiously prescribed to them by the duty of providing for the security of their own subjects and the general Tranquillity of Europe. (Hertslet 1875: 411)

These were some of the principal factors, and motives, which led the statesmen of 1815 to develop a peace that would be just about tolerable to all. In order to fully comprehend this attribute of the Vienna settlement, we need to examine yet more closely the precise relationship between consensus, concert, and the development of this principle of international legitimacy.

Consensus and Concert

As we have seen, it was to be the emergence of procedural disagreements that drove the quest for principles to resolve them and, in turn, raised more fundamental questions about the bases on which the powers were to relate towards each other. Operationally, legitimacy in its international aspect was coming to be conceived, less as adherence to law and treaties, and more as the expression of what the great powers were minded to think agreeable. Legitimacy could be claimed on the basis of a working consensus in support of any proposed action, and to be sanctioned by the very existence of that consensus. Thus it has been claimed of the concert that 'it was able to articulate some shared expectations and standards of legitimacy about the organization of European political order' (Ikenberry 2001: 106). The standards of legitimacy articulated were not some extraneous, and additional, ideas beyond the concert, but resided in respect for the essential idea of the concert itself. The concert was the standard of legitimacy, and did not simply give voice to it. 'The notion of international legitimacy', it is claimed, 'was revitalized in the Concert' (Bukovansky 2002: 223).

We need, however, to distinguish between the means and the end. To be sure, Castlereagh advocated a particular form of personal consultation (arising out of his own recent experience) as his preferred diplomatic method. He had outlined in early 1814 his own high hopes that such a practice would issue in

... a[n] habitual confidential and free intercourse between the Ministers of the Great Powers, *as a body*; and that many pretensions might be modified, asperities removed, and causes of irritation anticipated and met, by bringing the respective parties into unrestricted communications common to them all, and embracing in confidential and united discussions all the great points in which they were severally interested. (Bartlett 1996: 8)

This 'free intercourse' was to be the means. The greater purpose, however, was the attainment of consensual decisions, and it was to be the latter that would constitute the yardstick of legitimacy, however much the apparatus of the concert would create the necessary conditions for it to be realized. It was for this reason that the British delegation at the Aix-la-Chapelle Congress, in October 1818, felt it so necessary to reintegrate France. Such an addition to their company, stated their memorandum, would not make it 'too numerous for convenient concert', but—and much more to the point—'must add immensely to the moral weight and influence' of its activities (Albrecht-Carrié 1968: 43). Exactly the same sentiment was reiterated by the Plenipotentiaries of the four Powers, in a note to the Duke de Richelieu of 12 November 1818. Welcoming France's future participation in the periodic meetings of the Powers, as under Article VI of the Quadruple Alliance, they acknowledged that its force 'must spring from a perfect unanimity of principle and action', and to this end, that France's 'concurrence must add strength to the well-founded hope of the happy results which such an alliance must produce' (Hertslet 1875: 567–8). Critical to its success was not simply the method of the concert, but the scope of its embrace: a consensus from which France was indefinitely excluded would be forever tainted, and hence ineffectual in sustaining a collective policy on the part of the powers.

This leaves us with some interesting puzzles to resolve. If the concert was the embodiment of the new international legitimacy, why was it that significant sections of liberal opinion remained so hostile to it? To some critics, concert diplomacy appeared 'by its very nature, repressive and illiberal' (Palmer 1983: 25). Was it simply that the international procedure of consensus diplomacy remained too infected by the corollary principle of dynastic legitimacy, with its conservative and interventionist overtones? Or was it also that, even if in pursuit of a more benign set of political goals, any international mechanism based upon agreement amongst a handful of large powers remained too tenuous to enjoy genuine international authority and support? What we need to explore in the remainder of this chapter is the debate about the standing of this emergent European concert, and the sources of opposition to it. Both offer fertile sources of insight into contemporary doctrines of international legitimacy. New ideas about the balance of power were to be central to them.

A Just Equilibrium

There can be little doubt that balance-of-power concepts were integral to the settlement as a whole, enjoying, on one account, 'pride of place' (Osiander 1994: 223). Gentz characterized the grand design as one in which France and Russia posed the principal potential threats to the system, but could be contained by the *middle line* of Austria, Prussia and England, acting as the 'true rampart of the common security of Europe' (Walker 1968: 83–4). Not surprisingly, this echoed the views of Metternich himself (Kraehe 1983: 4–5). Balance language was also to be explicitly written into the treaties. Thus the secret articles of the first Paris Treaty provided for the allied powers to develop 'a system of real and permanent Balance of Power in Europe' (Hertslet 1875: 18), and in particular mandated that Holland be independently strong enough to play its part in 'a just Balance of Power' (Hertslet 1875: 19). Talleyrand, notably, made the cryptic comment of the use of the words 'real and permanent' in the treaty that they were 'bien vagues' (Talleyrand 1996: 308).

It has been claimed of the Vienna settlement that 'the principles of legitimacy and equilibrium jointly structured the new international order' (Reus-Smit 1999: 135). If so, we need a clearer conception of the respective contributions of each, and of the demarcation between them. We can again consider the analysis provided by Kissinger in this context. His contention was that an order enjoying legitimacy is distinct from one reliant upon power alone. Although he is clear that it is the very legitimacy of an order that is the key to its stability, and hence to its durability, his own understanding of this relationship remains a complex one. This much emerges in his various formulations of the order produced by the Vienna settlement:

Thus the new international order came to be created with a sufficient awareness of the connection between power and morality; between security and legitimacy. No attempt was made to found it entirely on submission to a legitimizing principle ... Rather, there was created a balance of forces which, because it conferred a relative security, came to be generally accepted. (Kissinger 1977: 318)

Elsewhere, and more succinctly, he talks of the post-Vienna order being predicated on 'not only a physical equilibrium but a moral one' (Kissinger 1995: 79).

What all this seems to suggest is that a physical balance of power is necessary, but not sufficient, for a secure and stable order. What is required, in addition, is a 'moral balance' which, given what is said elsewhere, presumably can express itself only through agreement and consensus. This is revealed in the possibilities for its peaceful transformation. In a legitimate order, change can be wrought 'through acceptance', based in turn on 'a consensus on the nature of a just arrangement' (Kissinger 1977: 172). In similar fashion, Schroeder discerns a revolutionary transformation between the eighteenth- and nineteenth-century international systems. This, he believes, must be attributed to a combination of factors, of which one was the transition from 'a competitive balance-of-power struggle', to one of 'political equilibrium based on benign shared hegemony' (Schroeder 1994: 580). In both the Kissinger and the Schroeder versions, the stability of the post-1815 system is attributed, either to a combination of legitimacy and a balance of power or, perhaps more accurately, to an idea of political equilibrium which itself incorporates a sense of legitimacy as a fundamental element.

Historians remain divided amongst themselves about how properly to understand the relationship between the balance of power and the consensus-based concert diplomacy of the period. Some, typically, see the prevailing distribution of power as 'one of the background conditions which rendered the Concert possible' in the first place (Richardson 1994: 228). Others take a different route and portray Talleyrand and Castlereagh as believing that 'consensus was more important for the stability of Europe than the actual distribution of material strength' (Osiander 1994: 228). Did the balance make a consensus possible? If so, how can we possibly know whether it was the balance or the consensus that generated the resulting stability (Schroeder 1992)?

What is the evidence to support these claims and counter-claims? The policy of Britain makes for an interesting case in point. Almost universally, British policy—and that of Castlereagh specifically—is understood to have been instrumental in the emergence of a moderate peace at Vienna, and to the possibility of consensual politics thereafter. But can this policy be detached from the privileged position in which Britain found itself in 1815? Some would have it that its policy was, in important respects, a reflection of the fact that British interests had already been satisfied by the outcome of war, and prior to the negotiation of the Vienna settlement. Britain alone, Webster attests, 'had secured her vital interest in the continental settlement before peace with France', and this made possible her 'future role as mediator' (Webster 1931: 269).

In another respect, what was not to be placed on the table for discussion is as revealing as the matters that were. Britain's strategic position within the coalition at the end of the war had allowed her to ensure that the American war specifically, and Britain's maritime standing more generally, did not fall within the purview of the Congress. These exclusions contributed, no doubt, to the success of Vienna by simplifying the agenda (Ikenberry 2001: 112). More generally, Schroeder (1994: 575) may also be right to suggest that the separation of European from extra-European issues at Vienna was a force for future stability. We should not, however, be blind to the interests served by this, nor to the exercise of power that had made such an outcome possible. It is for reasons such as these that the so-called 'equilibrium' of Vienna has been dismissed by one historian as 'fraudulent', as it left Britain 'supreme and unopposed' (Bridge 1979: 36). By the same token, the very 'pursuit of hegemony' on the part of Britain and Russia, that is said by Ikenberry (2001) to underlie the strategy of 'institutionalization' characteristic of the Vienna peace, casts the peace very much in the shadow of the power politics of the period. Others are equally dismissive of the 'disinterested' nature of the collaborative policies pursued at the time. Rather than driven by a commitment to a consensual outcome, 'each compromise was usually a pretty fair reflection of the realities of power' (Bartlett 1996: 23). If any of these claims is valid, it renders artificial the suggestion that the Vienna consensus can be understood in separation from the prevailing distribution of power. By this account, if consensus was the product of many states individually pursuing their own self-interests, then it was the balance of power, and not self-conscious adherence to a standard of legitimacy, that was the invisible hand behind the consensus that resulted.

Matters cannot, however, be left to rest there. If balance of power was part of the equation, it may still be regarded as only a *part* of it. Osiander is insistent that, at Vienna, and certainly in comparison to Utrecht, the balance-of-power principle was 'no longer the chief source of consensus'. It had by now come to be supplemented by something else, as revealed in the much-favoured expression of the age, a 'just equilibrium' (Osiander 1994: 231). We need next to consider this concept to see if it can shed any light on what that additional element might have been.

This term was certainly in widespread usage at Vienna. The preamble to the Chaumont Treaty recalled that the recent war had been undertaken to re-establish 'a just equilibrium of powers' (Osiander 1994: 224). The phrase was very much part of the personal idiom of Castlereagh. He informed his Cabinet colleagues in November 1814 that such a 'just equilibrium' was the main object of his policy (Webster 1945: 99), and his task was to move the notion beyond mere declarations and preambles 'to the map of Europe' (Webster 1931: 328). But what, if anything, did this concept amount to, beyond its fetching rhetorical flourish?

On closer scrutiny, we discover that the notion of 'just equilibrium' embraced, and replicated, the twin dimensions of legitimacy: one strand fastened upon issues of rightful possession and entitlement, the other amounted to an elaboration of the guiding principles of interstate conduct. It stands, in that sense, as a convenient synonym for the contemporary idea of legitimacy.

The former can be found in the utterances of various contemporary practitioners and commentators, with Talleyrand, unsurprisingly, foremost amongst them. As we have already seen, his doctrine was a composite of (domestic) legitimacy and balance of power, and this dovetailed neatly with the putative substance of an 'équilibre juste'. Essential to his position was that no equilibrium could be durable if it violated legitimacy. He wrote in his *Mémoires*, not a little woodenly, that any equilibrium 'can endure only so long as the proportions on which it is founded endure, and these proportions themselves can endure only so long as the rights of possession shall be transmitted in such a way that they are not changed' (Gulick 1967: 228). In practice, this meant that legitimacy should be incorporated into the equilibrium, not sacrificed to it. He wrote to Metternich in this very vein in December 1814, to urge upon him that the proper task of the Congress was to create 'a real and durable equilibrium'. To this end, he warned that a satisfactory outcome 'did not mean to sacrifice to the establishment of that equilibrium the rights which it should guarantee' (Metternich 1881: vol. 2, 510; Gulick 1967: 233–4). It was in the attainment of these twin objectives that the justness of the equilibrium would be achieved.

Other contemporary writers, such as Heeren (Holbraad 1970: 82) and Koch (Keene 2002: 20–1), likewise saw a just equilibrium to lie in the construction of a balance that respected, and succeeded in safeguarding, existing rights and entitlements. This did nothing to clarify what was to be done in hard cases of absolute incompatibility between the two demands, as was in fact to arise over Saxony. As against these publicists, Gentz struck a much more pragmatic note. 'Legitimacy is born in time', he reflected, and 'it can therefore be considered not in an absolute, but only in a relative, sense'. From this he drew the manifest conclusion—which Talleyrand would have denounced in principle, even if prepared to countenance in practice—that 'from time to time, like everything human, it must be modified' (Little 1996: 211). Accordingly some proponents treated the idea of a 'just equilibrium' as fixed, others as more flexible.

The second usage treated 'just equilibrium' as tantamount to the consensual practices of the great-power concert. Castlereagh broached this issue from a most interesting angle in his defence, before the House of Commons, of the policy he had adopted over Saxony. He presented himself as the staunchest of opponents to the swallowing up of all Saxony by Prussia, but was at pains to explain the grounds of his stance. This was not based on 'mere abstract right'. Indeed, he went so far as to assert that 'never was the principle of conquest more legitimately applicable, or more justifiably exercisable than in the case of Saxony' (Webster 1921: 400–1). He opposed Prussian demands, then, not because of the legitimate rights of the King of Saxony, nor yet because annexation would be an illegitimate conquest of war. He opposed it, in short, because it represented both an immoderate extension of Prussian power, and because that extension was intolerable to Austria and others. It thus violated the principle of 'just equilibrium' on the two combined grounds—it threatened the balance, *and* it violated the consensus. A 'just equilibrium' required respect for both.

In conclusion, the idea of a 'just equilibrium' symbolized the contemporary quest for a meaningful marriage between the needs of the balance of power, and its collective management in accordance with a shared concept of legitimacy. Schroeder has argued persuasively that the concept of equilibrium operated at multiple levels, and comprehended a broad range of desiderata, going well beyond the material distribution of power alone. 'A good European equilibrium', he attests, 'depended upon having one's honour and dignity recognized, one's national rights satisfied, treaties maintained, the great powers united, all the great powers equally represented in the Concert . . . ' (Schroeder 1989: 144). Legitimacy at Vienna can be understood as the shorthand expression for the aspiration to attain these conditions in some pragmatic combination. It stood not for the implementation of a single norm, but for some attainable combination of competing norms, consensually reached.

CONCLUSION

It is not unreasonable to conclude that it was such a synthesis that Vienna was seeking to achieve. This does not mean that the powers were to be required to abandon their individual interests for the sake of the collective enterprise of the concert. More realistically, what Castlereagh and others sought to foster was a recognition that all states stood to benefit from adherence to collective norms, and that this could indeed be factored into how interests were both formulated and pursued. This seemed, at the time, the only real prospect of avoiding a repetition of the recent wars.

Vienna managed some faltering steps in this direction, and this warrants due recognition. That said, even if legitimacy generated some rethinking of interests, it could scarcely be said to have trumped power. What held each state in check was not solely the collective animus of the age, but also the more general deterrence associated with that balance of power. At best, the two could work in tandem with each other. We need to be mindful of the restricted scope of the consensus that underpinned these new formulations of legitimacy. To be sure, some smaller states complied with the directorial role of the great powers, some of the time. There could be benefits for them in developing a degree of mutual restraint amongst the principal powers. For all that, however, the consensual principle at Vienna was restricted to those deemed equally strong, and manifestly did not extend to the weak. 'Their mandate was their power', insists Brown (2001: 94), 'their capacity to put into effect their collective will'. While it is important to acknowledge the sophisticated innovations that Vienna brought to the notion of international legitimacy, we should never lose sight of the bounds within which these diplomatic developments were to be set.

Almost all components of this legitimacy agenda were to be revisited a century later at the end of the First World War. For all the stark contrasts that are normally drawn between Vienna and Versailles, we should recognize also the common themes that were to arise in both. This is not, of course, to suggest that the peacemakers drew the same conclusions about what needed to be done on the issues that faced them. It is to a consideration of the Versailles settlement that the survey will now turn.

6

The Versailles Settlement: The Making of an Illegitimate Order?

Presenting the text of the Versailles Treaty to the German plenipotentiaries on 7 May 1919, French Prime Minister, Clemenceau, made the following emotional, and highly revealing, remarks. 'I am compelled to add that this Second Peace of Versailles . . . has been too dearly bought by the peoples represented here', he recalled, 'for us not to be unanimously resolved to secure by every means in our power all the legitimate satisfactions which are our due' (Hankey 1963: 153). The French leader encapsulated in these words the burdens that weighed upon the peace: the heavy sacrifices of the war; the popular dimensions of the new nationalist warfare, and the expectations to which they had led; the arduous search for agreement about the contents of the peace; and the strong sense on the part of the victors that what was being asked of Germany was the very least that was acceptable. Few treaties have been so voluminously discussed, and with such passion, by subsequent generations of historians. Strikingly, the theme of legitimacy is central to their debates.

If Vienna enjoys iconic status as the framer of a legitimate order, it is Versailles above all that is tainted with inaugurating an order considered to be highly unstable, because illegitimate. Its failures are thought to be multiple. More than any treaty so far, it stressed the conditions of rightful membership of international society, but in such a way that this domestic test undermined its simultaneous attempt to integrate the vanquished states into the new system. As far as its treatment of the international dimensions of legitimacy was concerned, Versailles faced problems in finding any effective consensus, around its treatment of Germany specifically, and in the procedural aspects of the treaty negotiations more generally. These features compounded the underlying problems that already awaited the peacemakers, as the Clemenceau quote makes clear. The war had been of such magnitude—affecting so many lives directly, creating both domestic and international divisions, and engendering insatiable expectations of the peace—that the peacemakers were all but impotent to deal sensibly with its consequences. This was not a settlement in which the peacemakers carelessly let the opportunity for consensus-building slip through their fingers: the basic problem of Versailles was that no such consensus could possibly be found. We must distinguish, however, between a consensus around principles of legitimacy, and the separate search to secure legitimation for what was to be done in their name.

THE SETTLEMENT AND ITS CONTEXT

Some doubt that Versailles deserves to be called a settlement at all. So little did it do to resolve the international problems of the period, it might better be considered a mere truce in an ongoing twenty or thirty years' war (Bell 1986). Its legacy 'was neither peace nor settlement' (Jacobson 1998: 451). This was not a consequence simply of its failure to deal with existing international disputes and balances of power. More fundamentally, what was left unresolved was the legitimacy of dominant domestic constitutional forms, and it was around this issue that the epochal war of the twentieth century was to rage until 1990.

The most common verdict upon Versailles is that the settlement was the victim of the incompatible victors' objectives, and hence of the necessary compromises to which negotiations were bound to lead. Different attitudes towards the war from its outset were carried over into the preparations for the peace. Indicatively, the United States had been at some pains to distance itself from other Allied war aims (and secret agreements) by becoming a belligerent as an 'associate' only, not as an 'ally' (Schulzinger 1994: 82). Since the war was a more limited one for the United States, American entry into the war heralded the prospect of a more moderate peace than any that could have been agreed by the previously existing coalition of powers (Stevenson 1998: 137–8).

This diversity of opinion had somehow to be reconciled with the simultaneous aspiration, if not universally shared, for a more 'integrated' conception of international society. Under the Versailles proposals, particularly with the inception of the League, the 'society of states was to remain as such', Armstrong contends. However, 'the limited *association* of the Westphalian conception was to evolve towards much closer *community*, sharing values, standards, practices, and institutions as well as interests' (Armstrong 1993: 161). In no small measure, such a conception arose from US President Woodrow Wilson's own belief that international society had not yet been fully realized, as it still lacked an effective legal basis. It was the task of the peacemakers to introduce this rule of law, and to create thereby an effective international society, in place of the deficient apparatus that had so far existed. In particular, the incorporation of certain key values was necessary, in Wilson's mind, 'because they were just, not because there was a consensus on their acceptability' (Osiander 1994: 266). In this respect, Wilson appealed to putative abstract and absolute values that stood apart from consensual state practice. He did so, nonetheless, in full expectation that such a 'process of consensual empowerment', if endorsed, would in turn result in the acceptance of his key principles into state practice, and permit the encouragement of new forms of state conduct.

Versailles offers that rare opportunity for bringing the theoretical discussion of legitimacy, and its practical application in the sphere of politics, into direct correspondence with each other. This opportunity is created in the person of none other than Weber who, as we have seen, represents a key perspective on the importance of legitimacy. Weber was a personal participant in the German peace delegation, a role only recently recovered (Mommsen 1998: 539). Tellingly, Weber found himself ranged on that wing of the delegation that eventually argued for rejection of the peace terms offered by the victor powers, as he felt that too many intolerable concessions had been made (Mommsen 1998: 540–1). Above all, Weber's 'perception' of the matter is doubly interesting for this discussion, exactly because he viewed the situation in terms of the critical linkage between the 'legitimacy' of the international conditions of the peace, and the impact this would have upon the domestic legitimacy of the new Weimar regime. In his estimation, 'acceptance of the treaty would have devastating effects on the domestic situation and would severely burden the new democratic order' (Mommsen 1998: 546). Since the fostering of such an order, both in Germany and elsewhere, was an important component of the Wilsonian project, we are led to confront this dual face of legitimacy in our assessment of this peace. The United States and Britain saw the process of the gradual accommodation of Germany (into what would then become an increasingly legitimate international order) to be conditional on German domestic change, whereas Weber's anxiety was that the treaty's international terms would themselves preclude the achievement of such internal change. The interplay between the international and domestic facets of legitimacy is thus central to the dilemma faced at Versailles, and tells us much about the nature of its failure.

The Paris conference—from which finally emerged the Versailles Treaty with Germany, and the four other individual peace treaties—was unquestionably the largest and most complex such gathering in human history. Its agenda was much more than a purely European one. It took place after a suspension of hostilities had already been agreed by the Armistice of 11 November 1918. There were precedents for such suspension before a peace conference was summoned, but equally there had been previous peace negotiations entered into while the fighting was still ongoing (Marston 1944: 13).

In addition to its incorporation of the Covenant of the League, Versailles provided for the territorial, military, economic, and colonial settlements. Germany lost the provinces of Alsace and Lorraine and, overall, some 13 per cent of its pre-1914 territory. Restrictions were imposed upon its army (an upper limit of 100,000, and these to be professional, not conscript), as well as on its navy. Some economic issues were dealt with by means of temporary expedients—such as administration of the Saar—but most contentiously was this done by the future efforts of the Reparations Commission to which the problem of determining a sum for reparations was passed. Finally, Germany was stripped of its former extra-European colonies, to be handed over as mandates to the administrative oversight of the League Mandates Commission, but in daily practice to the holders of this new colonial responsibility (Sharp 1991).

Beneath these formal provisions of the treaty is the rich vein of supporting principle on which it was purportedly to be based, and here the historian of international legitimacy is faced with a substantially larger archive of source material than is typically available. It is this Wilsonian rhetoric, shared or not in varying degrees by other participants, that sets the tone for the analysis of legitimacy in this particular settlement.

At the centre of Wilson's vision was to be found 'the principle of public right' (Holsti 1991: 177). If such could be articulated, then international society would be grounded on a shared value system that would itself make possible a dialogue about legitimacy. In conjunction with this, the very concept of international society was now broadened out to provide the requisite under-pinning for the new normative architecture it was to bear. It was to be under-stood as an international society of *peoples*, not simply of states. The future order was to be based not just on the acts of governments, but upon 'the will, the goodwill—of the people', of whom governments were simply the servants (Baker 1923: vol. 1, 103). It was the people who would have to be satisfied with the peace arrangements made on their behalf, and only in their satisfaction could the durability of the order be guaranteed. It followed equally that international society must genuinely represent the wishes of the people, and this demanded the adoption of democratic institutions, both domestically and internationally. Consent lay at the heart of the whole enterprise (Baker 1923: vol. 1, 11; Keylor 1998: 475). The League not only depended for its efficacy upon a worldwide democratic revolution, but would serve also to bring one about (Ikenberry 2001: 127). Democratic values were, after 1919, to become the equivalent of 'the coin of the realm' (Mayall 2000: 64).

There remained one final desideratum. For public opinion to be effective as a deterrent, people must have full information about the international deeds of their governments. This manifested itself in the demand for open against secret diplomacy. Only thus could the moral force of mankind be brought to bear. The actual negotiation of the peace settlement was to provide the first test of this new accountability. Sadly for its supporters, Wilson and his colleagues dis-played alarming tendencies towards recidivism when faced with hard decisions. The choice between the old and the new diplomacy was made in favour of the former, according to the then US Secretary of State, Robert Lansing, and 'secrecy was adopted' instead (Lansing 1921: 241). In this view, the conference was tainted from its outset by the 'extraordinary secrecy and arrogation of power by the Council of Four', which 'excited astonishment and complaint' (Lansing 1921: 218). This was bad enough, but doubly so when compounded by the high standards it had publicly set for itself, and the burden of expectation to which these had given rise. This was the background to the practice of legitimacy at Versailles.

THE HISTORICAL VERDICTS

Historical judgements upon Versailles have tended to concentrate explicitly on the notion of legitimacy. This is scarcely surprising, since President Wilson personally did so much to place this stamp upon the treaty, thereby to mark its historical departure from—as he saw it—the unfortunate precedents of the past. These had been preoccupied with spoils, and with the balance of power. As a result, they had dispensed victors' justice, which had served only to perpetuate the deformations of the international political system. The opportunity presented itself now, in contrast, for reconstituting the international order upon a real principle of justice. 'An evident principle runs through the whole programme I have outlined', he enunciated in his Fourteen Points. 'It is the principle of justice to all peoples' (Baker 1923: vol. 3, 45). The importation into the interstate discourse of legitimacy of this normative principle of justice was the hallmark of Wilson's modus operandi (Lentin 1985: 5; Holsti 1991: 185). Wilson self-consciously proceeded on the basis of the domestic analogy, and his self-assigned task was none other than the obliteration of any distinction between the real society of individuals within the state and the rudimentary society that was the international. An international society could be truly formed only by establishing within it the rule of law, rooted in a shared concept of justice. His political quest, as stated in his Mount Vernon address of 4 July 1918, was therefore to replicate by the 'consent of all nations' what were essentially 'the same principles of honor and of respect for the common law of civilized society that govern the individual citizen of all modern states in their relations with one another' (Baker 1923: vol. 3, 46). This is how he conceived of the creation of 'a stable and legitimate postwar order' (Ikenberry 2001: 160). It is, of course, the great paradox of the Versailles settlement that a peace so painstakingly based on explicit principles of legitimacy should have resulted in an order so poorly legitimated as a political condition. Seldom is there recognized to be such a wide gulf between aspiration and actual attainment. But what exactly was the nature of this failure?

It may be helpful at this point to return to the concept introduced in the context of the Vienna settlement of 1815: the notion of a just equilibrium. Was the key defect of Versailles its violation of its own declared principle of justice, or was it instead its adherence to justice to the consequent neglect of the actual balance of power? Or was it instead its failure to *combine* these two elements in some effective way? This issue is prompted by Kissinger's own analysis of the peace: its shortcomings, he felt sure, were 'structural'. The Vienna order had been so stable because it was supported by three pillars: 'a peace of conciliation with France, a balance of power; and a shared sense of legitimacy' (Kissinger 1995: 242). Versailles regrettably 'fulfilled none of these conditions' (1995: 242). Others have explained the matter somewhat differently. Osiander, for example, is less concerned with the failure to restore a balance of power.

The problem lay elsewhere in the inability to generate an effective international consensus (Osiander 1994: 329). But what was the reason for this? Was it, as Kissinger thought, the lack of a shared sense of legitimacy that made the reaching of a consensus impossible, or—as Osiander would have it—the failure to establish consensus that rendered agreed principles of legitimacy unattainable?

Holsti puts yet another gloss on it, and frames his explanation in terms of Wilson's abandonment of a key feature of his own notion of procedural justice:

By late 1918 he [Wilson] had also abandoned one of his critical moral maxims: peace must be based on justice. In practice, this meant that the peace would have to be negotiated between all the belligerents; it must be a peace between equals...The procedure was commonly recognized as a fundamental requirement for establishing legitimacy to a peace settlement and for assimilating the defeated power(s) into the postwar order. (Holsti 1991: 197–8)

In this version, the illegitimacy of the order was a function, not so much of the substantive harshness of the peace alone, but of the procedures followed in its making, and particularly of Germany's exclusion from that process.

Finally, there is the widely held judgement that Versailles was the victim of too many compromises. The theme of compromise is prominent in all accounts of Versailles. This derived, in turn, from incompatible war aims at the outset, and from the 'complication of coalition warfare' (Boemeke, Feldman, and Glaser 1998: 16). There were two types of compromise that were to prove damaging to the sustainability of the treaty. The first was the compromise between principle and execution. In practice, those great Wilsonian principles intended to subvert traditional European statecraft were found to have adapted parts of that tradition to their new purpose (Soutou 2001: 306–7). According to Lloyd George, the British Prime Minister, Wilson had to learn some pretty hard lessons, above all that 'the chronic troubles of Europe could not be settled by hanging round its neck the phylacteries of abstract justice' (George 1938: 238). Secondly, there were to be compromises between the various clashing principles themselves—how, for example, the new appeals to self-determination were to be reconciled with the other buttresses of order. The great betrayal, for some, was to be found in the elevation of justice as the supreme principle to which the securing of political equilibrium was to be sacrificed (Osiander 1994: 329). These compromises, as Soutou powerfully suggests, lent the treaty system a dynamic quality, and an unusual degree of 'suppleness', in the longer term (Soutou 2001: 312). This may well have been so. But possibly this very flexibility was its own undoing; it could bend in so many directions that the practitioners themselves became disoriented by the intricacy of their own artifice. For all these reasons, the practice of legitimacy at Versailles proved an especially complex and onerous undertaking. It was not that it was wanting for principles, but the politics of legitimation of the settlement proved exceptionally recalcitrant.

LEGITIMACY AT VERSAILLES

Rightful Membership

The Versailles settlement took yet a stage further the idea of international society's responsibility for its own composition, and the tutelage that was a necessary adjunct of that role. The act of admission into international society was not to be understood as unconditional: states had to conform to certain norms to accomplish this rite of passage. This much was scarcely new, and had become more firmly entrenched in the last third of the nineteenth century, after the Congress of Berlin of 1878, especially with regard to treatment of ethnic minorities (Soutou 2001: 308–9). Minorities had already been accorded, by these international instruments, certain basic religious freedoms as a matter of domestic constitutional practice of the states concerned. However, in 1919, the commingling of this with the new Wilsonian rhetoric raised the consciousness about issues of membership to even higher levels. It was also more explicit in relating this issue, not simply to domestic stability, but to international peace as well. Thus Krasner observes that the 1919 arrangements were 'explicitly designed to alter the domestic political arrangements of the new states', given the Wilsonian thinking about 'the relationship among the rights of minorities, national self-determination, democracy, and international peace' (Krasner 2001: 39).

This greater preoccupation with rightful membership had implications for Germany, and generally for 'the assimilation of the defeated power(s) into the international society' (Holsti 1991: 199). In 1815, the matter could be construed simply as the readmission of France into the diplomatic concert of the powers. Matters were much more complex in 1919, and this was particularly so with regard to the nature of the international society into which Germany now sought re-entry. It was no longer to be considered simply a club of great powers. It was, in Wilsonian terms, to be a society of people who bore responsibility for the good behaviour of their respective governments. Admission to this society set a higher threshold, and this was the obstacle that Germany now confronted. It was caught also in the pincer movement between the alternative means for securing future German compliance. For some observers, Germany would be subject to the new international norms and institutions under construction in 1919, and would be externally constrained in this way. For others, the essential constraint would be internal, and result from domestic transformations within Germany. Unhappily, these considerations operated in tandem in ways to prescribe a period of probation for Germany, until such time that the external constraints were sufficiently developed and robust, or until such time that the evidences of internal political change had become compelling. Germany was not to be permanently cast adrift from international society, but was required to wait patiently on the wings until its credentials could again be accepted. The external constraints could be modified when 'the Germans had been disciplined and democratized', and so once more 'become a part of the system' (Martel 1998: 615). This made perfect sense, as long as the external constraints did not themselves vitiate the democratic transformations awaited inside.

It is not possible fully to appreciate the Versailles architecture without a clear focus on this cardinal principle of democracy *as a proper concern of international society*. This underpinned all the aspirations for the League, but left its imprint also on the application of the principle of 'self-determination'. It was to be the key rationale for the treatment of Germany. In these ways, it pervades the settlement as a whole. Nor was this attitude confined narrowly to the Wilsonian camp. It was appealed to equally by the other peacemakers, whenever they had good reason to do so. We can note, for instance, the insistence on this requirement in the official French blueprint for the League of Nations. '[N]o nations can be admitted to the League', it stipulated, 'other than those which are constituted as States and provided with representative institutions such as will permit their being themselves considered responsible for the acts of their own Governments' (Baker 1923: vol. 3, 153). Despite the logic of collective security pointing towards universal inclusiveness, it is apparent that the insistence upon democratic institutions was deployed instead as a principle of international exclusion. The 'process of consensual empowerment' was thus coming to be focused explicitly upon this definition of rightful membership, exactly at the very moment when the constitutional struggle between different state forms and ideologies (liberal democratic, communist, and fascist) was moving towards its bloody climax (Bobbitt 2002: 608).

Democracy, in turn, was both the logical precondition, and the necessary vindication, of the principle of self-determination—that other momentous legitimating principle that played such a powerful discursive role within the framework of the settlement. Henry Kissinger (1977: 145), typically, has described national self-determination as 'the legitimizing principle of the new international order' after 1919. It became international society's 'new master principle' (Osiander 1994: 255), and operated as such in the specific sense that it provided 'the accepted criterion for membership of the system', thereby leaving a lasting impression on the future development of international society (Osiander 1994: 318). And yet this principle came late to the prominence that it was eventually to enjoy. Significantly, it was not listed amongst Wilson's Fourteen Points, making its appearance three days later (Keylor 1998: 475). Moreover, it could never be more than a general guide, rather than a set of specific prescriptions. Consequently, few other principles were to reveal such a gap between its apparent universalism—even if Wilson did not consider it in this way—and its limited delivery on the ground.

Its inherent problem was that, once enunciated, it sounded like an absolute principle. In practice, it was difficult to implement consistently, because it threatened other priorities. Wilson's secretary of state Lansing was highly suspicious of the principle. 'It is an evil thing', he declaimed, 'to permit the principle of "self-determination" to continue to have the apparent sanction of the nations when it has been in fact thoroughly discredited' (Lansing 1921: 104). This was on the grounds that it was either intractable in itself, or prone to be pushed aside by more powerful considerations. Wilson, it is said, gave up on the principle 'whenever competing principles or interests claimed a higher priority' (Keylor 1998: 493). It was also soon abundantly clear that self-determination for some would create national minorities of others, and there was no intent on Wilson's part to pursue self-determination to any kind of logical conclusion. Instead, the resulting problem of minorities had to be dealt with as a matter of civil rights (Preece 1998: 71). Nor yet was it any part of Wilson's programme to apply the principle outside of the new states in south-east Europe: this was no doctrine for dismantling the great European empires that bestrode the remainder of the globe.

All such criticisms can readily be made. Self-determination, for all that, was regularly appealed to as a legitimating principle to thwart the spoils of war. Italy is a good example, with reference to its log of territorial demands against the former Austro-Hungarian empire. These were advanced on a number of distinct grounds: the sanctity of treaties, and what had been promised by the Allies in the London Treaty; Italy's needs for rational borders, on both economic and security grounds; access to seaports to service the hinterland; and the future stability of the Italian government, claimed to depend on satisfaction of these demands. Such pressures came starkly up against a rival set of values: the Wilsonian insistence on the new, as opposed to the old, diplomacy and the discredit into which secret treaties like London had fallen; the principle of self-determination which Italian expansion would violate on ethnic and linguistic grounds; and above all the notion that for self-determination to have any 'normative pull', it would have to be applied consistently as between victors and vanquished. It could have no moral force if departures from it were seen to be motivated simply by the wish to punish the defeated states or to reward the victors (Osiander 1994: 289).

This then encapsulated the titanic clash between rival sets of normative principles, with immense consequences for the future. In Wilson's mind, the issue was very clear, as he explained when applying pressure on Italy to abandon its claim to the port of Fiume. The Armistice with Germany had already expressed the basic principles of the peace, and on these the settlement with Germany was in process of formulation. There could not then be a peace with Austria that was founded on a different set of principles. In short, there must be consistency not only within a specific treaty, but across the treaty system as a whole. 'We cannot ask the great bulk of powers to propose and effect peace with Austria', Wilson declared in a public statement of 23 April 1919, '...on principles of another kind' (Baker 1923: vol. 3, 287–8). This reflected the advice already tendered to him by a number of US experts, concerned as they were about the glaring contradiction that would emerge if the League were to be seen as 'a coalition to maintain an unjust settlement'.

This would undermine the integrity of the new world order, and saddle the League 'with the acceptance of the doctrines of Talleyrand and Metternich' (Baker 1923: vol. 3, 279). The appeal to Italy issued by Britain's erstwhile Prime Minister and current Foreign Secretary, A. J. Balfour, was an even more subtle blend. Fiume, to be sure, was not a part of the London Treaty, but for him that was not the central issue in any case:

It is for Italy, and not for the other signatories of the Pact of London, to say whether she will gain more in power, wealth and honour by strictly adhering to that part of the Pact of London which is in her favour, than by accepting modifications in it which would bring it into closer harmony with the principles which are governing the territorial decisions of the Allies in other parts of Europe. (Memorandum, 24 April 1919; Baker 1923: vol. 3, 285)

This appeal went beyond the matter of legality, and rested both on the consistency of the treaty framework as a whole, and the benefits that would accrue to all, including Italy, from a consensual stance upon their application. What Italy was being asked to do was to conform to the code contained in the Armistice document, as this was also the basis of expectation amongst the defeated. The invitation to Italy was to bring its future borders within the bounds of this consensus. It was in such a political condition that legitimacy would be found, not in adherence to legal niceties alone.

What all this amply revealed was that legitimacy required more than the application of any one principle in isolation. Legitimacy resided not in rigid adherence, say, to the idea of national self-determination, let alone to the terms of the war's secret treaties. It was ultimately derivative from the wider goals of international society, and was to be discovered in a broad reconciliation with them. Self-determination could be advanced to curb territorial demands that would generate future instability. In turn, it was itself to be tempered by notions of order and stability, understood as the avoidance of disruptive conflicts between states. This had much to do with the other unspoken values of international society. Legitimacy principles underwrote a conception of international order, and this of necessity set the bounds to the implementation of self-determination (Preece 1998: 89, 94). Wilson had expressed this candidly in a speech to Congress, long before the war had come to an end. He committed himself to the satisfaction of all 'well defined' national aspirations, but with the important qualification that this should be done 'without introducing new or perpetuating old elements of discord and antagonism that would be likely in time to break the peace of Europe and consequently the world' (Keylor 1998: 475). National self-determination could be regarded as a legitimating principle within international society only in so far as it was not itself disruptive of the order on which that international society rested. Both the principle and its qualification have resounded in international society ever since.

The corollary of self-determination was to be protection for minority rights. This was intended to address 'the shortcomings of national self-determination', paradoxically at the very same moment as the Paris peacemakers 'first hailed it as the new principle of legitimacy in international society' (Preece 1998: 94). In the same spirit, Wight had acknowledged the minorities' treaties to be the inevitable adjunct of national self-determination and, as such, 'a notable attempt to refine the new principle of legitimacy and to control its operation' (Wight 1972: 14). This refinement built on existing practice, but extended it beyond religious protection to include some measures of linguistic and cultural protection as well (Preece 1998: 72). What was critical about these instruments was, however, the fact that they represented a form of 'conditional recognition' for the new states of south-east Europe. The condition resided in the clear imposition on these states of 'certain principles of government' which, in turn, derived from 'fundamental principles to which all civilized states conformed' (Temperley 1924: vol. V, 116). As a principle of legitimacy, this insistence upon protection of minorities also had the effect of aggravating the issue of the relative status of the big and small powers, and presented itself as one of double standards. A draft clause in the Covenant of the League had required all members to sign up to religious toleration, but this had been rejected. Accordingly, it has been suggested, 'the question could be asked why an obligation which the Great Powers refused to undertake themselves should be imposed upon others' (Temperley 1924: vol. V, 129). In the same way, it was objected that civilized behaviour did not, apparently, extend to acceptance of racial equality, since efforts to include a statement to this effect were also defeated (A. Williams 1998: 262). Wilson himself played a decisive role in this regard, and for purely tactical political reasons. 'Wilson knew that any reference to racial equality would alienate key politicians on the west coast', is one comment, 'and he needed their votes to get the League through Congress' (Macmillan 2001: 329).

The practice of legitimacy looked for accommodation between often competing norms, of which self-determination was amongst the most prominent. If this search was often wayward, it nonetheless managed to establish a new priority for scrutiny of the organizational principles within the member states. States, in future, would be socialized into acceptance of this order by the power of international society to bestow, or withhold, membership.

An Immoderate Peace? The Treatment of Germany

To Wilson, justice dictated moderation in the treatment of Germany. 'We must not give our enemies even an impression of injustice', Wilson exhorted in March 1919, and this meant 'moderation and equity' (Mantoux 1964: 24). But if this was an appeal to natural justice, it was phrased also in the pragmatic language of consequentialism: to behave otherwise was to sow the seeds of future conflict. In his demands for a moderate peace, Wilson thus fluctuated between the argument that this was to be done because it was just, and the somewhat different argument that it was desirable to avoid future disruption to the international system, and future entanglements for the United States. 'Des stipulations excessives', he warned on 27 March 1919, 'jetteraient un germe certain de guerre' (Mantoux 1955: vol. 1, 41). The problem, as it became clear, was that German perceptions of what was acceptable, and the perceptions of the various victor powers, were not necessarily the same. Clemenceau was fully alert to this potential disparity. 'Il ne faut pas—dit le Président Wilson—donner aux Allemands le sentiment d'une injustice'. Clemenceau did not dissent from such a course. His concern was rather, as he put it in March 1919, that 'ce que nous trouverons juste ici, dans cette chambre, ne sera pas nécessairement accepté comme tel par les Allemands' (Mantoux 1955: vol. 1, 43). In short, there was a problem with Wilson's attempted application of justice, as if it were some objective standard. Legitimacy—on which the reception of the settlement would depend—was, instead, a matter of political perception.

The issue came to be encapsulated in the German resentment against the so-called 'war-guilt clause'. Lloyd George bluffly dismissed all such complaints, and sought to mollify his readers by reminding them that, at the time of the signing, the prevailing temper regarded the peace as too lenient, not too harsh (George 1938: vol. 1, 92–3). And yet the assignment of guilt rankled both at the time, and since, as it appeared to violate a cardinal principle once set out in the writings of Grotius. He had reminded his seventeenth-century readers that 'it is not customary for the parties to arrive at peace by a confession of wrong', and he thought it wise that 'in treaties that interpretation should be assumed which puts the parties as far as possible on an equality with regard to the justice of the war' (Grotius 1918: 809). The notion of the peace as a *Diktat* grew also from the perception, current at the time, that the Allies were in a position to make unconditional demands of Germany. US analysts had concluded, as early as the beginning of 1918, that they had the 'power to compel Germany's assent at the peace conference' (Baker 1923: vol. 3, 40). The problem for the legitimation of any order that was compelled was twofold. If one danger was that Germany would not be reconciled to it, the other was that it might also prove too harsh to opinion elsewhere, especially in Britain. 'What chance did it stand of durability', Lentin reflects rhetorically, 'if the victors themselves could not stomach it?' (Lentin 1985: 134–5).

What is so striking about Versailles is the tension between two operative frameworks of legitimacy: restrictive membership and inclusive consensus. If it is, in Kissingerian terms, the sine qua non of a legitimate order that a former great power, defeated in war, be speedily reintegrated into international society, then the stated reason for this not happening in Germany's case was to be that country's failure to meet the prevalent test for rightful membership. The principles of legitimacy were clear enough. What was lacking at Versailles was any available strategy of legitimation that could reconcile matters when those two principles found themselves pressing in opposite directions. In the remainder of this section, the treatment of Germany can be considered as a package of interconnected issues: its incorporation into international society; the consistency between the Armistice principles and the final form of the peace; and the substantive content of the peace itself. In each of these areas, we can see a demonstrable linkage between international treatment and the conditions for full membership.

We can take the matter of possible membership of the League as symbolic of Germany's wider standing within international society, although obviously the two are not identical. Germany existed as a legal entity, and there was no question about its recognition as such in international law. That, however, was not incompatible with the bestowal of 'second-class' citizenship, as far as enjoyment of the full benefits of international society was concerned. There was certainly a widespread feeling in 1919 that, *ceteris paribus*, German membership of the League was to be preferred to its exclusion. This derived in part from the very logic of collective security which functioned best on the assumption of threats from *within*, to be resisted by the whole community, as opposed to threats from *without*, which merely invited reinvention of alliances and other forms of balancing behaviour. The matter, of course, went beyond this formal logic alone. Put bluntly, Lloyd George's argument was that it was better 'to see the Germans in the League of Nations rather than outside', because that way 'we would have greater control over them' (Mantoux 1964: 2). But other things were not equal, and Clemenceau in particular was adamantly opposed to German membership. The German delegation protested, if not to the fact of their exclusion, then at least to the lack of specificity about the conditions to be met for their eventual inclusion (Baker 1923: vol. 3, 506; Mantoux 1955: vol. 2, 21). The response to this was fairly categorical. The draft Covenant was explicit that the League was open to 'toutes les nations qui se gouvernent vraiment elles-mêmes selon un régime démocratique' (Mantoux 1955: vol. 2, 21). Hence, and logically enough, as soon as Germany took on democratic constitutional form under Weimar, its representatives could then make the case for its immediate admission (Schwabe 1998: 42–3).

A second issue was the conformity of the final peace to the agreed governing principles as set out in the Armistice. By October 1918, the United States offered Germany the best prospects for a reasonable peace settlement, and that was why the *démarche* had been made in the German note of 4 October (Marston 1944: 13). The Fourteen Points were understood to indicate the nature of the peace to be expected. From the US point of view, the statement of these Points had been directed every bit as much to the other Allies as to Germany. 'The whole purpose of the American insistence on the Fourteen Points', it is recalled, 'was to tie the hands of the European Allies in the final peace negotiations and force them to accept a moderate peace' (Goemans 2000: 307–8). More specifically, the Fourteen Points were regarded by the Americans as a device for securing the abrogation of the various commitments entered into by the wartime treaties—all of which manifestly violated Wilsonian tenets for a properly conducted settlement (Temperley 1920: vol. I, 274). Above all, what the Fourteen Points had mandated was a peace 'without victors and van-

quished' (Lentin 1985: 3). There were, however, to be two obstacles to the
realization of such an outcome. First, by their very nature, the Fourteen Points
were statements of general, and somewhat vague, principle (Temperley 1920:
vol. I, 275). They allowed substantial latitude for manoeuvre. Second, not all
the Allies felt equally bound by these undertakings, as Wilson's close adviser,
Colonel House, was later to recall: 'the week following House's arrival in Paris
was marked by a steady effort on their part to evade any recognition of the
Fourteen Points as the basis for the peace' (House 1926: 164).

Nevertheless, German negotiators entered into armistice discussions in the
firm belief that the Fourteen Points constituted the legal basis of the future
peace (Mommsen 1998: 536). This appeared to be specifically confirmed in the
Lansing note of 5 November 1918 (Schwabe 1998: 41–2). It was to this
interpretation that House felt so deeply committed. He maintained that the
pre-Armistice agreement 'set forth in general principle the conditions with
which the ultimate peace must comply' and, above all, this gave Germany the
'right to a peace settlement based upon the Fourteen Points' (House 1926: 156,
152). The exchange of Armistice notes of 11 November included House's
specific intent that the German delegates would take part in the peace conference (Bobbitt 2002: 573–4). There had, in the meantime, been issued some
reservations about the meaning of the Fourteen Points on the part of the Allies,
and these had been set down in a memorandum of reservation of 4 November
(Marston 1944: 31). Intriguingly, House had not seen fit to communicate the
content of this explanatory note to the German negotiators, despite the important gloss that it placed upon the Fourteen Points as the basis of the peace
(Marston 1944: 25–6). General Smuts was later to write to Wilson on 30 May
1919, pointing out that the Allies could not afford to follow the German
example in its treatment of 'scraps of paper', and they would be held account-
able if they did. Accordingly, he enjoined Wilson that 'we are bound to make a
peace within the four corners of your Points and Principles' (Baker 1923: vol. 3,
466). But expectations and developments on the ground had, in the meantime,
moved in remorselessly opposed directions. The Armistice had fostered a set of
illusions whereby 'the Germans awaited a treaty of equals while in Paris the
Allies wrote a peace of victors' (Marks 2002: 83).

It is on these grounds that the case for a *Diktat* is generally mounted (Holsti
1991: 199). Lansing bitterly regretted the course that was followed at the time,
and contributed further to the critical mood that surrounded it. Because of the
procedure adopted—and in particular the absence of any negotiation with the
German delegation—he was to conclude in his memoir that 'it was evident that
it was to be a "dictated peace" and not a "negotiated peace"' (Lansing 1921:
238). Versailles has thus been credited with the unusual distinction of being 'the
first European multilateral war settlement that was not negotiated between all
the belligerents' (Holsti 1991: 199). So controversial had the settlement become *amongst* the Allies, that they feared a German contribution might destroy
it altogether. In short, to retain the minimal consensus amongst the victors

alone, any pretence at reaching a consensus to include the vanquished had to be sacrificed (Osiander 1994: 282).

The issue of how immoderate the peace was arose finally in the context of its substance. There can be no objective or absolute measure of this. It was the psychological expectations of the participants that were important, and these were fed directly by the procedural dimensions just discussed. The Fourteen Points had explicitly encouraged the expectation of a moderate peace between equals. It was against this standard alone that the final content could find any realistic measure. The notion that Versailles was finally to emerge as a 'harsh' peace has many elements to it. Three aspects are thought to have led to the greatest degree of German disaffection. First, there was the objection to the non-application of the principle of self-determination to Germans, both in the transfer of German nationals to new states, and in the preclusion of any unification between Germany and Austria. Second, there was Article 231 on 'war guilt'. There are many ironies about the drafting history of this clause. As is now widely accepted, the intention of the American drafters was to use the acceptance of moral guilt as a device for moderating the economic demands imposed through reparations. Paradoxically, however, since Germans were not reconciled to the implications of the clause, it evoked a more general objection to reparations, and to the imagined inequity of the peace as a whole (Keylor 1998: 501). The third critical issue was, of course, that of reparations itself. This is not the place to rehearse that debate. The relevant point for the present discussion is simply the extent to which the substantive issue of reparations caused disharmony on account of its perceived breach of existing undertakings. Wilson had been quite clear in his objective that, financially, this was not to be a punitive peace. No sooner, however, did the various delegations begin to arrive in Paris than rifts developed between the Americans, on the one hand, and Lloyd George and the Empire representatives (especially Billy Hughes of Australia), on the other. The Americans firmly believed that 'war costs and indemnity' had already been ruled out by the Lansing note on which the Armistice had been negotiated (Lentin 1985: 36). Others now mounted a campaign to find ways to rule them back in, lest any assessment solely in terms of direct war damage would confine reparations to France and Belgium. Evidently, the sense that a reopening of the scope of reparations was inequitable was not a German perception alone. British delegates reported about the conference in January that 'Wilson becomes quite furious when anyone mentions the word "indemnity" to him and says he will hear of nothing of the kind' (Headlam-Morley 1972: 6). He was in fact to hear much more of this kind.

The Format of the Negotiations

We have already considered some procedural aspects of the treatment of Germany. Procedural issues emerged more generally about whether or not this settlement—as had others in the past—was to have a two-stage format.

There was also the equally sensitive question of the scope of representation within the core decision-making structures of the conference. This touched on relations amongst the victor powers, as well as upon the relationship between the great and the small. In all these areas, important arguments were to arise about what was to count as an appropriate consensus, sufficiently broad to give the settlement some basis in legitimacy. Equally, in all those areas, there was to be a manifest disparity between the stated principles upon which the proced-ures were to be based and those actually put into practice. The conference generated its own organizational momentum as the recalcitrant practicalities of the peacemaking began to take over from declared values (Elcock 1972).

We can begin with the 'phases' of the settlement. This is a vexed issue in the literature which continues to paint a confusing picture. It is certainly the case that there had been past precedents for a sequence of separate stages. First, terms would be reached between the belligerents themselves (including the losing party). Subsequently, a more general congress would be held to ratify the settlement, and to decide on issues of concern to this wider constituency of states. Such was broadly the sequence previously pursued at the end of the Napoleonic War, allowing for the slight untidiness caused by the hundred days, and the resulting need for a second Paris Treaty. In the original scheme, the Paris Treaty negotiated the terms for France, and the Congress of Vienna then elaborated the more general constitutional order to be implemented. This was also, if less formally, the scheme enacted at Utrecht. The model typifying European nineteenth-century statecraft was that 'a peace negotiated directly between the participants in a war ultimately had to obtain the approval of the European community of states', and adherence to this procedure was considered vital 'for establishing legitimacy to a peace settlement' (Holsti 1991: 197–8).

Both at the time, and since, Versailles had been discussed as possibly entailing two distinct stages, but there is marked confusion as to what these stages were to be, and some presentations of them do not conform to Holsti's model (e.g. Marks 2002: 84). The nomenclature that pervades the histories of the confer-ence distinguishes between a preliminary and a final treaty. It also makes explicit reference to an Inter-Allied Conference. So what precisely was the intention of the peacemakers in this regard, and how did the actual practice unfold?

In much of the discussion at the time, the first phase was not at all to be as described above. This becomes apparent in Wilson's seeming rejection of an Inter-Allied Conference as the first stage, instead of holding a meeting between all belligerents. According to the British Prime Minister, Wilson was 'entirely opposed' to an Inter-Allied Conference, since he feared the 'general Peace Conference would be a sham if definite conclusions were simply arrived at beforehand, and these presented to Germany' (Hankey 1963: 17). Interestingly, both French and American participants were later to regret the loss of time between the armistice and the convening in Paris, and rued that a 'preliminary' peace had not immediately been struck in the interim (Tardieu 1921: 104; House 1926: 211–12). But given their respective positions, they were obviously not lamenting the failure to reach the same *kind* of preliminary peace. Was German participation to be allowed at this stage? This is not what the French had in mind. The historian of the conference procedures draws attention to the 'confusion' that reigned in this respect. Initially, during November 1918, it remained unclear as to whether there might be a conference whose task was to reach a 'preliminary' peace with Germany, which would then be ratified by a universal Congress. After the London meetings, there was evidently a change of course. Thereafter, in December, 'all preparation was for a "conference" of Allied and Associated Powers only' (Marston 1944: 28). The idea of a preliminary meeting involving Germany—which Wilson had championed against a restrictive Inter-Allied Conference—had disappeared from the agenda. If there was now to be a preliminary meeting, it was after all for the victors alone. In the event, this preliminary meeting turned out also to be the final one.

This resulted because the meeting of the Allies became so difficult and protracted (Marston 1944: 40–1). In part also, the idea of a two-stage treaty process came to be viewed as increasingly unattractive to the United States, given its complex ratification procedures and Wilson's worries about the Senate: two treaties, one preliminary and one final, would possibly entail running that gauntlet twice (Temperley 1920: vol. I, 261). There was also the matter of the priority that Wilson attached to the Covenant, as we shall see shortly, and this further complicated the issue, as he was reluctant to address the peace with Germany outside the framework of the League. What finally eventuated did so as much by contingency and political calculation as out of any consistent purpose. The preliminary agreement was 'so precarious', Bobbitt points out, that the Germans were excluded from it. Instead, this then 'metamorphosed into a final settlement driven by Allied fear that their domestic publics had lost patience' (Bobbitt 2002: 574).

The other significant aspect of conference procedure was the composition of its key organizational structures. As with the phases of the treaty, decisions about organizational structures also succumbed to a process of political evolution. Indeed, after the commencement of the conference, participants reported on a general sense of drift and lack of direction (Headlam-Morley 1972: 4). In this, as in so much else, the acceptability of what was to be done could not but be influenced by the expectations that the Allies had themselves engendered. They were to be judged, not by absolute standards, but by those they had firmly decreed themselves.

It is true that at the moment the conference first convened in January, very little had been already settled (Marston 1944: 53). There were, however, three strong indicators of likely directions. One was the Preliminary French plan of procedure for the conference, circulated in November 1918. This envisaged that Wilson's arrival in Paris would 'enable the four Great Powers to agree among themselves upon the conditions of the peace' which, as it stated unreservedly, could then be 'imposed severally on the enemy without discussion with him' (Baker 1923: vol. 3, 56). Initially, as we have seen, Wilson had distinct qualms about such a blunt instrument. The second was the Tardieu Plan which distinguished between those powers with 'general' interests (that would attend all sessions) and those with 'specific' interests (to attend by invitation only) (Tardieu 1921: 98; Marston 1944: 57). The third indicator was the procedure already adopted with regard to the Armistice. Key decisions about its content were taken, not by the complete War Council, but by a more informal coterie within it (House 1926: 98). It was during the negotiation of the Armistice that 'the existence of an inner cabinet became a definite feature of the organization' (Marston 1944: 14–15). The precedent was important, given the interesting continuity of personnel. Hankey, who served as secretary to the British War Cabinet, and also to the Supreme War Council, went on to become also the secretary of the inner cabinet that emerged at Versailles (Marston 1944: 1).

Subsequent events, in that light, possessed an air of inevitability. For the first two months, great-power direction of the conference was conducted through the medium of the Council of Ten (Marston 1944: 96). Thereafter, as from 24 March 1919, it relapsed into the confines of the Council of Four (Hankey 1963: 96, 103). If this was intended to speed up the sluggish pace of progress, then early reports were sceptical (Headlam-Morley 1972: 57).

To say that this concentration into a small circle of decision-making resulted from evolution is not to imply that it could have turned out otherwise. There was a powerful logic behind this from the outset. Clemenceau had made clear that the winning alliance would carry its work across from the war into the peace, with no 'separation in the peace of the four powers which have battled side by side' (Lansing 1921: 77). President Wilson, for all his commitment to a just peace, justly arrived at, did not disagree. There were certain basic rules of politics that could not be breached even in the pursuit of the loftiest ideals, and these demanded that the great victor powers have the final say on the key decisions, as he confirmed in a speech on 31 May 1919:

And back of that lies this fundamentally important fact that when the decisions are made, the allied and associated powers guarantee to maintain them. It is perfectly evident, upon a moment's reflection, that the chief burden of their maintenance will fall upon the greater powers. The chief burden of the war fell upon the greater powers, and if it had not been for their action, their military action, we would not be here to settle these questions. And, therefore, we must not close our eyes to the fact that in the last analysis the military and naval strength of the great powers will be the final guarantee of the peace of the world. (Temperley 1924: vol. V, 130)

The great powers had earned their right to broker the settlement both by their role in the war, and also by the responsibility that they now bore for the maintenance of the peace.

The Absence of Consensus

It was not only upon such procedural matters that the Versailles consensus remained precarious. This went to the heart also of many substantive issues, and above all to the very composition of a just peace. The attainment of consensus thus required the striking of compromises over fundamentals, not over mere incidentals. Without doubt, this did much to damage the integrity and consistency of the enterprise as a whole.

This is best demonstrated in their differing conceptions of a just order, in the differing priorities which resulted from them, and in their basically irreconcilable accounts of the purposes of the League. All could consent to the generality of a just peace, but this meant different things to the participants. As Clemenceau once pointedly remarked, he shared with Lloyd George the goal of a 'durable and consequently just peace', but dissented from his conclusion that this entailed 'moderate territorial conditions', in order to avoid 'a profound feeling of resentment after the peace' (Baker 1923: vol. 3, 249–50). His complaint was that Lloyd George had already achieved all his global goals for Britain, and his demand for justice boiled down to making concessions at others' expense, especially over French security.

This incompatibility was underscored by the contrasting French and American attitudes to the chronological sequence that was to prevail as between the peace proper with Germany and the construction of the wider international order. The preliminary French plan of procedure of November 1918 had set out its priorities unambiguously, envisaging the work of the conference in two phases: 'the settlement of the war' and the 'organization of the Society of Nations'. 'The examination of the second question', it bluntly recommended, 'no doubt calls for the settlement of the first' (Baker 1923: vol. 3, 59; Marston 1944: 53). Wilson would have none of this. The early discussions of this issue between Wilson and Clemenceau 'indicated how far apart were their ideas'. Wilson's resolve by early December was to make the League 'the centre of the whole programme', and to let 'everything revolve around that' (House 1926: 263). If for the French the construction of a new international order could await the resolution of the German problem, and the satisfaction of French security, for Wilson this separation did not exist: it was the new international order that would resolve everything else. The League would 'lock European states into a new type of order', and was in that sense 'the key to the entire settlement' (Ikenberry 2001: 139).

This gap spilled over into the rival conceptions of the League. Wilson was sufficiently realistic to appreciate that the community of the League would take time to develop and grow: it could not be legislated into being (Ikenberry 2001: 146). The French approached the matter in a less leisurely frame of mind: time was not on their side. Only if French security had been guaranteed already could the League be relied upon to play its subsidiary role of preserving those arrangements: it was no substitute for them. In pressing the French demand for a military frontier on the Rhine (which the United States and Britain were, in the event, to reject), Marshal Foch had commented that, in the fullness of time, 'the development of civilization' and the 'moral sense of nations' might curb wars of conquest. In the meantime, he protested, 'it is necessary that this society should receive, at once, a sufficiently secure basis and an especial strength that will ensure its development' (Baker 1923: vol. 3, 228).

In Kissingerian terms, if the Versailles order proved illegitimate, it was not because Germany was the only great power to be left dissatisfied. Bolshevik Russia was positively excluded from the peace. It was reported at the outset that Wilson 'had not shown any keenness on the idea that Russia should be represented at the Conference' (George 1938: 189). In this he was supported by the British delegation. The clearest reason why Russia should be cast aside came, as so often, from Clemenceau. He declared his intention to resist Russian representation 'with the greatest energy', on the grounds that Russia had 'betrayed the Allied cause'. Moreover, he was adamant, 'the peace which was to be settled did not concern her' (George 1938: 320). This is the point exactly. If it did not concern her, Russia could have no interest in its preservation, and to that extent it exercised no 'normative pull' over her future conduct. France was eventually to come to wish that the peace had concerned Russia more, but by then it was too late. What was even worse for the restricted consensus that became the peace was not just the non-incorporation of Germany and Russia, but its final abandonment by the United States as well.

CONCLUSION

In short, first things must come first, but evidently the principal great powers shared no common vision on that order of priority, either in importance or in time. This was the heavy burden that the peacemaking at Versailles had to carry upon its shoulders, and which set the limits to any possibilities for agreement. In the existing accounts, Versailles established an illegitimate order, either because it failed to incorporate Germany, or because there was an even wider lack of consensus amongst the great powers as a whole. Both are in a sense true, but only a part of the truth. They do not fully explain the nature of the problem. From another angle, it was the wider lack of consensus about the shape of a desirable international order that precluded Germany's integration into it. And from a yet deeper perspective still, views of the international order had been so profoundly shaken by the welter of revolutionary, and conflicting, ideas as to be unable to settle upon any one consistent version for the whole.

In these various ways, the tragedy of Versailles was its inability to translate principles of legitimacy into effective political legitimation. There was certainly no abrupt abandonment of the international societal project. If anything, the reverse was the case, namely that this project was pushed too far and too quickly. Taken in conjunction with the immense dislocations of the war, the consequence was that the required political accommodations between competing norms could not be found. If the practice of legitimacy is understood as 'a process of consensual empowerment', then it was international society as a whole that was debilitated by this failure, and for which it was eventually to pay a very high price indeed.

Versailles had gone to great lengths to integrate its concepts of rightful membership with its vision for rightful conduct. Even so, this was to be taken yet a stage further in the ideas that were in circulation at the close of the Second World War. In the final stage of this historical survey, we must consider the elements of legitimacy as they appeared to the peacemakers in 1944–5.

7

Legitimacy and the Dual
Settlement of 1945

The so-called settlement in the aftermath of the Second World War had a number of distinctive features. It is open to question whether any settlement was achieved at all, and if so, when. It also had more than one dimension, and hence the description of it here as a dual settlement. The two components were not—as in some earlier peace treaties—a set of arrangements agreed first amongst the belligerents, to be followed by a wider congress to deal with the new order more generally. Instead, the settlement after 1945 was dual in that it included a putatively universalistic component that, in practice, was to become confined initially to the West alone. In addition, it included a separate component, not amongst the former enemies, but amongst the former Allies. As Ikenberry (2001) has so convincingly suggested, its duality lay in its being simultaneously a 'bipolar', as well as a 'western', settlement.

More assiduously and self-consciously than any other preceding peace, this sought to calibrate the requirements of international order with the domestic political and socio-economic arrangements deemed necessary to support it. It extended the formal logic that had already been articulated in 1919. Woodrow Wilson had urged that the two faces of legitimacy were intimately connected. For there to be rightful conduct amongst the members of international society, there needed to be active adoption of a rightful membership criterion insisting upon democratic statehood: only genuinely democratic states could operate the newly institutionalized system that the League was to introduce. In short, within a system that defined the problems of security in classical military-political terms—the balance of power and how to manage it collectively—there was a need for states of a certain kind.

The post-1945 period certainly reaffirmed this logic. 'If the end of global peace needs the "means" of global democracy', Franck has elaborated, 'a Charter-based system established to ensure peace must also be presumed to have the authority to take measures necessary to promote universal adherence to democratic political rights' (Franck 1995: 137). Additionally, however, what the 1945 settlement so momentously did was to redefine the nature of the problem of international security. It did so in two directions. It expanded the agenda by incorporating within it an explicit human rights dimension. Moreover, it redefined international security to include the socio-economic agenda—and in particular management of the international economy—to take account of the disastrous security consequences of the failures in this regard during the 1930s. This theme had come to prominence as early as August 1941 in the Atlantic Charter which declared a commitment to furtherance 'of access, on equal terms, to the trade and to the raw materials of the world', as well as to 'the fullest collaboration between all nations in the economic field with the object of securing, for all, improved labor standards, economic advancement and social security' (Grenville 1974: 198).

Accordingly, those interrelated dimensions of legitimacy—as formerly expressed by Wilson—came into play once more, but with a different nuance. Since rightful international conduct was now to embrace an economic aspect—not collective security narrowly conceived—then there was a cognate requirement for a new concept of rightful membership to underpin this system. International society was thus being pressed to develop a more complex analysis of the conditions of its own sociability, and as a result explicitly to foster new qualities amongst its membership. It was to be the function of international legitimacy to render acceptable both the international and domestic bargains on which this was to be predicated, and hence the 'embedded liberalism' solution becomes a key focus of this enquiry. States had to pass this particular test to be fully acceptable to international society.

THE SETTLEMENT AND ITS CONTEXT

It is not possible to engage with legitimacy in the 1945 settlement without first tackling some inherently problematic aspects of that peace. Was there indeed such a settlement, and when was it put in place? Did the 1945 settlement successfully institute an agreed set of principles for international relations, or did it merely express a set of preferred principles that it then demonstrably failed to put into practice? Was it a universalistic peace, as so much of its rhetoric conveyed, or a particularistic one at best? Did the peace find acceptance as a legitimate order, and how might any such notion be reconciled with the immediate onset of the cold war? These are the issues that bedevil any straightforward assessment of the place of legitimacy in the forging of the peace at the end of the Second World War.

In terms of the strict formalities, we can say this much without too much contention. Peace settlements with a number of states (Italy, Romania, Hungary, Bulgaria, and Finland) were duly signed in 1947. A peace between the Western powers (but not the Soviet Union) and Japan was completed in 1951, and a 'State Treaty' with Austria in 1955 (Grenville 1974: 265–9). As to Germany, the Potsdam Conference had established the Council of Foreign Ministers with a remit of 'preparation of a peace settlement for Germany to be accepted by the Government of Germany when a Government adequate for the purpose is established' (Grenville 1974: 231). Thereafter, there is little agreement on whether, or when, a settlement with Germany was finally reached.

This requires some brief incursions into the troubled history of cold war origins. What certainly sets the peacemaking in the Second World War apart from that of 1919 was its self-declared intent of making an early start. The sober recollection had been that, after the Great War, too much had been left unsettled until too late, then leaving too little time adequately to address them. This was not to happen a second time around. 'This time', President Roosevelt advised a Joint Session of Congress on 1 March 1945, reporting on the Yalta conference, 'we are not making the mistake of waiting until the end of the war to set up the machinery of peace' (Challener 1970: 128). Arguably, this process had begun as early as the Moscow meeting in 1943. On that occasion, British and US delegates were eager to discuss key aspects of post-war relations, only to discover that the Soviets were interested only in the timetable for opening of the second front, in order to accelerate the ending of the war (Kennedy-Pipe 1995: 35–6). Not for the last time were the pressures of ongoing war-making to get in the way of future peacemaking. Matters were taken further at the subsequent Teheran summit, at which Roosevelt elaborated his plans for the post-war settlement, and for the creation of a new world organization in particular. We are told that Stalin 'approved the scheme in general', although raising objections to the inclusion of China as one of the major powers (Kennedy-Pipe 1995: 41). By the time of the Yalta meeting in February 1945, Roosevelt reported to Congress that, while the participants had argued freely on many issues, 'at the end, on every point, unanimous agreement was reached' (Challener 1970: 126–7). On this account, there would appear at that stage to have been every prospect of a consensual agreement. What then went wrong? It might be said that Yalta succeeded only in so far as it fudged the issues—its provisions 'lacked precision and were vague' is a common verdict (Grenville 1974: 223)—and that this was in any case its primary intent. At that moment, the key players remained too preoccupied with successful conclusion of the war—and with keeping the Allies on side to achieve this—to want to face the full implications of peace. What was expressed at Yalta was no more than 'an outward show of unanimity' (Grenville 1974: 218). Why it unravelled is the very stuff of cold war historiography. Subsequently, one or more parties may have reneged on their commitments. Stalin was to cheat, or the transition from Roosevelt to Truman saw the introduction of a much tougher US stance. And so on.

The treatment of Germany raises once more the general point about 'inclusiveness' as an aspect of legitimacy in the conclusion of peace settlements. The case of 1945 fits but awkwardly into analyses of this kind. Generally, it has been thought that there is some correlation between a direct negotiation with the enemy, as part of the peace procedure, and the moderateness of its resulting terms. Thus, in the cases of Utrecht and Vienna, a deal was essentially struck with the former enemy (in both cases France), in direct negotiation, as a preliminary to the more general settlement. In both cases, a reasonable historical argument can also be made that the terms were moderate, and did not seek to alienate the defeated party in the longer term. Indeed, it is precisely on these grounds that the claims to the success of Vienna are explicitly made. The contrast, in turn, is then frequently drawn with the procedure adopted in 1919, when there was no preliminary negotiation with Germany, and Germany was not represented until the end, when it was offered the treaty on a 'take-it-or-leave-it' basis. Such a correlation encourages the thought of a causal connection. Is inclusion of the defeated party in the formalities of the peace negotiation itself a necessary precondition of a consensual peace, both in the sense of recognizing the continuing status of the defeated party, and of inducing restraint on what is demanded of it? Alternatively, there could be just as good reason for thinking that this argument confuses cause and effect. Otherwise formulated, it might be the existence of a sufficient degree of consensus amongst the victors on the need for moderate terms of peace that makes it possible, in turn, for the vanquished to be included in the negotiation in the first place. Thus understood, inclusion in the peace settlement is not the cause of moderation in terms, but merely symptomatic of an already existing predisposition towards such an outcome.

The case of 1945 demonstrates the complexity of this issue, as it otherwise generates a paradoxical result. As we know, the war aims of the Allies were expressed as a demand for 'unconditional surrender'. Explicitly, there would be no dialogue with the enemy on the terms of peace. It would appear on the face of it that the peace settlements with Germany and Japan were to be as 'exclusive' as any in history, and if anything more so than the 'failed' procedure of 1919. And yet, despite this unconditional surrender, and the absence of negotiation, 1945 was to issue for both Japan and (West) Germany in a remarkably moderate, and highly resuscitative, peace. This makes the point that it is not only the presence or absence of the defeated at the peace table that is the determinant of its final severity, but rather the intent and predispositions of the victors more broadly construed. Whether or not claims to legitimation can be successfully made depends critically upon these prevailing conditions, not simply upon the correspondence of actions to absolute norms.

HISTORICAL VERDICTS

There is a broad spectrum of historical opinion about the timing and the degree of success of the post–Second World War settlement, and it is useful to distinguish five sets of those at the outset. At the one end is the harshest judgement that there was to be no settlement at all in 1945, and in this fundamental sense it stood for a failed peace. Uniquely, it has been pointed out, 'this was the first major war in history that did not end with a single comprehensive peace settlement' (Ikenberry 2001: 162). There was little that was agreed about the post-war order, and what was could not then be implemented. Instead of reaching a settlement, the wartime Allies fell out catastrophically amongst themselves and the world slid precipitously from peacemaking into cold-war making in one continuous action. If legitimacy, in the Kissingerian sense, is a product of all the great powers being satisfied with the shape of the new order, then this scarcely fitted a situation wherein the Big Three rapidly descended into acrimonious dissension. To the extent that post-war developments threatened to turn a cold war into a hot one, this gave all the appearance of being the most 'revolutionary'—and unstable—of orders.

Second, one major contribution to the historical literature (Trachtenberg 1999) has contended that the post-war settlement was effectively put in place, not in 1945 at war's end, but much later. There seemed to be the fleeting prospect of a settlement based on spheres in 1945, but 'a settlement of this sort did not come into being, not until 1963 at any rate' (Trachtenberg 1999: 4). The peace terms were not to be agreed at any single conference—as had been the traditional practice—but rather were 'constructed' over the long period of the cold war. This corresponds with the implicit verdict that the post-1945 peace settlement was 'fragmented' and 'protracted' (Ikenberry 2001: 163, 263). From such a point of view, the cold war does not represent the refutation of the idea of a post-war settlement. Instead, it becomes the central mechanism whereby the actualities of the peace were to be put in place. In similar vein, others have pointed to the abandonment of the quest for 'a final peace treaty and comprehensive settlement', and its substitution by an 'interim settlement' in the shape of the treaties signed with the two Germanys in 1972 (Grenville 1974: 263).

Third, we have the view, widely proclaimed in 1990, that it was to be the end of the cold war that would bring the final settlement to the issues of the Second World War. 'A true peace settlement of the scars of World War II', we are told, 'was finally reached when the Berlin Wall was torn down in 1989' (Kegley and Raymond 1999: 196). The cold war had been, in that sense, not a settlement, merely an agreement to differ. It was only with the sweeping away of the entire structure of the cold war that the mess left behind by the war—what to do about Germany, and the artificial division of Europe as a whole—could finally be addressed. The cold war had not been the peace, but its evasion.

A fourth perspective—and the one adopted here—is that, far from failing to reach a settlement, the post-war period was to be twice blessed, and gave birth to two settlements, not just one. This is the core argument that runs through Ikenberry's (2001) important contribution to the debate. He maintains that there was indeed a bipolar settlement that sought to regulate the balance of power in East–West terms at the end of the war. There was also, and with a longer preceding history, the Western settlement that had been driven by the agenda of the 1930s, and the conditions thought to have led to the collapse of the internationalist project during that period.

Fifth, a number of historians, including John Gaddis (1998), were to suggest that 1945 falls within that broad category of successful peace settlements wherein the former enemy was to be fully reintegrated into the club of the victors. In turn, this is believed to have contributed a key element of stability to post-war international relations. From this point of view, 1945 stands side by side with 1815 as a model peace of this kind, and is in this regard to be sharply distinguished from the 'failure' of 1919.

So there we have it. Opinions range from the failure to reach any peace in 1945, to the grounds for its manifest success. Chronologically, the settlement is considered to have taken place in 1945, in 1963, in 1972, or not finally until 1989. As they stand, these interpretations bring quite different perspectives to bear on the matter of legitimacy. They might imply that the failure to generate an effective settlement in 1945 was itself symptomatic of the absence of an agreed framework of legitimacy at the time. If legitimacy is intimately connected with the existence, or production, of a degree of operative consensus, then 1945 represented a serious failure in this respect. Alternatively, we could say that the principles of legitimacy were broadly agreed, but as a matter of practical international politics not the geographical scope within which they were to be applied. In the context of Ikenberry's distinctive argument, the Western peace was suffused by a number of important legitimacy principles of its own, but these would not necessarily carry across into the bipolar settlement.

In the remainder of this chapter, we need to consider the application of legitimacy principles within the context of this dual settlement. This entails an exploration of the new elements of rightful membership, within the areas of human rights and what is often referred to as embedded liberalism. On the side of rightful conduct, the key areas for discussion are trends in then current thinking about consensus, and how it was to be attained. This had resonance within both the bipolar and the Western settlements: how instrumental was consensus in forging the cold-war division of Europe, and how was it to be applied in the new international order more generally. In virtually all of these areas, the interface between the domestic and the international became subject to much closer scrutiny, and pressure, than at any time hitherto.

RIGHTFUL MEMBERSHIP

Human Rights

Ideas about human rights had already been in wide circulation for at least the preceding two centuries: they were scarcely some invention at the end of the Second World War. Nonetheless, in the Declaration by the United Nations of 1 January 1942, the Allies expressed their conviction in the necessity for complete victory in order 'to defend life, liberty, independence and religious freedom, and to preserve human rights and justice in their own lands as well as in other lands' (Grenville 1974: 212). These preliminary ideals were to be further developed in immediate post-war practice. For example, the United States declared in its Initial Post-War Surrender Policy for Japan, that 'the Japanese people shall be encouraged to develop a desire for individual liberties and respect for fundamental human rights' (Dennett and Turner 1948: 267).

Evidently, international society had previously concerned itself with rights issues—on such matters as slavery, religious, and other minority rights protection, and within the ambit of bodies like the International Labour Organization set up after the First World War. What is interesting about 1945, in comparison, was the rapid retreat from international action within a framework of group rights or minority protection, and its replacement by a framework of universal human rights instead (Preece 1998). There may have been a pragmatic calculation in this of seeking to distance the new venture from the tarnished reputation of the inter-war machinery, but there were also more deep-seated motives at work reflecting the unprecedented civilian horrors of the recent war.

The war marked a milestone in this regard for two principal reasons. The first was the flagrant violation of human rights in the course of the war, and the felt need to codify their existence and content as part of a practical policy of avoiding future such infringements (Donnelly 1993, 1999). The invention of a new category of 'crimes against humanity' in the post-war military tribunals logically entailed the articulation of those rights of humanity against which the crimes had been committed. Second, there was also an obvious sense in which the issue of human rights took on a more pronounced international dimension after 1945. If the discussion of human rights had thus far proceeded within the relatively safe confines of the development of the liberal state, as the appropriate vessel for both defining and protecting them, the Second World War placed squarely on the agenda the issue of human rights 'beyond borders', in so far as the war provided a chilling demonstration of just how far human rights were at the mercy of the international system itself. For these reasons, as US Secretary of State Stettinius emphasized at the San Francisco meeting in May 1945, human rights provisions in the UN Charter 'are not mere general expressions in a preamble', but are actually 'woven through and through the document' (Goodrich and Carroll 1947: 432). Accordingly, the period of the 'human rights settlement' can be considered as that falling between 1945 and 1948 (the Universal Declaration), and its importance to lie in the first serious attempt to embed the notion of human rights within an international context. Human rights, in a much more demonstrative way than ever before, had now become the business of international society itself.

Another area in which the force of this new framework revealed itself was that of racial equality. At first glance, this might seem to press in the opposite direction of deriving rights from group status—in this case from racial groups. The logic, however, was precisely the reverse, and reveals the victory of the human rights framework once more. Attempts at formal international endorsement of a principle of racial equality failed in 1919, when the temper was not yet ready for declarations that might have unsettling implications for the dominant European empires, as well as for domestic US politics. By 1945, all that had sharply changed, and the UN Charter confirmed racial equality to be 'now part of the official doctrine of international society' (Vincent 1984*b*: 252). In part, the revolution was wrought by the 'abhorrence felt at the working-out of a noxious doctrine of racial superiority' in Europe (Vincent 1984*b*: 252). More generally, however, racial equality was logically entailed by a conception of human rights. If these rights are enjoyed by human beings as individuals, and equally so enjoyed, members of distinct races cannot possess them in varying degrees. Racial equality is firmly grounded in a concept of human rights, rather than in membership of a racial group, and was thus contingent upon that more fundamental reappraisal.

It is the explicit discussion of human rights in 1945, and their inclusion in the UN Charter, that has led many commentators to highlight the purported resulting tension within the Charter between its appeals to two contradictory legitimacy principles. The tension is claimed to exist between respect for human rights—in which the subjects are people—and the respect for sovereignty—within which the subjects are states. The highlighted tension is thus between, for example, the second paragraph of the Preamble (which reaffirms faith in fundamental human rights), and the provisions in Chapter 1, Article 2.1 (the principle of sovereign equality) and Article 2.7 (which excludes matters essentially within the domestic jurisdiction of a state). Many of the contradictions in the post-1945 discussion of international legitimacy are thus thought to derive from this basic inconsistency.

Embedded Liberalism

The second area in which new legitimacy principles were to be expressed related to the so-called 'embedded liberalism' compromise (Ruggie 1998), and this was to become a key feature of the Western settlement. If, in 1919, the concern had been to elaborate principles for conduct within a new system of collective security, then the experience of the 1930s had stressed the intimate connection between the international economy and international security. 'No machinery for combined action to prevent or suppress aggression will work for any length of time', Secretary Stettinius insisted in April 1945, 'in a world in which the causes of war—particularly the economic causes—are permitted to poison relations between countries' (Goodrich and Carroll 1947: 31). 'Economic stability and political security are, consequently', the Panamanian Government commented in the deliberations over the Dumbarton Oaks proposals for the new UN, 'different aspects of the same problem' (UNIO 1945: vol. III, 260). Accordingly, by the Bretton Woods conference in 1944, there had already developed a reasonable consensus around the need to institute a system of international economic collective security as well:

The postwar planners strove as much to eliminate the causes of economic crisis as international conflict... Wilsonian political leaders in World War I had made the connection between political democracy and a peaceful international order, but not between a democracy and an international economic order free of deflationary pressures. The political leadership of World War II understood the second connection as well and thus achieved a more robust settlement. (Maier 1996: 14)

Ruggie has done more than most to set this argument within a context of legitimacy. It is fundamental to his argument that the decisions taken at Bretton Woods, and the policies followed in the years thereafter, are significant not simply for their substantive content, but more so for the *legitimate social purpose* that infused them. 'In sum, to say anything sensible about the *content* of international economic orders and about the regimes that serve them', he stresses, 'it is necessary to look at how power and legitimate social purpose become fused to project political authority into the international system' (Ruggie 1998: 65). This is what makes his analysis so germane to the present discussion. The adjustments to the management of the international economy were not to be undertaken simply as policy enactments, but as expressions of new legitimacy principles. The core of the bargain or compromise is again best summarized by Ruggie (1998: 72–3):

The task of postwar institutional reconstruction was to maneuver between these two extremes and to devise a framework which would safeguard and even aid the quest for domestic stability without, at the same time, triggering the mutually destructive external consequences that had plagued the interwar period. This was the essence of the embedded liberalism compromise; unlike the economic nationalism of the thirties, it would be multilateral in character; unlike the liberalism of the gold standard and free trade, its multilateralism would be predicated upon domestic interventionism.

In short, the essence of the compromise lay in a balanced solution that would safeguard both the requirements of international economic stability (within a multilateral order), and also domestic social and economic stability (within a degree of governmental interventionism). It is the duality of this compromise that is so central to the present discussion. The idea of international legitimacy was thereby to be extended to embrace rightful international conduct within the economic sphere. A perfect illustration of this can be discovered in a public statement issued by the Federal Council of the Churches of Christ in America, as early as March 1943. Its Commission on a Just and Durable Peace reported on a set of political propositions deemed necessary for the ensuing peace. The second of these demanded that the peace 'make provision for bringing within the scope of international agreement those economic and financial acts of national governments which have widespread international repercussions' (Challener 1970: 121). This is as clear an expression as can be found of the intent to bring international economic conduct within the scope of consensus building, and in conformity with the broadened remit of international society's purpose. Rightful conduct would no longer be restricted to the political and security domain.

The other side of the coin was what this then prescribed for rightful membership. It has been said of the 'constitutional' order developed after 1945 that 'there was an explicit presumption among American and European officials that binding postwar institutions...would only operate effectively to provide restraints and assurances if the participating states were democratic' (Ikenberry 2001: 213). This reiterates the earlier Wilsonian logic, but does not go quite far enough to capture the altered context of 1945. Thinking had by then moved outside the narrow confines of collective security as depicted at the end of the First World War. Stable international order depended on more than a politico-security structure alone, and consequently required states also to be more than merely democratic: states needed to adapt to particular forms, incorporating degrees of social welfare, as a safety net for domestic stability. As international society reinvented its purpose, it sought also to reproduce the type of state that would best carry it out. Under embedded liberalism, the criteria of rightful membership had moved beyond those of 1919.

The same point can be directly reinforced with regard to the treatment of the former enemy states specifically. As we have seen, the issue of how to deal with the defeated enemy impacts upon the nature of international legitimacy in several respects. The idea of a speedy resurrection and reintegration of the enemy is often regarded as the sine qua non of the creation of a legitimate international order. By this measure, the treatment of the enemy is likely to determine the legitimacy of any particular settlement. However, the very notion of the *treatment* of the defeated states has two distinct aspects to it. The first concerns, as it were, the external impositions to be placed upon the state, by way of territorial, military, and financial exactions. This defines the regime of international tutelage to which the defeated party is now to be subjected, and normally as a guarantee of its future good behaviour. The second dimension is that of internal constitutional transformation. Appeals to these twin aspects of legitimacy can be made simultaneously, as they had overtly been in 1815. The demanding political task is, of course, to strike a balance in the application of the two instruments. Notoriously, a harsh international regime can have the effect of undermining measures taken to bring about desirable domestic changes, not least because it can damage the legitimacy of the new governmental apparatus in the eyes of its own citizens. In the best of all possible worlds, internal transformation might replace the need for international tutelage altogether. In the case of Japan, the prohibition on the maintenance of armed forces became a matter of the Japanese constitution of 1946, thereby removing the need for any military clauses of this kind in the final peace treaty of 1951 (Grenville 1974: 270). In the Draft Treaty of Disarmament and Demilitarization of Germany, submitted by the United States to the Council of Foreign Ministers on 29 April 1946, the same logic was on display. International controls were to operate upon Germany for twenty-five years in the first instance; they would then be reviewed to determine 'whether the German people have so far progressed in the reconstruction of their life on a democratic and peaceful basis that the continued imposition of the controls defined herein is no longer necessary' (Dennett and Turner 1948: 208).

As argued, the theme in embedded liberalism generally was to reach an equilibrium point between international and domestic instruments. As applied specifically to the defeated former enemy, this expressed itself in domestic measures that went well beyond the limited programme of democratization that had been encouraged in 1919, although this certainly continued to be present. In its statement of Initial Post-Surrender Policy for Japan on 29 August 1945, the United States outlined as a fundamental objective the emergence of a Japanese government that 'should conform as closely as may be to principles of democratic self-government' and, to this end, declared that the 'Japanese people shall be afforded opportunity and encouraged to become familiar with the history, institutions, culture, and the accomplishments of the United States and the other democracies' (Dennett and Turner 1948: 267). General MacArthur, in a further statement on Occupation Policy on 9 September 1945, also undertook to encourage 'liberal tendencies and processes' (Dennett and Turner 1948: 275). All of this, however, went beyond the narrowly civic or political domain. It would embrace the economic sphere as well, inasmuch as 'those forms of economic activity, organization and leadership shall be favored that are deemed likely to strengthen the peaceful disposition of the Japanese people' (Dennet and Turner 1948: 271).

At one level, these simply reiterated the standard point that domestic changes would be insisted upon in the peace treaty to fit the former enemy for readmission into international society. The statement issued at the end of the Yalta meeting on 11 February 1945 made this connection in explicit fashion: 'It is not our purpose to destroy the people of Germany, but only when Nazism and militarism have been extirpated, will there be hope for a decent life for Germans, and a place for them in the comity of nations' (Grenville 1974: 227). However, it was the nature and scale of this domestic transformation that was to have important implications for the domestic face of legitimacy in 1945. This also had significant, and possibly negative, impacts on the search amongst the victors for consensus about how to treat the former enemy. Thus, it has been said, 'the United States and Great Britain undertook steps to resuscitate their former enemies', a policy that caused 'dismay' in the Soviet Union 'which clung tenaciously to the Allies' prior agreement to exact revenge' (Kegley and Raymond 1999: 184).

RIGHTFUL CONDUCT

Consensus and the Division of Europe

Since the theme of consensus, and what is acceptable as a representation of one, has been central to this ongoing investigation, we need to begin by making some sense of this aspect of the situation in 1945. Any attempt to follow the dynamics of peacemaking in the final stages of the war, and its elements of consensus, risks being sucked into the maelstrom of the origins of the cold war. Exactly what did the major victor powers want to emerge from the post-war order, and how widely were their views shared? Did they agree on key international principles, but not about their area of operability? Can the cold war be understood as a process of 'consensual empowerment', or does it by definition stand for the failure to reach any such consensus? Was it a solution, or a non-solution? The key to resolving these conundrums lies presumably in some assessment of the decision-making dynamics that led to the spheres of influence upon which the cold-war settlement came effectively to rest. If these were the self-conscious outcomes of consensual agreements amongst the key powers, then that is one thing. However, if they were the unintended consequences of failures to reach accord on a preferred outcome, then that is quite another.

It has been argued that it was certainly the US intention to establish a consensual order after 1945, one which assumed 'a set of *common* interests that would cause other countries to *want* to be affiliated with it rather than to resist it' (Gaddis 1997: 38). Analogously, we have previously encountered the various elements at work in Kissinger's analysis of the post-1815 settlement. In one exegesis of his work, it is remarked that the ideas of a legitimate and stable order 'presuppose a balance of power, which induces self-restraint', while at the same time, 'legitimacy also requires the existence of a *principle* of legitimacy capable of justifying the adjustment of conflicting claims'. In this exposition, the author then goes on to point to the difficulty to which this leads, in that 'a reader of the book never quite finds out whether self-restraint results merely from the constraints of the balance, or also from the acceptance of a common principle' (Hoffmann 1978: 38). The comment is particularly apposite for an analysis of events after 1945, especially with regard to the so-called bipolar settlement. Was the imposed solution the result of the working of a common principle, or simply an effect of the balance of power?

What is critical is whether or not anything was agreed about the scope within which general principles were to be applied. This is germane both to the general issue of 'universalism' versus 'spheres' in Europe as a whole, and particularly so with regard to the future of Germany. There is now much reassessment of these issues in the light of the new (post-cold war) cold war history. Are we any closer to resolving these fundamental questions about what the principals wanted from the settlement, as opposed to what actually eventuated?

Roosevelt's 1 March 1945 address to Congress can be read as a quintessential statement of the universalistic aspirations embodied in US goals at the time:

The Crimean Conference was a successful effort by the three leading Nations to find a common ground for peace. It ought to spell the end of the system of unilateral action, the exclusive alliances, the spheres of influence, the balances of power, and all other expedients that have been tried for centuries—and have always failed.

We propose to substitute for all these, a universal organization in which all peace-loving Nations will finally have a chance to join. (Challener 1970: 133)

Is this to be understood to mean that the face of the US administration was finally and irreversibly set against the adoption of any 'spheres' solutions to the problems of the post-war order? A generation ago, such a view remained commonplace. It could be stated then, with some confidence, that in his last days as president, Roosevelt believed that 'Yalta was certainly still the symbol of the universalist concept, not that of the partition of Europe into spheres of influence' (Aron 1974: 18–19). It is less clear that this commitment survived the change of president, or for that matter that it would have survived the ending of the war, even under the same president. Recent scholarship reinforces this scepticism. According to Trachtenberg's magisterial study, a settlement based on mutual recognition of spheres was in the offing by late 1945, crafted by Truman's Secretary of State Byrnes. In this version, 'it might have seemed that a more or less permanent settlement was taking shape', and it was one predicated upon agreement that 'each side would have a free hand in the area it dominated' (Trachtenberg 1999: 4). If this were so, we are forced to conclude that the Truman presidency had abandoned the key principles advanced so recently by Roosevelt. But why then did not a settlement eventuate, such as was currently being planned? Trachtenberg's book continues to argue that such a division was deserted by the US administration itself, and the world had then to await 1963 before a settlement on that basis could finally be reached.

This interpretation, plausible enough in its own terms, becomes slightly more perplexing when set against recent work on the nature of Soviet objectives, especially with regard to Germany. The thrust of Trachtenberg's analysis is that the post-war peace had to be deferred because the United States turned cold on its provisional acceptance of spheres. If this meant a return to a policy of universalism, and especially one of treating Germany as a unity, it is then hard to see what the difficulty was because, as the recent historiography informs us, *this is precisely what Stalin himself desired*. The puzzle is why then a US abandonment of spheres should have resulted in a *disagreement* with the Soviet Union?

It remains premature to reach definitive conclusions about Soviet policy. Nonetheless, some major reassessments are now emerging. We have, for instance, much more detailed accounts of the nature of Soviet planning for the post-war peace, in the shape of the deliberations of the Litvinov, Voroshilov, and Maisky Commissions during 1944 (Filitov 1996: 4; Mastny 1996: 18). These provide patchy insights into Soviet thinking—not necessarily Stalin's—but are instructive nonetheless. There is a telling account of the Soviet concept of 'legitimate' treatment of the defeated enemy in the Maisky Commission's fundamental principle: 'To take from Germany and its allies everything that can be taken' (Filitov 1996: 6). Equally revealing is the Soviet order of priorities. The United States defined its strategic interests in terms of the construction of a suitable international order: national security was to be derived from an international and multilateral system. The contrast with Soviet thinking could not have been sharper. Soviet planners started from Soviet interests, narrowly construed, and moved gingerly outwards from that point. In a Maisky memorandum of 11 January 1944, the fundamental aim of the peace was stipulated as a 'guarantee for a long period of Soviet security', and the main condition for its attainment was defined as the emergence of the USSR 'from the war with favorable strategic frontiers' (Filitov 1996: 7).

Germany occupied central stage in Soviet designs, but recent thinking on this issue does not fit into orthodox models. If the United States became reluctant to follow through on the Byrnes policy of pragmatic recognition of spheres of domination, there was nothing inherent in this shift in Washington's policy to have upset Stalin. If anything, this seemed to accord with Soviet preferences. In a general sense, Stalin was not committed to expelling all US military presence from Germany, but rather welcomed this as a guarantee of Washington's resolve to ensure against German military resurgence (Kennedy-Pipe 1995: 3). In detail, there is substantial Soviet documentation to suggest their priority was to retain the unity of Germany, not its division (Raack 1995: 141; Mastny 1996: 24; Gaddis 1997: 116). Soviet diplomacy, we are told, 'proceeded on the basis of maintaining Germany as one state' (Filitov 1996: 19). Others agree that 'the unity of occupied Germany was a declared aim of Soviet policy', and attest that what was 'quite remarkable' was the 'stubbornness with which Stalin stuck to his vision of a unified Germany' (Loth 1996: 24, 28–9). That this was born of a desire to extend Soviet influence through socialism throughout the entire country, and a wish for access to economic resources in Germany's western half, rather than out of a general commitment to universalism as such, is not the point. In practice, such a reading of Soviet policy implies its potential reconcilability with US goals and values.

If the decision to 'divide' Europe could in some sense be seen as reflecting a basic agreement amongst the major powers, and in some degree thereby to have been sanctioned by international society, the 1945 settlement emerges in one particular light. If, instead, and against the agreed principles of the peace, a set of pragmatic 'non-solutions' was imposed, as it were, by *force majeure* and unilateral action, our judgement of the post-1945 settlement needs to vary accordingly. As we await the verdict on the nature of this bipolar settlement, the evidential jury remains obdurately out. On such evidence as there is, the argument that the division of Europe into spheres was consensually reached at the time does not appear very convincing.

Consensus and Universal Organization

Given the sorry history of the League of Nations, it was all the more remark-able that a policy of collective security was even essayed a second time around. It was no less so for the formal separation that was to take place between the

UN Charter and the completion of the peace settlement properly understood, in order to avoid repetition of what was seen to be the tactical mistake made in 1919. This putative separation was to be demonstrated in two distinct ways. Firstly, and most obviously, the UN Charter was not to be incorporated into the peace treaties, after the fashion of 1919. Secondly, the UN was to be given the task of maintaining the peace, once it had been settled, but was not itself to be the instrument for reaching that settlement. This is highly revealing. Given that the UN was to become a permanent congress for international society, one might think, on historical analogy, that once the particulars of the settlement had been reached with individual states, it should be the task of this general congress to determine the more general provisions of the settlement as a whole. However, the United States, for one, was fully adamant that this was not to happen, as President Truman affirmed in a statement to the General Assembly on 23 October 1946. 'The United Nations...was *not* intended to settle the problems arising immediately out of the war', he reminded his audience, whereas it '*was* intended to provide the means for maintaining international peace in the future after just settlements have been made'. The former task, he underscored, 'was deliberately consigned to negotiations among the Allies' (Dennett and Turner 1948: 519). This had already become a cause of some complaint during the review of the Dumbarton Oaks proposals. 'As was done at Versailles, the United Nations reserve to themselves full liberty of action for the settlement of the questions to be decided at the end of the war', the Venezuelan Government had tartly remarked in a paper of 31 October 1944, whilst 'there is left to the new institution the task of defending and perpetuating the peace that is concluded, without any intervention in the negotiation thereof' (UNIO 1945: vol. III, 190). But if some complained that the separation between the peace settlement and the new organization was only too sharp, others worried instead that the transition from the wartime alliance to the new organization might not be distinct enough. In the same way that the Quadruple Alliance of 1814 had become the basis of the new congress system in 1815— and the winners of the war thus identified with those responsible for preserving the peace—some now expressed anxiety about the duplication in name as between the United Nations (as wartime allies) and The United Nations (as the new international organization). To sceptical ears, this made the international organization sound too much like a 'system of transitory alliance' (UNIO 1945: vol. III, 397).

At the same time, the UN Charter presented a conspicuously realist face, and explicitly sanctioned a society whose members enjoyed unequal powers. This was permitted by appeal to the lessons of recent history, and the vindication of the role of the great powers, both as the effective victors in the war and as the necessary custodians of future security. All this yielded a complex, and often contradictory, concept of consensus and of how it was to be demonstrated. This pushed in two different directions. It gave substantial power to a collective security system, led by the Security Council, to enforce the peace in those situations in which major-power consensus was attainable. And it demobilized that same system, in the interests of everyone, in situations where that consensus could not be reached. It is this permanent-member veto power that strikes such an ambivalent chord in the UN's overall design. At the time, this was met with the charge of 'privileging' the great powers. In defence of the measure, it was therefore countered that it was not a matter of privilege, but of practical necessity. US secretary Stettinius insisted in 1945 that the permanent members must 'bear the principal responsibility for action' (Goodrich and Carroll 1947: 415). Moreover, this was not a 'new' power to be given to the permanent members: it was one that they had already enjoyed under the old League structure. On substantive peace enforcement issues, the League's voting system has been one of unanimity within the Council and, as such, everyone enjoyed a veto. Accordingly, in an explanatory statement issued at San Francisco in June 1945, the Delegates of the Four Sponsoring Governments (US, USSR, UK, and China) justified the proposed voting procedure as an enhancement of the possibility of taking action, rather than as any augmentation of the rights of the great powers:

The Yalta voting formula substitutes for the rule of complete unanimity of the League Council a system of qualified majority voting in the Security Council. Under this system non-permanent members of the Security Council individually would have no 'veto'. As regards the permanent members, there is no question under the Yalta formula of investing them with a new right...The formula proposed for the taking of action in the Security Council by a majority of seven would make the operation of the Council less subject to obstruction than was the case under the League of Nations rule of complete unanimity. (Goodrich and Carroll 1947: 449)

Thus viewed, the P5-veto was sold as a relaxation, not a tightening, of international society's requirements for what could reasonably represent international consensus. Additionally, the measure was to serve the purpose of averting the damaging spate of departures that had characterized the short lifespan of the League. The veto would lock the great powers in, by providing them with the reassurance of a weapon to thwart unacceptable collective action. A dissatisfied major power could now express its dissatisfaction, and would be much better served by doing so, from inside instead of outside. What might this be if not a subtle extension of the logic of a 'legitimate' order as later expounded by Kissinger and others? Anything that was not blocked by a veto would, by definition, be deemed acceptable to international society. Anything proposed that *was* unacceptable to one or more of the major powers would, by extension, be prevented in the interests of international society as a whole, as robust action against a dissident major power could be in nobody's interests in the nuclear age.

These provide fascinating insights into the practical adaptations of a requirement for consensus to meet the contemporary needs of an evolving international society. In the face of repeated uses of the veto by late 1946, the US delegate to the General Assembly admonished his fellow permanent members to behave 'responsibly'. He reminded them of their undertaking not to use the veto 'wilfully to obstruct the operation of the Council'. He advised them that unanimity of the great powers was a requirement to facilitate the operation of the UN, not to obstruct it. He cajoled them that the permanent members 'in good conscience do not represent in the Security Council their own governments', but rather they represented 'the entire membership of the United Nations' (Dennett and Turner 1948: 527–30). This reiterated key parts of a major statement made by President Truman to the General Assembly on 23 October 1946. This had grappled, in a revealing way, with the issue of international consensus, how it was to be reached, and the role of the Security Council in relation to it. It stands as a good statement of a concept of legitimacy, regarded as a process of consensual agreement expressed through agreed procedures, but going beyond them in its appeal to wider purposes and values. It neatly juxtaposes the veto, as an aspect of the constitutional procedure of the UN, with the purpose of the UN to pursue the declared objectives of the Charter:

The United States believes that the rule of unanimous accord among the five permanent members of the Security Council imposes upon these members a special obligation. This obligation is to seek and reach agreements that will enable them and the Security Council to fulfil the responsibilities they have assumed under the Charter... The exercise of neither veto rights nor majority rights can make peace secure. There is no substitute for agreements that are universally acceptable because they are just to all concerned. The Security Council is intended to provide that kind of agreement. (Dennett and Turner 1948: 521)

It is possible to discern, in these various deliberations, two different accounts of the relationship between legitimacy and consensus. In one of these versions, it would be legitimate for the Security Council to take action if this was giving expression to an extant consensus within that body, and, as a corollary, illegitimate for it to proceed in the absence of such consensus. In the second version, the relationship is otherwise construed. It becomes here a key role and responsibility of the Council to reach such a consensus, especially in cases where none was already in existence, to enable the Council to perform its legitimate tasks. The view of what could be rightfully done by exercise of the veto very much depended on which of these doctrines was being embraced.

The respective powers of the great and small states were to be discussed heatedly in the drafting of the UN Charter, and yet another bargain struck. There appeared to be a significant accretion of the role of the great powers, at least in relative terms, because non-permanent members lost the veto that they formerly had enjoyed under the League system. Accordingly, some governments objected to the entire principle of 'permanent' membership of the Council, and sought instead to implement a status of 'semi-permanence', to be reviewed after a specified period of say eight years, as in Mexican proposals

(UNIO 1945: vol. III, 111). More commonly, the contentious issue was the voting system itself, and the permanent-member veto. Certainly, some small states protested, as did Ecuador, that the great-power veto, in effect, disregarded 'the juridical equality of member states, reducing those which obtain non-permanent seats to a sad and decorative function within the Council' (UNIO 1945: vol. III, 408). The other side of the coin was the debate over the precise number of elected, and non-permanent, members to be on the Council. There were many demands for a number larger than six, but that was the figure finally incorporated in the Charter, although subsequently expanded.

For all their deficiencies, these proved broadly acceptable compromises to a representative cross section of international society. That this was an imperfect curb on great power unsociability is scarcely in doubt. The reality, however, was that in the absence of those imperfect institutional restraints, the small powers would still have inhabited a world dominated by the great. The alternative to institutionalized inequality was not perfect equality, but a yet more unbridled and ruthless form of inequality—'a world in anarchy in which lawless power runs riot and small nations are the first to be trampled underfoot', as Stettinius argued before the Council on Foreign Relations in April 1945 (Goodrich and Carroll 1947: 421). The Norwegian government, with its own recent and painful experience at the sharp end of international relations, concurred in this realist logic. It posed the key question: 'Can a small state risk to place its destiny in the hands of the Security Council to be instituted by the Dumbarton Oaks plan?' Its own unequivocal response was that 'we are tempted to say: It cannot risk *not* to do it' (UNIO 1945: vol. III, 354). Since each small power might now expect to enjoy at least an occasional day in the sun, when its turn for Council membership came up, it would be no worse off, and arguably slightly better, by the protection afforded by such an institutional outcome, however unequal it might seem.

There is yet one further strand in the drafting of the UN Charter that sheds a fascinating light upon the general concerns of this book. In the Dumbarton Oaks version of the Charter, the emphasis had been strictly upon maintaining the peace and taking such actions as were necessary to this end. This had evoked criticisms from a large number of states worried about what they saw as a normative void at the heart of the Charter. These debates provoked interesting reflections upon legitimacy, and its relationship to such things as law and morality. At one level, this expressed itself straightforwardly in a complaint that the draft Charter omitted those values on the basis of which peaceful settlements should be sought. This is nicely captured in the positions adopted by both the Greek and the Turkish governments. The Greek comments of 3 May 1945 urged the insertion of a reference to the 'principles of international law, justice and morality' (UNIO 1945: vol. III, 531). Almost identically, the Turkish government sought the inclusion of a statement about 'justice and the general principles of law' (UNIO 1945: vol. III, 481). In each case, the underlying objection to the existing version was that it promoted *peaceful* settlement, but was otherwise silent on the principles by which this was to be secured. The wording 'in conformity with the principles of justice and international law' was therefore incorporated in the final draft (UNDPI 1995: 14). Legitimacy, in that sense, apparently needed to be anchored in other consensual norms of international society, albeit that it did not seek merely to replicate them.

The richest commentary on these broad issues, within the context of the drafting of the Charter, was to be provided by the Netherlands government in January 1945. It, too, lamented the absence of any normative underpinning, beyond that of peaceful settlement, in the existing draft. What its paper insisted upon was, in addition, affirmation of 'some acceptable standard of conduct in international affairs'. Interestingly, it argued, this could not be in the form of international law: this was inadequate both 'because it would exclude relevant considerations of another nature', but, more generally, because law could not be relied upon 'at all times and in all circumstances'. It then objected that 'legitimacy as a standard would undoubtedly be too static where a notion is needed allowing for growth and development'. Be it noted, that in dismissing legitimacy as the appropriate standard, the paper was in fact dismissing a legalist view of legitimacy. Turning this around, what it was in fact saying was that legitimacy needs to embrace values other than legality, and it needed to do so because legitimacy is *dynamic*. As it groped its way towards an adequate formulation of these needs, it candidly admitted that the best it could suggest was inclusion of 'a reference to those feelings of right and wrong, those moral principles which live in every human heart' (UNIO1945: vol. III, 312–13). In short, what emerges from these discussions was a sense that international legitimacy is a dynamic process that is based not exclusively upon peaceful settlement, nor upon existing law, but embracing other substantive values of morality and justice as well. Legitimacy, in short, is about finding a consensual accommodation amongst these elements, not about asserting any one to the exclusion of the others.

CONCLUSION

The paradox of the 1945 settlement begins to resolve itself when we explore the conditions that seemingly facilitated a 'successful' outcome in 1945, in ways that had not proved possible in 1919. The predisposing conditions that helped foster the nature of the peace in 1945 need not be detailed at length. They are to be found, in some combination, in the following three factors: the actual experience of the 1930s, and the subsequent lessons drawn from this collapse of the international security and economic orders; the new pre-eminence of the United States as the world's foremost military and economic power, in conjunction with a newly found willingness to mobilize that power for international purposes; and the rapid emergence of difficulties amongst the victors, leading to the onset of the cold war. In short, these factors pressed collectively in ways that made compromises, especially those between the United States and its European allies, more readily available in 1945 than had proved possible in 1919.

The domestic face of embedded liberalism, as well as the reinvention of the former enemy states, was a critical facet of *both* settlements in 1945, the Western and the bipolar. The seeds of the Western settlement predated the war, and had their origins in the experience of economic collapse in the 1930s. It followed that the concept of international legitimacy had to be extended to outlaw unilateral 'beggar-my-neighbour' policies in the interests of international society as a whole. At the same time, the negative consequences of international constraints could not be dumped solely in the domestic domain, without first introducing there significant measures of social protection. Simultaneously, and in order to allow Germany and Japan to play their key roles in this resurrected Western system, both states had to be tied into future good behaviour by interlocking international and domestic regimes. Internationally, their roles as economic and civil centres within a Western system would thus render them safe as future international actors. Domestically, this goal would be promoted also by the profound changes in German and Japanese societies. The former enemy states could then be readmitted into international society with those safeguards. This replicated the twin logic of the embedded liberalism solution as it applied to the other main participants in the Western system.

And yet the Western settlement cannot be understood in isolation from the bipolar: both fed off each other. The Western settlement became the more readily acceptable to those included within it because of the external challenge from the Soviet Union, and perceptions of this emerging 'threat'. In turn, the bipolar settlement made the resuscitation of Germany and Japan an ever more pressing matter: they were needed as counterweights to the USSR, in Europe and Asia respectively. However, the Western system would have undermined a bipolar settlement had the relationship between them been purely antagonistic, as this might imply. Instead, there was an element of positive reinforcement as well. While an effective Western system certainly represented a challenge to Soviet power, it was necessary also as a guarantee of Soviet security against its former enemies. 'If the western countries could create a political system of their own in which German power was limited', notes Trachtenberg, 'this was something the USSR could live with' (Trachtenberg 1999: vii). Fundamentally, therefore, a successful Western settlement became the necessary precondition for the bipolar settlement as well. The trick was to bring about the '"double" containment of Germany and the Soviet Union' (Lundestad 1998: 4), and the formation of a Western system, including European integration, was the key to that overall design. That Western settlement was to prove remarkably robust and durable, and many of its elements persist to this day. The bipolar settlement would dissipate as it became detached from the former, gradually during the 1970s and 1980s, and then finally with great speed in 1989–90.

In the meantime, the newly articulated principles of 1945 survived the experience of cold war. The ongoing revolutions in rightful membership continued apace in the spheres of democracy and human rights, and with all their as yet unforeseen implications for rightful conduct. The standard of consensus that had been forged in 1945 was largely driven underground during the long decades of the cold war, but was to resurface into a bewilderingly different world after 1990. All these principles were then to be subjected to the most demanding of tests, in the altered circumstances of the post-cold war world. With the completion of this historical survey, it is now time to move forward to the complex practices of legitimacy in contemporary international society.

Part II

Contemporary International Society

8

Legitimacy after the Cold War

Part I has reviewed some historical dimensions of the international practice of legitimacy. Part II now considers its status in contemporary international society. It will cover the conduct of the legitimacy debate since the end of the cold war, its elaboration of principles of legitimacy, and also the diplomatic practice accompanying some of the major international events of this period. The focus of its illustrative case studies will be upon key episodes of international security, although clearly practices of legitimacy extend into other areas—such as management of the international economy, development and distribution, cultural interactions, and environmental protection—as well. The basis of this selection is simply that if legitimacy is taken seriously by international society in the context of the great issues of war and peace, its relevance elsewhere follows straightforwardly.

This stage of the analysis needs a more explicit integration of the theoretical schemes that were elaborated at the outset. In particular, how does contemporary international society apply a principle of rightful membership? How does it deal with the nature of consensus, and what is considered an adequate representation of one? How is legitimacy related to other international norms at present? Finally, what problems face contemporary international society on account of its currently distinctive, and highly uneven, distribution of power? This chapter maps out the theoretical terrain to be reviewed in the remainder of the book in order to trace what has been happening to international legitimacy since the end of the cold war.

THE POST-COLD WAR REVIVAL OF LEGITIMACY

The place to begin is the recent resurgence of legitimacy talk, noted in the Introduction. What does this signify for contemporary international relations? One intuitive estimate is that this has been related in some way to the end of the cold war. 'What is and is not "legitimate" in international politics', reflects one of the few writers to have addressed this issue, 'is becoming a more important question as the certainties of the Cold War disappear' (Williams 1996: 40). If understood as a claim that those very certainties of the cold-war era forestalled legitimacy talk—presumably because it did not seem appropriate in these conditions—this appears persuasive enough. Why then should the resulting 'uncertainties' have been any more conducive? Does legitimacy talk thrive in twilight zones?

At first glance, it is possible to hypothesize two quite different characteristics of the post-cold war era that encouraged resort to the language of legitimacy. One major contribution to the study of international society set out in its agenda of future research the distinction between 'consensual solidarism' and 'coercive solidarism' (Alderson and Hurrell 2000b: 67). What was conveyed by the first was an intensification of shared values within international society, arising spontaneously from normative integration. In contrast, the coercive form suggested an imposition of hegemonic power. In these opposed terms, what change did the end of the cold war make?

According to the first, what transpired with the ending of the cold war was the possibility of a world of values 'whole and free'. The artificial divisions that had bifurcated international society for the past several decades had now been removed, and there was the potential for international society to express a more cohesive vision of its purpose. Much of the grandiose rhetoric at the time reflected this mood. In the context of this newly discovered harmony of international values, talk of legitimacy began to carry a greater sense of conviction. In short, the flourishing of the legitimacy dialogue resulted from the greater normative universalism to which the end of the cold war had given rise. The potential for a single integrated international society had once before been present when 'Europe unified the globe' (Bull and Watson 1984b: 5–6), but was thereafter stymied by the onset of the cold war. The events of 1990 finally permitted international society to resume its course towards unity. 'Today everybody is an insider of international society', was one proud boast to this effect (Jackson 2000: 13).

The 'coercive' account stands as a counterpoint to this benign image. It shares the surface phenomenon of solidarism, but differs radically as to the conditions that have brought this about. 'The paradox of universalism is that the successful promotion of "universal" or "global" values', is one telling comment, 'will often depend on the willingness of particularly powerful states to promote them' (Hurrell 1999: 291). From this perspective, the end of the cold war has exercised its normative influence at one remove. The degree of solidarism in its wake results primarily from the new distribution of power, not from a spontaneous consolidation of shared norms. The proponents of Western values have found themselves in the fortunate position of being able now to chivvy, without heed or hindrance, the rest of international society. This has been accomplished either through subtle processes of hegemonic power, or through instruments of overt military coercion, or some combination of both. In any case, we now talk the shared language of legitimacy precisely because political power has enabled such a 'hegemonic discourse' to take place.

Clearly, given this stark choice, what legitimacy talk means for international society can be interpreted in radically different ways. Both accounts, *contra*

Williams, locate legitimacy in the greater certainties of the post-cold war world, not in its remaining uncertainties. In the first, we now have greater certainty about the shared values; according to the second, we now have even greater certitude about the location of power in the international system. The resurgence of legitimacy is driven by one or other of these individually, or by both in some combination.

Nonetheless, there remain good reasons to take the theme of uncertainty seriously. There are at least three ways in which the radical uncertainties of the post-cold war period might be thought to have contributed to the rise of recent legitimacy talk.

The first asserts a connection between resort to the language of legitimacy and a perception of fundamental crisis. As has often been remarked, we are much more likely to discuss legitimacy when least confident that the conditions for its realization are present. On this suggestion, we dwell on issues of legitimacy when things appear to be going wrong. 'Discussions of legitimacy have been most vigorous', we have been warned, 'at just those times when the order and justice which a normative theory of legitimacy appears to offer seem . . . to be most endangered' (Barker 1990: 4). To this extent, the presently voluble dialogue may serve only to confirm our fears and anxieties. The present author has elsewhere set out the detailed argument that, although not a hot war, the cold war was functionally similar in kind, and accordingly gave rise to a cold peace at its end (Clark 2001*a*). On the historical precedents, we should not be surprised to find a phase of introspection after the cold war, as international society attempted to come to terms with the full implications of that most recent challenge.

A second uncertainty produces equally paradoxical results. Our loss of bearings is, in part, a consequence of the very integration within international society that has already taken place. International society has traditionally operated to foster low expectations. It is widely claimed to have been 'pluralistic' about fundamental values, and to have contented itself with the practicalities of coexistence. However, this is less tenable now than before. International society is currently faced 'with tasks that go beyond a shared responsibility for international stability' (Osiander 1994: 8). Ironically, it is this very increased solidarism that has spawned uncertainty and division about the scope of these new purposes, and about the extent to which they have found acceptance. It is the heightened ambition of international society that is placing strain upon its cohesion and testing its resolve. The lapse into the language of legitimacy is but a measure of this deeply unsettled state of affairs.

This is compounded where the quest for new purpose appears to founder upon the rock of cultural diversity. International society has expanded too quickly to have consolidated fully the variety now within its embrace. Doubt has been cast on the existence today of a 'globally meaningful system', because of the plurality of the 'culture-specific concepts' that continue to prevail (Bozeman 1984: 404–5). While international society remained in some way

European international society (writ large or small), this presented less of a problem. Now, however, the challenge is one of achieving a 'universal society' in the absence of a 'common cultural framework' (Hoffmann 1990: 26). International society is being asked to do much more, at the very moment when its own cohesion is increasingly suspect.

A third aspect is that the underlying uncertainty is less about the diversity within, and more about the legitimacy *of*, international society. This goes well beyond the scope of the present study (Clark 2003). However, as an explanation of the heightened resort to the language of legitimacy, it has considerable credence. The entire 'Westphalian' image of international society, predicated upon sovereignty and territoriality, is widely called into question (Zacher 1992; Hassner 1993: 52–3; Lyons and Mastanduno 1995). When people now discuss legitimacy, it is frequently not from *within* the confines of international society, but explicitly *about* the appropriateness of this frame of reference. The great uncertainty is whether, with the declining relevance of the old conception of international society, we can yet rediscover any meaning for legitimacy within an increasingly global order.

For these reasons, there is no doubt that heightened sensitivity to legitimacy has been spawned by the peculiar conditions present since the end of the cold war. However, it would be rash to conclude that this places us in a novel situation. What is so striking is the extent to which the format of the practice of legitimacy after the cold war has conformed to traditional patterns. We should, for that reason, be less impressed by the novelty of what is now taking place, and more so by the important continuities with earlier ideas and practices. This emerges from an outline of the key theoretical concerns that have been revealed in the post-cold war discussion.

THE ELEMENTS OF CONTEMPORARY LEGITIMACY

How is the contemporary practice of legitimacy best considered? The basic approach of this book to international legitimacy has already been set out in Chapter 1. To further set the scene for the remaining chapters, an outline of its principal analytical elements can be presented at this stage. These map the range of factors that impinge upon the practice of legitimacy with regard to both membership and conduct. Central to these is the working out of an acceptable form of consensus. They encompass also the specific international norms—legality, morality, and constitutionality—that supply most of the substantive content, and the actual language, of the process of legitimation. However, as we have seen, the practice of legitimacy does not correspond directly with any of these norms in particular: it is instead mediated through a political process of contestation and consensus-building. This process, in turn, is filtered through prevailing distributions of power.

The following section will dismantle those elements of international legitimacy to help understand how the pieces are best fitted together again. Existing accounts of international society, as we have seen, remain unsatisfactory. They seek to reduce it either to specific institutions (often that of international law, or sovereignty) or to its shared values (be they pluralist or solidarist). What this analysis suggests instead is that it is legitimacy that constitutes international society. Legitimacy, in turn, is not reducible to any one institution, or norm, but depicts a highly volatile condition of political balance amongst the diverse elements that seek to capture it. The focus on legitimacy in international society thus enables us to understand its practice in a highly dynamic and political way. This draws on institutions and other norms, but goes beyond them. It introduces the additional factor of the search for consensus which is central to the enterprise as a whole.

Rightful Membership

Where does contemporary international society stand with regard to this particular dimension of legitimacy? Are we currently experiencing a revolution in international society's concept of rightful membership? In so far as the period after the end of the cold war can be regarded as the functional equivalent of a peace settlement, it is at these moments exactly that we might expect such revolutions to become manifest. The end of the First World War offers an example. 'The Peace of Paris', Bobbitt (2002: 638) submits, 'provides the source of an overarching constitutional order that sets the standard to which all national legal and political institutions must conform'. It is within the context of the 'upheavals' represented by such periodic bouts of peacemaking that there is posed the fundamental question: 'What constitutes a legitimate state?' (Reus-Smit 1999: 134). In the case of the end of the cold war, the answer was liberal democracy (Clark 2001a: 217).

Accordingly, the imprint of contemporary notions of international legitimacy is most readily to be discovered in this working out of the Wightian criteria for rightful membership. It was suggested earlier that, after a period of expansion of international society to become virtually all-embracing (at least, in terms of states), we are now experiencing a new phase in which there is the potential for a contraction of that membership. While in the formal diplomatic sense no change has been made in the conditions for international recognition, informally there now operates a set of principles that justify a more restrictive concept of international society. Otherwise expressed, within the still universal ideal of international society, there has increasingly been articulated the doctrinal rationale for an 'inner' grouping entitled to the fullest enjoyment of the rights of membership, and also to be the interpreters and executors of the wishes of international society as a whole. By its nature, this is the most contentious aspect of contemporary international legitimacy, and there is a profound political struggle to secure acceptance for any such concept. This is, nonetheless, a shift of considerable proportions and the task of this chapter is both to document its occurrence and to explore its wider significance and implications.

Many of the key issues that have exercised policymakers since 1990—such as humanitarian intervention, democracy promotion, the development/security interface, post-conflict reconstruction, the identification and treatment of rogue states, and regime change—are all at base symptomatic of the paradigm shift currently being experienced in international society's conception of rightful membership. To the extent that international society has it in its capacity to legitimize certain types of state, this in turn specifies the precise relationship between the member states and international society itself. It is the rationale upon which the rights and duties of the states, as well as the rights and duties of international society, are necessarily founded.

It is in this area of rightful membership that the most profound transformations in international society's conception of legitimacy are presently underway. These are surfacing as challenges to, or erosions of, sovereignty, but to portray them thus is to misunderstand their more fundamental nature. Sovereignty is not a 'self-referential value'; instead, sovereignty 'has always been justified with reference to particular conceptions of legitimate statehood' (Reus-Smit 2001: 520). Unsurprisingly, these changing conceptions are now manifesting themselves as apparent revolutions in sovereignty: at base, however, they are actually about the proper form and function of the state which, hitherto, have been expressed through the medium of doctrines of sovereignty. The developing principle of the 1990s, implemented in faltering and inconsistent ways, was that 'national governments are subject to international sanction if they violate certain basic norms within their own borders' (Talbott 2003: 1040). To the extent that this was to be so, it posed a whole set of consequent questions about the nature of rightful conduct in today's international society.

To be sure, a major part of what was driving all this was the continuity in normative concerns about human rights. But recent manifestations of this go to the heart of the relationship between states and international society. This has two principal facets, and they correspond to the twin dimensions of legitimacy: the extent of international society's remit to prescribe the domestic state constitutions needed to protect these human rights; and the extent of international society's remit to act on behalf of those rights in situations where the state in question lacks the means, or possibly the will, to so act by itself. Even if the ultimate concern is the human rights of individuals, international society expresses this primarily through its approval, or disapproval, of forms of state. This has become much more conspicuous since the end of the cold war. '[L]iberalism, within the international realm', is one representative assessment, '...is of growing importance because of its dominance as a value system against which state forms are legitimised' (Robinson 1999: 143).

This development within international society can be presented in Weberian terms. It has been pointed out that, like Wight, Weber's concept of membership of international society possessed a social dimension. Whilst formally and diplomatically the society may be universal, Weber understood the necessity to cultivate appropriate domestic conditions within those member states.

'Weber's most fundamental claim', it is stated, 'was that European inter-national society could *only* be successfully reproduced once an "ethic of responsibility" governed state behaviour' (Hobson and Seabrooke 2001: 240–1). As with Wight, Weber conceived of international legitimacy as having an internal or domestic aspect. 'European international society', he believed, 'can only be successfully reproduced once the state–society relations of its members acquire a specific conception of social legitimacy' (Hobson and Seabrooke 2001: 241). While individual societies have their own interest in creating such conditions, international society has its separate interest in encouraging this development. This has been expressed through attempts at proactive state socialization. However, the wish of international society to promote the emergence of particular state forms is now expressed more candidly and recurrently than at any earlier historical period. This is acknowledged in a wide array of contemporary commentaries, all of which point to an attempted ' "homogenization" of domestic structures in accordance with those prevailing internationally' (Armstrong 1993: 7; Keal 2000: 63–4; Bukovansky 2002: 35; Colas 2002: 124). Notions about what international society may legitimately do are now such that, inescapably, they demand 'the creation of international rules that deeply affect the domestic structures and organization of states' (Hurrell 2003: 32).

The reproduction of a society of *states* has always been an essential part of the remit of international society, and that aspect of international legitimacy concerned with rightful membership has been its chosen means to this end. It was most powerfully demonstrated during the process of decolonization from the 1940s to the 1960s. As is widely accepted, the so-called 'revolt' against the West was far from absolute, and resulted in the paradoxical reaffirmation of the Western state form as the ticket for admission into international society (Bull 1984*b*: 224). In this respect, Mayall (1990: 49) is rightly persuaded that 'it is the traditional society of states which has had the greater impact on anti-colonial nationalism rather than the other way round'. While decolonization reflected the delegitimation of the former practices of colonialism, it also endorsed other traditional principles, especially those pertaining to sovereignty and non-intervention (Von Laue 1987: 307; Colas 2002: 128). These became more deeply entrenched as part of the process of validation of international society as one now predicated on universal equality of membership (Bain 2003*b*: 65–6).

Much of this is now under renewed pressure, as the criteria for rightful membership have been more fully elaborated. As will be demonstrated in Chapter 9, this theme has become much more prominent in the post-cold war practice of states.

Consensus

The keystone of this whole edifice is the highly problematic search for a working consensus. In some rudimentary sense, the attainment of legitimacy in international society is concerned with the production of such a consensus, although its pertinent demonstrations have shifted historically. What is to count as an acceptable representation of consensus is endlessly negotiable, and remains highly fluid. International society pretends that consensus is an 'objective' criterion that itself confers legitimacy on international actions. However, this consensus is itself subject to constant review, and is part of the problem to which it is routinely offered as the solution.

Some historians of international society tend to speak the language of consensus, in preference to that of legitimacy, or treat the one as tantamount to the other. This is very much the case in the work of Osiander (1994). His abiding concern is with the '*consensus agenda*', the '*consensus notions*', and the '*consensus principles*' that have been developed within international society from time to time (Osiander 1994: 9). Although he speaks only occasionally of legitimacy, he employs consensus in such a way that is scarcely distinguishable from it. Additionally, he attributes stability to those phases of international society in which there has been a strong consensus about these principles. In short, consensus is claimed to have the same causal effect as is often attributed to legitimacy.

More fundamentally—and in parallel with the present argument—Osiander asserts that consensus is essential to the existence of an international society. When states do not share the consensus agenda, he pronounces, 'international society then ceases to exist, at least as between these actors and those willing to uphold the existing consensus notions' (Osiander 1994: 10). This is so because consensus forms the central part of his definition of an international society. 'International society may be defined', he insists, 'as a situation of general acceptance by the international actors of a consensus agenda' (Osiander 1994: 10). This is very close to the present claim that it is legitimacy that constitutes international society.

How then do we get from legitimacy to consensus? Are they indeed the same thing? Are these various historical practices of consensus already reviewed the closest that international society can ever approximate to an ideal of legitimacy, and is this what legitimacy actually means for international relations? If not, what precisely is the relationship between them? It had long been held by political theorists, and theorists of democracy in particular, that legitimacy resided in any political relationship only if marked by consent—the doctrine that 'only those governments which enjoy the consent of their subjects possess rightful authority and can legitimately demand or expect obedience' (Partridge 1971: 9). It is precisely this linkage between legitimacy and consent that is made in the wider argument advanced by Linklater about contemporary global governance. '[G]lobal structures violate commitments to the politics of consent', he suggests, and it is this 'democratic deficit' that needs to be eliminated, if 'worldwide arrangements are to be legitimate' (Linklater 1999: 477). However, political theory has recognized also the many difficulties with the notion of consent, and the highly problematic nature of what counts as reliable evidence for its expression (Partridge 1971).

Both political theory and sociology, if for slightly different reasons, have therefore shifted much of their attention away from consent, and towards consensus instead (Partridge 1971: 72). Consensus provides a different, and less demanding, criterion for the creation or maintenance of legitimacy. It fits well with the Weberian approach in that consensus, unlike consent, 'is a more purely descriptive term', and points towards 'empirical constituents of the structure of a society' (Partridge 1971: 71). In the case of individual political systems or regimes, 'the "legitimacy" of an authority derives from the social consensus in which the rightful authority of the ruler is generally recognized'; this is different from saying that the authority is based on the explicit consent of the governed (Partridge 1971: 23). This shift correspondingly diminishes the significance of the (hard to specify) 'act' of political consent by the affected parties. Sociologists, in particular, have been drawn to this idea of consensus 'to explain the cohesiveness of a society—a form of agreement that falls short of explicitly expressed consent but which nevertheless represents a willing acceptance of what is the subject of the consensus' (Partridge 1971: 17).

Where does the willingness come from? It may appear that any property of legitimacy is vitiated in conditions of what is often referred to as 'structural consensus' (Mueller 1973: 92–4). In this situation, elites are taken to operate in such a way that society reproduces its own value system, and this ensures a significant social consensus in support of it (Partidge 1971: 118). This description approximates to the Gramscian notion of hegemony, in which 'power takes a primarily consensual form' (Cox 1981, reproduced in Cox 1996: 120, fn. 24), and is expressed in notions that have enjoyed some international currency, such as the so-called 'Washington consensus'. In such frameworks, consensus is suffused with power relations, and it is hard to see where coercion stops and voluntarism starts in the production of it. It is an easy step from this position to the view that legitimacy is simply what is in the interests of the dominant social forces. Is this the trap into which any consensus-based empirical theory of legitimacy is bound to fall?

This poses a number of central questions about the relationship between legitimacy and consensus, and these will be a key preoccupation of Chapters 10 and 11. They relate to the fundamental issue of whether what is important for legitimacy is the *fact* of agreement, or rather the content of the *norm* to which it gives expression. In sum, the key questions are:

1. Does the importance of consensus reside purely in its embodiment of social agreement, irrespective of the particular values contained within it? Is it the agreement that validates the content, because it encapsulates the commitment to proceed consensually, even if the actual course adopted might otherwise be 'wrong'?

2. Is the consensus important instead, or additionally, because it gives voice to other core norms? In this case, agreement is less important for itself than for

being indicative of the 'rightness' of what is to be done. What makes it 'right' is its correspondence with other fundamental norms.

These are matters in which social theorists have long expressed an interest, if not normally in connection with international affairs. It has commonly been held that consensus is fundamental to social order because it is itself the product of the shared values of a society. 'Consensus on the political means', we are told, '. . . is not the most basic kind of agreement'. Rather, 'the political "rules of the game" are derived from and undergirded by a broad ethical consensus' (Willhoite 1963: 304). This is a clear statement of the claim that, as a dimension of legitimacy, consensus cannot be about procedural matters alone. The consensus must express the substantive values of the society more generally. This is similar to Morgenthau's discussion, which also assigned a prime role to consensus. Morgenthau considered that the balance of power could operate effectively only in conditions where a consensus already existed and was operatively strong, as this had the effect of 'strengthening the tendencies toward moderation and equilibrium' (Morgenthau 1973: 219). Crucially, he insisted that this consensus adhered to basic and shared moral standards, but in a complex way. 'It is this consensus', he suggested, '—both child and father, as it were, of common moral standards and a common civilization as well as of common interests—that kept in check the limitless desire for power' (Morgenthau 1973: 220). On this reckoning, it is their origin in common values that makes for the closeness between consensus and legitimacy. Others, however, make the distinction *between* legitimacy and consensus exactly on this issue. The difference is that 'legitimacy cannot viably be reduced to a product of the political system as a consensus can be' (Mueller 1973: 132). What this suggests is that legitimacy is embedded in fundamental principle(s), in a way that a social consensus is not.

These are difficult issues to disentangle, especially as matters of international political practice. In summary, they invite two different assessments of the relationship between legitimacy and consensus. According to the one, consensus is important because it is the means by which society articulates its most basic purposes and values. Consensus is the benchmark of legitimacy in so far as it corresponds with these values, but these values have an objective existence beyond the fact of the consensus itself. Ultimately, the consensus is subject to testing by these absolute values. In the second case, consensus is a measure of social cohesion, and that measure has its own autonomous importance, especially within an international society possibly lacking in fundamentally shared values much beyond that point. In this latter conception, consensus is valuable wherever it can be found. As between these two versions, legitimacy and consensus become radically realigned. According to the former, legitimacy exists through the medium of valid normative principles, and social consensus is taken to represent a faltering movement towards their expression and realization. Ultimately, the consensus can be judged and challenged by this standard which exists external to the consensus itself. In the latter version, it is conformity to the consensus that constitutes the principal test of validity, and hence of legitimacy. What makes any position or action legitimate is its adherence to the consensual position. Any appeal to values and principles beyond this will be destructive of the consensus, and of social cohesion, and is to be avoided.

A good illustration of these dilemmas is provided in the response to the terrorist attacks of 11 September 2001, and to the encouragement thereafter of a consensual 'war against terror'. There were, in the aftermath of the attacks, repeated calls for an international consensus against terrorism, as the necessary foundation of an effective international societal response. Commentators appealed for a bolstering of international society to counter the threat, and this was to entail recommitment to 'legitimizing institutions', like the UN, as well as encouragement of 'a broad consensus on democracy, markets, and human-rights norms' (Hirsh 2003: 7).

The UN Secretary-General, Kofi Annan, painted a complex picture of the relationship between legitimacy and consensus in this global struggle against terror. Seeking to place the UN at the centre of international responses to terrorism, he envisioned the UN as the 'forum necessary for building a universal coalition', which, in turn, would 'ensure global legitimacy for the long-term response to terrorism' (*New York Times*, 21 September 2001: A.35). There needed to be a consensus so that the struggle against terrorism would be legitimate. This chimed with the advice tendered by other commentators to the Bush administration to adhere to an international consensus, not 'as an end in itself', but instrumentally to 'gain the legitimacy that comes from operating through an international consensus' (Zakaria 2002).

Elsewhere, Annan painted a different picture, and appeared to reverse the relationship. On these occasions, he was persuaded that the task was one of fostering legitimacy for the war against terror, as a means of making it possible for as many countries as possible to adhere to the consensus position. The UN, he pronounced, must have a strategy that would 'ensure global legitimacy for the struggle ahead'. This was necessary, he continued, since 'the legitimacy that the United Nations conveys can ensure that the greatest number of states are able and willing to take the necessary and difficult steps' (*International Herald Tribune*, 2 October 2001: 6). From this point of view, legitimacy is understood to have its own distinct quality, one that would in turn then make the creation of an international consensus possible. What, it needs to be asked, would be the nature of that legitimacy, if different from its source in an already present consensus? Is it created instead by its conformity to other norms, whatever the consensus position? Clearly, practitioners and analysts alike have some difficulty in discerning the operative relationship between these two concepts in contemporary international society. As the next step, we need to explore further the relationship between legitimacy and the substantive norms which many regard as its foundation.

International norms

The normative substance of legitimacy continues to be supplied by a trio of contemporary norms—legality, morality, and constitutionality. These exist in a dynamic relationship and often pull in opposite directions. For that reason, none of these norms individually holds the key to legitimacy. While it might appear that legitimacy is wholly derivative from these standards, this misunderstands the relationship in important ways. These norms are certainly appealed to as part of the process of legitimation but, as practice, this introduces the additional element of political brokerage. At this point, the quest for consensus is reinserted.

The practice of legitimacy responds to concerns raised under all three normative headings, without being predetermined by any one. Moreover, and fundamental to this argument, legitimacy exists in a hierarchic relationship to these other norms; it is not co-equal with them. That is to say that legitimacy does not possess its separate normative content, distinct from what they supply. Since it is not co-equal with them, legitimacy should not be set against any one in particular, as this implies a false opposition. At any one moment in time, legitimacy draws more strongly upon one norm than another, but it is never in opposition to the remainder. When this is claimed, it is usually a means to creating a new normative equilibrium. Indeed, it can confidently be suggested that it is the legitimacy discourse that is itself instrumental in contributing to the shifting content of these other norms, as well as to their periodic realignments. The struggle to achieve legitimation contributes to the reconfiguration of the principles of legitimacy.

Suggestions of a direct conflict between legitimacy and any one of its supporting norms should be read as a strategy of legitimization of this kind. These make appeal to a purported *constant* standard of legitimacy as a means to effecting *change* within it. The idea that legitimacy possesses its own distinctive normative content is a device to bring about a relative reordering of priorities amongst its constitutive norms. It pretends that there is a permanent normative order of things as a way of gaining endorsement for what in effect is a transient recalibration.

In part, this works on the basis of consensus. 'The creation of new norms in international politics', it is held, '. . . essentially involves a numbers game', since 'the larger the size of the coalition that subscribes to a new set of norms, principles, and institutions the greater the sense of legitimacy that is accorded to those norms' (Hampson 2002: 177–8). The situation, however, is more complex than this suggests, as it is not entirely reducible to numbers either, as this would exclude the element of normative appeal altogether. The size of a coalition behind a new norm may well be a function of the intuitive appeal of that norm, and of a sense of its rightness: it may become widely endorsed exactly because it is thought to accord with legal practice, or with standards of justice, or with the constitutional demands of international society. Equally, the formation of a coalition around a new norm is also part of a deeper political process in which norms, consensus, and power are all implicated in the outcome.

During the 1990s, for example, we witnessed an attempt to shift the norms pertaining to domestic jurisdiction and humanitarian intervention (Wheeler 2000). This 'normative evolution was stronger amongst the Western states than elsewhere', and was 'resisted by a coalition that included Russia, China and the bulk of the states of the South' (MacFarlane 2002: 60). The 'rightness' of the shift was appealed to in order to extend the scope of the consensus in its support while, at the same time, the scope of the consensus was presented by others as evidence of its inherent rightness. This attests the dynamic relationship between legitimacy, consensus, norms, and power. 'Legitimacy should also reflect human values and aspirations', opined the prominent Arab commentator, Mohamed Heikal, 'and the fact that these change with the times' (*The Times*, 12 September 1990).

Equilibrium

There is a complex circularity at work in the many depictions of the crucial relations of power and legitimacy. 'Power, order and peace grow out of legitimacy', we are told in one case, but at the same time 'this has all to be backed by force' (Cooper 2003: 150). Legitimacy is thereby deemed to be a source of power, or a type of power multiplier, while it remains ultimately dependent upon the exercise of a material form of power—force—to sustain it. Theorists, including international relations theorists, have long wrestled to make sense of this complexity. There are several facets of their deliberations that relate to this particular inquiry.

The first is whether legitimacy is to be treated as a 'unit-level' or 'system-level' phenomenon. It was on this ground that Waltz was to distance himself from Morgenthau and Kissinger: their concept of legitimacy, he believed, was ultimately reductionist. Although Kissinger had framed his argument in terms of the legitimate or revolutionary nature of the international order as such, his account depended finally, in Waltz's assessment, on 'the attitudes and the internal characteristics of states'. This became clear, he maintained, in Kissinger's characterization of a revolutionary order as one 'in which one or more of the major states refuses to deal with other states according to the conventional rules of the game'. As a result, the determinant of whether an order is legitimate or revolutionary is ultimately 'the dispositions of the states that constitute it' (Waltz 1979: 62–3). If Waltz is correct in this suggestion, then neither Morgenthau nor Kissinger can be understood to argue that legitimacy is a product of the balance of power per se, since the balance of power is an element within the structure of the international system and, as such, is a system-level characteristic, not a unit-level one. On Waltz's reading, legitimacy is deemed by both these writers to be a unit-level, not system-level, creation. Is Waltz then correct in his assessment of Morgenthau and Kissinger?

To answer this we need to open up a second issue that goes beyond the unit–system opposition, and is about the relationship between balance of power and moral consensus. As so often, Morgenthau's position is much richer than is warranted by his conventional assignment to the camp of realist power politics. Stability in international relations, in his view, is not merely the contrivance of the balance of power, but is instead the product of the reciprocal action between the balance, on the one hand, and the degree of moral consensus within international society, on the other. Morgenthau was at pains to insist upon this point. The chronic instability of periods, such as that from 1772 to 1815, and again from 1933 to 1945, was exactly located in the absence of a moral consensus, not in the balance of power as such. 'The confidence in the stability of the modern state system', he pronounced categorically, ' ... derives ... not from the balance of power, but from a number of elements, intellectual and moral in nature, upon which both the balance of power and the stability of the modern state system repose' (Morgenthau 1973: 217). He explained further: 'Before the balance of power could impose its restraints upon the power aspirations of nations through the mechanical interplay of opposing forces, the competing nations had first to restrain themselves by accepting the system of the balance of power as the common framework of their endeavours' (Morgenthau 1973: 219). In short, it was not the material balance of power alone that held things in check, but additionally the moral consensus on the *value* of the balance of power: the material balance of power could operate effectively provided only that a normative consensus in its support already existed. It was on the basis of this analysis that he felt able to frame his burning question about the post-1945 order. 'What kind of consensus unites the nations of the world in the period following the Second World War?', he reflected, and then he proffered his own telling answer: 'Upon the examination of the component elements of this consensus will depend the estimate of the role that the balance of power can be expected to play today for the freedom and stability of the community of nations' (Morgenthau 1973: 221). Evidently, the degree of shared principle must come first in the order of analysis, before we can then arrive at judgements about the capacity of the balance of power to play any effective role.

We can thus reach two pertinent conclusions about Morgenthau. First, he is convinced that legitimacy is not primarily the creation of a balance of power. Second, and *pace* Waltz, neither is it for him in any obvious sense a 'unit-level' creation, since the extent of moral consensus seems no more nor less a 'system-level' characteristic than is the distribution of power itself. It is composed of the distribution and density of particular values within international society, and it is only Waltz's narrow and prescriptive methodology that blinds him to the significance of this fact. These theoretical reflections, in turn, have a direct bearing on our assessment of the role of the United States, and of US power, in today's world (Chace 2002: 8).

What can be said in the case of Kissinger? We have already had several previous occasions to draw Kissinger into the discussion, and have encountered the opaqueness of his thought on this particular relationship. He certainly declares himself very close in spirit to Morgenthau, in so far as he likewise describes a legitimate order as one predicated upon *both* a moral and a material balance, but he is less clear on the priority between the two. Morgenthau, as we have seen, is consistent in giving precedence to the role of a moral consensus as the key underlying factor. Kissinger is more circumspect, hesitant, and downright equivocal. This is the complaint that Stanley Hoffmann registered back in the 1970s. Noting that Kissinger accepted the balance of power as a major source of restraint, he acknowledged also that, in Kissinger's scheme, 'legitimacy also requires the existence of a *principle* of legitimacy'. Hoffmann then proceeded to chastise Kissinger for imprecision as to 'whether self-restraint results merely from the constraints of the balance, or also from the acceptance of a common principle' (Hoffmann 1978: 38). This is the point that Morgenthau had specifically addressed. And yet Kissinger's writing on this same issue two decades later hardly satisfied Hoffmann's complaint. In the world of the 1990s, we were now told, we could hope for a quasi-Metternichian system 'in which a balance of power is reinforced by a shared sense of values' (Kissinger 1995: 166). However, unlike in the argument of Morgenthau, this shared sense of values did not already exist, but would have to be created. It was to be 'reinforced' *ex post facto*, rather than being in existence *ab initio*. 'It is reasonable for the United States', he continued, 'to try to buttress equilibrium with moral consensus. To be true to itself, America must try to forge the widest possible moral consensus around a global commitment to democracy'. In doing so, however, it was imperative not to 'neglect the analysis of the balance of power' (Kissinger 1995: 166).

What are we to make of all this? In so far as anything is clear, the emphasis here is evidently different from that in Morgenthau. While both are adamant that legitimate orders require a moral and material dimension, Morgenthau is much firmer in his conclusion that it is the former that makes the latter effective. Kissinger is less certain as to how the two interact. In the end, where a balance of power is not predicated on a moral consensus, the predominant state is said to have a responsibility to create such a consensus. In short, for Morgenthau, a moral consensus must exist for the balance of power to be operative. For Kissinger, an imbalance of power can be exploited to manufacture a moral consensus around the preferred value system of the leading state. This can most readily be done, and the circle seemingly squared, if it is assumed that 'American values are universal' (Rice 2000: 49). In this case, the moral consensus exists implicitly, but remains merely to be brought to full consciousness by the encouragement of the leading state. This, however, is symptomatic, in some eyes, of an emerging sense in the United States of 'moral and military superiority' (Hassner 2002: 30). There is potentially a world of difference between these two conceptions of legitimate order—one founded upon an extant moral consensus, the other on the power that can forge one—and contemporary international society can be regarded as perched precariously on these two stools, trying awkwardly to straddle the widening separation between them.

Posing the issue in these terms reinvents the original puzzle. Do contemporary stresses in international society result from the absence of a moral consensus or from the lack of any balance of power? Is US power, and the order which it sustains, durable in the absence of the former? This is the question posed by William Pfaff when he asked, as the Iraq crisis reached a head in October 2002, whether the US destiny as global hegemon would be 'well assumed and acknowledged as legitimate', as only thus could it endure in the longer term (*International Herald Tribune*, 26 October 2002: 8). Alternatively, is it the US predominance which by itself forestalls such a consensus from emerging, since it is that much harder to reach when the leading player always has the option of acting outside it. According to Watson, legitimacy in international society, since the seventeenth century, has been powerfully bound up with 'anti-hegemonial' assumptions (Watson 1992: 315). In this case, the core problem for today's international society can be conceived as the need to adjust traditionally anti-hegemonial principles to meet the new realities of this US preponderance.

Can legitimacy be refashioned in such a context? A fundamental dimension of the moral consensus must be that no one actor, however powerful, can routinely impose its will. Thus viewed, disequilibrium gets in the way of attainment of any moral consensus, as the hegemon may be too readily seduced by the attractions of imposition instead. In the words of one Chinese commentator, what is intolerable is the view that 'I'm the sole superpower, no one can restrain me' (*People's Daily*, 1 June 1999: 6). As the *Japan Times* editorialized, in order 'to remain the global leader both in name and spirit, the US needs to share common values, instead of imposing its own' (*Japan Times*, 23 July 1999). Unhappily, the temptation to resort to the latter is likely to be encouraged by the very power differentials that exist.

In these respects, US power presents itself as a possibly fundamental problem for the contemporary practice of legitimacy. On the European side, the view has been regularly expressed that 'the difficulty with the American monopoly of force in the world community is that it is American', and 'this will not be seen as legitimate' (Cooper 2003: 167). On the US side, a robust defender of US unilateralism has insisted equally that the 11 September 2001 attacks were planned at a time when the US administration 'did its utmost to subordinate American hegemony and smother unipolarity'. The reason this did not avert an orgy of violence against the United States was that the underlying resentment was fomented by 'the very structure of the international system, not by the details of our management of it' (Krauthammer 2003: 605). The first viewpoint sees exceptional US power demanding particular skills in its exercise to be tolerable to international society; the second sees the preponderance of US power making the manner of its exercise irrelevant. The conclusions differ sharply: what they share is the starting point that today's legitimacy crisis is a function of a unique constellation of power.

CONCLUSION

This chapter has set out the analytical building blocks for the unfolding discussion. In the remainder of Part II, a thematic framework is adopted to amplify this argument. Legitimacy in contemporary international society will be investigated through the medium of those principal elements. Chapter 9 will revisit the recurrent matter of rightful membership as it now manifests itself in contemporary conditions, and demonstrate that this dimension of legitimacy enjoys, if anything, an even higher profile today than in the past. The next two chapters turn instead to aspects of rightful conduct. Chapter 10 explores the issue of consensus, and what this means for contemporary society. About what matters is international consensus needed, and what can be taken as appropriate demonstrations of it? This is followed, in Chapter 11, by an analysis of the relationship between legitimacy and its cognate norms; namely, those of legality, morality, and constitutionality. How does legitimacy deal with the tensions between those other norms? Finally, Chapter 12 develops the idea that legitimacy is intimately related to power, and considers the extent to which contemporary problems affecting international legitimacy simply reflect the current distribution of power. If today's world is characterized by a radical disequilibrium, or what is commonly described as an American hegemony, what might this portend for international legitimacy?

9

Legitimacy and Rightful Membership

As already encountered, there are a number of theorists of international legitimacy who regard the core history of the subject to be concerned largely with
evolving notions about the 'moral purpose' or 'constitutional order' of the
states themselves (Reus-Smit 1999; Bobbitt 2002). From this point of view, it
might be said that what states are, or, more specifically, what international
society endorses them as being, is possibly more important than what they do,
as far as international legitimacy is concerned. Accordingly, the great revolutions in international legitimacy have mainly been related to the revolutions in
the domestic structures of states, with the most successful of these gaining
sponsorship, and further propagation, at the hands of international society
(Bukovansky 2002). In this duality, revolutions in domestic legitimacy, as
sanctioned by international society, in turn contribute to new constitutional
orders for international society as well (Bobbitt 2002: 777). How precisely do
such revolutions in rightful membership pertain to thinking about rightful
conduct? This chapter examines the contemporary 'domestic' face of legitimacy, and its implications for the kind of external behaviour that is deemed to be
acceptable to international society.

THE END OF THE COLD WAR, GOOD GOVERNANCE, AND RIGHTFUL MEMBERSHIP

Since the end of the cold war, rightful membership has been expressed, not
simply about *states*, but about certain *types* of state. Accompanying this, there
has also been the re-emergence of doctrines positing a hierarchical form of
international society, rather than one based on universality and equality. The
precise form of international society's tutelage over the composition of its
various members can itself vary. Commonly, when we speak of socialization,
we have in mind the exposure to, and the internalization of, the norms and
behavioural patterns of any particular society: members simply absorb what
they see around them. But socialization can also take more self-conscious
forms. The leading, and more successful, states set an example that may
then be purposefully emulated by others. International society, by policing its

membership, in effect holds out inducements to would-be members to conform to certain norms: the main inducement it has to offer are the benefits that derive from membership itself. Implicit in the act of deciding 'who gets to count as a member' is international society's veiled sanction of the potential consequences to 'follow from acts of deviancy' (Dunne 2001: 89). Finally, of course, international society may interfere in domestic arrangements in a more overt way. The idea of regime change from the outside, if sanctioned by international society, would obviously fall towards the coercive end of the 'socialization' spectrum.

The evidence for the promulgation of a more pronounced set of domestic legitimacy tests since the end of the cold war is overwhelming. In large measure, and in US official parlance, this became possible because the cold war issued in 'a single sustainable model for national success' (USNSC 2002). The key features of this 'model' have been variously depicted, often in terms of its calibration to the requirements of the global economy, and the resulting state has been defined, for example, as the 'market-state' (Bobbitt 2002: 228) or as the 'virtual state' (Rosecrance 2002: 449). In similar fashion, a deluge of globalization literature makes the claim that the generic state of today has been fashioned by the 'socialization' exercised upon it by the global economy (Armstrong 1998; Clark 1999). However, if not wholly separate from this aspect, the central motif of most post-cold war discussions of rightful membership has been couched in terms of conformity to democratic standards of good governance (Fierlbeck 1998: 12). These imply at least a degree of accountability, and also a minimum adherence to concepts of human rights. Such concerns were given a further stimulus by the events of the1990s. They lay at the heart of the reactions to the 'ethnic wars' of the period, and drove the international community's policies on protection of the rights of religious and ethnic minorities (Preece 1998: 11, 137). They permeated discussion of the 'new wars' of the post-cold war era by highlighting the seemingly more direct encounter between security and development: international society pronounced a decidedly instrumental view of liberal values, as the prerequisite for addressing the problems of international security (Duffield 2001: 16). More pervasively, the concern with good governance went to the heart of the increasingly clear affirmation by international society of its belief in the liberal peace, not just as academic theory, but as the basis of international policy. 'Wolfowitz, Rice, Powell and their colleagues', we have been sharply reminded, 'embrace the idea of a democratic peace' (Leffler 2003: 1055). When analysts speak of political liberalism as a 'transnational movement' that has penetrated a large number of states, this should not be understood as an incidental development (Owen 2001/2: 120–1). Principles of international legitimacy have accordingly been framed ever more explicitly such as to emphasize these concerns with good governance: this has fostered a preoccupation with domestic conditions (Foot 2003: 5).

The policy expression of this new orientation was, initially, the 'democracy promotion' programmes that flourished in the 1990s (Cox, Ikenberry, and

Inoguchi 2000; Patrick 2002). To be sure, this was no sudden or radical innovation. Political conditionality, as a test for development aid, had been part of the European Union discourse since the 1980s, and this was presented as an explicit form of promotion of democratic and human rights norms (Youngs 2001). However, the end of the cold war engendered ever greater self-confidence in the declaration of such social purposes, and gave much greater prominence to the idea of democracy promotion as an international civic duty. In 1993, the then US National Security Adviser, Anthony Lake, testified that, in US national strategy, the idea of containment had now been replaced by 'a strategy of enlargement of the world's free community of market democracies' (Patrick 2001: 120–1). This was to be accomplished by strategic interventions, on behalf of pro-democracy and pro-market forces, in the evolving domestic situations of countries like Russia. More generically, however, it took the form of the enunciation of legitimacy principles by various international financial bodies and a host of other international organizations. Typically, if without attracting much attention, there have been the sponsoring activities of bodies, such as the so-called Community of Democracies, that held meetings in 2000 and again in 2002. This was initially encouraged by the Clinton administration, but subsequently has been supported by its Republican successor as well (Hirsh 2003: 108).

These democratic ideals now lie deeply embedded in contemporary international policies on economic development, on post-conflict reconstruction and nation-building, and also explicitly in those actual admissions that have taken place, to such 'mini-international societies' as NATO and the European Union. In those cases, tests of an explicitly democratic nature have been imposed on would-be members, and this has been symptomatic of the tendencies present in international society more generally. These are demonstrated also in the Constitutive Act of African Union, the declared objective of which, in Article 3(g), is to 'promote democratic principles and institutions, popular participation and good governance'. Article 30 insists that 'Governments which shall come to power through unconstitutional means shall not be allowed to participate in the activities of the Union' (African Union 2000; Bain 2003a: 157–8). Similarly, the Inter-American Democratic Charter, adopted by the Organization of American States in 2001, roundly declared in Article 1 that 'the peoples of the Americas have a right to democracy and their governments have an obligation to promote and defend it'. Its Articles 19 and 20 allowed for suspension in any case where 'there has been an unconstitutional interruption of the democratic order of a member state' (Organization of American States 2001).

At the same time that international society exercises its rights over inclusion, the corollary has been a more visible trend towards exclusion. During the 1970s and 1980s, it was common enough to hear international condemnation of the so-called pariah states, but these were unsystematic instances, such as Israel and South Africa, that had been ostracized by parts of the international community. Since the end of the cold war, the specification of separate *categories* of 'failed', 'outlaw', and 'rogue' states has been developed much more purposefully (Chomsky 2000; Litwak, *Washington Post*, 20 February 2000: B3; Litwak 2000). Its full import has been to designate a group of countries that either do not belong within international society at all, or, if they do, exist within it on conditional terms and with less than full rights of membership (Simpson 2004). 'States that are viewed as being hostile to the partnership underlying the society of states', it has been noted, 'are typically deprecated as rogue states', and, as such, as 'little more than international outlaws' (Bain 2003*b*: 73). Such status carries with it two distinctive sets of implications. The first is that these countries may be treated in a manner different from full members. In other words, the rules of engagement with such countries differ from those applying to the 'insiders' of civilized international society. Thus Iraq was designated as one of the rogue states that 'were stripped of their internationally recognized sovereign rights, which otherwise should have protected them from attack' (Barber 2003: 106). Since then, some commentators have advanced a 'duty', on the part of the international community, to take preventive action against WMD on the part of those states 'run by rulers without internal checks on their power' (Feinstein and Slaughter 2004). Secondly, the designation gives expression to a putative entitlement on the part of international society to normalize its relationship with these states in some way. Where an existing democratic regime has been unconstitutionally overthrown, international society—acting through sundry regional organizations—now asserts an entitlement to act to restore the democratic order. *In extremis*, this has amounted additionally to an attempt to elaborate a right of international society to bring about regime change in those states that do not qualify for full membership as presently configured. Any such entitlement is far from being recognized by the majority of states at the moment, but it has been implicitly, and increasingly, appealed to by a powerful group of leading states.

The focus on rogue states in US policy sharpened during the 1990s. Interestingly, it has been pointed out that the criteria then elaborated to classify a rogue state had nothing to do with domestic political conditions, but were wholly related to external behaviour: pursuit of weapons of mass destruction; use of international terrorism as state policy; representing a threat to key US regional interests (Litwak 2000: 49). If anything, this reflected a tension between the Wilsonian thrust of the Clinton administration in the promotion of democracy, and its insistence that rogue states were states that simply behaved badly (Litwak 2000: 62). Nonetheless, even at that time, National Security Adviser Lake (1994), in a much-noted piece, had drawn attention to the shared domestic political characteristics of such states, and believed that it was these characteristics that gave rise to the bad conduct. By the end of the decade, and then under the successor administration of George W. Bush, the motif of the domestic sources of rogue behaviour had become paramount, issuing in an 'aggressive push to bring freedom and democracy to countries where evil lurks' (Ikenberry 2004: 7).

As noted, these formulations can be regarded as a self-conscious attempt to create a tiered or hierarchical international society, constituted by a core and a periphery, or more loosely by insiders and outsiders. The strategy of the leading states has been to secure widespread support for concepts of legitimacy that would specify civilized international behaviour, and thereby outlaw those states that fall short of the requisite standards. The bestowal of legitimacy, in this sense of rightful membership, thus becomes an integral part of the ongoing international political process. One characterization of the policies of President George W. Bush remarks that 'a core of like-minded, democratic, free-market-orientated nations is building norms and rules to govern their own behaviour as well as imposing those rules on, and trying to bring into their own number, the still developing or still-unfree "peripheral" states'. In this endeavour, the core dispenses with state sovereignty when it 'is enforcing one of its rules on the periphery' (Mazarr 2003: 507). This form of proactive state socialization can be witnessed through the current practices of peacebuilding in post-conflict societies. In these, we are told, is exemplified the 'core continuing to define the standards of acceptable behaviour, and international peacebuilding agencies serving as "transmission belts" that convey these standards to the periphery' (Paris 2002: 653).

Beyond these specific policies, the relationship is demonstrated above all in the practices of inclusion and exclusion which the very issue of membership brings to the fore. The matter of who counts for full membership, and who does not, represents itself a powerful stick and carrot of international politics, and has become increasingly so in the post-cold war situation (Schroeder 1995: 375). The carrot, as former President Jimmy Carter expressed it, was that leaders of states that did not otherwise conform to international norms could be offered 'the promise of reward—at least legitimacy within the international community' (*New York Times*, 27 May 1999: 33), to induce compliant behaviour. It is precisely in these terms of inclusion and exclusion that various parties have understood the underlying structures of international politics. Nowhere is this more so than in the case of the Palestinians, and, as one report was to put it, their 'hunger for international legitimacy'. Legitimacy, for the Palestinians, makes itself felt above all as an issue of membership and belonging—who is inside and who is outside. This emerges clearly in one reported interview with Radwan Abu Ayyash, chairman of the Palestine Journalists Association in Jerusalem. Asked to condemn the Iraqi occupation of Kuwait in 1990, he responded in these terms: 'But the Americans, by cutting the dialogue, pushed us outside the circle of international legitimacy. We are outside international legitimacy. How come everybody is asking us to take a position which fits the international legitimacy we are denied?' (*Jerusalem Post*, 24 August 1990: 11). A very powerful demonstration of this relationship is provided by the announcements in December 2003 that Libya had abandoned its quest for weapons of mass destruction. In a telling comment, Prime Minister Tony Blair remarked in a broadcast statement that 'Libya's actions entitle it to rejoin the international community' (CNN, 20 December 2003). It was not just that Libya's policy reversal should be welcomed, but this served as the reason for its readmission to membership of international society. The British Prime Minister has had frequent recourse to this telling idiom. With regard to Iraq, he again made clear that his quarrel was with the regime, not the Iraqi people, and he looked forward to 'welcoming a liberated Iraq to the international community of nations' (Blair 2002*b*: 2–3; 2003*c*: 3)

For much of the Clinton period, the international policy towards rogue states was one of containment, but coexistence. By the late 1990s, however, this had hardened into one of potential regime change. It was a policy prescription by no means confined to policymakers in the United States, as the various phases of the Yugoslav war were to make abundantly clear. During 1995, the Bosnian Serbs held several hundred UN hostages, and this was naturally protested by the Russian UN spokesman in Sarajevo, Aleksandr Ivanko. He condemned the hostage-taking in terms that evoked the need of those who would belong to international society to respect its codes. 'The Bosnian Serb leadership continues to seek international legitimacy, international recognition', he admonished, 'and at the same time declaring void international law and civilised rules of behaviour' (*The Times*, 31 May 1995). The issue was clearly one of rightful membership, and due responsibility of action to warrant entitlement to it. Even more explicitly was the link to regime change made during the Kosovo war, in this case by the French Foreign Minister, Hubert Védrine. Asked if Kosovo could be saved without taking the war to the regime in Belgrade, he replied candidly: 'We have to pursue our objectives one at a time. Our general goal, shared by all the Western countries, including the Russians, I believe, is to see ex-Yugoslavia come into line with European norms and become democratic. That means a change of regime in Serbia. But that long-term objective is different from the air strikes' purpose, which is to break the military strength that the regime is using for repression' (*International Herald Tribune*, 20 April 1999: 5).

Historically, international society has indeed sanctioned various regime changes, but commonly does so at the end of periods of war, and with the intention of thus shoring up the future peace. It did so in the case of France in 1815, and again in the cases of Germany and Japan in 1945. More recently, however, the policy of regime change, notoriously, became central to the prosecution of the war against Iraq in 2003. This revealed how far things had moved from the eruption of the first crisis over Iraq and Kuwait in 1990. At that time, the US ambassador in Baghdad, April Glaspie, was famously forced into making a humiliating retraction to Iraq's Deputy Prime Minister, Tariq Aziz, at the behest of US Secretary of State James Baker. 'It is absolutely not United States policy', she wrote, 'to question the legitimacy of the Government of Iraq nor to interfere in any way in the domestic concerns of the Iraqi people and Government' (*New York Times*, 10 September 1990: A23). Such diffidence had certainly evaporated a decade later, and the matter of potential regime changes had become a prominent part of the US foreign policy debate prior to the election in 2000. In one much-reported commentary, two analysts enjoined the United States to deal with rogue states not by 'coexistence but transformation'. It described as 'eminently realistic' a policy of 'America using its power to promote changes of regime in nations ruled by dictators' (Kagan and Kristol 2000: 66). Interestingly, at the same time, the future under-secretary for defense, Paul Wolfowitz, struck a much more circumspect note, certainly much at odds with the policy actually to be pursued against Iraq in 2003. Wolfowitz cautioned about the 'limitations of US leverage' in bringing about democratic change in regimes. Moreover, he pointedly dismissed the post-1945 examples of Japan and Germany, as they did not 'offer a model that applies in other circumstances' (Wolfowitz 2000: 39–40). These reservations appeared no longer to be heeded when the war came. At least in the case of Iraq, Washington lost whatever inhibitions it might previously have had about the limited prospects for successful regime change. What is important for the present discussion, however, is the possibility of such changes being sanctioned by international society, as the logical extension of the illegitimacy that certain regimes are purported to enjoy. Those that do not qualify for rightful membership do not qualify either for the protection that international society normally accords its members, above all through its principles of sovereignty and self-determination.

Retrospectively, key leaders have denied that changing the Iraqi regime was the motive for war in 2003. Prime Minister Tony Blair is adamant that 'however abhorrent and foul the regime . . . regime change alone could not be and was not our justification for war' (Blair 2004: 2). At the same time, he made indirect appeal to his doctrine of international community for implicit additional endorsement for the actions taken. 'It may well be that under international law as presently constituted', he reflected, 'a regime can systematically brutalise and oppress its people, and there is nothing anyone can do'. He conceded that 'this may be the law', but then went on to query whether 'it should be' (Blair 2004: 4).

In the context of a discussion of international legitimacy, such developments are best understood as a counter-revolutionary strategy, and it seems clear that a number of states have enjoined international society to adopt such a stance. The revolutionary state, in Kissinger's terms, is one that violates international society's legitimacy criteria, as regards both its domestic constitution and its international conduct. Kissinger, of course, was interested only in revolutionary great powers, and the threat that they posed to the remainder of international society. His preference, on the Vienna model, was for such great powers to be co-opted back into the system. Instead, in contemporary international society, the concern has been with revolutionary small powers. Rogue states, in the present conception, are 'relatively marginalized states', that pose a threat to their immediate region, not to the wider system as a whole, however much this might be complicated by their possession of weapons of mass destruction (Litwak 2000: 47). This offers the prospect of an alternative counter-revolutionary strategy. There are fewer dangers in keeping them on the outside, and hence legitimacy has been used purposefully as an instrument for excluding, effectively if not in a formal diplomatic sense, some states from the full embrace of international society. In the exceptional case, as in Iraq, rightful membership has been deployed as the rationale to vindicate a change in the target state's regime: either the regime precludes admission to international society, or international society can proactively admit it on its own terms by effecting its own change of regime. Given the intense conflict over the Iraq war, however, it is certainly far from the case that such a strategy has found widespread adherence at present.

THE REINVENTION OF A RESTRICTIVE INTERNATIONAL SOCIETY

After a generation during which the formal rationale of international society was one of equality and universality, it now appears that contemporary international society has reverted to a more limited, or at least unequal, membership: either some states are potentially excluded, or, if they belong at all, they belong on qualitatively different terms from the rest. If we all remain 'insiders' of today's international society, then this is at the expense of its becoming a society 'of mixed character and uneven depth'. It may have become more solidarist, but only in parts (Jackson 2000: 13, 127). What were formerly *external* differences between groups of states—those inside and those outside—have now been *internalized*: all are members of international society, but not equally so. Either way, the differences still remain. In Keene's terms, the task is now to pursue the goal of 'civilization', not 'toleration', even amongst the insiders (Keene 2002).

This can most readily be seen in the designation of some states as 'failed', and in the proposed remedial action to be taken on their behalf. Underlying these developments is the rediscovery of the former concept of trusteeship, something that had been expurgated from the litany of international society during the period of decolonization. The reintroduction of this concept marks a hugely significant development within international society. 'If trusteeship is once again to be recognized as a legitimate practice of international society', writes the principal recent historian of this idea, 'then we must rethink how we theorize something called "international society" ' (Bain 2003*b*: 69). At the very least, it seems to mark the end of the inclusive arrangement in which there 'are no barbarians, savages, infidels, or pagans standing outside' (Bain 2003*b*: 71). This rediscovery is driven in part by security concerns which, as the US National Security Strategy of September 2002 expressed it, mean that 'America is now threatened less by conquering states than we are by failing ones'

(USNSC 2002). It is driven also by the revival of a civilizing mission, as part of international society's role as trustee. This reveals itself in the UN peace-building operations conducted in the aftermath of recent wars and civil strife. Missions, such as those of the UN in East Timor and Kosovo, have far out-stripped previous forms of international administration in the level of authority invested in them. Kosovo has been described by Strobe Talbott as a 'ward of the international community' (Bain 2003*b*: 69), and by others as a 'protectorate' in which 'actual sovereignty is exercised by a UN viceroy' (Ignatieff 2003: 71). In the case of Timor, 'UNTAET effectively constitutes the legal sovereign' (Caplan 2002: 16). In these cases, the sovereign acts, not just to bring order and effective administration to these war-torn societies, but to import into them one inter-nationally approved type of political order. They are the instruments of inter-national society in seeking to reproduce its own standards of rightful membership. In one radical appraisal of this situation, 'soldiers and humani-tarians are troubleshooters for an international society structured to sustain inequality and denial of human needs' (Pugh 2002: 228). The same general point is made, if more moderately, elsewhere:

One way of thinking about the actions of peacebuilders is to conceive of liberal market democracy as an internationally sanctioned model of 'legitimate' domestic governance. Peace-builders promote this model in the domestic affairs of war shattered states as the prevailing 'standard of civilization' that states must accept in order to gain full rights and recognition in the international community. (Paris 2002: 650)

These tendencies in contemporary international society highlight a concept of legitimacy, as rightful membership, that emphasizes the duty of international society to instil certain standards of domestic political order. The other side of the coin, and the other instrument of international socialization, is the encouragement of a right on the part of all peoples to a democratic system of government. In these terms, international society acts merely as the instru-ment on behalf of the prior rights of all people to be represented in such a political system. At the fringes of international legal theory, such a notion has now become accepted, if remaining contested elsewhere. Its most vocal expo-nent is Franck. 'Both textually and in practice', he contends, 'the international system is moving towards a clearly defined democratic entitlement, with na-tional governance validated by international standards and systematic moni-toring of compliance' (Franck 1995: 139). To the extent that this doctrine comes to be realized, it would be the strongest possible affirmation yet of contemporary international society's adherence to a concept of legitimacy as entailing its right to specify particular qualifications for full membership. Although couched in terms of the rights of peoples to democratic government, its secondary dimension is the duty of international society to monitor this development, and to impose its attainment as a qualification for membership. This is potentially a very powerful instrument of international compliance. In one judgement, such 'an emergent right, if established' would 'augur a major transformation of the ground rules of the international system' (Fox and Roth 2001: 335).

However, one final link in this chain remains to be established. This criterion of the democratic entitlement, as a test for fit membership of international society, is not to be understood merely as an end in itself, but also as a means to a wider social purpose. In the same way that the great Wilsonian mission was to democratize the world in the greater cause of peace, rightful membership is being deployed by international society today with the same ostensible purpose. It is not peoples alone who enjoy their separate national rights to democratic governance, but international society itself claims a collective right to ensure such national democracy, by dint of its entitlement to enjoy international peace. Franck provides a succinct and trenchant summary of this perspective:

> ... compliance with the norms prohibiting war-making is inextricably linked to observance of human rights and the democratic entitlement. None of these basic objectives of the international community can be achieved in any lasting sense without the realization of all. This suggests that the democratic entitlement's legitimacy is increased by its hierarchic relation to the peremptory norm of global peace. (Franck 1995: 137)

If so, then rightful membership stands as the mainstay of the whole enterprise of international legitimacy at present. In this sense, it is unsurprising that so many commentators should speak of the contemporary situation as tantamount to the readoption of another standard of civilization, in succession to that of the nineteenth century. Typically, the resemblance is drawn between that earlier standard and thinking today, inasmuch as 'societies that do not honour Western liberal practices regarding governance and rights are legitimate targets of reformative international action' (MacFarlane 2002: 79).

By way of concrete example, this parallel was explicitly drawn at the time of China's prospective adhesion to the World Trade Organization (WTO). The nineteenth-century standard sought, amongst other things, to secure adequate legal protection for the conduct of commerce in countries such as China, and made the case for degrees of legal extraterritoriality towards this end, until such time as expatriate individuals and commercial enterprises could be adequately protected by local law. China's entry to the WTO was heralded as serving the same essential purpose, with the WTO in the role of custodian of the proper standards of commercial and regulatory law, and the transmission belt for 'civilized' legal standards worldwide. Just as the foreign commercial community, and the extraterritoriality that it entailed, was said to have stimulated legal reform within China a century ago, so it was now maintained the WTO could bring about the same effect today. The need to comply with WTO legal standards would lead to an overhaul, to Western standards, of the Chinese legal system. 'China's entry into the WTO', it was reported, 'is being used by some Chinese political groupings as an engine to push through necessary legal reforms' (*South China Morning Post*, 12 November 2001: 12). More generally, trade analysts insisted that this was indeed a fundamental purpose of the WTO—to implant acceptable standards of legal practice worldwide. Commentators urged that the Doha round of trade talks provided an opportunity 'for the WTO to build a worldwide consensus on strengthening core principles of legal conduct' (*Financial Times*, 17 February 2003: 13). Any existing deficiencies lay, not in the WTO apparatus itself, but in the failure of national members to implement sound and transparent legal practice. The task of the WTO was, accordingly, to promote acceptable standards of behaviour globally, so fitting members of the world trading community to meet their international social responsibilities. This logic of rightful membership within the commercial sphere thus replicated exactly that found elsewhere, in other civic and security dimensions of international society. By this logic, the WTO would serve as the handmaiden of the standard of civilization, just as trade and commerce were understood to have done in that earlier period. And in the event that member states 'failed' to meet these standards, the logic entailed also that they could not enjoy full membership, but must instead be subject to international tutelage and potentially to new forms of extraterritoriality.

There remain, however, conflicting understandings of how the contemporary notion of rightful membership relates to that earlier standard of civilization. Donnelly presents this relationship in the more positive light. He understands the contemporary version of the standard to be linked intimately to the cause of human rights, and is broadly supportive of this development. The source of his hope is that 'human rights have become a (small) part of the post-cold war calculus of political legitimacy', and, as such, 'unlike the classic standard...they link national and international legitimacy to an inclusive, positive model of civilized behaviour' (Donnelly 1998: 20). In contrast, Jackson has been much more wary in his assessment, reflecting no doubt his own preference for a pluralistic international society. Commenting upon the particular conception underpinning the theory of international community adumbrated by Prime Minister Tony Blair, Jackson drew the parallel between this and the earlier standard in a more negative way. For him, the parallel was to be found in the extent to which the Blairite concept is 'pre-liberal'. 'It is really a doctrine of Western international community', Jackson objects, and it is in this regrettable sense that 'it is clearly recognizable as the descendant of the old European "standard of civilization"' (Jackson 2000: 359). Whether for better (as Donnelly sees it), of for worse (in Jackson's estimation), the connection with that earlier standard is repeatedly made, and is so because contemporary practices of international legitimacy place the matter of membership, and of living up to acceptable international standards, so very much to the forefront. These practices clearly imply a more restrictive concept of international society, or at least of variable rights and entitlements within it. It remains to be considered how this emphasis upon rightful membership impacts upon other aspects of international legitimacy, such as the traditional commitment to some kind of consensus within international society.

LEGITIMACY, DEMOCRACY, AND INTERNATIONAL CONSENSUS

Such a prominent insistence upon good governance as the essential qualification for membership of international society, derivative as it is from a certain understanding of human rights, brings a number of problems in its wake. Not the least is how international society is to reconcile this requirement with other contending sources of legitimacy. In this section, three aspects of this dilemma will be explored. First, how is this international endorsement and promotion of certain types of state to be reconciled with other 'internal' sources of state legitimation? Second, as a matter of international practice, how does the notion that legitimacy is what international society sanctions fit with the seemingly competing idea that legitimacy expresses itself through norms of democracy, and hence through the wishes of the 'sovereign people'? This implies a contradiction between international society's endorsement of democratic statehood, and its own modus operandi. Third, how might the normative pull towards democracy square with the notion of the desirability of securing a broadly based international consensus, itself blind to any requirement of democracy in the composition of the consensus constituency? These three problems are profoundly interconnected with each other, and reflect some of the principal tensions within contemporary international society's efforts to reconcile its domestic with its international aspect of legitimacy.

It is in international society's quest to establish criteria for rightful membership, and hence to intrude into the 'self-determination' of the individual member states, that the potential for a clash with other sources of state legitimacy is greatest. It is for this reason that international society has, historically, tended to express itself in a pluralistic form, if by no means strictly so. However, it is clear that now, as far as domestic good governance and the democratic entitlement are concerned, international society remains far from indifferent to the internal composition of states. For this reason, there is a much sharper confrontation today between domestic legitimacy norms, and international social norms, than in any preceding period.

The idea of state socialization at the contemporary period encapsulates many of the tensions marked more generically by complaints about globalization, Westernization, or Americanization. It is the state system itself that is deemed guilty of reproducing the secular nation-state in surroundings in which it enjoys no local legitimacy. Ideas of 'national self-determination', secularism, and individual human rights all have the potential to clash with other local or universal sources of legitimacy. Typically, much of the Arab world—but by no means it alone—has been unsettled by an emergent Islam regarded by many adherents as the only source of legitimacy for its society and political regimes (*Al-Ahram Weekly*, 486, 15–21 June 2000). The state, in this context, risks becoming disembedded from local social context and can be seen, by those disenchanted with it, as part of a more general problem of external imposition. This may be tolerable in some benign circumstances, such as conditions of rapid economic growth, when regimes continue to enjoy a residual 'performance-based' legitimacy (*International Herald Tribune*, 26 April 1999: 8), but it leaves them highly vulnerable to economic downturn, such as in the East Asian financial crisis at the end of the twentieth century.

Second, and as a matter of international practice, there is a wide potential gulf between the express will of the sovereign people, as postulated in democratic theory and as endorsed by international society also, and the notion of legitimacy as having its source in expressions by international society of its 'opinion'—however far removed that opinion might be from any basis in democratic will. From the point of view of the sceptics, international society's theory of rightful membership is sharply at odds with its own international practice. The scope for dissent within international society on this score grew substantially during the 1990s, precisely in proportion to the higher profile that international society itself was giving to democratic credentials. These disagreements came to a head over such issues as NATO's military campaign over Kosovo in 1999, and again in the war against Iraq in 2003. 'The priorities', Will Hutton was to comment of the Iraqi situation, 'must be legitimacy, legitimacy and legitimacy' (*Observer*, 24 August 2003: 29).

But which concept of legitimacy was to be brought to bear? One of the most striking features of the Iraq war was not just the quest to acquire legitimacy for certain policies and courses of action, but the struggle to find acceptance for a more foundational account of what could provide such legitimacy in the first place. In the course of this political process, appeal was made self-consciously to quite different founts of legitimacy. In the present context, two versions only of the argument need be considered (others will be discussed in subsequent chapters), one appealing to domestic democratic credentials, and the other to a commitment to international consensus.

The domestic argument, widespread in the United States, has it that the only proper source of legitimacy is the democratic sanction of the people themselves: legitimacy has its source in the domestic polity, not in the abstractions of the international community. Senator Jesse Helms had persistently articulated this point of view, well ahead of the Iraq events. 'No UN institution', he insisted, '...is competent to judge the foreign policy and national security decisions of the United States...There is only one source of legitimacy of the US government's policies—and that is the consent of the American people' (Helms 2000/2001: 33). In similar vein, Condoleezza Rice, before becoming George W. Bush's National Security Advisor, had already dismissed the notion that 'the support of many states—or even better of institutions like the United Nations—is essential to the legitimate exercise of power' (Rice 2000: 47). Perhaps most bluntly of all, John Bolton, US under-secretary for arms control and international security, addressed an audience from the Federalist Society with these words: 'Our actions, taken consistently with Constitutional principles, require no separate, external validation to make them legitimate' (Bolton 2003: 4). With US policymakers starting from this premise, no one should have been in the least surprised at the actual conduct of US diplomacy over Iraq.

In sharp contrast to this viewpoint is the multiplicity of claims that international legitimacy, if it is to mean anything at all, must be detached from such a national perspective. Legitimacy, in this alternative account, is a property of international society, not of its individual members: it is bestowed by international approval, not asserted as of democratic right. In some sense, it must be an expression of an acceptable consensus within that society (however much debate there might still be about the appropriate forum for the expression of that consensus). Much of the discussion of the Iraq war was conducted in these terms, as will later be reviewed in detail, and the focus tended to be upon the Security Council as the only acceptable expression, however imperfect, of the views of international society. Unsurprisingly, UN Secretary-General Kofi Annan opined that the Security Council was the only body 'that can provide the unique legitimacy that one needs to act' over Iraq (BBC, 11 September 2002).

These two concepts are wholly at odds with each other. The one postulates legitimacy as a product of 'domestic' political values; the other sees it as something conferred by international norms and decisions. In the former, international institutions derive their legitimacy from the democratic credentials of the individual states; in the latter, the actions of individual states derive their legitimacy from international society. It is on this basis that some commentators regarded Washington's policies over Iraq, and other matters in the early 2000s, as tantamount to an opting out of international society, or as portending the demise of international society altogether (T. Dunne 2003). In a nutshell, the problem is why the democratic will of a sovereign people should be subject to veto by any unaccountable and undemocratic international society.

Third, the logical extension of this position is that—pending the creation of an international society composed wholly of democratic states—the pertinent international society should be considered to be, not the totality of states, but rather the more restricted grouping of democratic states within it. 'In our day', it is noted, '... democratically legitimated states have shown a growing ... tendency to restrict some forms of international discourses and co-operation to their own circle' (Sadeniemi 1995: 227–8). These arguments emerged also during the Iraq war, as they already had over Kosovo: democratic consensus was deemed in some quarters to be more important than general international consensus, and this could serve also as the basis for a possible reinvention of international society. The idea that a foreign policy action can be legitimated by 'international' support was to be denigrated precisely on the grounds that such a procedure lacked any democratic credibility. Columnist Charles Krauthammer played this card to considerable rhetorical effect by demanding to know what legitimacy would have been conferred on the war in Iraq if supported by France, Russia, and China, since 'China's leaders are the butchers of Tiananmen Square' (*Daily Camera*, 4 October 2002). Senator Helms had similarly dismissed the authority of the UN on grounds of its being populated by dictatorial tyrants. In these arguments, domestic democratic legitimacy was advanced as the reason why national policy should remain internationally unaccountable. In so doing, it directly attacked the very notion that any special legitimacy attached to expressions of international approval, or disapproval, in general.

Going beyond this, the same logic has been appealed to in support of a project for constructing an alternative and more congenial—if also more restricted—international society. This concedes some legitimacy to a constituency of democratic states, but not to international society indiscriminately. As the Iraq issue came to a head in March 2003, President Bush's press secretary, Ari Fleischer, warned that 'there are many ways to form international coalitions', and 'the United Nations Security Council is but one of them' (*New York Times*, 11 March 2003: A1). What this implied was that military action might enjoy legitimacy, if supported by a democratic coalition of the willing, regardless of whether or not it had been authorized by the Security Council alone. While the justifications of the war did not (initially) have the same humanitarian overtones as had those of Kosovo in 1999, there was a similar logic to the contention made then that a consensus within democratic NATO trumped whatever view the Security Council might express. Over Kosovo, as Brown attests, it was possible to see the 'coalition as the agent of a new conception of international society based on a substantial understanding of the requirements of humanitarianism' (Brown 2001: 97). Implicitly, the suggestion here was that humanitarian purposes counted for more than a general consensus expressed through the Security Council. As part of the build-up to the war on Iraq, the argument was somewhat different: it appealed not so much to humanitarianism, as to the authority of an international society of democratic states, whatever international society as a whole might think. In this respect, the argument was that international society speaks with several voices, and we should listen more attentively to the voice that speaks with a democratic accent. As an editorial in the *Jerusalem Post* (4 October 2002: 6A) put it, 'votes among dictators cannot be treated as the pinnacle of international legitimacy', but instead 'the democracies must band together to reflect their true power and legitimacy'. What we are witnessing in these statements is not so much the abandonment of international society per se. Instead, this amounts to an attempted invention of a more restricted international society to take the place of the universal one. Rice had expressed sentiments fully consonant with such a suggestion. In dismissing the 'illusory international community', she had expressed her own preference for the US to work 'in concert with those who share its core values' (Rice 2000: 62). The corollary of international society's expressed preference for good governance in the domestic constitution of its members, on this logic, was that this section of international society possessed a greater entitlement to speak on behalf of the whole. This was the full force of the New Wilsonianism in American thinking: it coupled the traditional Wilsonian agenda of promoting a wide democratic community internationally with the less internationalist objective of stipulating the limits that were to be imposed on international society's freedom to speak for itself (Pfaff 2001: 221). The problem with such a doctrine, when applied in the Iraq war of 2003 was, of course, that the democratic international society was to be just as divided as was its broader counterpart, and this is why the failure of the United States and United Kingdom to achieve endorsement from the democratic community for their action in Iraq was to prove so damaging (Kagan 2004: 85).

CONCLUSION

Recent tendencies in international society's development of that aspect of international legitimacy that deals with rightful membership point towards two starkly different conclusions. On the one hand, they invite the judgement that, more so than at any earlier historical period, the two dimensions of legitimacy—the domestic and the international—have been brought into intimate relationship with each other. To the extent that international society has become 'thicker', and more solidarist, in recent decades, the most powerful expression of such tendencies has been in the greater rhetorical commitment, within a broadly based section of international society, to the credentials of good governance.

As noted, this reflects the ideals of democratic self-determination, and of the promotion of human rights, that have been such important bedrocks of post-1945 international society as a whole. The commitment to these ideals was expressed with even greater resolution in the more auspicious geopolitical circumstances that emerged after the end of the cold war. However, these were never visualized as ends in themselves, whatever their inherent importance. They were originally seen, and have more recently been affirmed, as means to the wider international purpose of securing order and peace. The logic that has united these two ambitions is the assumed intimate connection between adherence to domestic legitimacy precepts and legitimate international conduct. The overarching theory that makes sense of both is that it is only in the former that there can be any proper guarantee of the latter. In a nutshell, this is the all-embracing legitimacy theory to which international society has increasingly, if intermittently, subscribed over the past century. It has reached an important culmination point at the end of the twentieth century, and in the early years of the twenty-first.

On the other hand, such a conception has given rise to its own contradictions. Above all, this has brought to the fore the tension between international society's own commitment to a certain form of state, as appropriate for membership, and the seemingly divergent basis of its own pragmatic and pluralistic activities. In a word, how can international society profess faith in an increasingly solidarist view of rightful membership, while simultaneously adhering to pluralist procedures on the matter of how state action is to be approved or disapproved? On the former front, the explicit doctrine of international society privileges the emergence of individual states capable of good governance, and committed to democratic accountability and responsibility. Only in this way can international order be guaranteed. On the latter front, however, it has traditionally operated on the pragmatic basis of a search for consensus that was blind to the constitutional make-up of the individual states that were called upon to participate within it. In this sense, the substantive content of the current criteria for rightful membership now present a challenge to the procedural norms of legitimacy as hitherto understood within international society. The tension alluded to above between democracy and international society, as well as the putative quest to reinvent international society on a more selective democratic basis, is a clear expression of this difficulty. It points to a contradiction between international society's preference for democracy as the constitutive form of the state, and its own inability to operate on that basis in matters of international action.

As a result, rightful membership and rightful conduct have fallen increasingly out of alignment, the greater has been the attempt to integrate them. There are now serious tensions between those two parameters of legitimacy. The explanation is the rapid development of legitimacy as rightful membership in a purportedly solidarist direction, at a time when legitimacy as rightful conduct has lagged behind, and remains firmly rooted in pluralist processes. To resolve the tension, the procedures of rightful conduct would need also to take on a more solidarist hue, and that is precisely what underlies the recent attempts to reinvent international society. The notion that the voice of international society can best be expressed through its democratic members is an attempt to square this particular circle.

In order to trace this further, we must now move on to the various dimensions of the international face of legitimacy. In the first instance, we need to consider the means for finding an adequate expression of international consensus. This chapter has highlighted the tension between a preferred democratic model for the states internally, and the procedural requirement that they operate on the basis of consensus in their international relationships. What, more generally, is the present status of international society's thinking about the nature of this consensus, and how does this relate to matters of international legitimacy?

10

Legitimacy and Consensus

It is abundantly clear that, as a matter of state practice, legitimacy has historically been viewed as implying a measure of social consensus. Consensus
touches upon legitimacy in both the substantive and the procedural senses, in
that there may be a requirement for consensus around the substance of normative principles, and separately a consensus about how they are to be implemented, or actions authorized in their name. In other words, while consensus may
be a historical constant, *how* it has been put into practice has demonstrated
considerable historical variation. Moreover, while legitimacy and consensus
can be taken to be intimately connected, they are not identical. If they were,
legitimacy would be simply whatever the relevant constituency of states agreed
it to be. To suggest this would be to disregard wholly the constraints of other
social norms, as will be discussed in Chapter 11. While legitimacy clearly
subsumes a measure of social consensus, consensus by itself is not sufficient
for legitimacy to pertain. Evidently, there is something more to legitimacy than
consensus alone. It is in the very closeness of the two ideas, but also in the slight
separation between them, that the complexities of this relationship are to be
found. It is the task of this chapter to explore that specific relationship in the
circumstances of contemporary international society.

THE NATURE OF CONSENSUS

So what is the nature of consensus? At the most basic level, we can safely
presume that 'consensus is a matter of agreement' (Rescher 1993: 5). Others
stress that it connotes the 'voluntaristic' nature of social organization (Partridge
1971: 78). Others yet again feel that 'political consensus refers . . . to agreement
. . . on the ends and means of political organization and activity' (Willhoite
1963: 295). So 'agreement' is the common denominator, but more problemat-
ically some would add that the agreement is 'voluntaristic', and encompasses
both 'ends and means'. How does consensus manifest itself within international
society, and what significance attaches to such manifestations?

   Is consensus something that is already extant and immanent within society,
or something that needs to be created? Does it need to be teased *out*, or does it

need to be worked *in*? If we start with the first conception, it might be thought that the achievement of consensus amounts largely to the working out of philosophical aphorisms to capture those values that already inhere within international society. The task is simply that of bringing international society around to the practical consequences of the principles upon which it is already agreed. From this point of view, the international political process is tantamount to a seminar in which truth will eventually out, and become the foundation of international policy. However, if we start with the second formulation, we assume instead that consensus is a project of political construction, not of philosophical discovery. The project is to create something that did not hitherto exist, and its basis may be found in other things than truth alone. Indeed, legitimacy resides exactly in this acceptance of a social responsibility to strive for such a consensus. It is reported, for instance, of the Westphalia proceedings that 'an adequate consensus agenda was lacking', but that 'one did emerge to some extent as a result of the negotiations' (Osiander 1994: 21). Such an outcome might best be regarded as a measure of success, not of failure. International legitimacy is less about expressing a consensus already present, than it is about accepting the obligation to produce a consensus where none might otherwise have seemed possible. We have already encountered such a notion, as part of the original design for the P5 veto, in the drafting of the UN Charter. The right of the permanent members to exercise a veto, so it was thought, was less important than their responsibility to achieve a consensus to avoid its use.

There are evidently a number of quite different ways in which a consensus might be formed, and each implies a different relationship to legitimacy. What does a consensus signify? It might, for instance, be taken to indicate a correspondence with truth. For that to pertain, the consensus needs to have been arrived at in a particular way. 'What matters for rationality is not *that* people accept something in common', we are reminded, 'but *how* they came to do so' (Rescher 1993: 56). If the appropriate standard is the rational quest for truth, then a consensus will have validity in so far as it has been reached in this way, and may be considered to embody an enlightened assessment of the situation. 'It is never *just* consensus we want but the *right sort* of consensus' (Rescher 1993: 15–16), runs one version of this argument.

In actuality, we know only too well that international consensus is promoted by means that often have little to do with such rationality. Consensus can be encouraged, and thwarted, by a range of power-political, self-interested, and coercive means. Non-permanent members of the Security Council may be offered tangible inducements to subscribe to a particular position, and to cast their votes in a particular way. Permanent members may, from time to time, seek to bandwagon with the most powerful. In any case, all states are assumed to vote in international organizations in support of their own interests. During the diplomatic manoeuvrings in the Security Council ahead of the war against Iraq in 2003, it was often remarked, as Richard Perle suggested, that the P5 'are not a judicial body. They're not expected to make moral or legal judgements, but to advance the respective interests of their countries'. The thought that lurked behind these remarks was Perle's underlying question: 'So how much legitimacy attaches to a French veto?' (*Observer*, 23 February 2003: 4). But the question could just as equally be turned around. Had there been a consensus amongst the members of the Security Council on that occasion, such as to authorize the use of armed force against Iraq, what would have been the moral force of that approval, if it amounted to no more than a coincidence of self-interests? In this case, legitimacy cannot be imagined to inhere in any putative 'truth correspondence', if the process of consensus formation is critically vulnerable to the vagaries and vicissitudes of self-interest. The legitimacy of the consensus, on this reading, must depend, instead, on factors that are separate from the process by which it comes into being.

These reflections return us once again to contemplation of the central issue of what kind of validation it is that the existence of a consensus provides. The core concern is whether it is the *agreement* that is important, as a social value in its own right, or whether that agreement is thought somehow to *validate* action in some other way, by implying its soundness or conformity with other norms. At this point, we can explore three alternative answers to this question—respectively the normative, the sociological, and the political accounts of consensus.

According to the normative perspective, the importance of a consensus inheres in its being assumed to express, in some rationally determined way, an ultimate value or norm. What commands universal respect is not the fact of agreement, but its concurrence with some other deeply held societal belief(s). It is not right simply because it is agreed, but is in some prior sense right, and the agreement lends further credence to its being so. What is right, from that point of view, stands outside society itself, and is subject to evidential confirmation against some absolute standard. 'In opinion formation our duty is surely not towards a coordination with others as an independent desideratum of its own', opines one philosopher, 'but simply towards the truth' (Rescher 1993: 17).

The sociological perspective eschews such objectivist and absolutist groundings for consensus, and interprets it instead from a purely social point of view. Any claim to knowledge rests precariously upon a social consensus (Kuhn 1970), as it is such a consensus alone that can lend validity to the claim. Society, in this sense, is the ultimate custodian of its own truth claims. Accordingly, since there can be no validation from the outside, consensus is the best validation that is available. According to one account of the epistemological pragmatism of Richard Rorty, 'consensus is a *substitute* for an inherently unavailable rationality' (Rescher 1993: 15). Since we can never truly know, 'communal consensus is the most and the best that we can achieve in its place' (Rescher 1993: 14–15). In this second case, the status of consensus is quite different from the first. In the normative account, consensus is indicative of value, but not its source. Accordingly, the claim to legitimacy derives only indirectly from the consensus itself. In the sociological version, there can be no absolute values or truth claims outside the consensus and, to that extent, consensus acquires a greater normative power, as the validation of the claims made: the fact of agreement creates its own value.

The political stance is the most pragmatic of all. In this third case, consensus is to be privileged not because it is indicative of ultimate value, nor because it is constitutive of society's truth claims. Instead, and more prosaically, consensus matters because in a world in which it is in short supply, it should be pursued wherever possible. Its value, and hence its affinity to legitimacy, resides in the procedural benefit that it offers to international society, rather than in any absolute (normative), or social (sociological), grounding in truth. The question, to which we will return in Chapter 11, is whether such an instrumental view of legitimacy is fully plausible on international society's own terms, or whether the political appeal of such a deal is not itself indirectly dependent upon the reinsertion of ultimate values and standards by the back door.

LEGITIMACY, CONSENSUS, AND POST-COLD WAR INTERNATIONAL SECURITY

What kind of consensus is important to international society, or about what matters is the relevant consensus required to be? 'The consensus legitimacy requires', as Hoffmann once explained of Kissinger's account of the post-1815 period, 'is not a consensus of statesmen on the principles of domestic government, on the internal social order' (Hoffmann 1978: 39). In this version, it is evident that consensus can be effective, even if limited and selective in its purview. It need not cover the entire spectrum of potential international concerns. In this section, the focus will be upon one aspect of consensus alone—the procedural norm of how the existence of consensus is to be established, and acted upon, in matters of international security.

More specifically, it will concentrate upon the activity of the Security Council in response to three post-cold war crises: in Iraq, during 1990–1; in relation to Kosovo, in 1999; and again in Iraq, during 2002–3. Prior to the end of the cold war, it would not have been thought very plausible to consider the Security Council as the appropriate vehicle for demonstrating the consensus of international society, albeit that the UN's function of 'collective legitimization' was already deemed important even in those inauspicious circumstances (Claude 1966: 379). However, the surge of renewed confidence in UN structures that accompanied the end of the cold war meant that it once again seemed possible for international actions to be sanctioned through that body. In that context, Security Council votes and resolutions could credibly be interpreted as indicating the temper of international society as a whole, and as indicative of the presence or absence of international consensus on any particular issue. It remains to be considered whether adherence to the judgements of this body was widely considered to be just a procedural device—the best, albeit imperfect, demonstration of any consensus—or whether the authorization of the

Council was considered to carry some substantive validation as well: to be a measure of the 'rightness' of a particular course of action.

But what was the consensus to be about? It would appear, at first glance, that the legitimacy of the Security Council is a clear instance of a procedural norm: there is a widely held belief—however many qualms there are about the representative degree of the Council—that its votes and resolutions can be taken as appropriate demonstrations of the existence of any consensus or not. In this sense, the consensus is limited to support of a particular procedural device. This seems to reveal, in practice, the oft-remarked preference of international society for privileging process over substance. Indeed, political theorists have suggested that this is a tendency of complex modern political societies in general (Partridge 1971: 92; Mueller 1973: 137–8; Rescher 1993: 167). But this has always been considered to be a dominant tendency within international society in particular. As we have seen, Franck roots community notions of legitimacy in the acceptance of a 'right process as defined by a community' (Franck 1995: 26). This seems to be corroborated in the similar claim that, for international society, 'fair process matters more than substantive consensus' (Hurrell 2003: 44), and in the views of Hedley Bull, whose concern was with 'a *procedural* and not a *substantive* value consensus' (Alderson and Hurrell 2000*b*: 6).

There was certainly a widespread opinion throughout this period that the UN, and the UN alone, carried a special legitimacy as the uniquely recognized voice of international society on security matters. 'Only the Security Council can legitimize the use of force', declaimed President Chirac of France over the Iraq imbroglio in March 2003 (*Times of India*, 18 March 2003), even if that had not been his position on Kosovo. Many academic commentators agreed. Conceding that occasionally other bodies apart from the UN might act as 'validating authorities for decisions on the use of force', Roberts insisted nonetheless that these were the exceptions that proved the general rule, that 'no other body commands quite the same degree of international legitimacy' (Roberts 2003: 52; Berdal 2003: 10). This is not, of course, to suggest that its role in this regard was to go unquestioned (Slocombe 2003: 121).

That said, the perceived legitimacy of the Security Council is recognized to rest on a complex blend of factors. Its claim to be the voice of international consensus on matters of international security is rooted in the processes defined by the Charter. At the same time, the legitimacy of this procedure is itself regularly challenged on the basis of the unbalanced composition, and lack of representation, of the Security Council, and of the P5 in particular. Whatever merits this group might have collectively possessed back in 1945, its credentials for exercising the unique rights and responsibilities of permanent membership seem increasingly suspect to many critics in the new millennium (Camilleri et al. 2000: 26–7). While this representational argument has regularly pressed for an expansion in Council membership, it has also been understood that the Council's effectiveness depends upon its ability to attain consensus, and any augmentation of the P5 could complicate this task. From this point of view, 'consensual' legitimacy stands somewhat at odds with 'representational' legitimacy.

Moreover, the legitimacy of this particular expression of consensus has, not infrequently, been questioned even from within the ranks of the P5 itself, not least by the United States. 'It follows that to require United Nations approval as an absolute condition of legitimate use of military force', the argument runs, 'is to say that no military action of which Russia or China...strongly disapproves is legitimate, no matter how broadly the action is otherwise supported' (Slocombe 2003: 122). There may be found, in other words, better expressions of consensus outside the Council chamber, than the imperfect one that is 'artificially' and 'politically' voiced within it. Nye has similarly advised that the 'United States should reject multilateral initiatives that are recipes for inaction', on the grounds that 'sometimes multilateral procedures are obstructive', and he condoned the undertaking of the Kosovo operation by NATO for this reason (Nye 2002: 161–2). These arguments may be read as a kind of response to the rhetorical question that Kissinger had posed about how receptive the United States should be to multilateral expressions of consensus, if these conflicted with American values. The nub issue, as he posed it, was 'what, to be true to ourselves, must we try to accomplish no matter how small the attainable international consensus' (Kissinger 2001: 17).

The irony, of course, is that the P5, individually and collectively, has most to lose from a circumvention of the Council (Berdal 2003: 20). This means that there is a cost to them, either in promoting other expressions of consensus outside the framework of the Council—by appeals, for instance, to the General Assembly—or in thwarting the attainment of consensus from within. In the former case, encouragement of the idea that there are other legitimate expressions of the consensus within international society, apart from the Security Council, risks becoming a self-fulfilling prophecy. Likewise, as the dispute over the course of action to be taken over Iraq in the spring of 2003 revealed, the Council can be damned if it does, and damned if it does not. If it cannot consensually support the policy preferred by its most important player, it may be condemned to irrelevance, and systematic delegitimation on that score. If, from the perspective of France, the Council had sullied its reputation by an unprincipled adhesion to a consensus, it would likewise have lost its moral authority. Although these countervailing constraints did not produce 'agreement' in the Council in March 2003, they served to limit the 'dissension' that might otherwise have been expressed (the United States went further down the UN route than many had feared, and France did not issue calls for a ceasefire after the war was initiated, nor seek a resolution condemning the action). Tony Blair (2004: 3) recalled of the Security Council efforts that 'we strove hard for agreement', and perhaps somewhat optimistically, that 'we very nearly achieved it'. In part, this was because no P5-party had any interest in inflicting irreversible damage on a procedure which gave it a privileged status. These issues can now be traced briefly in three case studies of the post-cold war period.

The Gulf War 1991

The war in 1991, following upon Iraq's military occupation of Kuwait, seems to reflect one of the clearest examples of a genuine consensus within international society about the need to resort to armed force to overturn an illegal state of affairs. However, even this consensus was more problematic than it seemed. It was not unanimously supported in the Security Council, and there remained some ambiguity about the nature of the authorization for force dispensed by it (Weston 1991: 519–21).

On 2 August 1990, UNSC resolution 660 condemned the Iraqi invasion of Kuwait, with fourteen in favour and none against. When it moved to impose economic sanctions against Iraq (UNSCR 661, 6 August 1990), this was carried by thirteen in favour and two abstentions (Cuba and Yemen). By the time the Council authorized the use of 'all necessary means' (UNSCR 678, 29 November 1990), this was supported by twelve, with two votes against (Cuba and Yemen) and one abstention (China). Resolution 678 was subsequently described as 'one of borderline legitimacy at best', mainly because of its indeterminate legal authority, and the extent to which the consensus was created by great-power pressure (Weston 1991: 518).

There were two main sources of unease. The first was that while most states—including France, the Soviet Union, and China—condemned the Iraqi action, they wanted to ensure that the United States was not simply handed a blank cheque by the UN to undertake whatever military action it saw fit. From their point of view, an authorizing resolution by the UN was desirable in itself, but was needed also as 'the best way to impose limits on American military action' (Freedman and Karsh 1993: 145).

On the US side, Secretary of State, James Baker, above all appeared eager to adhere to this route, not least because it would best facilitate domestic support for military action. Baker intimated that maintaining widespread international support was politically vital for firm presidential action. 'I think he would want to move in a manner', he commented in September 1990, 'that would seek to preserve as much of the international consensus as we could—and, hopefully, all of it' (Freedman and Karsh 1993: 229).

This gave rise to the second form of unease. To request authorization from the Security Council was to imply that the use of force to liberate Kuwait was an action under Article 42 of the Charter (collective security, mandated by the Security Council), and not under Article 51 (individual or collective self-defence, requiring no such authorization). Some, including Mrs Thatcher, the British Prime Minister, until late 1990, were eager that any action in support of Kuwait be viewed as being taken under Article 51. UNSCR 661 had, in imposing sanctions, affirmed Article 51, and Mrs Thatcher argued that it was inconsistent, already possessing a right to use force, to be returning to the Council for yet further confirmation of it. The more that the Security Council was called upon formally to sanction armed force, the less would it appear to be an action under Article 51 (Freedman and Karsh 1993: 84, 148, 228). There remains a residual ambiguity on this issue, as Rosalyn Higgins explains: 'Its application in the Gulf remained ambiguous, because the Resolutions eventually authorized the use of force if Saddam Hussein had not withdrawn from Kuwait by 15 January 1991. Although no mention is made in the resolution of Article 42, this appears to be an authorization of military sanctions. No prior authorization of an Article 51 action would be necessary' (Higgins 1994: 262). In a sense, the ambiguity was creative. As long as there remained some danger of a veto in the Council, most likely by China, it was politic to keep both articles in play, and there was no disadvantage in blurring the distinction between them. In both these respects, the consensus on how to deal with the Gulf crisis was less complete than is often imagined. That said, by any historical comparison, the show of unity it evoked was unprecedented.

This was additionally demonstrated by the nature of the military coalition, or of those who acted in coordination with it. This achieved the symbolically important inclusion of a number of key Arab states. There was widespread acknowledgement at the time that this served a crucial political purpose of symbolizing an international consensus that cut across the Arab world, and embraced key states from within its ranks. This was clearly the case with Egypt. President Mubarak was instrumental in securing condemnation by the Arab League of the invasion of Kuwait, and his commitment of peacekeeping forces was felt to have 'provided a critical patina of Arab legitimacy for the deep American military intervention in the gulf' (*New York Times*, 5 September 1990: A1). Even more so, given the standing of Syria as a 'radical' voice, was its participation believed to raise 'the operation's legitimacy in Arab political circles' (*New York Times*, 14 September 1990: A10).

In sum, there were to be two pertinent demonstrations of consensus that were considered important for the legitimacy of the coalition war against Iraq. The first was the securing of a UN mandate from the Security Council. As was reported at the onset of the crisis, this reflected a conscious policy on the part of the United States and other leading coalition members of creating a 'global consensus', and staying within 'the boundaries of UN legitimacy' (*The Times*, 5 September 1990). The other face of consensus, that had a different resonance from agreement within the UN, was to secure military participation in the coalition from within the ranks of the Arab states. Both dimensions fed off each other and, collectively, made it easier for the leading coalition members to galvanize public support domestically. In contrast, for the Arab states, participation in the international consensus was a liability, not an asset, in terms of domestic politics.

In the aftermath of the war, it proved much more difficult to sustain those elements of consensus. On 5 April 1991, UNSCR 688 condemned 'the repression of the Iraqi civilian population in many parts of Iraq, including most recently in Kurdish populated areas'. However, there was little agreement as to how to follow up on this condemnation. The setting up of security zones within Iraq, and later the enforcement of no-fly zones of parts of the country, was done without any explicit Security Council authorization 'because of disagreement between Security Council members' (Higgins 1994: 256), even if UNSCR 688 had provided some kind of fig-leaf for the military actions taken.

Kosovo 1999

The use of NATO armed force in 1999 in Kosovo, and against the rest of the Federal Republic of Yugoslavia, was significant because it was the 'first time that a group of states, acting without explicit Security Council authority, defended a breach of the sovereignty rule primarily on humanitarian grounds' (Wheeler 2001*a*: 113). The problem for NATO was that it was increasingly faced by an unpalatable choice. It must either take no action at all, because it became abundantly clear during the second half of 1998 that Russia and China would not approve Security Council authorization of the use of armed force. Alternatively, if action were to be taken, it would have to be without explicit authorization of this kind. In UNSCR 1199 of 23 September 1998, the Council (with the abstention of China) expressed its seizure of the seriousness of the situation, confirmed the threat to international peace and security, and demanded an immediate cessation of hostilities. This left entirely open the question of what was to be done in the event of non-compliance, on which the resolution was purposefully silent, given Russian and Chinese reservations.

NATO had operated under the UN umbrella in Bosnia since 1995, but it enjoyed no specific mandate for dealing with the situation which erupted in Kosovo in 1998–9. The military operation did, however, enjoy unanimous support within NATO ranks, even if that consensus proved hard to sustain once the military operation was underway (Kagan 2003: 48). Many saw such a consensus, within a multilateral and democratic coalition, as an important safeguard that its actions would not infringe the purposes of the UN Charter (Farer 2003*a*: 76). Thus, in a very stark fashion, the handling of the Kosovo situation posed the issue of which consensus was to be the decisive one for purposes of action. NATO was condemned in some quarters for not seeking a UN resolution that would authorize it to act, but was dissuaded from this course by the expectation that no such resolution would be forthcoming, given the likelihood of a Russian veto. The calculation was that it would then be politically even more difficult to mount the operation in the face of a failed resolution, than in the absence of one altogether (Roberts 1999: 104). This determination to proceed was reinforced by two other considerations, over and above the political imperative to 'do something', in the words of UNSCR 1199, to 'avert an impending humanitarian catastrophe' (Wheeler 2001*a*: 113). The first was that there was a putative majority in support of military action within the Council, and from that perspective it was the 'unreasonable' Russian veto that was blocking the expression of the consensus position. In the event, this contention was lent seemingly even greater force by the failure of a resolution to condemn the NATO action, once underway. Russia, Belarus, and India tabled this critical motion on 26 March 1999, but it was defeated by twelve votes to three (Russia, China, and Namibia) (Wheeler 2000: 279). Instructively, the Canadian representative warned any potential supporters of the resolution that doing so would place them 'outside the international consensus' (Wheeler 2001*b*: 156). Indirectly, this outcome was argued to be tantamount to a vote in support of the operation, and hence it was Russia, not NATO, that was acting reprehensibly in the face of a clear consensus position. Second, play was also made of the argument that the consensus within NATO had a greater validity than the lack of consensus within the Council, given NATO's democratic credentials. The doctrine was invoked that a consensus amongst democratic states somehow trumped a lack of consensus within an inherently undemocratic Council (Roberts 1999: 107), although this did not prevent an increasing European desire to come back within the UN ambit in due course (*International Herald Tribune*, 15 April 1999: 1). Some commentators remained convinced that NATO would have been right to act, even against the express wishes of the Council. 'For to say that a UNSC resolution is essential', it has been protested, 'amounts to saying that not "the international community" but Russia and China... are the absolute custodians of the legitimacy of international force' (Slocombe 2003: 122). It is also to give undue weight to the voice of the Council, again for the reason that this is 'tainted' by political calculations and interests (Brown 2001: 92).

The Iraq War 2003

The issue of consensus, and what it meant for legitimacy, arose in a number of discrete ways in the course of the diplomacy preceding the Iraq war, during the hostilities, and again in its diplomatic aftermath. The terms of reference remained in flux, as did the exact subject of the legitimacy debate. At some times, the matter of concern was the legitimacy of using armed force against Iraq. At others, attention shifted to the legitimacy of the UN, and of the Security Council in particular. At yet others, and certainly during the post-war phase, attention once more shifted to the legitimacy of a new Iraqi regime, although that issue was not to be considered in separation from all that had transpired before. For presentational purposes, the discussion will proceed on the basis of these three issues: the legitimacy of the war; the legitimacy of the UN; and the legitimacy of the successor regime in Iraq. In practice, the three issues were tightly interwoven with each other.

The dominant diplomatic and public debate concentrated on the first of these. At stake was the entitlement of members of international society to act forcefully against Iraq in furtherance of preceding Security Council resolutions about disarmament. The post-Gulf war 1991 international consensus on the handling of Iraq had been under strain since at least 1994, and had explicitly broken down in 1998 (Berdal 2003: 15; M. Dunne 2003: 268; Kagan 2003: 44). Nonetheless, the unanimous resolution 1441 was agreed in November 2002. This was after Colin Powell, US Secretary of State, had successfully persuaded an otherwise reluctant administration to pursue the issue through the UN-consensus route (Berdal 2003: 22; Talbott 2003: 1044), and quite possibly in response to British diplomatic pressure. The issue that developed over the winter of 2002–3 was what action would then follow should the arms inspectors report that Iraq was in 'material breach' of its undertakings under 1441 (and earlier resolutions). This was the main framework of the intense legitimacy debate that was to be conducted over the use of armed force against Iraq during these months. Once again, what lay at its heart was which demonstrations of consensus were to be accepted as authoritative.

It is also interesting to note the complex arguments that were to unfold about the precise relationship between legitimacy and consensus, and which provided good illustrations of the theoretical problems addressed above. As we have seen, the widely held view has been that legitimacy itself in some sense derives from the existence of a consensus, even if not from consensus alone. Interestingly, as regards the legitimacy of the Iraq war, it was as common to find the argument taking the reverse form, namely that it was important to secure legitimacy for armed action in order to facilitate a consensus in favour of it. Instead of consensus being the fount of legitimacy, it was apparently held that legitimacy would be the fount of consensus. What, the question remains, would be the source of this legitimacy? As we shall see, when deployed in this way, legitimacy has usually been a coded expression for conformity with international law, and in particular, for adherence to UN procedure.

The most salient issue was to be whether or not Security Council backing was mandatory for the legitimate undertaking of force against Iraq, and the battle lines were soon sharply drawn over this. In particular, in the event of a breach by Iraq of the conditions of 1441, the question was whether or not a second Security Council resolution was required to authorize 'all necessary means', since the letter of the former resolution was certainly silent on that matter. Kofi Annan repeatedly made the point that if military action 'is taken without the authority of the Security Council, the legitimacy of … any action will be seriously impaired' (*The Hindu*, 25 February 2003). When the war started, he came as close as he felt able to go in open criticism of it, when he commented that 'many people around the world are seriously questioning whether it was legitimate for some member states to proceed to such fatal action now … without first reaching a collective decision of the Council' (*New York Times*, 27 March 2003: A1). Subsequently, the UN chief arms inspector, Hans Blix, was to concur. The fact that action was taken without Council authorization resulted in its 'compromised legitimacy' (Blix 2004: 274). In a nutshell, what was at stake was 'how many votes does it take to confer an aura of international legitimacy on an attack against Iraq' (*New York Times*, 13 March 2003: A12). If legitimacy depends upon a wide consensus, 'how wide is wide', and 'who decides what is wide enough'? (Kagan 2004: 83) How many votes make up a consensus, and can there be such a thing as a negative consensus, if there is no actual vote carried *against* a course of action, as was occasionally argued? (Roberts 2003: 38). The implication in all of this was that, if a consensus existed, it would find expression through the rightful channel, and of necessity this had to be the Security Council. Interestingly, of course, when the second resolution failed to materialize, the United States and Britain did not publicly claim to be discounting the UN in their decision to resort to war. On the contrary, they appealed to the authority of prior Security Council resolutions, and to Iraq's failure to respond adequately to them (Roberts 2003: 39–40). As Tony Blair (2004: 1) has insisted, 'we went to war to enforce compliance with UN Resolutions'.

The more common view held that it was the expression of international consensus through the medium of the Security Council that was needed to establish the legitimacy of the use of force against Iraq. This was very clearly set out in a joint letter sent by the British and US trade unions (TUC and AFL-CIO) to Tony Blair and George W. Bush. 'It is vital that a firm and broad consensus be forged and sustained', they cautioned, 'to ensure the legitimacy required should any future action be considered' (*The Times*, 31 January 2003: 16). A British Home Office Minister, John Denham, in resigning from the government, lamented the failure 'to put together the international consensus' on the need for military action at that point, and warned that it would undermine the legitimacy of future policy (*The Times*, 19 March 2003: 4). Japanese Prime Minister, Junichiro Koizumi, publicly confirmed that he had asked Bush to establish an international consensus before any attack on Iraq since 'international cooperation and legitimacy are essential for any war' (*Daily Yomiuri*, 11 September 2002: 1). Underpinning all such typical assessments was the need for that consensus to be expressed through the Security Council. 'From the point of view of international order, that's the only way to do it', insisted Karl Kaiser, Director of the German Council on Foreign Relations. 'It gives it a very powerful legitimation' (*New York Times*, 2 February 2003: 13). Whether this required a positive vote in favour of an authorization, or might conceivably be satisfied with a mere majority on the Council—any veto notwithstanding—remained a moot point (*Guardian*, 12 March 2003: 3). In the event, this was never put to the test, as the draft second resolution was withdrawn.

In an indirect fashion, this same argument that legitimacy was derivative of consensus was made by the Russian Foreign Minister, Igor Ivanov. After the outbreak of hostilities, he remarked that 'attempts will be undoubtedly made in the Security Council to find ways that would help legitimize the military operations'. Pointedly, he made clear the Russian position that 'we will not, of course, give legitimacy to this action in the Security Council' (*Moscow*

Times, 24 March 2003). In other words, Russia would not be a party to any consensus that, retrospectively, might legitimize the action that had already been undertaken. What this logic evinced was that abstention from a consensus would, by that act alone, deprive military action of the legitimacy it sought.

The UN Secretary-General, however, appeared to develop a different line of argument. His concern was that a lack of legitimacy would make it that much more difficult for international society to develop a consensual position, and to secure support for the new situation. If action was taken without the authority of the Council, 'the legitimacy and support for any such action will be seriously impaired' (*New York Times*, 11 March 2003: A10). Here we find legitimacy used in the very specific sense of legality. The Secretary-General was taking a more legalistic approach, and suggested that the consequence of any such infraction would be a lack of international support. On his reasoning, it is legitimacy (in this more formally legal sense) that begets consensus, rather than the other way round. This returned the issue to a more explicitly procedural one, in that the pursuit of 'right process' was considered to be the necessary precondition for the attraction of wide international support. In the absence of second-order agreement about what to do about Iraq, the important thing was to maintain the first-order consensus in support of dealing with the issue by the proper means. As explained by the French ambassador to Japan, Bernard de Montferrand, what was 'at stake today when dealing with the Iraqi crisis, is the international community's ability to ensure that its rules are fully complied with' (*Daily Yomiuri*, 25 February 2003: 8). The warning was clearly intended for an audience wider than the Iraqi regime. Another French ambassador, this time to the United Kingdom, later repeated the same admonition: 'We have to have rules, international rules, decided in common and applicable to all' (*Independent*, 12 May 2003: 18).

When the participants were not arguing that it was the UN alone that could bestow legitimacy upon military action, their attention turned instead to the implications of unauthorized use of armed force for the UN: it was the legitimacy of the UN, not of the war, that became the subject of concern. This was in no small measure the consequence of an overt political strategy on the part of the United States, as is well captured by Reus-Smit. 'Instead of support from the United Nations Security Council being the measure of the legitimacy of Washington's preferred strategy', he concludes, 'the Administration tried to turn the tables, to make compliance with its strategy the test of the United Nations' legitimacy' (Reus-Smit 2004*a*: 53; *Korea Herald*, 15 March 2003). This strategy was deployed at the height of the crisis over the second resolution in mid-March 2003. 'If the United Nations fails to act', warned the President's press secretary, Ari Fleischer, '... another international body will disarm Saddam Hussein'. He then placed this in the context of earlier failures to act on the part of the Council, over the Balkans and Rwanda. 'If you judge legitimacy by whether the United Nations Security Council acted', he added, 'then you would think you'd need to restore Slobodan Milosevic to power, because he was removed without the United Nations Security Council approval' (*New York Times*, 11 March 2003: A1). Following this logic, an otherwise 'rightful' course of action, sanctioned by other demonstrations of international 'consensus', possessed its own inherent legitimacy, and if the UN failed to act in support of it, so much the worse for the legitimacy of the UN. The problem with this logic, for the UN, was that it was a double-edged sword. In the eyes of the opponents of military action, if it were seen to endorse unilateralism of this kind, as Ramesh Thakur pointed out, 'instead of UN legitimacy being stamped on military action against Iraq, the legitimacy of the UN itself will be eroded' (*Japan Times*, 9 February 2003).

Oddly, this strategy did meet with a measure of success, even amongst those least sympathetic to the reasoning behind the American position. It led to a concerted campaign to ensure that the UN once again became involved in the Iraqi situation, not to legitimize the war, but rather to relegitimize the UN itself. The defensiveness of this posture revealed the extent to which the tables had, in fact, been turned. Typically, then, Indian Prime Minister Vajpayee appealed for consensus in the Security Council—but not to legitimize any military action. 'We hope that the members of the Security Council will harmonise their positions', was his considered analysis, 'to ensure that its final decision enhances the legitimacy and credibility of the United Nations' (*The Hindu*, 13 March 2003). The Malaysian Foreign Minister called for UN re-engagement in Iraq 'to restore the confidence of the international community towards the world body' (*New Straits Times*, 10 April 2003: 2). The reasoning was not quite as Washington saw it, but it nonetheless shifted the focus to the legitimacy of the UN, instead of the war. As a Korean newspaper reported, 'if the United States is allowed to go to war unilaterally, the concept of a community of nations bound by collective norms and subject to consensual procedures would become untenable'. In such circumstances, 'the United Nations would lose its legitimacy and its very reason for being' (*Korea Herald*, 13 January 2003).

Finally, the legitimacy debate turned its attention towards the importance of UN-expressed consensus for the future legitimacy of the post-war Iraqi regime. The view that the Iraqi regime needed legitimacy, and that this could be found only through UN involvement, was widely expressed during and after the war. A chorus of diplomatic voices concurred. Indonesian Foreign Minister, Hassan Wirayuda, was insistent that the UN 'should determine the legitimacy of the new government in the country' (*Jakarta Post*, 9 April 2003). German Chancellor Gerhard Schroeder apparently told Japanese Prime Minister Koizumi that 'United Nations leadership in the reconstruction process was necessary to give legitimacy to the new government of Iraq' (*Asahi Shimbun*, 1 May 2003). The Malaysian Government, through its acting Prime Minister, made a public statement to this same effect: 'Malaysia believes that the UN must play a leading role in the future of Iraq', it affirmed, on the grounds that 'as the organization which embodies the will of the international community, the

UN will provide legitimacy to these efforts' (*Malaysia General News*, 10 April 2003). Speaking in London at the IISS, the French Foreign Minister, Dominique de Villepin, was adamant that the UN be placed at the heart of the reconstruction effort, since 'the legitimacy of our action depends upon it' (*Independent*, 28 March 2003: 9). He subsequently elaborated that the 'future administration of Iraq presupposes the support from both the Iraqi people and the entire international community—a condition under which necessary legitimacy can be given. This legitimacy cannot exist outside the United Nations' (*Asahi Shimbun*, 14 April 2003). Britain's former UN ambassador, David Hannay, was equally persuaded that the legitimacy of an Iraqi interim governmental authority depended upon agreement through the UN, so that it should not be seen as 'the creation of the United States alone' (*The Times*, 7 April 2003: 10). Colin Powell's ill-advised characterization of the need for the UN to act as a *chapeau* in this reconstruction process both recognized, and belittled, the seriousness of the point (*New York Times*, 29 March 2003: B10; 2 April 2003: B12). Discussing the prospective handover of power to a new Iraqi sovereign authority, Tony Blair informed a news conference that 'the UN is the body that has the international legitimacy to be able to certify and help guide the process of political transition' (*BBC News*, 22 April 2004).

Once again, however, in this specific context of the legitimacy of the future Iraqi regime, there was displayed also a tendency to reverse the relationship between legitimacy and consensus. Whereas the predominant argument was that it was the UN voicing of an international consensus that could confer legitimacy upon the regime, there was also a more subdued suggestion that legitimacy was the prerequisite for the attainment of international consensus. The UN Secretary-General once more voiced the clearest statements to this effect, concerned as he no doubt was with facilitating the post-war reconstruction effort. He made no demand for a comprehensive UN administration of the country, but insisted upon some UN sanction for the process, in order to bestow legitimacy on the regime. The point, however, was precisely to make possible a wider international consensus in support of the new administration. It would help 'European, Arab and other governments' to come to the party. Even more tellingly, it was felt that this could 'mend the breach' in the Security Council (*Washington Post*, 8 April 2003: A32). Legitimacy might thereby issue in consensus, rather than the other way round. This, in part, recalled the Kosovo experience, wherein the UN had not authorized the war, but approved the postwar administrative arrangements, 'in a way that conferred international legitimacy upon them and encouraged all nations to extend support and resources to the enterprise' (*Independent*, 6 March 2003).

CONCLUSION

In these various manoeuvrings, we confront the complexity of the relationship between consensus and legitimacy as a matter of diplomatic practice. The predominant perspective throughout these crises has been that legitimacy is derivative of consensus, and consensus is best expressed through the voice of the Security Council. This was deemed the safest route, since it was predicated upon a first-order procedural consensus that affirms a right way of doing things, separate from the merits or otherwise of the individual case. This view, however, has not commanded universal respect. It has been increasingly challenged by appeals to other possible demonstrations of consensus within international society. It has been modified also by appeals to a standard of legitimacy that apparently exists at one remove from international consensus, but is presented as the necessary and desired instrument for securing such consensus. Appeals, in this form, have usually been to norms of legality or morality. Accordingly, consensus has been variably viewed both as the source of legitimacy, and as a possible effect and outcome of it. Whether this reflects a deep-seated confusion and misunderstanding about these issues within contemporary international society, or merely tactical sparring for political position, is very much a moot point.

Consensus is clearly important for legitimacy. But just how decisive is it? As has been repeatedly foreshadowed in this chapter, the answer to that question depends on whether consensus is valuable in its own right, or, more fundamentally, because it is thought to indicate a correspondence with the other norms of international society. In the latter case, consensus is only indirectly important for international legitimacy. What counts above all is the conformity of international actions with those other accepted norms. These, as adumbrated earlier, are the norms of legality, morality, and constitutionality. The quest for consensus to which so much of the legitimacy talk is directed can then be understood as an effort to extend, or realign, the normative bounds themselves. It is to a consideration of this dimension of the problem that the next chapter will turn.

11

Legitimacy and Norms

In addition to its affinity to consensus, legitimacy is closely related to a number of other international norms: these will be discussed as the norms of legality, morality, and constitutionality. Legitimacy is cognate to all, but does not equate to any one in particular. Logically, it could not be identical to all three, given the disparities amongst them. It is the purpose of this chapter to explore the relationship between legitimacy and these diverse norms in the present circumstances of international society. In doing so, it will demonstrate the confusions in existing usages. It will show also, as a matter of practice, how the appeal to norms as part of the process of legitimization is itself fundamental to normative change.

In sum, the chapter will criticize propositions to the effect that a choice can be made between legitimacy, on the one hand, and particular norms, on the other. It does so for several reasons. First, legitimacy possesses no independent normative content of its own that would make such a choice meaningful. Second, the notion of legitimacy is always mediated through a composite of other norms, and cannot be ranged against them individually. Third, the tensions that arise are amongst those discrete norms themselves, rather than between each individually and legitimacy. Finally, it is important to detach legitimacy from these individual norms since recognition of it as an aggregate is fundamental to understanding the process of normative change.

THE RELATIONSHIP BETWEEN LEGITIMACY AND NORMS

The central argument of this chapter will be that it is a serious misapprehension that there is any such thing as a distinctive scale of legitimacy values as such. Accordingly, all attempts to posit a specific tension between legitimacy per se, and other norms such as legality or morality, rest on a major confusion. Legitimacy is a composite of, and an accommodation between, a number of other norms, both procedural and substantive, and does not possess its own independent standard against which actions can be measured. For that reason, it is never in direct tension with other norms: it is amongst those norms that any tension exists. To say, for example, that there is a conflict between legitimacy and legality is, from this point of view, confusing. It implies that there is a separate legitimacy scale of values, in the same and equal sense that there is a legality set of values. What is instead at work here is a sleight of hand in which legitimacy, in this context, is read to mean something else, such as morality. To claim, as was said after the Kosovo campaign, that there is an 'unacceptable gap between what international law allows and what morality requires' is perfectly understandable (Buchanan 2003: 131). However, to portray this as a gap between legitimacy and legality is misleading, since legality can never be more than *one* of the elements of which legitimacy is composed. As an aggregate, legitimacy does not enjoy any kind of antagonistic relationship with its individual components.

So what are the pertinent norms, and how does legitimacy relate to them? In a telling commentary on the prospect of war against Iraq in early 2003, the former Australian Foreign Minister, Gareth Evans, commented that if it could not be demonstrated that the Iraqi leadership posed such a threat to international security as to require military action for its removal, then 'war on Iraq will lack legality, legitimacy, morality and sense' (*International Herald Tribune*, 3 February 2003: 8). What is of interest is the general structure of this argument. It suggests that legitimacy is one normative standard amongst several, co-equal with the others, and possesses its own normative independence. This implies that we can have a discussion about the legitimacy of the Iraq war in the very same way that we can have a discussion about, say, its legality or morality. But can this be so? To what values does legitimacy then make appeal? In what terms is the legitimacy talk to be conducted?

In another commentary upon the Iraq war of 2003, Lawrence Freedman had described legitimacy as 'that magic quality to be found somewhere in the vicinity of legality and morality' (*Independent*, 29 March 2003: 23). We need, however, to be clear about the nature of the 'vicinity' in which it falls. Legitimacy is not to be placed on the same plane as the others, but instead exists in a hierarchic relationship to them. From this point of view, legitimacy denotes a combination of values, and represents some balance amongst them, when these individual normative standards might tend to pull in opposite directions. The tension is to be found between those norms, not between any one of them and legitimacy. This presentation draws our attention to the inescapably political nature of legitimacy, as being about the exercise of choice in a realm of indeterminate values. It was on precisely these grounds that the failure of the peacekeeping efforts of the 1990s had been explained. The UN, we were told, 'was not willing to choose a decisive course of action among the various legitimacies that formed the umbrella under which it was working'. This reflected the wider reality that international society at the time was itself 'unwilling to have one source of its legitimacy taking precedent over the others' (Coicaud 2001*b*: 284).

In order to examine those various issues in greater detail, the remainder of this chapter will examine the relationship between legitimacy and three important international norms: legality, morality, and constitutionality. The first of these starts from the commonly asserted position that legitimacy betokens conformity with the law: what is legitimate is what is sanctioned by international law, and maintenance of the value of legality is the highest norm of international society. 'Defenders of international society argue', we are reminded, 'that the existence of international legal rules is the best indicator of the presence of society' (T. Dunne 2003: 314). If so, actions regarded as legitimate are essentially those that conform to such legal prescriptions.

Second, however, it is commonly accepted that the law may be unjust, or fail some wider test about ultimate moral principles. In Freedman's conception, legitimacy is to be found in the vicinity of both morality and legality, and thus cannot be a matter of legality alone. It was on this issue in particular that the legitimacy of NATO's military action in Kosovo in 1998 was to be explicitly debated. Where does legitimacy lie if legality and morality pull in opposing directions, and what 'new actions' are permitted in such conditions of normative uncertainty? Since the end of the cold war, international society has repeatedly engaged with the legitimacy of various acts of war, in language that implies that legitimate war is but a pseudonym for just war. This implies a degree of equivalence between legitimacy and a conception of morality or justice, within which the legal rules may not necessarily be paramount.

Third, the pertinent strictures of international society are not captured fully by the norms of legality and morality. For a degree of completeness, a third category needs to be introduced, and it will be referred to as that of constitutionality. This is not to be construed in the narrow sense as the legal foundations of the political order, as this would simply return us to legality by yet another route. Instead, it refers to the mutual political expectations on which international society is from time to time founded, and which are not fixed in legal rules. For instance, the early eighteenth-century subscription to the attainment of a balance of power was a political ideal of that phase of international society, but scarcely a matter of international law. Nonetheless, various international actions were most definitely legitimized by reference to it. Likewise, the nineteenth-century European concert asserted a standard of legitimacy as part of an innovative political procedure of consultation and consent amongst the great powers. Once again, this was hardly a matter of international law, as the foundations and day-to-day operations of the concert were avowedly too informal for any such legal transcription. We might then think of constitutionality as a norm based on the political constraints that are voluntarily entered into within international society, and that have a basis recognizably different from legal or moral prescription, however much the political play may be rhetorically coloured by legal and moral language. If there has been a recent crisis of legitimacy within contemporary international society, then arguably it has been brought about by a shock to this informal norm of constitutionality, rather than to legality or morality as such.

This point can be made by way of brief allusion to the two wars against Iraq, in 1991 and 2003 respectively. It may be felt that the former of these enjoyed a much less contentious claim to legitimacy than the latter, on the grounds that the legal and moral cases were that much more secure in 1991. And yet even moderate commentators blithely pronounce that, in 1991, the 'reason for fighting this war was *not* that Iraq had violated the norms of international behaviour', but was instead the result of 'a collective defence of interests by the West' (Cooper 2003: 57–8). If so, why did the West get away with it comparatively cheaply in 1991, but not again in 2003? One answer is that the legal and moral bases of legitimacy were far from unambiguous in either of the two cases. Critically, what then distinguished them was that the war in 2003 generated a crisis of constitutionality in a way that the 1991 war did not. Constitutionality, in the second case, played a more conspicuous role in the determination of legitimacy than did either legality or morality. Generally, then, what is considered to be legitimate in any one case very much depends on this shifting balance between the three norms, and on the extent of the consensus around any one point of equilibrium.

LEGITIMACY AND LEGALITY

'The relationship between legality and legitimacy', we are told, 'is one of the most important themes in legal and political philosophy' (Dyzenhaus 1997: 1). To many, these terms are synonymous: what is legitimate is what the law ordains. Accordingly, in the eyes of legal realists, any claimed distinction between legitimacy and legality 'dissolves' (Farer 2003a: 68). Such had always been the case in the tradition of legal positivism handed down from Hans Kelsen in which the law had its own autonomy, distinct from the political or moral universe that might surround it. This is opposed to the Schmittian perspective in which law is inescapably rooted in politics. In the first, legitimacy is enclosed within the legal order; in the second, it opens out to other considerations (Dyzenhaus 1997: 162–7). Weber too subscribed to the identity between the two concepts. 'Weber denied that there is a morality beyond the law by which it can be judged', and held instead that 'a *de facto* legal order is also legitimate' (Dyzenhaus 1997: 238).

Any such complete identification, however, raises two immediate problems. If they are identical, the concept of legitimacy becomes essentially redundant, and we might as well speak exclusively of conformity to law. The fact that the representatives of international society so regularly speak of legitimacy and, separately, of legality clearly suggests that they are taken to be cognate, but not identical, terms—even if, as argued, there is artifice in some of the posited oppositions between them. For example, as part of the build-up to the war with Iraq, senior Whitehall officials insisted that 'lawful and legitimate are not necessarily the same thing' (*Guardian*, 8 October 2002: 12; *The Times*, 8 October 2002: 1). Second, any identification between them would disable an important instrument of international change. It is precisely the political space between the two concepts that contributes to normative change in international society, to refinements of international law, and to developments in actual state practice. The gap is one of the dynamic instruments in the evolution of international society, and this is widely understood by those who participate within it. Rather than being the same, legitimacy is one vehicle for redefining legality, by appeal to *other* norms.

There is one further reason why legitimacy should not be straitjacketed into a legal framework. The legitimacy discourse is as likely to be driven by legal uncertainty as by certainty, and the idea of legitimacy has a greater role to play precisely at those moments when the legal ground appears least secure, or possibly is in flux. This is confirmed in accounts of Security Council practice during the post-cold war period, as one well-placed analyst judiciously points out. 'Increasing references to the concept of legitimacy in legal literature', he contends, 'would be a clear indication that the legality or constitutionality of various activities by the Security Council is ambiguous or fragile at best' (Sato 2001: 340). What this again seems to indicate is that the language of legitimacy is employed to reach those parts that cannot be reached by the language of legality alone. However, to assert that legitimacy is not narrowly bound by the norm of legality is far from saying that legality is wholly excluded from international society's operative concepts of legitimacy. This general argument can now be illustrated with reference to the Kosovo crisis of 1998–9.

Kosovo 1999

Kosovo has been considered to mark a major milestone in international relations. It did so for two interconnected reasons. First, it was the 'first time a major use of destructive armed force had been undertaken with the stated purpose of implementing UN Security Council resolutions but without Security Council authorisation' (Roberts 1999: 102). Second, the use of force 'was intended to bring a halt to crimes against humanity being committed by a state within its own borders' (Roberts 1999: 102). If Kosovo was, indeed, such a landmark event, what did it signify for international legitimacy?

No case better illustrates the problems with the claimed opposition between legality and legitimacy than this. The predominant debate about that crisis was explicitly so framed. Famously, the Independent International Commission (IIC) on Kosovo was to conclude that the NATO intervention, and air campaign against both Kosovo and the rest of the Federal Republic of Yugoslavia (FRY), was 'illegal but legitimate' (*Guardian*, 27 October 2000: 24), thereby making a clear separation between the two normative categories. The report certainly questioned the legality of the war, noting that 'it remains difficult to reconcile NATO's recourse to armed intervention on behalf of Kosovo with the general framework of rights and duties which determines the legality of the use of force' (IIC 2000: 167). At the same time, it drew attention to the argument that 'given the unfolding humanitarian catastrophe...the use of force by NATO was legitimate' (IIC 2000: 167). Other commentators have developed this same theme. Notably, in his elaboration of a theory of humanitarian intervention, Nick Wheeler noted 'the conflict between legality and legitimacy posed by NATO's military intervention in Kosovo' (Wheeler 2001*b*: 145). Richard Falk was similarly to observe that 'the Kosovo dilemma disclosed an undesirable gap between legitimacy and legality' (Falk 2003: xvi). The IIC report, in Franck's estimation, was a step towards 'bridging the gap...between legality and legitimacy' (Franck 2002: 182)

This perception is deeply embedded in current debates. Gareth Evans, for example, has appealed for the development of a 'group of principles which have to be satisfied if any decision to use military force is to be not just legal, but *legitimate*...The distinction—if it can be operationalised, with criteria of legitimacy simplified, standardised and commonly accepted—is an important one' (Evans 2004: 11).

But what might legitimacy signify in such a context? To make sense of it, it needs be transcribed as a coded word for morality, thus capturing the tension between morality and legality, not the purported one between legitimacy and legality. Franck, disarmingly, transcribes the gap between legality and legitimacy as one between 'strict legal positivism and a common sense of moral justice' (Franck 2002: 182). In his own gloss upon the IIC Report, of which he had been a member, Falk restated the issue more precisely. He explained that he had come round to the view that the NATO war 'while technically illegal, was politically and morally legitimate' (Falk 2003: xvi). That is a different, and more acceptable, formulation of the argument. In effect, the tension lay between legality and morality, and a rounded assessment of legitimacy was to be found in some balance between the two. What it was not was any direct conflict between legitimacy and legality, since such a claim has no apparent meaning.

This is not to suggest that legality was an insignificant ingredient of the Kosovo legitimacy debate. Certainly, at the official level, NATO governments mostly assumed the legality of their action, although some stated this more explicitly than others. When the IIC concluded in favour of legitimacy, despite illegality, it employed legitimacy in this context as a substitute for a moral or humanitarian objective. Thus reconfigured, the operation might not have been strictly legal, but could be sanctioned by its compelling moral purpose. Frequently, it was in those terms that the issue was presented—not as a conflict between legitimacy and legality, but as one between morality and legality. The humanitarian crisis, from this point of view, was deemed to trump the legal niceties in this particular case. Such a perspective was widely expressed in France. A columnist in *Le Monde* captured it neatly: 'Devant le scandale humanitaire (les mauvais traitements infligés a la communauté albanaise du Kosovo), le scandale juridique (l'absence d'un mandat clair de l'ONU) s'efface, disait-on a l'Elysee. Des lors qu'on était convaincu de la légitimé politique, voire de l'obligation morale, d'une intervention au Kosovo, pouvait-on y renoncer sous pretexte de légalité onusienne...' (*Le Monde*, 19 November 2001). The French President concurred and gave voice to his belief that, the absence of explicit UN authority for action notwithstanding, 'the humanitarian situation constitutes a ground that can justify an exception to a rule, however firm and strong it is' (Henrikson 2000: 49). The rule itself was not to be jettisoned. The British Prime Minister, Tony Blair, explicitly stated as much in his insistence that this 'is a just war, based not on any territorial ambitions but on values' (Blair 1999: 1; Chomsky 1999: 3), and, as such, should not be stymied by the incapacity of the UN to act in support of its own resolutions (Brown 2001: 93; Patrick 2001: 12). Likewise, US Secretary of State, Madeleine Albright, asserted that 'the alliance has the legitimacy to act to stop a catastrophe', even without further UN authorization (*International Herald Tribune*, 9 October 1998: 1). However, such a defence of the NATO action (legality tempered by morality/humanitarianism) was not that employed by NATO as a whole. 'At no point during the Security Council debates in March 1999', attests Wheeler, 'did NATO governments try to advance the argument that the bombing of the FRY was illegal but morally justified' (Wheeler 2001*b*: 154). As NATO governments affirmed their willingness to take part in NATO action in October 1998, President Clinton reportedly confirmed that action 'would be within the framework of UN decisions', and other NATO diplomats acknowledged that they had 'started working on the legal basis for action' (*International Herald Tribune*, 9 October 1998: 1).

From the official NATO point of view, armed intervention was in conformity with international law on two discrete grounds. The first was that the repression of the Kosovar Albanian population threatened regional stability and, under Chapter VII of the UN Charter, represented a threat to 'international peace and security', as UN resolutions had already accepted. In this light, it might have been argued—although in fact was not (Franck 2002: 167)—that NATO reserved the right to initiate measures of collective self-defence. Second, under international law and conventions on human rights and genocide, military intervention 'was lawful on the basis of overwhelming humanitarian necessity' (Henrikson 2000: 52). This was the position held to by Britain's UN ambassador, Sir Jeremy Greenstock, in the Security Council meeting of 24 March 1999: 'The action being taken is legal ... It is justified as an exceptional measure to prevent an overwhelming humanitarian catastrophe' (quoted in Franck 2002: 167). Some international lawyers, while holding this view to be 'controversial', concede that the argument can still be made (Weller 1999/2000: 81). Even some sceptics have admitted that 'the prior authorization of NATO by the UN Security Council as its enforcement arm earlier in the 1990s, plus the evolutionary nature of Security Council resolutions directed at Serbia, meant that NATO could claim to be acting at least in a "semi-permissive" legal environment' (Thakur and Schnabel 2000: 502).

This purported opposition between legitimacy and legality might then be a construct of various observers, but appears not to have been accepted by most of the central players, and this too is instructive. Those who supported the NATO action sought to legitimize it as legal, while additionally in support of humanitarian objectives; those who opposed it viewed it as illegal, whatever the moral grounds, and hence denied its claim to legitimacy. Amongst the practitioners, on both sides of the argument, the idea of the war as 'illegal but legitimate' was not, in any case, the operative framework.

We have previously considered the role of the UN in Kosovo as an aspect of consensus-based legitimacy. From the current perspective, the role of the UN emerges also as part of the legality of the NATO campaign, focused as this was on the need for authorization by the Security Council. This acted as a double-edged sword. To be sure, there was a major potential cost to the UN in any attempt by NATO to circumvent the Security Council procedure. At the same time, it was recognized both then and since that inaction, under the shadow of Russian and possibly Chinese vetoes, could be just as damaging. Since the Security Council had condemned the policy of the FRY in successive resolutions, and demanded remedial action, allowing Milosevic to 'flout the core ideals of the UN would have eroded its legitimacy' (*International Herald Tribune*, 25 June 1999: 8; Wheeler 2001a: 119). As the war reached its denouement, the circle was squared with the adoption by the Security Council of Resolution 1244 on 10 June 1999. As this prepared the ground for the post-war phase, it authorized 'relevant international organizations to establish the international security presence in Kosovo'. Importantly, it enjoined them to do so 'with all necessary means' (S/RES/1244, 10 June 1999: 2), arguably lending some degree of retrospective 'absolution' to NATO's role hitherto. As previously discussed, the draft resolution of 26 March 1999, condemning the NATO action, had already failed. On 9 April, the Secretary-General submitted the text of a letter to the President of the Security Council. This enumerated a number of demands of the Yugoslav authorities. Once these had been accepted, the letter urged 'the leaders of the North Atlantic Alliance to suspend immediately the air bombardments upon the territory of the Federal Republic of Yugoslavia' (S/1999/402, 9 April 1999). There was no demand for a cessation of these hostilities before the conditions had been fully satisfied. Even before Resolution 1244, it could be said that the UN was already acquiescing in the NATO action, even if it had not explicitly authorized it. To this extent, the legal status of the intervention remained obscure, but far from irrelevant.

Beyond the central issue of UN authority, the legality of the Kosovo campaign was additionally questioned from other angles, especially after the military operation was underway. These framed the discussion largely in terms of the ends/means relationship: whatever the merits of the purported ends, the means to securing them were inappropriate and/or illegal in themselves. These arguments came in two main varieties. The first condemned the resort to military force as being in itself the major cause of the acceleration of the humanitarian and refugee crisis. If the war was motivated by humanitarian concerns, commented the Chinese press, then 'this excuse is downright hypo-critical, because it is NATO ... has created unprecedented "humanitarian dis-aster" ... and has caused the biggest tide of refugees ever since World War II' (*People's Daily*, 13 May 1999: 2). This assessment was given further weight by the findings of the UN Secretary-General's Inter-Agency Needs Assessment Mission, despatched in May. It reported back that by 24 March 1999, UNHCR estimated that some 260,000 people had been displaced in Kosovo, but that the crisis then 'entered a new phase with the commencement of NATO air strikes' on that day. Over the next eight days, a further 222,000 people were expelled, and by the end of May the total figure had reached approximately 850,000 (S/1999/662, 14 June 1999: Annex 12–13).

The second dimension was a specific critique of the conduct of the military operation, and above all a condemnation of its 'high air' character. There was little willingness on the part of NATO to engage in a major ground campaign, and so the air assault extended over several weeks, both within Kosovo and elsewhere in the FRY. The standard objection was that this maximized the safety of air crews, only at the expense of minimizing the safety of civilians on the ground. The moral ground of the campaign 'could be shaken if more civilians get killed or wounded while the attacking side is exposed to minimum danger', commented one report, and concluded that 'if civilians face a greater danger because of this policy pivoting on protecting the lives of NATO's armed forces, the whole campaign loses its moral legitimacy' (*Korea Herald*, 17 April 1999). The UN Inter-Agency Mission repeatedly drew attention to the high human and economic costs of the air war for the people of Kosovo and the FRY generally. The 'aerial bombardment' rendered the country 'severely debili-tated'. This included the civilian loss of life, as well as the 'devastating impact on industry, employment, the environment, essential services and agriculture' (S/1999/662, 14 June 1999: Annex 5–6). Unease was further compounded by the bombing of the Chinese Embassy in Belgrade on 7 May 1999, which prompted the Security Council President to issue a statement of sorrow and regret, noting NATO's announced investigation into the matter (S/PRST/1999/12, 14 May 1999).

These aspects of the conduct of the war contributed great intensity to the debate over the legitimacy of the war. However, while conducted in the language of legitimacy, this was essentially a just-war dialogue by other means. At stake was the *ius in bello*, and in particular questions about the targeting of civilians, about collateral damage, and about the proportionality of the means to the ends. While often appealing to legal principles, this was primarily a just-war debate about the morality of the war's means. This is in no way to denigrate the force of the issues at stake, but merely to point out that such an ethical debate, by itself, does not amount to a debate about the war's legitimacy.

We have already encountered the view that the authority of the Security Council is related to the 'consensus' that it demonstrates procedurally. In cases of humanitarian emergencies, it might be felt that the general responsibility of the permanent members to reach a consensus in support of international action is, if anything, even more compelling. Indeed, there have been suggestions that, in such situations, the right to the veto should be suspended (Linklater 2000: 490; ICISS 2001). In no small measure, the feeling amongst NATO governments was that further resort to Security Council approval might, *in extremis*, be pushed aside. This, in turn, was fuelled by the perception that the much-vaunted Russian veto was, in the circumstances, unreasonable. If unauthorized action placed a question mark over the legality of the war, then the veto offended against the requirement for consensus given the high humanitarian stakes. Thus was one legitimacy narrative set against another.

This returns us to the inescapably political, and dynamic, quality of international legitimacy, within which the norm of legality remains but one consideration. 'It should be emphasized that the collective legitimization function acquired by the United Nations', it has been aptly recalled, 'is not mainly a matter of legality or of judicial proceeding, although international law is hardly irrelevant to the process... The key elements of it... are its *collective* and its *political* aspects' (Henrikson 2000: 44). The first of these recalls the need for consensus; the second stresses the arbitration between interests, and between multiple, but often inconsistent, norms. Legality, morality, and constitutionality need to be reconciled, and legitimacy encapsulates that political perception of where the balance lies at any one time. The Kosovo crisis, rooted in time and place, demonstrates well those general perspectives.

LEGITIMACY AND MORALITY

What is the relationship between legitimacy and morality? Does international society's approval of any action depend upon its correspondence with moral values, and do they hold the key to international legitimacy? Alternatively, is legitimacy distinct from morality, while still enjoying an intimate but complex coexistence with it? The UN Secretary-General, Kofi Annan, implicitly distinguished between them in remarks he had made about Kosovo in early 1999. He spoke then of the necessity for the world to be clear about the 'credibility, legitimacy and morality of intervention' in that situation (*The Times*, 29 January 1999). If we take these words literally, legitimacy must refer to something different from shared moral values. If so, what then is the relationship between them?

Some writers distinguish between legitimacy and morality on essentially the same basis as that between process and substance. Franck, in particular, had been insistent that while justice and legitimacy 'have something in common'— since both encourage 'non-coerced compliance'—they are nonetheless 'discrete phenomena' (Franck 1990: 209–10). What separates them is best illustrated in his discussion of one of the basic rules of international society, the principle of *pacta sunt servanda*:

This rule... exerts a strong pull towards compliance powered *both by its justice and its legitimacy*. The *justice*-based claim, nevertheless, is different from the *legitimacy*-based one...

The legitimacy-based claim... derives from a *secular* political community's preference for, and dependence on, order and predictability. The identical-appearing justice-based claim, in contrast, derives from the belief of a community of *shared moral values*... that fairness requires the honouring of commitments... In any community of moral values, promises are sacred because trust and reciprocity are believed to be instrumental in advancing not order, but *fairness*. (Franck 1990: 234)

In this version, legitimacy stands on the side of existing law, predictability, and order, and is to be contrasted with the normative quest for justice as fairness. But why should legitimacy be conceived in this way? Why should it stand as a counterpoint to morality, in the same way claimed above of legality? The contemporary notion of legitimacy tends not to make that separation. Instead, contemporary international society views legitimacy as a political accommodation between competing norms, with no greater prior commitment to any. All are equally in play, although international society may be more responsive to one or other in any given situation.

Thus understood, we have an answer to the same hypothetical question already posed above with regard to legality. If it were to be said now that an action was immoral but legitimate, this would be but the mirror-image of the claim to illegality but legitimacy. In the latter case, as seen, the claim is predicated on identification between legitimacy and morality, such that action may be considered legitimate even if illegal. In the present case, the play on words works in reverse. To assert that something is immoral but legitimate is to claim simply that, while not corresponding to some moral values, what has been done is perfectly legal. Legitimacy, in this case, is transcribed as legality. By way of illustration, many felt morally unsure about the Iraq war in 1991, and yet—in legal terms—there was a predominant sense that the war was 'legitimate'. Let us briefly examine international society's treatment of this war as an illustration of the limits of the argument that an action can be considered immoral but legitimate.

The Iraq War 1991

On the face of it, the case for the war to expel Iraq from Kuwait in 1991 was widely accepted. It rested upon a broad conjunction of legal and political factors. In the first case, Iraq's unprovoked armed occupation of Kuwait— whatever the muddied history of territorial claims—was readily adjudged by the Security Council to have constituted a breach of international peace and security, and to be a violation of the territorial integrity of a sovereign member of the UN, namely Kuwait. This permitted the Council to initiate economic and military sanctions and, as we have seen, eventually to approve 'all necessary means' to restore the status quo ante. There was dissent, to be sure, to the relatively short period of notice contained in the final ultimatum to Iraq, as some states considered diplomacy not yet to have been exhausted, and insisted upon going the extra mile for peace. However, there was virtually no objection to the basic legal assessment that Iraq had breached international law by its invasion, must withdraw from Kuwait, and must make good the damage it had caused. The legal input was thus especially strong in shaping the framework of the legitimacy debate at the time.

Second, and procedurally, the political climate facilitated unprecedented P5 collaboration within the Security Council. There was virtually no dispute about the *authorization* of military action. The Council had been charged of the issue from the outset, had set out its unequivocal demands, and finally permitted its resolutions to be enforced by military means. To be sure, the military operation was not then undertaken by the UN itself, and there were degrees of unease expressed about the delegation of this function (Weston 1991: 517), but there was little dissent to the validity of the authorization that had been given. US defense secretary, Dick Cheney, announcing the start of the military campaign, confirmed that its objectives were 'to liberate Kuwait and enforce the resolutions of the UN Security Council' (*New York Times*, 17 January 1991: A17).

Third, and in a more political sense, the war gained considerable support from the make-up of the international coalition that, at least symbolically, participated in the military campaign. This was partly a function of numbers, in that the coalition was deemed representative of international society, and not seen as a purely sectional interest. It was partly also a function of its diversity. As earlier noted, the adhesion of Arab states lent the coalition respectability as a cross-section of international society, and was broadly representative in that sense.

It was on such grounds that the war enjoyed relatively high levels of legitimacy internationally, at least at official levels. However, its moral standing was much more equivocal. Again, there are a number of different reasons for this. First, the indignation expressed at the Iraqi regime's behaviour sat awkwardly with the toleration/support lent by many of the P5 powers to Saddam's equally aggressive earlier war against Iran. Throughout the 1980s, this had been viewed by the international community with a high degree of equanimity, and arms had been supplied to Iraq by the Western powers, as well as by the Soviet Union.

Second, successive UNSC resolutions emphasized the legitimacy of the Kuwaiti regime in international legal terms (S/661/1990, 6 August 1990; S/662/1990, 9 August 1990; S/665/1990, 25 August 1990; etc.). However, this was not a regime that otherwise scored well on informal membership criteria, such as human rights and democracy. Since the Western powers routinely deployed these concerns elsewhere, this if anything magnified the disparity with the 'new world order' rhetoric that was then so much in the air.

Third, there was extensive speculation that, while the illegal occupation of Kuwait was the 'permissive' condition for the war, it was not the actual reason.

What turned the dispute into an actual political commitment to fight was the strategic location of the infringement. If it was the case that the war was driven mainly by a defence of Western interests in the region, then any moral case was that much more questionable.

Fourth, this directly raised the moral issue of double standards. To fight a war in defence of a legal principle was one thing. To act quite differently in other comparable cases posed questions about consistency. Accordingly, many challenged the war on those grounds, particularly with reference to the Palestine/Israeli dispute. Addressing the General Assembly a few weeks after the invasion of Kuwait, the Saudi Foreign Minister, Prince Saud al-Faisal, stressed that 'it is for Palestine that Iraq should withdraw from Kuwait and adhere to international legitimacy so that we can mobilize international legality to realize for the people of Palestine what will be realized for the people of Kuwait' (*New York Times*, 3 October 1990: A13). Although couched in legal language, the point was about differential treatment of like cases. Given his own political difficulties, King Hussein of Jordan made repeated reference to this same point. Appealing for a Palestinian settlement on the heels of a Kuwaiti one, he demanded 'it is high time for all to defend international legitimacy by upholding it, and for the security council to show that it applies one, and not two, yardsticks' (*The Times*, 11 December 1990). Unsurprisingly, Saddam Hussein was more than eager to play the same card. 'Many have spoken of international legitimacy and law', he suggested to a conference of Islamic leaders, 'but if we are reviewing international legitimacy and laws, let us start with Palestine' (*New York Times*, 12 January 1991: A9). There were many tactical reasons for such appeals at the time, but there is no denying that the point struck a powerful chord in the region, and has continued to do so since. Speaking in 1998, Crown Prince Hassan of Jordan spoke of the frustration of the Arab peoples at the 'UN duality in enforcing international legitimacy in the region' (*Jordan Times*, 17 February 1998). In that sense, part of the moral squeamishness about the Gulf war in 1991 was not about what was done there, but about what was being seen not to be done elsewhere.

Finally, as in the case of Kosovo, the moral objection to the war was often stated as a set of specific objections to the manner in which it was conducted. The issue of civilian casualties became prominent, as did the political strategy of encouraging insurrection on the part of the Kurdish and Shiite communities, both of which were then left to the mercy of the regime.

On these grounds, the war evoked mixed moral reactions. However, to present this as a tension between legitimacy and morality per se is again to miss the more important point. What needs to be emphasized instead is that each of these arguments—illegal but legitimate, immoral but legitimate—is seriously imbalanced. What both do is privilege one component of legitimacy, and then set it up against a supposedly alternative normative principle. The evidence suggests that this is not how legitimacy is understood and practised in contemporary international society. Legitimacy does not possess its own separate Richter scale of values against which an action can be judged, but is necessarily parasitic upon the other norms that are embedded in international society. Legitimacy is international society's aggregate instrument for seeking an accommodation between competing norms, and is essentially a political condition grounded in degrees of consensus about what is considered acceptable. Other norms, such as that of morality, feed into this overall process, without necessarily determining its outcome.

LEGITIMACY AND CONSTITUTIONALITY

The third norm to be considered is the most overtly political, that of constitutionality. This is the realm neither of legal norms, nor of moral prescriptions. Instead, it is the political realm of conventions, informal understandings, and mutual expectations. At its core are political sensibilities about what can properly be done, and how affairs should be conducted. Perceptions of the legal and moral state of play make their presence felt, but are neither separately nor collectively the determining factor. Constitutionality captures the wider context of political mediation through which these perceptions must pass, and is itself subject to the quest for consensus. Just as legitimacy cannot be wholly identified with either legality or morality, neither can it be entirely identified with constitutionality. Nonetheless, now the practice of legitimacy is very much concerned with codes of constitutionality, and with claims about their violation.

John Ikenberry's analysis of constitutional orders provides a good demonstration of this category of norm. He suggests that, at the end of the Second World War, the United States exercised strategic restraint to establish a constitutional, rather than a victor's, order. Constitutional orders 'serve to reduce the returns to power', and have three principal characteristics: shared agreement about the principles and rules of order; authoritative limits on the exercise of power; and the entrenchment of these rules in a wider political system (Ikenberry 2001: 29–32). Through a multiplicity of multilateral institutions, the United States traded off elements of its (unilateral) power for the greater authority it would derive in return from the acceptability of this order to most states. So successful was this that, with the cold war won, it not only survived but was actively expanded. Incorporation into this order became the chosen instrument for stabilizing the new Europe to emerge from the east (Ikenberry 2001: 235). Essentially, just as in the earlier concert of Europe, the constitutionality of the order was to be found in mutual expectations about multilateral forms of action (in the political, security, and socio-economic fields). In so far as all participating states subscribed to those modalities, the order was less costly for the United States to maintain, since it rested upon compliance and not coercion. In a very direct way, legitimacy was understood to be a function of the constitutional bargain. Other commentators share this perspective. 'American preponderance is softened when it is embodied in a web of multilateral institutions that allow others to participate in decisions', Nye reassures us, 'and that act as a sort of world constitution to limit the capriciousness of American power' (Nye 2002: 17). The contemporary debate about legitimacy is extremely sensitive to the maintenance of this constitutionality, and, as is implicit in Nye's remark—and will be further discussed in Chapter 12—is largely so because of the discrepancies in power on which it now rests. The worry is that the United States is so strong 'that it can resist the constitutionalist pressures of the system' (Hurrell 2002: 190).

While the norms of legality and morality change over time, the norm of constitutionality has the greatest capacity for rapid change. The climate of mutual expectations can alter within a relatively short period of time. Despite his insistence that constitutional rules are 'not easily altered' (Ikenberry 2001: 31), this claim must be offset against his qualification that constitutionality is more problematic in an international context, not least because 'limits on power are never clear-cut, absolute, or fully guaranteed in relations between states' (Ikenberry 2001: 29). For example, the foundational documents of the concert were barely a few years old when, operationally, the concert began to falter in the early 1820s. In no small measure, this is so because what is politically acceptable reflects changing circumstances and opportunities, and is certainly not immune to shifts in the distribution of power: what is acceptable is a function of the room for manoeuvre. Russia found itself accepting things in the 1990s—such as a unified Germany within NATO—that would have been inconceivable a few years earlier. Hence also the widespread argument that the humanitarian interventionism of the 1990s was less a reflection of a new moral purpose in international society, but driven largely by the more permissive international distribution of power. Constitutions bridle power, but are themselves devised in the context of existing distributions of it. Nonetheless, there is compelling justification for including constitutionality in the discussion of contemporary legitimacy. Its impact is best illustrated by the diplomacy surrounding the Iraq war in 2003.

The Iraq War 2003

However ambiguous and indeterminate the legal and moral arguments deployed in the context of what became the war against Iraq, the resort to war failed the additional test of constitutionality, and it was this norm—more so than the others—that provoked the air of crisis surrounding this episode. The norm of constitutionality is not derivable from the other two, but has a real existence independently of them. It was the palpable sense of infringement of this norm—in a sense irrespective of the force of the legal and moral arguments—that was such a prominent feature of this particular sequence of events. On this, even those on the opposite sides of the fence can agree. The disagreements over Iraq, Kagan tells us, were not just 'about policy', but also 'about first principles' (Kagan 2004: 65). Germany's ambassador to the United States concurred: 'By raising doubts about power, legitimacy, and credibility', the Iraq war 'challenged the existing international order more than any other event since the cold war' (Ischinger 2004: 1). The leading coalition powers tried to sustain a case that the war was possibly unconstitutional, but still legitimate—in legal and moral terms—but no effective consensus developed around their position.

There was clearly a mainstream preoccupation with legality in the international community's response. Iraq had been subject to a succession of UNSC resolutions since the end of the first Iraq war in 1991, and these constituted the scope of the legal demands made of that country. These covered a range of subjects, including disarmament (in the areas of missile technology and weapons of mass destruction), and related also to various acts of restitution required in the aftermath of the original war, as well as to economic embargos. As the crisis culminated in late 2002 and early 2003, the key questions concerned the degree of Iraq's compliance with these resolutions, and what further measures might be taken against it in the event of clear evidence of material breaches of its undertakings. The inspection regime for illicit armaments was to become the core issue of concern. A large number of states insisted that the inspection regime had not yet run its full course, and that it yet held out the best prospects for a peaceful resolution of the problem. A smaller number of states, especially the United States and United Kingdom, became increasingly restive about further delays, and pressed for the UN to take more urgent measures.

The diplomacy came down finally to the matter of whether or not existing UNSC resolutions did, or did not, authorize military enforcement, and if so by whom. There was to be no express resolution in 2002–3, as there had been in 1990, to authorize the use of 'all necessary means'. Nonetheless, the specific legal argument was decidedly not about the importance or otherwise of UNSC authorization, but rather about whether or not it already existed. The United States and Britain claimed to act in support of existing UN resolutions, and suggested that this legal authority dated back to ceasefire resolutions in 1991. 'What was at issue regarding Iraq in 2003', says Roberts (2003: 43), 'was as much a claim of "existing authority" or "continuing authority" as of "implied authority" '. It is interesting in this light to note the content of the draft 'second' resolution of 2003 (in succession to Resolution 1441 of 8 November 2002, which had already warned Iraq of 'serious consequences' if it did not comply). If, to satisfy domestic publics in the United States, United Kingdom, and elsewhere, as well as international demands from other countries, no military action was to be taken without express Security Council approval, one would have expected this draft to contain the coded 'all necessary means' terminology. It did not do so, and presumably for two good reasons. First, it was evidently proving extremely difficult to secure any second resolution, and countries like France had made very clear their opposition to one that would unleash immediate military action. Second, since the argument was that this authority already existed, it could be thought contradictory to secure it a second time.

Accordingly, the text stated simply that the Council '*Decides* that Iraq has failed to take the final opportunity afforded it in resolution 1441 (2002)', and left the rest to the imagination (Sifry and Cerf 2003: 499–500).

In large measure, the case made against Iraq was that, on the basis of past actions and presumed policies, it constituted a threat to regional and global peace and security, as existing UNSC resolutions had attested. It was this potential threat which, if not removed to the international community's satisfaction, would provide the legal grounds for action against the country. However, just as in 1990–1, the issue of double standards was raised over Iraq's putative security threat. The comparison that was made on this occasion was with North Korea. Internationally, commentators asked why action should be taken against Iraq, but apparently not against North Korea. Typically, it was pointed out that 'Washington should be preparing to attack Iraq, even though Baghdad's capabilities in the weapons of mass destruction field are unproven, while doing so much less to deal with the nuclear weapon capability that North Korea has itself declared' (*The Hindu*, 25 February 2003). Others suggested that 'the contrasting US approach to Iraq and North Korea...further undermines the legitimacy of a US military strike on Iraq' (*Korea Herald*, 17 January 2003).

Other moral issues entered into the debate at various stages. Although the key issue was ostensibly the legal one, this was to some extent also turned around by the proponents of the war to be a matter of the moral authority of the UN itself. It had spoken in its resolutions, so it was claimed, and now it needed to follow through on its intent. Even Kofi Annan admitted to this serious concern. In his much-heralded speech to the General Assembly on 12 September 2002, Annan urged that 'if Iraq's defiance continues, the Security Council must face its responsibilities' (Sifry and Cerf 2003: 312). It was less noteworthy that US President George W. Bush should also emphasize the same point, to the same body, on the same occasion. 'The conduct of the Iraqi regime is a threat to the authority of the United Nations', he insisted, and asked rhetorically 'Are Security Council resolutions to be honoured and enforced, or cast aside without consequence?' (Sifry and Cerf 2003: 316–17).

More directly, there were to be attempts to present the key problem with Iraq as predominantly moral or humanitarian. At issue was the heinous domestic behaviour of the regime against its own people. This note had already been struck before the war started. In his General Assembly address in September 2002, President Bush protested that 'liberty for the Iraqi people is a great moral cause' (Sifry and Cerf 2003: 317). However, as the war progressed, and in its immediate aftermath, there was an even more assertive emphasis upon this dimension, not least in the absence of any immediate finds of weapons of mass destruction. From being initially a concern for international peace and security, Iraq came increasingly to be discussed as a great humanitarian cause, in ways that suggested parallels with the Kosovo operation. We should, for example, note seriously the codename given to the military campaign: *Operation Iraqi*

Freedom. It was this goal that was to justify the regime change that had become the implicit objective of the war, and certainly its proximate outcome. However, in terms of the legalities of UN resolutions, it must be recalled that each and every one of the resolutions carried on the subject of Iraq included the ritual affirmation of the sovereignty and territorial integrity of that country.

In the case of Britain's Tony Blair, we can trace this evolution in proportion to the mounting difficulties faced by his preferred UN strategy, and as his hopes of a second resolution evaporated. Initially, Blair was categorical that, whatever might be felt about the evils of Saddam's regime, this was not the principal issue. In a statement to parliament, he made the categorical distinction that, while 'the ending of the regime would be the cause of regret for no-one other than Saddam...our purpose is disarmament' (Blair 2002*a*: 6). He reiterated this stand on the adoption of UNSCR 1441. 'I may find this regime abhorrent...But the survival of it is in his hands. Conflict is not inevitable. Disarmament is' (Blair 2002*b*: 2). During the winter and the early spring of 2003, there was a detectable shift of emphasis towards the humanitarian situation within Iraq. Implicitly, as the prospect of new Security Council authorization disappeared, Blair felt more comfortable to mount this plea in mitigation. Opening the key debate in the House of Commons, Blair was consistent in his statement that 'I have never put our justification for action as regime change. We have to act within the terms set out in Resolution 1441. That is our legal case'. However, he then immediately added the following comment: 'But it is the reason, I say frankly, why if we do act we should do so with a clear conscience and strong heart' (Blair 2003*a*: 12).

Clearly, then, there were substantial legal and moral dimensions to the legitimacy debate over the war, and these were deployed on both sides of the argument. Nonetheless, the norm of constitutionality lay at the core of the problem. From this perspective, the role and authority of the UN was the *symptom*, rather than the *cause*, of this crisis. The point can be illustrated with reference to France. As we have seen, President Chirac was the NATO leader who came closest to espousing the argument that the moral/humanitarian catastrophe in Kosovo created an exceptional circumstance in which normal UN procedure might have to be bypassed, and yet he resolutely resisted all versions of similar arguments when used by the United States and Britain over Iraq. On the outbreak of war, he bluntly chided that 'to cast off the legitimacy of the United Nations, and put the use of force above the rule of law is to assume a heavy responsibility' (*Independent*, 19 March 2003: 7). How is this different French attitude to be explained? It could be that France simply saw no parallel, as there was no moral emergency, let alone immediate threat to international security in the case of Iraq that might warrant such an exception. Given that the Kosovo war was legally as contentious as that in Iraq in its absence of explicit UN authorization, was it then the 'moral purpose' that made the difference with regard to Kosovo, and made it relatively less contentious? Alternatively, it could simply be a matter of the numbers. The use of force in

Kosovo was supported by a clear majority in the Security Council, and unanimously within NATO. In the case of Iraq, the draft second resolution was dropped presumably because not even a 'moral majority' was available, even in the face of a veto, and the resulting coalition was, by comparison with 1991, a tawdry affair, both in absolute numbers and as a cross section of international society. It could then be said that France and others opposed the war because of the very limited degree of international support that it mustered. But this may get it the wrong way round. It is equally plausible to argue that the coalition became so small because of the impact of the already emerging legitimacy deficit induced by the crisis of constitutionality.

The pertinent factor here was one of political context, and this accounts for the differing reactions to the situations in Kosovo and Iraq. In 1998–9, Europe carried the burden of its none-too-illustrious role in Yugoslavia during the 1990s, plus the more positive memory of NATO's eventual role in Bosnia as the handmaiden of the UN. France, in particular, had its own political skeletons in the cupboard, some left over from Rwanda. Moreover, it was very welcome that the United States had been prepared to act through NATO in Kosovo, rather than go it alone. It was against this backdrop that the norm of constitutionality was understood in 1999.

The world in 2002–3 appeared quite a different place, and the crisis in the UN over Iraq reflected the transformations over the previous three years. What made many practitioners so sensitive to the norm of constitutionality in 2003 was exactly the extent to which it had already been stretched across the preceding period (Ikenberry 2004). The crisis over Iraq would not have been so serious had it not been regarded as the *culmination* of a tendency, rather than as an isolated departure. It was therefore against this background of the pre-existing evidence of unilateralism in US policy that the events over Iraq were to unfold in such a damaging way.

Concerns about US unilateralism were already widespread by this stage. In the Chinese press, Bush's foreign policy was dismissed as 'reeking of isolationism and unilateralism' (*People's Daily*, 1 April 2003). This was perhaps to be expected. More surprising was the reaction in Europe. The crisis of constitutionality affected Europe particularly: it stood to lose most, as being central to the existing constitutional order. Even the rapprochement with Russia and China, following upon the 11 September attacks on the United States, had been substantially dissipated by the perceived lack of constitutionality which the 'war on terror' was thought to be fostering. Decisions about Iraq were then taken in a context in which basic confidence in the constitutional order had already been deeply shaken.

CONCLUSION

In sum, the legalities were no more clear-cut over Iraq in 2003 than they had been over Kosovo in 1999, and the moral agenda remained equally opaque.

What distinguished the two episodes was the much wider concern in 2003 that the informal norm of constitutionality was being tested beyond acceptable levels, and eventually breached. It was these existing concerns that became manifest in the crisis in the UN, rather than the events in the UN being the cause of them. While the issue was debated in terms of the legalities of resort to military action, and increasingly also in terms of the moral purpose of liberating the people of Iraq, the underlying problem was demonstrably that wider shock to the confidence of mutual expectations that the erosion of constitutionality was producing. This was to be the principal benchmark in terms of which legitimacy would be bestowed or withheld, and this accounts for the prominent dissent to the war on the part of leading European states, such as France and Germany. Legality and morality were manageable elements, provided only that they were underpinned by a reasonable consensus about, and confidence in, the basic constitutional order. It was this final element that was so manifestly missing in 2003 as to trigger the legitimacy crisis of that year.

This chapter has demonstrated that legitimacy is close to the norms of legality, morality, and constitutionality, but not so close that we are unable to distinguish between them. When people speak the language of legitimacy, the substance of what they say is perforce drawn from these three norms. Legitimacy, however, is more than the sum of their total, as it incorporates the element of political accommodation amongst their competing pulls. This accommodation is voiced through degrees of consensus. While legitimacy draws upon these norms, it also stands at one remove, and it is this consensual quality about the validity of their respective normative claims that marks this separation.

Why, finally, had international society become so vulnerable to a crisis of legitimacy over Iraq? There is a widespread view that this was a symptom of a yet deeper shift in international society. This shift had occurred in the international distribution of power, and its result was a new age of US hegemony. It was this that had unsettled the norms of international society, and made the attainment of international consensus so much more difficult. It is to this relationship between legitimacy and (dis)equilibrium that we must finally turn.

12

Legitimacy and Equilibrium

At various junctures, we have already encountered aspects of the problematic relationship between legitimacy, on the one hand, and power, consensus, and norms, on the other. These preceding reflections now invite a final set of questions. If the attainment of legitimacy is dependent upon the realization of satisfactory degrees of consensus, and this in turn expressive of some kind of normative congruence, in what ways might such consensus and normative unity be related to power? More particularly, might it be the case that they are both dependent upon particular distributions of power, and possibly most attainable in conditions of equilibrium? It was certainly the case that nineteenth-century international thought developed a close connection between the concept of legitimacy and the achievement of what it called a 'just equilibrium'. How important, then, is the balance of power for notions of legitimacy in contemporary international society, and might its currently troubled quest for consensus, and the unsettled condition of its norms, both be rooted in profound disquiet about the unequal distribution of power in today's world? This chapter will explore these connections, both theoretically and also in terms of the specific debate about US hegemony in the contemporary world situation. To what extent is legitimacy challenged by the very fact of US predominance, and, conversely, to what extent is the current search for legitimacy driven by the felt need to constrain that power?

As already acknowledged, power and legitimacy are fundamentally inseparable ideas. The need for legitimacy arises only in the context of the exercise of relations of power, and legitimacy enhances power by making its maintenance less costly. Legitimacy does not simply constrain power: it makes it more effective through 'consensual empowerment'. However, can it be claimed also that there is a direct relationship between legitimacy and specific *distributions* of power? Is an international consensus about norms and procedures more likely to be discovered in conditions of relative equilibrium? Is disequilibrium in *itself* an obstacle to development of legitimacy principles, or does it merely impede attempts at legitimation by appeal to them? If the hegemony is too complete, and amounts to an imperial order, can there be any effective constraint at all on power in such a situation?

These questions are particularly pertinent in today's conditions of manifest disequilibrium: this distribution is regularly captured by the language of unipolarity, hegemony, and empire. If this diagnosis is accurate, it raises key issues for the attainment of viable principles of legitimacy in contemporary international society. Indeed, to some minds, it goes yet further in raising fundamental questions about the viability of international society itself, and whether it is now being supplanted by hierarchy instead (T. Dunne 2003: 308). In accordance with the argument of this book, if principles of legitimacy are unattainable in conditions of hegemony, then the bonds of international society would indeed be seriously ruptured. Is this actually the case?

If the disparity in US power presents some kind of problem for legitimacy, we need to explore its precise nature before reaching such apocalyptic judgements. For initial presentation, we can consider the core issue to be expressed in the following three ways. Each pinpoints the difficulty in slightly different terms:

1. It is the *fact* of US preponderance that impedes the search for consensus, and destabilizes contemporary international norms.
2. It is the *content* of US policy that is disruptive of contemporary norms because the United States is behaving as a 'revolutionary' state.
3. It is the ambivalent demands on the United States in its role as the *leader* in contemporary international society that makes contemporary legitimacy so problematic.

Each of these provides a different gloss upon the situation, and each gives rise to its own set of policy implications for international society. These will need to be examined in detail in the course of this chapter, and the scheme will provide an analytical framework to structure this discussion.

Ironically, as against the traditional European notion of a just equilibrium, the United States has historically displayed a penchant for its alternative vision of what might be termed a just disequilibrium: at least since Woodrow Wilson, its preferred model of the ideal international society has been one in which there is not a balance of power, but rather an imbalance in favour of the forces of peace and justice, as viewed from Washington's perspective (Claude 1962; Talbott 2003: 1038). This is an idiom that has powerfully re-emerged in recent US official thinking, as is nicely displayed in President Bush's covering letter to the 2002 National Security Strategy document. 'We seek instead', he affirmed, 'to create a balance of power that favors human freedom' (USNSC 2002: 1). Support for this kind of logic had already been candidly, and vocally, canvassed by sympathetic publicists. They had decried any possible attractions in a multipolar world, and urgently reminded the US people that 'their support for American pre-eminence' is itself a crucial 'boost for international justice' (Kagan and Kristol 2000: 69), words that were to prefigure closely the sentiments subsequently expressed by the President. Its critics have dismissed this formulation as 'a confused, even meaningless concept' (Leffler 2003: 1057). Be that as it may, what it certainly appeals to is an image of a just disequilibrium in which there is to be preponderance, not a balance of power. This preponderance, moreover, is construed to enhance normative values: its real attraction is that the preponderance is on the side of 'freedom'.

Why does such a US presentation of its vision place great strains on contemporary international society's notion of legitimacy? Unfortunately, again in the eyes of the critics, this formulation itself constitutes the essence of the problem, because it is the very imbalance that it promotes that has facilitated the disruptive policies now pursued by the United States. 'At no time in the last 50 years', is one such stark judgment, 'has the United States stood in such antagonism to both the primary norms and the central institutions of international society' (Hendrickson 2002: 4–5). 'Bush and his advisers', echoes Leffler, 'display a disdain for the norms, institutions and rules that bind the community in whose interests they are ostensibly acting' (Leffler 2003: 1061). Supporters, naturally enough, demur from any notion that 'legitimacy derives from international consensus', and exhort the US administration instead to 'be guided by its independent judgment, both about its own interest and about the global interest' (Krauthammer 2003: 605–6). The critics, in riposte, retort that any 'US primacy that is not embedded in a legitimate world order undermines US security' (Guzzini 2002: 296). In a nutshell, the issue to be addressed is whether, in the eyes of contemporary international society, US primacy is part of the solution or part of the problem, as far as legitimacy is concerned. As will be demonstrated, it is necessarily both.

THE DEBATE ABOUT US POWER

The predominant position of the United States in international society had accelerated markedly after the end of the cold war, both absolutely and relatively. As is often remarked, the United States enjoyed a good 1990s in terms of its rapid economic expansion. By the early 2000s, this was being reflected in the scale of defence expenditure which then stood at a total equivalent to that of the next fifteen or so states combined. At the same time, in qualitative terms, US armed forces enjoyed an ever widening technological gap over all other contenders. Relatively, US primacy had been substantially reinforced by the travails of others. Russia descended into medium-powerhood during the 1990s as it sought, slowly and painfully, to reinvent itself after the Communist collapse. Japan's economy stagnated through the 1990s, and the East Asian economies suffered collectively from the financial crisis at century's end. In consequence, the earlier fears of an irresistible Japanese economic challenge to the United States virtually dissipated. The European Union both deepened and widened, but this did nothing to disguise its proclivity to political immobilism during international crises, nor to reduce its ultimate dependence upon US military power to resolve problems, even those within Europe, such as in Bosnia and Kosovo. Chinese power remained a semi-distant prospect. Instead of balancing against the United States, there was at least a short-lived tendency in the aftermath of the 11 September attacks for the major powers—and especially Russia and China—to bandwagon with it by committing themselves to the war on terror. By 2003, most analysts could agree with Krauthammer (2003) that his unipolar 'moment' had now taken on a yet starker form, and had settled in for the duration: the moment was more likely to capture an 'age'.

But was it this unipolarity that was frustrating legitimacy? On this first reckoning, it is the stark realities of US power that are very much at stake in the contemporary search for legitimacy. Moreover, and to be precise, it is US *power* that is the problem, rather than the content or the style of US foreign and security policy. The issue is not one of US 'arrogance', it is said. Instead, it is the 'inescapable reality of American power', and 'those who suggest that these international resentments could somehow be eliminated by a more restrained American foreign policy are engaging in pleasant delusions' (Kagan and Kristol 2000: 67). Kagan reminds us that it was during the Clinton years of relatively assiduous US multilateralism that French Foreign Minister, Hubert Védrine, coined the term *hyperpuissance* to characterize the 'American behemoth' (Kagan 2003: 43). Indeed, Védrine had himself explained at the time that 'the predominant weight of the United States and the absence for the moment of a counterweight' was 'the major fact of the global world today' (*International Herald Tribune*, 3 February 1999: 1). Underlying the French concept of a restored multipolarity was therefore the explicit logic that international society 'can derive its greatest legitimacy from structured dialogue among these poles leading to some form of universal consensus around agreed norms of international behaviour' (Howorth 2003–4: 184).

The suspicion, however, must be that this version exonerates US policy too much: style and content matter, just as much as do any crude power differentials. Power does not directly translate into anything else, except in so far as it is mediated through policy and actions. Thus a second perspective seeks to shift the emphasis away from the 'determinants' of the structure of power, and towards the 'voluntarism' of policy. As we have been aptly reminded, 'there are ways and ways of hegemons exercising power', and the root cause of today's malaise is not simply the power disequilibrium, but rather the fact that 'many people outside the United States simply do not trust America to use its enormous power wisely or well' (Cox 2003a: 532). Preponderance may be the backdrop against which the play is set, but it is policy that is the real source of dissension. In turn, the cause of this, especially under the Bush administration, had been its own misplaced belief that predominance, by itself, was the necessary and sufficient element in forging a desirable international order, and that 'the confident assertion of that power made it less necessary for the US to rely on structural arrangements' (Talbott 2003: 1040). Existing tendencies in this direction were then mightily reinforced by the events of 11 September which sent the United States 'veering from humility to supremacy' (*The Times*, 13 September 2002: 24). This marked, be it carefully noted, a change not in the power of the United States, but in its political reading of how that power was now to be deployed. It was in the content and style of policy that the crucial shift took place. Power was to become the new legitimacy, and not something that needed to be negotiated into a legitimate order.

In the remainder of this section, we can explore various aspects of US policy during the early 2000s: the war on terror; its role in the UN; instances of the revival of unilateralism; and the condition of its relations with Europe. Within each, the aim will be to explore the dialectic between power and policy, as the underlying source of tension in today's quest for international legitimacy. However, as already foreshadowed, instead of within this stark opposition alone, the issue will be posed also in terms of the unique responsibilities of leadership in a hegemonic world. Does this third consideration present a middle position between the determinants of power, and the discretionary options of policy, such as to make sense both of US behaviour and of the response of the remainder of international society to it?

The war on terror offers a good illustration of these themes. The fact that the terrorist attacks of 11 September were responded to by the declaration of a generic and global war on terror was itself symptomatic of the capacity of the United States to exercise such a choice; and the modalities of this response both captured the new mood of US policy, and served further to crystallize the political will to act upon it. In short, the United States had the power to universalize its reaction to those specific attacks, and established a policy framework that would do precisely that. In President Bush's words, in his covering letter to the National Security Strategy statement of 2002, the war would be a 'global enterprise of uncertain duration' (USNSC 2002: 1). Weaker states would have had to settle for less in framing their response. At the same time, the war on terror highlighted issues that extended beyond the mere power or policy of the United States. These articulated concerns that the United States was the principal victim of the attack for the very reason of its symbolic role as world leader; and the expectation of global support for the war could hence be justified in the same terms. It was the hegemon that was under attack, not the United States, and those who benefited from the order it provided had a shared responsibility to contribute to its defence. This demanded recognition that the United States should enjoy certain rights and responsibilities—not because it was the United States, nor yet through any acceptance of a doctrine of US exceptionalism—but precisely because of the functional role that the United States now played as the world's leading power. What mattered were not so much the details of US power and policy, but the symbolic importance of its social role as leader. What is vital to appreciate is that the response of the United States—by reasserting its hegemonic role—was tacit recognition that it was this role that had been directly attacked, not just the geographical space of the United States. The attacks, it has been claimed, were 'a consequence of the new unipolar world...Because America is "No. 1", it is also target No.1' (Zakaria 2002).

The conjunction of the new post-attack normative possibilities, along with this test of US leadership, created the dynamic of the ensuing situation. There was a widely shared perception in the aftermath of 11 September that the agreed rules of international security conduct would need to be redrawn. Not least was this because those events were understood to be 'norm-shattering' (Falk 2003: 94–5). They evoked, in turn, a number of policy statements about the entitlement to resort to pre-emption in order to prevent future terrorist attacks, and these became collectively known as the Bush Doctrine. 'The Bush Doctrine', it has been suggested, 'is a revolutionary response to revolutionary times' (Wheeler 2003: 201). Existing codes were to be suspended, and their replacements were now subject to renegotiation. If, as international relations theorists have argued, certain states can play the role of 'norm entrepreneurs', then the greatest opportunity for filling this role fell to the United States. In a world where the conventional boundaries on the use of force had been desta-bilized, what was so noteworthy after 11 September was the 'particular power of a hegemonic state to influence the character of customary legal norms' (Hurrell 2002: 188). This was especially so with regard to those norms defining the use of force in self-defence, and what might properly be done pre-emptively as a means to this end. Was the United States to be allowed the opportunity to redefine these rules, and if so what might this then say about the restraints upon the role of the predominant state? These were the issues that were to preoccupy international society, and its debate about legitimacy, in the early 2000s.

Even the critics had been happy to acknowledge the extent to which in its early phase—during the war against Afghanistan—the war on terror had taken on a pronounced multilateral aspect. The United States sought 'general en-dorsement at the UN', and rallied other countries as active supporters, if not as participants, of the military campaign against al-Qaeda and the Taliban (Falk 2003: 73). At the same time, it was made clear also that the operational decisions would be taken by the United States alone. Despite NATO's invoca-tion of Article 5, the United States wished to make no formal use of the alliance in the prosecution of the war, mindful as it was of its Kosovo experience, and determined also to reassert its own leading role. The strategy of the war was therefore reserved to the United States alone. The key question was how long it would be possible to sustain a legitimacy that depended upon a 'general endorsement' by others, but in which they were clearly excluded from the key decisions. In one verdict, the United States succeeded well enough in grasping the conditions necessary for an 'effective' international response, but displayed 'monumental insensitivity to the equally important need to fashion a *legitimate* response' (Falk 2003: 98). For Falk, the illegitimacy resided in the failure on the part of the United States adequately to justify and explain its own departures from existing legal norms in the conduct of the war on terror, and from the seemingly limitless scope of the project. If correct, what this would seem to indicate is either that international society failed to see or accept the case made by the United States about its symbolic role as leader, or simply disagreed about the extent of its consequential entitlement to rewrite the rules. What was missing was an acceptable framework that would define the rights and duties of both leader and society at large, in these normatively unsettled times. At the very least, the response of international society to date suggests that the US entrepreneurial role in this regard has, for the moment, been rebuffed.

Any review of the diplomatic conduct of the war on terror slides seamlessly into a discussion of the specific role accorded the UN in this venture. Immediately after the 11 September attacks, UN Secretary-General Annan insisted that the UN was the only proper organ through which the international effort against terrorism could be conducted. In this sense, the war on terror has presented a key test of the performance of *both* the UN and the United States. In this regard, the tripartite frames of reference—power, policy, and leadership—again assist the inquiry. These themes are apparent in one interpretation of the UN's post-cold war function, as being 'simultaneously to restrain and legitimise the global hegemony of the US' (*The Times*, 13 March 2003: 22). This is less paradoxical than it might otherwise appear. In the context of unipolarity, the UN has no choice but to make use of US power for its own collective ends, and thus has its own interest in legitimizing US power. Former President Clinton had appreciated this in his acknowledgement that 'America truly is the world's indispensable nation' (*Daily Yomiuri*, 20 November 1996: 7). This was not so much a boast about the fact of American power, as it was an admission of the social responsibility that flowed from it. At the same time, the notion of societal legitimation is inescapably bound up with the idea of restraint. The United States is an irreplaceable source of community power, but the community as a whole has an interest in how that power is to be deployed. Without the United States, the UN is effectively disempowered; without the UN, the exercise of US primacy will be more costly than it needs to be. It is within this framework of mutuality that the bargain of contemporary international legitimacy needs to be struck.

In the years since the 11 September attacks, there has been a conspicuous tension between the United States and the UN and this, as we have seen, reached its head over Iraq in 2002–3. But what was the underlying problem? Was it simply that the United States was so dominant that it potentially undermined any credible role for the UN at all? In this case, as some have seen it, the key task for the Security Council is to work 'to restrain American power' (Rodman 2000: 34). Thus conceived, some degree of tension between the two is inevitable, as the UN structure is being called upon to compensate for the disequilibrium that otherwise exists, and to substitute an institutional balance for the imbalance that operates elsewhere. This is no easy task.

The second perspective is to emphasize the distinctive tendencies of US policy under the Bush administration, and to suggest that there has been nothing structurally inevitable about this situation. Symptomatic of this policy was the president's own penchant for speaking of the United States *and* the UN, as if the two were wholly discrete, and the United States not a part of it

(Hoffmann 2003: 1033). This verbal gap denoted the intellectual gap that had emerged in US policy, but was not in itself an inevitable facet of US policy.

The third perspective draws attention once again to the requisite accommodation between recognition of US power, the preferences of US policy, and a realistic appraisal of the leadership role that the United States was structurally required to play in the current UN system. From this point of view, it was not simply the fact of US predominant power that mattered, but additionally the responsibility of leadership that went with it. Critically, this raised the issue of international society's assessment of the allowance that needs to be made in recognition of this role. It is this 'burden of responsibility' (*Japan Times*, 17 February 2002) that needs to lie at the heart of any current legitimacy bargain, and this has so far proved elusive. Such responsibility cuts both ways. It takes the form of the responsibility upon the United States for making possible the enforcement of authorized UN decisions, while operating within social norms in the execution of this function. On the other hand, there is equally the responsibility of international society to come to terms with the extra costs that this imposes on the United States, and to make due allowance for them in tolerating some degree of US discretion.

This relationship between the United States and the UN encapsulates the broader, and much discussed, theme of unilateralism versus multilateralism in contemporary US behaviour. Unilateralism is scarcely a new tendency in US policy. Even a multilaterally-disposed administration, like that of President Clinton, was not immune to its attractions. In the economic sphere, commentators had already complained of the erosion of multilateralism by the end of the 1990s, and its displacement by what was viewed as a US economic policy that was 'unilateral and self-centred' (Gilpin 2000: 11). In 1996, when the possibility of reappointing Boutros-Ghali for a second term as UN Secretary-General was under review, the United States demonstrated its displeasure with the candidate by vetoing the appointment in a vote of 14 to 1 in his favour (Guyatt 2000: 91). It was equally the Clinton administration that stood aloof in 1998 from the newly created International Criminal Court (ICC), as part of a small minority against the 120 states that agreed to submit to its authority (Guyatt 2000: 72).

Nonetheless, the political response within the United States to 11 September sharply intensified any existing predispositions in this direction. 'Taken together', these responses, in the view of one pundit not at all critical of the trend, 'amount to an unprecedented assertion of American freedom of action and a definitive statement of a new American unilateralism' (Krauthammer 2003: 598). In its prosecution of the war on terror, instead of trying to bring about a general shift in the rules for self-defence, the United States, it is argued, was bolstering its own 'exceptionalism': rather than change the rules for all, it sought only 'to exempt itself' (Wheeler 2003: 212). To be sure, such unilateral policies tended to be 'costly in blood and treasure', as Haas had warned, and it remained to be seen how sustainable this could be as the basis of US behaviour in the longer term (Haas 1997: 89). From the other side of the fence, what made unilateralism possible in the first place was also what made its pursuit seem that much more necessary. This can be illustrated in the US attitude to the ICC. Once more, as in the case of 11 September, the matter was presented not as one of simple pre-dominance, but as about the specific responsibilities attached to it. US under-secretary of state, John Bolton, a leading opponent of the ICC, explained why US concerns about the Court were different from assessments prevailing in Europe. 'Because they're not the world's only remaining super-power', he explained. 'The responsibilities we have and the attacks we receive . . . leave us, perhaps, more aware of the risks' (*International Herald Tribune*, 25 September 2002). In the recrudescence of US opposition to the ICC during 2002, there was a period when the United States threatened to pull peace-keepers out of UN missions, in Bosnia and elsewhere, putting these operations temporarily at risk (*The Times*, 2 July 2002: 15). This may have helped the United States eventually to get its own way on the Court, but at some cost to its relationship with erstwhile friends and allies. A Human Rights Watch spokes-person in New York had commented of the whole affair that 'a court that exempts the world's superpower risks losing its legitimacy' (*International Herald Tribune*, 30 September 2002: 8). It might just as well be said that such exemption would entail a loss of legitimacy for the role of the United States as well.

This same trend of unilateralism emerged openly in the Bush administration's final denunciation of the ABM Treaty in late 2001 (*International Herald Tribune*, 15 December 2001: 6). It was these expressions of unilateralism that most worried the administration's critics. 'In its first two years', it was lamented, 'it has reneged on more international treaties than any previous Administration' (Zakaria 2002: 3). European critics, in particular, made much of this theme of unilateralism, and of its potential costs. The *IHT*, for example, quoted Robert Cooper's comment that the 'international order requires international legitimacy', but this was unlikely to be achieved 'by a single power taking decisions on its own' (*International Herald Tribune*, 3 January 2003).

Finally, assessments of the recent trends in Washington's policy can be approached in the context of what many have seen as a widening rift between the United States and its formerly close allies in Europe. Both US and European analysts have warmed to this particular theme. Their reflections tap into wider concerns than those about US unilateralism alone, although they are intended to provide insight into the deeper forces from which this unilateralism might be thought to spring. Above all, the relevance of this debate lies precisely in the importance it attaches to US power as an explanation of US behaviour, and of that of its allies. If there is a contemporary problem in attaining a legitimate international order, based upon a reconciliation of US leadership with the constraints demanded by the remainder of international society, then the current disarray in US–European relations can shed some light on its basic nature.

It is interesting to note in this context the arguments advanced by Tony Blair. He too lamented the difficulties in US–European relations, and suggested that the world as a whole would be the loser by them. In particular, he has repeatedly stressed that a reversion to multipolarity would be an undesirable development, as he felt the case of Iraq had already demonstrated. 'The loser will be the wider world', he admonished, 'because on every single issue that comes up there will be rival poles of power to which people can gravitate. It will be far harder to make the international order stable and secure' (Blair 2003*b*: 15). He had already explained the divisions in the UN over Iraq as the product of this misguided search for multipolarity. 'And at the heart of it has been the concept of a world in which there are rival poles of power. The United States and its allies in one corner. France, Germany, Russia and its allies in the other' (Blair 2003*a*: 11). To the British Prime Minister, disequilibrium was not the problem. It was rather the attempt to displace it with a resurrected multipolar equilibrium.

Tracing the trajectory of recent disagreements between the United States and its European allies, the most prominent critic is adamant that 'these disagreements reflect, above all, the disparity of power' (Kagan 2003: 29). In short, it is the absence of equilibrium which makes the attainment of a legitimate order so problematic in contemporary conditions. Europeans are obsessed, we are told, by the wish for a 'handcuffing of American power', and this is no less than is to be expected 'given Europe's weakness and America's power' (Krauthammer 2003: 601). 'Today's debate over multilateralism and legitimacy', Kagan opines, '...is Europe's response to the unipolar predicament' (Kagan 2004: 83). So is US power, after all, the key to understanding what is now going wrong?

Kagan's account is rooted in a realist understanding of power. The United States displays 'Martian' tendencies because it is the predominant state. The Europeans have become 'Venutian', not just because of culture and history, but because of their relative weakness, and the interests that reflect their present predicament. Accordingly, while one European observer plots the tensions in accordance with Europe's new 'postmodern' characteristics (Cooper 2003), and Francis Fukuyama describes an ideological chasm over national versus multilateral sources of legitimacy (*International Herald Tribune*, 9 August 2002: 4), Kagan (2003: 38) remains convinced that the Europeans' 'hostility to unilateralism is also self-interested'. What prevents any accommodation of these interests, such that a consensus around legitimacy principles might emerge, is exactly the power differential between them: this gives rise to an American interest in unilateralism and a European interest in multilateralism. As long as this gulf persists, their expectations of the international order will remain incompatible, and no accommodation is obtainable. 'America's power and its willingness to exercise that power', he elaborates, '...constitute a threat to Europe's new sense of mission' (Kagan 2003: 61). The concatenation of events around the Security Council—as in the case of Iraq—should then be understood, not as the real crux of the legitimacy contest, but instead as its shadow play. 'For Europeans', the logic runs, 'the UN Security Council is a substitute for the power they lack' (Kagan 2003: 40). In short, we should not be deceived into imagining that disputes about the authority of the UNSC represent a clash between international legitimacy, on the one hand, as against a 'revolutionary' US unilateralism, on the other. What is instead at stake is whether or not a legitimate order can be forged at the interstices of these two sets of preferences. In the meantime, UN diplomacy is but the continuation of this more basic power struggle by other means: it is the fundamental absence of equilibrium that stands in the way of any moral consensus about appropriate international procedures.

Is the argument convincing? Alternatively, is this just a sophisticated realist defence of US primacy? Underlying Kagan's analysis is an assumption of moral equivalence: rooted in power differentials, and their corresponding interests, the US preference for unilateralism is on a par with European, and other, demands for multilateralism. The problem is that any such assessment is buttressed by a naive, or disingenuous, set of beliefs about how the United States, given its preponderance, has 'no choice' but to act in certain ways, as do also the Europeans. This fails to take due account of that important strand of realist thought, expressed by Morgenthau and others, which places equal weight upon the responsibilities of statecraft, and in particular upon the responsibilities of leadership. In this respect, what is deficient about the analysis is its attempt to explain everything in terms of power, resulting in a highly deficient analysis of the concept of power itself (Reus-Smit 2004*a*). It is scarcely unthinkable that there could be shifts in US policy that would soften emerging US–European antagonisms. Moreover, it is equally plausible that new bargains could be struck about the responsibilities of US leadership that would accommodate, in some degree, both US and European needs. Kagan's analysis does not take seriously enough the extent to which his prescriptions are likely to be corrosive of US power—and detrimental to its interests—in the longer term. The disparities of power are real enough, but that is the starting point, not the end point, of any adequate analysis. These power differentials are the backdrop against which policy must be formed, and responsible leadership developed: they are not themselves a set of policies.

This is a theme to which the chapter must finally return. In the meantime, it is now necessary to locate this debate about American power, and its implications for legitimacy, in the context of some of the current gross evaluations of the character of that US power in the international system. Given the salience of the United States, how is that power best to be depicted, and what might this mean for the prospects of creating a just disequilibrium?

There is a plethora of terminology in current usage to describe today's international distribution of power. Amongst the most common terms are those of primacy, unipolarity, preponderance, hegemony, and empire. These can be variously defined, and this is not the moment for any extended semantic excursus. What is important is to tease from them any important implications for the nature of the legitimacy principles that might be available to contemporary international society. For this purpose, these terms can be considered loosely to fall along a spectrum, with the opposite ends of the spectrum carrying quite distinct implications for the kind of international legitimacy principles that might be obtainable.

Arguably, notions such as those of primacy, unipolarity, preponderance, and hegemony cluster towards a part of the spectrum that is, at least in principle, reconcilable with a logic of pluralism, and some residual concept of a balance of power. If Watson (1992) is correct in his diagnosis that the fundamental legitimacy principles of the state system have been anti-hegemonial in nature, then today's principles of legitimacy remain minimally intelligible within such frameworks, however much they might be stretched by such notions. However, once we make the move towards the ever more widespread term of empire, we edge towards an end of the spectrum marked by a stratified hierarchy, rather than by the interaction of sovereign equals. Hierarchy, in this sense, undermines traditional notions of international society (T. Dunne 2003), and can scarcely express itself in legitimacy principles of a conventional kind. Accordingly, within the domain of empire, we must expect to encounter a concept of legitimacy that pertains to the logic of rule, rather than to the logic of 'anarchy' and pluralism. Legitimacy, in this different setting, and as in domestic political systems, will give rise to authority structures of a kind not normally associated with international society.

In the immediate post-cold war period—and at a time when an eventual reversion to some kind of multipolarity was a widespread expectation—the language of primacy and unipolarity was the most common. By the early 2000s, and as US primacy intensified and appeared to be more durable, the idiom shifted to that of hegemony and empire. 'Today's international system', we were categorically informed, 'is built not around a balance of power but around American hegemony' (Kagan and Kristol 2000: 61). Despite the array of terms on offer, there are a number of interlocking reasons why the topic is best approached through the lenses of this hegemony.

It is true that others have been as happy to speak the language of US empire (*Guardian*, 13 September 2002: 17; Callinicos 2002; Cox 2003*b*). But what is at stake in doing so for our understanding of legitimacy? The complexity arises in the current fashion for the concept of empire itself, and in the attempted exegeses of the contemporary international order in its terms. Popular works, such as that of Hardt and Negri (2001), have raised this profile. There are two points in their account that are of immediate importance to the present discussion. First, they insist that the model of empire is an accurate depiction of the world today because it operates around 'a single logic of rule' (Hardt and Negri 2001: xii). This, as noted, must set today's imperial order apart from classical models of international society. If this logic were adopted, traditional conceptions of international legitimacy could have little purchase, and the full extent of the challenge which disequilibrium presents to legitimacy would come to the fore. There is little that this book can say on that topic. Second, however, we need to consider what Hardt and Negri say about the nature and source of this single logic of rule. What is so striking is that they distance it from US power, as do some other cognate descriptions of the so-called international or global state (Shaw 2000). '*The United States does not*', insist Hardt and Negri, '*and indeed no nation-state can today, form the center of an imperialist project*' (Hardt and Negri 2001: xiii–xiv). This is a world of global network power, rather than of power contained within separate states, such as the United States, however much its opponents like to give it the name 'America' (Brown 2002: xiii). For proponents of the global state, it is equally this issue of American power that divides them. Shaw agrees with Hardt and Negri 'that contemporary global power is quite a lot *more* than American empire' (Shaw 2002: 328). Others dissent, and prefer to speak in terms of an 'international state dominated by the US' (Barkawi and Laffey 2002: 34).

The name by which it is called matters less than the reality that it describes. If we understand empire to be global network power, divorced from the United States, then international society as such can do precious little to negotiate the terms of this rule. This is self-evident, since it is international society itself that is threatened and undermined by this very development. Only to the extent that this empire is American, or can be partially controlled by the United States, can it be addressed by international society. Even then, if US rule is genuinely imperial in nature, its logic remains stubbornly different from that normally pertaining in international society. The world of difference between these two versions of empire is that there can be no accommodation with global network power, while there remains yet the prospect of an accommodation with the United States. Any such accommodation is best conceived within the terms of hegemony. Thus, it has been argued that 'states will agree to specific forms of hegemonic leadership', and accordingly, 'hegemony is an institution that arises within an international society of states' (Cronin 2001: 108). In principle, hegemony can be legitimated within the context of international society as traditionally understood. In reality, many of those who speak of empire have precisely such an arrangement in mind. If the first US empire was one by invitation (Lundestad 1986), thought needs now to be given to the terms in which the second set is to be issued. How is such a legitimate hegemonic order to be devised?

LEGITIMACY AS JUST DISEQUILIBRIUM

The first US hegemony, during the cold war, was a highly selective affair: those in receipt of an invitation, and with whom the bargain had to be struck, were confined to Western Europe and a handful of strategic allies elsewhere. It was in relation to these states alone that the United States displayed strategic restraint in shaping its new constitutional order (Ikenberry 2001). If there is now to be yet another constitutional order, it must be more broadly based. The bargain cannot be restricted to clients within a particular camp, but must appeal to a broad cross-section of international society. From this perspective, the architecture for legitimizing US power in the new hegemony is substantially more complex and baroque than in the case of the first.

Those who assume that the legitimacy of US action is somehow a product of domestic factors (US power, and the democratic will of the Americans) make the very same mistake as those who conceive of US power as a domestic resource, possessed in isolation (Reus-Smit 2004*a*). Power is an attribute of a relationship, not a thing unilaterally possessed, in the same way as is legitimacy a characterization of a relationship between states, and not something produced by any one of them in isolation. The paradox then is that, as the wielder of the greatest potential power, the United States has the strongest incentive to establish widely accepted principles of legitimacy. As has been aptly noted, 'even the most powerful need to legitimize their power' (Hurrell 2002: 188–9). *Al-Ahram Weekly* approvingly quoted Zbigniew Brzezinski as saying: 'I am a great supporter of American power... But our power is not so enormous that we can afford progressively to lose the element of legitimacy of that power' (*Al-Ahram Weekly*, 6–12 February 2003). Nye has repeatedly enjoined the United States to provide global public goods because 'they legitimize our power in the eyes of others' (Nye 2002: 143–4). It is for exactly these reasons that the various critics of the Bush security policy have warned of its recent acts of unilateralism 'inviting a fundamental de-legitimation of American power' (Hendrickson 2002: 2). In the aftermath of the Iraq crisis, the German ambassador to the United States warned his US listeners that 'for such a superpower, multilateralism, functioning alliances, and strong international institutions are... fundamental components of a foreign policy based on legitimacy and consensus' (Ischinger 2004: 3).

What is at stake is not a narrowly conceived US interest in its own power, but the setting of US power in a framework that is acceptable to the broad range of other parties affected by it. In short, even if we are now in a second US hegemonic age, the terms of the invitation to participate remain crucial. We must return, at this point, to the norm of constitutionality as confronted in the previous chapter. It is this constitutionality that must lie at the heart of the acceptability of the order to the participants within it. Nye, once again, makes his case in terms of US interests. Conceding that multilateralism reduces US policy autonomy, he nonetheless points to the benefit to be derived from such a 'constitutional bargain', insofar as 'the multilateralism of US pre-eminence reduces the incentives for constructing alliances against America' (*International Herald Tribune*, 13 June 2002: 8). This remains then a balancing tactic, albeit by pre-emption, in a context wherein the hegemon might have been thought to have no need for such defensive action. That it nonetheless might see such a need is testimony both to the limits of its power, and to the *difference* that a United States policy of accommodation is able to make:

By exercising leadership through consensual institutions that give voice and satisfaction to the less powerful and that place modest constraints on its own policy autonomy and sovereign prerogatives, the United States can reassure weaker states that fear exploitation or abandonment, increase their willingness to follow the American lead, and consolidate a world order that promises to serve US interests even after America's dominance fades. (Patrick 2001: 11–12)

A situation of disequilibrium, such as currently exists, demands at the very least a return to constitutionality of this kind for legitimacy to pertain. This is, to be clear, a two-way process, and not simply a matter of the most powerful state making concessions to appease the weaker. Reciprocally, it needs to be based upon recognition of the requirements of leadership on the part of the predominant state. This is not just to kow-tow to US hegemony, nor is it to accept with resignation all of the vagaries of US policy. It is, however, to make realistic allowance for the leading role that the hegemon plays in the maintenance of international order as a whole. If, as English-school theorists have long held, the great powers enjoy certain special rights and responsibilities within international society, it follows likewise that there are special rights and responsibilities attached to a hegemon as well. Even those most worried by the recent directions of US policy explicitly draw attention to this side of the equation. '[T]he community cannot expect America to exercise self-restraint in support of community values, or to make sacrifices in support of its values', it has been aptly remarked, 'if the community trivializes the risks, costs and dangers that inhere in the US leadership role' (Leffler 2003: 1062). It should also be accepted that framing a constitutional order for hegemony is, without doubt, a harder political project than framing one for equilibrium.

This constitutionality should not be narrowly understood to refer solely to conduct within an institutional setting, such as at the UN. It pertains crucially to more informal settings, such as the multilateral deployment and use of armed force. This had been a vexed issue in the early 2000s. Reflecting upon various unhappy experiences in the conduct of the Kosovo war, the Bush administration was very guarded about committing itself to any formal involvement of allied organizations, such as NATO, in military operations. In the preferred idiom of the times, instead of the coalition determining the mission, it was to be the mission that would determine the scope and nature of the coalition. At one level, this could be regarded as just another illustration of US unilateralism since, in this latter case, 'Washington would not necessarily be bound by the view of its allies' (*Al-Ahram Weekly*, 6–12 February 2003). A powerful United States would thereby simply garner ad hoc support, as needed, and where it was to be found. On the other hand, the US—intent upon sidelining NATO with regard to Iraq, as it had over the war on terror more generally—still insisted upon a show of NATO loyalty in support of the US policy. Speaking ahead of the NATO summit that was held in Prague in November 2002, the US deputy national security adviser, Stephen Hadley, pointedly emphasized, with reference to Iraq, that 'the summit will be a valuable opportunity to show allied solidarity in the face of this common threat' (*The Times*, 4 October 2002: 19). While the US exercised discretion over the composition of the coalition, all were to feel equally committed to the value of the mission that this coalition devised. This was the inherent contradiction in the position. Nor was this a simple spat between erstwhile allies. What was at stake was not merely how to deal with the whims of US power, but whether in such a context it was at all possible to develop an acceptable framework for defining the nature, burdens, and recompenses of US leadership.

The point can be made in slightly different terms. What precisely is this constitutionality that needs to be restored? As we have already seen, the balance of power can be conceived in two distinct senses; first, as the raw distribution on the ground; second, as a moral acceptance of the idea of a balance of power as a collective good of international society. This was the important message that Morgenthau sought to deliver, however much it has subsequently been misunderstood. The principle of the balance of power facilitates the working of the balance of power, but in the end—and happily—adherence to the principle is reinforced by the actuality.

By analogy, much the same might be said of a condition of hegemony, but the connection in this case has rarely been explored or explained. In almost all discussions—including, importantly, the policy texts of the United States—its predominance or hegemony has been treated as a statement about the raw distribution on the ground. This pays no heed to its other dimension: a moral acceptance of an idea of hegemony as a constitutional practice of international society. Constitutionality specifies the duties that the United States must bear as the key upholder of community values; it stipulates also the duty of the remainder of international society to make full acknowledgment of the costs to the leading state entailed by this role. This is the core of the constitutional bargain to be sought, and it is rooted in a *principle* of hegemony, not simply a reality of hegemony. Only in this way is a just disequilibrium to be achieved. What makes the task so much more difficult of realization is that, unlike the balance of power, the reality of hegemony does not reinforce the principle, but is instead in constant tension with it.

CONCLUSION

The problem for legitimacy in contemporary international society does indeed reside in disequilibrium, but not in any straightforward sense. It is not simply a matter of international society coming to terms with the lack of a balance of power. Nor, for that matter, is it the case of international society having to adjust to the preferences and vagaries of US policy, as they variably reflect these underlying power conditions. Much more importantly, the contemporary idea of legitimacy attaches itself to a notion of acceptable leadership in conditions of hegemony. That is to say that it must be a leadership that is acceptable both to international society at large, and also to the predominant state called upon to play that role. If the current conditions of disequilibrium are treated merely as a raw distribution of power—as much of current US policy and its many realist publicists would have us believe—then the prospects for a generally acceptable constitutional order are far from bright. What is required additionally is that this actuality gives expression to a principle of hegemony that is broadly tolerable to most concerned and affected states.

It is not too much to say that the tribulations of international society in the early 2000s concern the basis on which the actuality of hegemony can be translated into an agreed principle: in Morgenthau's terms, we already have hegemony, but no moral consensus to sustain it. If such a moral consensus is the necessary underpinning of an effective hegemony, we remain still at some distance from its attainment. This has certainly handicapped the practice of legitimacy, and prevented the legitimation of major international undertakings, such as the war in Iraq. It may yet be far too gloomy to conclude that there remain no other accepted principles of legitimacy, or that this heralds the demise of international society altogether.

Conclusion

This study makes the case for IR to take legitimacy seriously. It registers this claim by locating legitimacy within the framework of international society, both as a theoretical construct and as a set of continuing historical practices. In the first place, it suggests that legitimacy is stripped of any meaning outside such a societal framework. Secondly, and conversely, it has developed the case that legitimacy constitutes international society: by studying its principles of international legitimacy—and how in turn these are translated into practice—we demonstrate that such a society exists. Where principles of legitimacy are to be found, the theoretical case for an international society is made; where there are practices of legitimacy, we can see the reality of international society on a day-to-day basis.

Even when the important role of legitimacy is already acknowledged, it is too often misunderstood. This is especially so in the confusion between legitimacy as a feature of international society, and legitimation which attaches to the acts performed in its name. The attainment of legitimate status is commonly treated as a matter of its direct correspondence to certain international norms. This fails to understand the extent to which legitimacy resides in the belief of international society and, as such, reflects the condition of international society at any one time: norms form part of that condition, but do not amount to its total sum. To appreciate why some claims to legitimacy are successfully made, we need to be aware also of other characteristics, including international society's notions and degrees of consensus, as well as its distribution of power.

WHY LEGITIMACY MATTERS

By way of summary, let us revisit the reasons—outlined at the beginning—why legitimacy might be thought to matter. The first was the view that the evolution of specific legitimacy formations forms the essential history of international society: if its systemic changes occur around its legitimacy principles, we can document significant stages in its development by this means. Second, this study has engaged more generally with claims that ideas shape state conduct: behaviour is influenced by prevailing principles of legitimacy, and IR needs to treat it seriously on this count. Third, we return to the purported relationship between legitimacy and stability, and to the pervasive argument that those international orders most successfully grounded in legitimacy best achieve stability. What conclusions can be reached about these claims in the light of this study?

Of the three, the first is least contentious. If it is, indeed, accepted that its principles of legitimacy constitute what is meant by international society, it follows readily that we can recount an important part of its history in these terms. For instance, the lineage of concepts about rightful membership provides a detailed account of shifting ideas about statehood, and how international society has acted as midwife to particular types of state. In the realm of rightful conduct, there is a rich history to be told about the role of great powers, and their relationship to the small. This emerges above all in the variable historical encounters with what is to count as an acceptable consensus, and how this has related in turn to other international norms.

There is one caveat in order. The focus throughout has been upon the discrete international society of states, but this is not, and never has been, a self-contained sphere. Although this survey has traced issues that have preoccupied the practitioners of international society at its moments of greatest historical challenge, there has been no assumption that such encounters have been driven exclusively by sources within international society, so narrowly conceived. International society has always been porous. Its early deliberations make no sense if thought to exclude traditions of natural law that insisted upon all humankind as members, not states alone. International society has been pushed and prodded by various facets of civil society throughout its history, including most obviously in the economic sphere (Teschke 2003). This interface looms larger than ever today, as international society interacts with other components of a world or global society (Clark 2003; Buzan 2004). A history of its legitimacy formations tells us a great deal indeed about what has been going on within international society; it does not tell us everything we need to know about what has been going on around it.

Second, any verdict on the relationship between legitimacy and state conduct is necessarily less straightforward. Those who hold that ideas matter in shaping behaviour regard legitimacy as both constraining and enabling: it both discourages states from acting in certain ways, while also permitting actions that would otherwise not have been possible. The idea of legitimacy does most certainly affect behaviour: only given acceptance of certain principles can a practice of legitimacy be formed at all. This, of course, does not translate into any universal prescription that, where principles of legitimacy are to be found, nobody transgresses set limits. The fact that we can identify particular crises of legitimacy—say after 1919, and again in the early 2000s—suggests that these frameworks are sometimes seriously challenged. However, the occurrence of these crises should not be misunderstood: they signify that the issues of legitimacy raised are highly significant for state practice, not that they are irrelevant. Had they been irrelevant, it is not apparent why there should have been any sense of crisis over their violation. As with other social rules and norms, principles of legitimacy are not nullified by acts of deviance (Farer 2003*b*). They may actually be reinforced as a result.

This, however, is only part of the point. In this study, we have been interested also in attempts to secure legitimation, whereby the actors seek to represent their actions, or the order more generally, as in conformity with core principles. This practice does not entail that all such claims are equally successful, but there could be no such practice at all without subscription to some rudimentary belief in the existence and value of those principles. What matters less is the outcomes of these individual claims to legitimation; of greater consequence is the identification of behaviour that acts *consciously to maintain an international society, defined by its principles of legitimacy, and reflects a belief in being bound by such a social enterprise.* It is in this more fundamental sense that the behaviour of states in relation to legitimacy is to be assessed. Where that commitment is widely present, we can say that an international society exists. Moreover, if states feel themselves so bound, then this means that their behaviour is already affected. This is not a claim that all actors necessarily conform to particular rules or norms of that society; nor does it mean that they will be uniformly successful in their efforts to secure legitimation by appeal to these rules and norms. If legitimacy affects behaviour, so likewise do the practices of legitimacy help to reconfigure its principles.

Third, there is the matter of legitimacy and stability. This is connected to the previous point. Only if legitimacy is assumed to shape behaviour in general could it be thought to affect behaviour by producing stability in particular. Nonetheless, this book has struck a sceptical note about the strong version of such claims. It does so not to disparage legitimacy, but to encourage an understanding of it in a particular light. It is not that legitimacy creates stability, but in stable conditions successful claims to legitimation are more likely to be secured. A logically similar version of the present argument has been set out cogently by Barker, with reference to regime legitimacy, in his dismissal of the notion that erosions of legitimacy *cause* crises and collapses of regimes. He objects to any conceptualization that the withdrawal of consent (and hence a legitimacy deficit) is a separate event from the governmental crisis in which it is thought to issue: that the one is causally related to the other. Instead, he argues that 'crises do not occur as a result of these events, but rather the confluence of those events is what a crisis is... Crises or erosion of legitimacy do not cause crises or erosions of government' (Barker 2001: 24). This is helpful, and is logically identical to the relationship between legitimacy and stability in an international setting. In the same way that erosion of legitimacy does not lead to crisis of government, so the bestowal of legitimacy does not cause international stability: it is but another way of describing such stability as already exists. In short, legitimacy and stability are not two separate, and causally related, political conditions.

The apparent circularity in Kissinger's argument is to make stability a con-sequence of great power agreement, while in effect explaining that agreement in terms of the stable conditions that have made it possible in the first place. He does this by defining a stable international order as in the interests of great powers, but this holds true only as long as it holds true. This was the objection that Hoffmann (1978) had long ago raised to Kissinger's reasoning. What was missing from it, Hoffmann complained, was that while it tells us 'what the order must be like in order *not* to induce a power to become revolutionary', it does not 'tell us how a revolutionary power is induced to accept a moderate world order'. In a stable international order, the great powers may well reach such agreement but Kissinger's analysis does not explain the conditions which make this possible, nor what role legitimacy can thereafter play in sustaining it. Legitimacy, so understood, is a restatement of an extant consensus (as long as it lasts), with no additional insight into why the consensus existed in the first place, nor any account of how it can inhibit its own demise. It is merely descriptive of stability, not an explanation of it. Indeed, it makes as much sense to argue that it is the stability of the order that gives rise to the possibility of shared principles of legitimacy, as it does to posit the causality working in the opposite direction.

The politics of legitimacy may indeed be associated with characteristics that we describe as stability, but it makes little sense to see this as the product of a causal relationship. These are not two separate sets of political conditions, the former resulting in the latter. They are the same state of affairs, otherwise described. Where there are principles of legitimacy, we can reasonably con-clude that international society exists. Where there is a high level of successful claims to legitimation, there will also be conditions favouring high levels of stability. However, it is those historical conditions that determine the legitim-ation, as well as the stability, rather than the existence of the principles of legitimacy as such.

To pull these points together we need to return to the continuing theme of legitimacy and its relationship to international society. What is it that justifies the claim that legitimacy is *primary* to a conception of international society, and what difference does it then make to think about the matter in this way? The book has presented first a historical, and second a theoretical, answer to those questions.

HISTORICAL INTERNATIONAL SOCIETY

Historically, we can map a gradual shift in the normative bases of legitimacy. In its earliest beginnings, legitimacy drew foremost from a moral-theological conception rooted in a divine cosmology. Increasingly, and mainly during the seventeenth and eighteenth centuries, legitimacy was attached to a conception of a legal order. From Vienna onwards, both of these were to some degree relegated by a notion of legitimacy located in constitutionality: it was what the great powers consensually agreed it to be. These shifts, however, should be viewed as ones of degree, not of kind. By the beginning of the twenty-first century, norms of constitutionality were of considerable importance, but they jostled alongside those of legality and morality, and had not displaced those others.

It is wholly artificial to imagine that there was any single moment when the European system of states suddenly coalesced into something that can be described as a European international society. What produced this was a gradual transformation extending over a considerable period of time. Nonetheless, a convincing case can be made that this formative period occurred during the sixteenth century and the first half of the seventeenth. As has been argued, it was this great age of discovery, and the practical agenda to which it gave rise, that generated a body of conscious reflection both upon Europe's relationship to the outer world, and concomitantly upon the nature of Europe's own sociability. We find in the arguments about 'legitimate possession' of the new lands, and the various titles to them, early treatments of the basis in legitimacy of any international society.

This was given more formal expression in the proceedings of the Peace of Westphalia. Its treaties have always enjoyed landmark status in the history of international relations, but largely for mistaken reasons. The claim that Westphalia was essentially about the elaboration and implementation of a modern doctrine of sovereignty is misplaced, or grossly overstated. At the time, if there was any 'consensus principle', it was rooted in a shared concept of legality, not in one of sovereignty. Even that, however, is not the key point. It matters less the precise principle through which the embryonic concept of international legitimacy was then expressed, and much more that there did emerge at this point a sense of underlying *bond* on which any such principle could then be based. It is in this sense alone that the European system, in Wight's formulation, 'came of age' at Westphalia. Instead of developing a systematic doctrine of sovereignty, Westphalia gave voice to 'the common bonds of society' and, in that way, stood for 'the constitutional foundation of international society' (Bull 1990: 93, 76).

Utrecht bore witness to the more mature international society of the early eighteenth century. Of its many salient points, two in particular stand out. With regard to rightful membership, Utrecht was highly significant in imposing an agreed principle of limitation upon the otherwise sacrosanct idea of legitimate dynastic succession: it did so with regard to the French, Spanish, and British crowns. Again, the significance of this lay not in what was decided about these crowns in particular, but in the prior acceptance that it was fit for international society to dispose of these entitlements. It could do so, secondly, on the agreed principle of rightful conduct of the time: namely, that the best interests of international society lay in the collective promotion of a balance of power. There was certainly no invention of any idea of balance in 1713. What Utrecht symbolized was the acceptance of this doctrine as an appropriate expression of international society's common bond.

Much of this agenda was revisited a century later at Vienna. On the face of it, Vienna enjoys a reputation as having in some key respects *revised* what had been done at Utrecht. This is especially so with regard to the treatment of rightful membership. The great principle deployed at Vienna, especially by Talleyrand, was precisely that of legitimacy, as a prescriptive entitlement to rule. This doctrine was itself a reinvention of the more traditional principle. However, Vienna's challenge to the Utrecht formula was more apparent than real: it certainly did not question the entitlement of international society so to dispose. Even Talleyrand acknowledged as much. 'No title of sovereignty', he conceded, '... has any reality for other states unless they recognise it' (Talleyrand 1996: 317). As a result, after 1815 'the legitimacy of states ... rested ... on the treaty system and its guarantees, backed by the consent of Europe' (Schroeder 1994: 578). Its doctrinal statements about legitimacy notwithstanding, Vienna did not disturb the principle already established at Utrecht.

Vienna was equally revealing in other areas. It went much further in formalizing a notion of consensus explicitly confined to the great powers, although appealing to the interests also of the small powers in making this stipulation. This was given a degree of institutional expression through the resulting concert. In this respect, Vienna edged the normative influences upon legitimacy away from legality and morality—as predominantly conceived in the seventeenth and eighteenth centuries—and increasingly towards the notion of constitutionality. This was to become the principal test of rightful conduct. At the same time, in presenting its arguments in the language of the quest for a just equilibrium, Vienna both acknowledged the need for a balance of power (as Utrecht had already done), and moved beyond it. A just equilibrium was to encompass much more than any simple, and material, balance of power. Once again, we can see in this formulation the imprint of the concerns with constitutionality.

Yet another century further along, international society essayed a much more ambitious programme, but achieved considerably less. Versailles appears to be the hard test case for the present discussion. If it is accepted that the settlement failed to establish a legitimate order (as so many say), does this mean that international society literally collapsed at that point? Any such suggestion can be rejected on the basis of the distinction between legitimacy in international society, and the construction of a legitimate order. Versailles certainly failed on the second score. It seems much less convincing that it consciously abandoned the international societal project altogether. So far was this from being the case that its main shortcoming was to push the project too far, not too little.

Its basic difficulty was its inability to generate a working consensus, either between victor and vanquished, or amongst the ranks of the victors themselves. The peacemakers were unable to overcome this fundamental condition, and to a degree further exacerbated it. This resulted in a palpable failure of legitimation—to make the claim to legitimacy stick; it did not signify that core principles of legitimacy, concerning rightful membership and rightful conduct, had been jettisoned. That we can discuss Versailles at all as creating an 'illegitimate' order makes sense only on the assumption that these principles remained intact; without them, how was any claim to illegitimacy to be sustained?

The heightened ambition shone through above all in the confident assertion of democracy as the key principle of rightful membership. The entire logic of the League was predicated on this. Unhappily, the forceful promotion of this requirement served to undercut other dimensions of legitimacy, such as universal membership. The principle had a greater purity; it resulted in a more restrictive practice. In the immediate term, this had a damaging impact on the format of the peace negotiations. If a consensual order required inclusion, the imposition of a test for democracy led to exclusion, and this tension ran through many facets of the peacemaking. In the longer term, this was to be equally costly for the efficacy of the League as well. Collective security required universality; a democratic principle of rightful membership pushed towards selectivity.

In retrospect, Versailles is a case of the ambitions of international society outstripping its real possibilities. These heightened ambitions were driven by political circumstance, arising out of the nature of the war. Its sheer scale and impact fundamentally destabilized the existing conception of a self-contained international society, and the peacemakers proved impotent to deal with the resulting pressures. International society was being challenged by more powerful forces from the outside: by the great surge of popular pressure created by the combustible experiences of war; by the spread of new ideologies that seemed to place people above states; and by the accumulated discontents brought about by rapid, and unevenly distributed, economic growth. The Great Experiment was born of the sheer scale of the problems then countenanced, not by any sensible appraisal of the possibilities for addressing them.

Finally, the settlement in the aftermath of the Second World War demonstrated further striking modifications in international society's practice of legitimacy. It reached a more complex set of compromises. First, it opened the prospect for a universal international society. Second—and to a degree paradoxically—there was pronounced continuity with the democratic criteria for rightful membership as established in 1919. Third, to this was added—with momentous implications for future international society—a much more explicit acknowledgement of human rights. Fourth, principles of legitimacy were functionally extended to embrace other forms of social protection, principally in the economic domain: embedded liberalism integrated the requirements for rightful membership and rightful conduct in the socio-economic sphere, going beyond the liberal peace as previously advocated by Wilson.

Elsewhere, the post-1945 settlement grappled with a more traditional agenda. In its attempt to resurrect collective security, it reconfigured the requirements for consensus in a more restrictive fashion, pushing ideas about constitutionality back towards the 1815 model. In practice, a workable implementation remained largely unattainable for the duration of the cold war.

There was instead a complex interweaving of two separate settlements, one to govern the bipolar order, and the other to address the novel developments within the West. Each embodied its own distinct set of legitimacy principles.

CONTEMPORARY INTERNATIONAL SOCIETY

In all these phases, the book has sought to demonstrate that its principles of legitimacy—instantiated in its politically mediated practices—gave substance to the existence of an international society. This same point can now be established in a more theoretical way. This was the explicit burden of the argument in Part II. In exploring the nature of legitimacy in contemporary international society, it suggested that—as previously—this has been expressed through principles of both rightful membership and rightful conduct. If anything, the stipulations under the former have become even more prominent since the end of the cold war. As the substance that holds international society together, legitimacy is a compound of various ingredients. Specifically, it is an amalgam of sundry normative claims. It is mediated through a quest for consensus. And it is influenced by distributions of power.

Principles of rightful membership have been expounded more vigorously since the end of the cold war. These have normally been presented as criteria of good governance, and as subscription to basic tenets of democratic rights. So visible has this tendency become that some international lawyers even speak of a democratic entitlement, to be supervised and acted upon by international society. The application of this set of principles has had the effect of bringing about renewed shrinkage in the scope of international society, as some states fail to meet its tests, and international society has become correspondingly more exclusionary as a result.

These conditions have been adduced largely to enhance respect for principles of rightful conduct, and to this extent there has been greater attempted integration of the two strands of legitimacy. This, however, has incurred costs. First, the greater the emphasis upon the democratic requirements for rightful membership, the greater the danger that some members—especially potent ones, such as the United States—will account for the legitimacy of their own actions solely in terms of domestic constitutional requirements. Second, the greater the integration between membership and conduct, the greater also has been the potential for tension between the two. They have increasingly fallen out of alignment, the more that membership criteria have conformed to soli-darist imperatives, while, at the same time, principles of conduct continue to respond to pluralist needs.

This has placed pressure on the concept of consensus from two distinct directions. The first is by the notion that a consensus within the democratic sector of international society may have some inherently greater cogency than a wider consensus amongst all members. Such an issue emerged during the course of the war in Kosovo in 1999. In the same way, consensus—as a largely procedural value—has also been subject to intensified scrutiny from the direction of shared substantive norms. As we have seen, consensus always opens up to normative considerations on the one side—what counts is *what* is agreed—while being subject to political arm-twisting and coercion towards the other. What matters in this latter case is *that* there is agreement, less so its content.

As a result, the always highly complex relationship between legitimacy and consensus has become, if anything, even more problematic still. Does a consensus emerge around courses of action that are deemed to be already legitimate (because of conformity to norms), and so does legitimacy spawn consensus? Or does the legitimacy reside in the consensus, and so is it the consensus that gives rise to legitimacy? Contemporary international society has, in practice, great difficulty sorting such ideas out, and has been quite inconsistent in its understandings of the position, as some of the case studies have revealed. Deep down, it is sharply torn between the choice that it is the basic values that matter—and the consensus is only secondary—as against a wish to prioritize the procedural rules, because that is where the consensus principle is most clearly expressed. A similar tension emerges in the various proposals to restructure the Security Council, especially as regards its permanent membership. Here, the antagonism expresses itself between a notion of representational legitimacy—the Council should be broadly representative of international society—as against its adherence to consensual legitimacy; it can effectively act only with consensus, and this is less likely to be achieved the wider the representation on it.

Throughout this study, the most consistently difficult task has been to reach a clear conceptualization—both in principle and in practice—of the relationship between legitimacy and other international norms. There is no doubt that legitimacy has an irreducibly normative quality. It remains, however, misleading to identify it with those norms. This is, however, a common misunderstanding. Legitimacy is often discussed as if it were a substantial scale of values, as with legality, morality, or constitutionality. It is frequently suggested that we can devise sets of 'legitimacy principles', in exactly the same way that we can codify the laws of war, or set out ethical principles for its just conduct. This confuses the relationship amongst the principles of legitimacy, the practice of legitimacy, and the claims to legitimation made on behalf of actors and particular actions. Specific normative principles are appealed to in the quest for such legitimation, and philosophical judgements made about the degree of conformity of an action to a particular normative rule. In practice, legitimacy is a factual matter about how international society perceives a situation: its degree of belief is open to normative persuasion, but may well not be fully determined by it.

In the early 2000s, and as epitomized by the events over Iraq, international society did suffer a crisis in its sense of legitimacy. This was encouraged above all by the apparent infringement of prevailing notions of constitutionality, more so than by any violation of legal and moral norms as such, as these remained ambivalent throughout. Such was this the case that the ruptures in the UN can be more properly regarded as the symptom of the crisis, rather than its substantial cause.

This led to the final area for consideration. Was it the case that the problematic encounter between consensus and norms—engendering a sense of crisis in the early years of the twenty-first century—was driven by the disequilibrium in power that had become so marked across the period? In turn, this opened up questions about whether it was the fact of US power—its hegemony—or rather its policy, and disagreements about its leadership role, that lay at the root of the problem. Morgenthau had argued that what was important was not just the actuality of a balance of power, but a moral consensus in support of it. In the same spirit, the book developed the argument that the fundamental problem was not American hegemony as such, but the failure as yet to develop a satisfactory *principle of hegemony*—rooted in a plausibly wide consensus—in which that actuality would be enshrined.

A common thread unites all these suggestions: an insistence upon the strong linkage between legitimacy and international society. This is necessary to enable us to distinguish between the core principles of legitimacy, and the strategies of legitimation pursued by individual actors. These spheres are separated by the practices of legitimacy that have been the principal focus of this book. In turn, this matters critically because we should never confuse legitimacy with the component elements that feed into its practice.

The abiding error is to treat legitimacy as a property of individual actions, and to imagine that we can set up criteria for assessing them in accordance with an independent legitimacy scale. This ignores the fact that legitimacy is a *social* property—not an attribute of an action. Those norms that feed into the claims to legitimation are mediated through politics and consensus. To ask whether a particular international action is legitimate is not to ask a question of moral philosophy or jurisprudence. It is to ask a factual question about how it is regarded by the members of international society—even if there is no easy factual answer to that question. One can devise sets of criteria for determining whether an action conforms to acceptable moral, legal, or constitutional standards or not. But we should not confuse this with its degree of legitimacy. This latter judgement is influenced by such norms, but is not determined by them alone. When they enter the realm of the practice of legitimacy, these norms encounter a complex universe of politics, consensus, and power. To imagine that this can be wholly governed by appeal to a set of principles is to impose a rationalist paradigm upon a politically indeterminate sphere. This is a recipe for disillusion and disenchantment. Setting up abstract principles is therefore not the same as the attainment of legitimacy, as this disregards the murky world of politics. To equate legitimacy with legal and moral principles is to pretend that the political task is thereby accomplished: this is where it starts, not where it finishes.

There are profound normative questions to be asked about all facets of international life, including its usage of force, for humanitarian and other purposes. It is wholly appropriate to debate these in terms of the best standards and criteria that we can devise. The great models here are the traditions of international law, and the cognate but independent tradition of just war. The quest for criteria to assess actions (on the use of force generally, or humanitarian intervention more specifically) draws directly upon both traditions, and has much to offer in this respect. What these do not, however, represent are criteria of legitimacy. To pretend that legitimacy can be pinned down in this way is to elide all politics from the process, and to conjure up an artificial image of what legitimacy entails.

In sum, we are led to acknowledge the essentially political, and hence indeterminate, nature of legitimacy. Far from making it less important to international society, recognition of this character makes it all the more so. The attainment of legitimacy is a practical political activity; it can be encouraged by appeal to specific normative principles, but it is not the same as them.

The point can be made with reference to the situation in Iraq. As of this writing (August 2004), the Security Council had unanimously passed resolution 1546 on 8 June 2004, endorsing arrangements for the transfer of authority to take place at the end of that month. From the division and acrimony of early 2003, the Security Council had re-emerged into the bright sunlight of unanimous agreement. Reports widely commented on the significance of this resolution as bestowing 'international legitimacy' on the arrangements for Iraq (*Independent*, 9 June 2004; *The Age*, 10 June 2004). Included amongst these, the Security Council charged the 'multinational force' with the responsibility to 'take all necessary measures to contribute to the maintenance of security and stability in Iraq'. There was some similarity here with the aftermath of Kosovo. Inasmuch as the Security Council then provided token retrospective authority for NATO's role, so SCR 1546—while certainly not condoning the war— acknowledged the role that outside forces could now play in providing for that country's security.

What brought about this change of heart? It was not that there had been some immense improvement in the situation in Iraq, nor that the former protagonists had become fully agreed about what was best to be done. If international action enjoyed in mid-2004 an acceptance that had been so demonstrably lacking fifteen months before, the change had taken place in the *disposition* of international society, not in the *facts* on the ground, nor in the *principles* in terms of which these facts were to be understood. It is safe to suggest that, by scrutiny of the norms of legality, morality, and constitutionality, one would have been unable to demonstrate the reason for this shift in international society's attitude.

This is the point in a nutshell. The practice of legitimacy signifies a point of political equilibrium, but there is much more to its determination than the validity of the normative principles to which appeal is made. Principles are mediated through consensus, and subject to the play of power. The outcome is inherently political.

In the case of Iraq, many considerations contributed to the new situation. All involved in the 2003 imbroglio had paid a heavy price for their actions. Germany and France experienced political and economic costs in their subsequent treatment by the United States. Both the US President and the British Prime Minister suffered substantial domestic political damage. Internationally, US standing massively eroded, as also did the credibility of the UN; there could be little doubt that the global war on terror, even on its own terms, had suffered a serious setback. Above all, the people of Iraq had a heavy price exacted from them, on account of the international divisions about what was to be done. The facts on the ground in mid-2004 no more corresponded with the requirements of legality, morality, and constitutionality than a year before. And yet, at least insofar as one key institution of international society was concerned, it now felt able to bestow its blessing upon the internal and international arrangements for that country. That blessing remains of critical importance to future outcomes, and that is why legitimacy matters so much. We should, however, have no illusions about what it signifies.

Those diverse costs were part of the political fallout from the Iraq crisis, but should not be understood as factors wholly independent of the workings of legitimacy. Instead, these costs are a measure of its importance. It is, of course, common to distinguish between compliance for reasons of legitimacy, and compliance for reasons of self-interest (Hurd 1999). To this extent, the avoidance of future costs may well be seen as self-interested behaviour that has nothing to do with legitimacy. This misses the central point: the costs are directly attributable to preceding failures of legitimation, and have been incurred because principles of legitimacy did matter to the actors concerned. It is not simply that the costs of unilateralism over Iraq have encouraged a return to multilateralism: unilateralism incurred costs in the first place because it had infringed generally held precepts about how affairs should be rightfully conducted, at a time when the predisposition of international society was to be especially sensitive to the issues of constitutionality that they raised. Norms matter, but so does the condition of international society when it responds to them.

In sum, there are three principal conclusions to emerge from this study. The first is that principles of legitimacy are integral to the concept of an international society. Second, the working through of these principles is part of the day-to-day practice of international society. Finally, because this is a realm of contested politics, there can be no direct appeal to superior international norms at this stage. Principles of legitimacy draw upon these other norms, but are at one remove from them, distanced as they are by the practice of legitimacy. This is what makes the attainment of legitimacy so highly indeterminate, but it is no less important for being so.

References

African Union (2000). *Constitutive Act of African Union*. 11 July, at www.africa-union.org.

Albrecht-Carrié, R. (1965). *A Diplomatic History of Europe since the Congress of Vienna*, 2nd edn. London.

—— (1968). *The Concert of Europe, 1815–1914*. New York.

Alderson, K. and Hurrell, A. (eds.) (2000a). *Hedley Bull on International Society*. Basingstoke.

—— (2000b). 'Introduction', in Alderson and Hurrell (2000a).

Alexandrowicz, C. (1967). *An Introduction to the History of the Law of Nations in the East Indies*. Oxford.

Anderson, M.S. (1972). *The Ascendancy of Europe: Aspects of European History, 1815–1914*. London.

—— (1976). *Europe in the Eighteenth Century*, 2nd edn. London.

—— (1993). *The Rise of Modern Diplomacy, 1450–1919*. London.

—— (1998). *Origins of the Modern European States System, 1494–1618*. London.

Applbaum, A. I. (2000). 'Culture, Identity, and Legitimacy', in Nye and Donohue (2000).

Arend, A. C. (1999). *Legal Rules and International Society*. New York.

Armitage, D. (ed.) (1998). *Theories of Empire, 1450–1800*, Vol. 20: *An Expanding World: The European Impact on World History 1450–1800*. Aldershot.

Armstrong, D. (1993). *Revolution and World Order: The Revolutionary State in International Society*. Oxford.

—— (1998). 'Globalization and the Social State', *Review of International Studies*, 24 (4).

—— (1999). 'Law, Justice and the Idea of a World Society', *International Affairs*, 75 (3).

Aron, R. (1966). *Peace and War: A Theory of International Relations*. New York.

—— (1974). *The Imperial Republic: The United States and the World, 1945–1973*. Englewood Cliffs, NJ.

Avalon (1996–). 'The Avalon Project at Yale Law School', at www.yale.edu/lawweb/avalon/westphal.htm.

Bain, W. (2003a). *Between Anarchy and Society: Trusteeship and the Obligations of Power*. Oxford.

—— (2003b). 'The Political Theory of Trusteeship and the Twilight of International Equality', *International Relations*, 17 (1).

Baker. R. S. (1923). *Woodrow Wilson and World Settlement*, 3 vols. London.

Barber, B. R. (2003). *Fear's Empire: War, Terrorism, and Democracy*. New York.

Barkawi, T. and Laffey, M. (2002). 'Retrieving the Imperial: *Empire* and International Relations', *Millennium*, 31 (1).

Barker, R. (1990). *Political Legitimacy and the State*. Oxford.

—— (2001). *Legitimating Identities: The Self-Presentations of Rulers and Subjects*. Cambridge.

Barnett, M. N. (1997). 'Bringing in the New World Order: Liberalism, Legitimacy, and the United Nations', *World Politics*, 49 (4).

Bartlett, C. J. (1996). *Peace, War and the European Powers, 1814–1914*. Basingstoke.

Beetham, D. (1991). *The Legitimation of Power*. Basingstoke.

—— and Lord, C. (1998). *Legitimacy and the EU*. London.

Bell, P. M. H. (1986). *The Origins of the Second World War in Europe*. London.

Bellamy, A. (2003). 'Humanitarian Responsibilities and Interventionist Claims in International Society', *Review of International Studies*, 29 (3).

—— (ed.) (2004). *International Society and its Critics*. Oxford.

Bély, L. (2000). 'La négociation comme idéal et comme art: un model westphalien?', in Bély and Richefort (2000).

—— and Richefort, I. (eds.). (2000). *L'Europe des traités de Westphalie*. Paris.

Berdal, M. (2003). 'The UN Security Council: Ineffective but Indispensable', *Survival*, 45 (2).

Bergin, J. (ed.) (2001). *Short Oxford History of Europe: The Seventeenth Century; Europe 1598–1715*. Oxford.

Bernard, J. F. (1973). *Talleyrand: A Biography*. London.

Black, J. (1990). *The Rise of the European Powers, 1679–1793*. London.

—— (2002). *European International Relations, 1648–1815*. Basingstoke.

Blair, T. (1999). 'PM's Speech: Doctrine of the International Community', Chicago, 24 April 1999, at www.number-10.gov.uk (visited 16 March 2004).

—— (2003a). 'PM Statement in Parliament Opening Iraq Debate', 18 March 2003, at www.number-10.gov.uk (visited 16 March 2004).

—— (2003b). 'Press Conference', 25 March 2003, at www.number-10.gov.uk (visited 16 March 2004).

—— (2003c). 'Jt Statement by PM Tony Blair and President Bush on future of Iraq', 8 April 2003, at www.number-10.gov.uk (visited 16 March 2004).

—— (2004). 'PM Warns of Continuing Global Terror Threat', 5 March 2004, at www.number-10.gov.uk (visited 10 March 2004).

—— (2002a). 'PM's Iraq Statement to Parliament', 24 September 2002, at www.number-10.gov.uk (visited 16 March 2004).

—— (2002b). 'PM Statement on Iraq Following UNSC Resolution', 8 November 2002, at www.number-10.gov.uk (visited 16 March 2004).

Blix, H. (2004). *Disarming Iraq: The Search for Weapons of Mass Destruction*. London.

Bobbitt, P. (2002). *The Shield of Achilles: War, Peace and the Course of History*. London.

Boemeke, M. F. (1998). 'Introduction', in Boemeke, Feldman, and Glaser (1998).

—— Feldman, G. D., and Glaser, E. (eds.). (1998). *The Treaty of Versailles: A Reassessment after 75 Years*. Cambridge.

Bolingbroke, Viscount H. St. J. (1932). *Letters in the Study and Use of History* (letters vi–viii). Cambridge.

Bolton, J. R. (2003). ' "Legitimacy" in International Affairs: The American Perspective. Theory and Operation', remarks to the Federalist Society, Washington, DC, 13 November 2003, at www.state.gov(visited 18 May 2004).

Bonney, R. (1991). *The European Dynastic States, 1494–1660*. Oxford.

Booth, K. (ed.) (2001). *The Kosovo Tragedy: The Human Rights Dimensions*. London.

—— and Dunne, T. (eds.) (2002). *Worlds in Collision: Terror and the Future of Global Order*. Basingstoke.

Bozeman, A. (1984). 'The International Order in a Multicultural World', in Bull and Watson (1984a).

Bridge, R. (1979). 'Allied Diplomacy in Peacetime; the Failure of the Congress "System", 1815–23', in Sked (1979a).

Broers, M. (1996). *Europe after Napoleon: Revolution, Reaction and Romanticism, 1814–1848*. Manchester.

Bromley, J. S. (ed.) (1971). *The Rise of Great Britain and Russia, 1688–1715/25: New Cambridge Modern History*, Vol. VI. Cambridge.

Brown, C. (1998). 'Contractarian Thought and the Constitution of International Society', in Mapel and Nardin (1998a).

—— (2001). 'World Society and the English School: An "International Society" Perspective on World Society', *European Journal of International Relations*, 7 (4).

—— (2002). *Sovereignty, Rights and Justice: International Political Theory Today*. Cambridge.

Buchanan, A. (1999). 'Recognitional Legitimacy and the State System', *Philosophy and Public Affairs*, 28.

—— (2003). 'Reforming the international law of humanitarian intervention', in Holzgrefe and Keohane (2003).

Bukovansky, M. (2002). *Legitimacy and Power Politics: The American and French Revolutions in International Political Culture*. Princeton, NJ.

Bull, H. (1977). *The Anarchical Society: A Study of Order in World Politics*. London.

—— (1984). 'The Revolt against the West', in Bull and Watson (1984a).

—— (1990). 'The Importance of Grotius in the Study of International Relations', in Bull, Kingsbury, and Roberts (1990).

—— and Watson, A. (eds.) (1984a). *The Expansion of International Society*. Oxford.

—— (1984b). 'Introduction' in Bull and Watson (1984a).

—— Kingsbury, B., and Roberts, A. (eds.) (1990). *Hugo Grotius and International Relations*. Oxford.

Bullen, R. (1979). 'France and Europe, 1815–48: The Problems of Defeat and Recovery', in Sked (1979a).

Burkhardt, J. (1998). 'The Summitless Pyramid: War Aims and Peace Compromise Among Europe's Universalist Powers', in Bussmann and Schilling (1998).

Bussmann, K. and Schilling, H. (eds.) (1998). *1648: War and Peace in Europe*, Vol. I. Münster.

Butler, P. F. (1978). 'Legitimacy in a States-System: Vattel's *Law of Nations*', in Donelan (ed.) (1978).

Buzan, B. (2004). *From International to World Society? English School Theory and the Social Structure of Globalization*. Cambridge.

Callinicos, A. (2002). 'The Actuality of Imperialism', *Millennium*, 31 (2).

Callières, F. De. (1983). *The Art of Diplomacy*. M. A. Keens-Soper and K. W. Schweizer (eds.). Leicester.

Cameron, R. (ed.). (1971). *Civilization since Waterloo: A Book of Source Readings*. Ithaca, NY.

Camilleri, J.A., Mahlrota, K., and Tehranian, M. (2000). *Reimagining the Future: Towards Democratic Governance*. Bundoora, Victoria.

Caplan, R. (2002). *A New Trusteeship? The International Administration of War-torn Territories*. IISS Adelphi Paper 341. Oxford.

Carlier, C. and Soutou, G. H. (eds.) (2001). *1918–1925: Comment Faire La Paix?* Paris.

Caron, D. D. (1993). 'The Legitimacy of the Collective Authority of the Security Council', *American Journal of International Law*, 87.

Cecil, A. (1923). *Metternich 1773–1859: A Study of his Period and Personality*. London.

Chace, J. (2002). 'Imperial America and the Common Interest', *World Policy Journal*, 19 (1).

Challener, R. D. (ed.) (1970). *Documents of Modern History: From Isolation to Containment 1921–1952*. London.

Charvet, J. (1998). 'International Society from a Contractarian Perspective', in Mapel and Nardin (1998*a*).

Chomsky, N. (1999). *The New Military Humanism: Lessons from Kosovo*. London.

—— (2000). *Rogue States: The Rule of Force in World Affairs*. London.

Clark, I. (1999). *Globalization and International Relations Theory*. Oxford.

—— (2001*a*). *The Post-Cold War Order: The Spoils of Peace*. Oxford.

—— (2001*b*). 'Another "double movement": the great transformation after the Cold War?', *Review of International Studies* 27 (special issue).

—— (2003). 'Legitimacy in a Global Order', *Review of International Sudies*, 29 (special issue).

—— and Neumann, I. (eds.) (1996). *Classical Theories of International Relations*. Basingstoke.

Claude, I. L. (1962). *Power and International Relations*. New York.

—— (1966). 'Collective Legitimization as a Political Function of the United Nations', *International Organization*, 20 (3).

Coicaud, J-M. (2001*a*). 'International Democratic Culture and Its Sources of Legitimacy: The Case of Collective Security and Peacekeeping Operations in the 1990s', in Coicaud and Heiskenen (2001).

—— (2001*b*). 'Conclusion', in Coicaud and Heiskenen (2001).

—— (2002). *Legitimacy and Politics: A Contribution to the Study of Political Right and Political Responsibility*. Cambridge.

—— and Heiskenen, V. (eds.) (2001). *The Legitimacy of International Organizations*. Tokyo.

Colas. A. (2002). *International Civil Society: Social Movements in World Politics*. Cambridge.

Connolly, W. (ed.) (1984*a*). *Legitimacy and the State*. Oxford.

—— (1984*b*). 'The Dilemma of Legitimacy', in Connolly (1984*a*).

Cooper, R. (2003). *The Breaking of Nations: Order and Chaos in the Twenty-First Century*. London.

Cox, M. (2003*a*). 'Commentary: Martians and Venutians in the New World Order', *International Affairs*, 79 (3).

—— (2003*b*). 'The Empire's Back in Town: Or America's Imperial Temptation—Again', *Millennium*, 32 (1).

——, Ikenberry, G. John, and Inoguchi, T. (eds.) (2000). *American Democracy Promotion: Impulses, Strategies, and Impacts*. New York.

Cox, R. W. (1981). 'Social Forces, States, and World Orders: Beyond International Relations Theory', *Millennium*, 10 (2).

—— (1996). *Approaches to World Order* (with T. J. Sinclair). Cambridge.

Cronin, B. (2001). 'The Paradox of Hegemony: America's Ambiguous Relationship with the United Nations', *European Journal of International Relations*, 7 (1).

Croxton, D. (1999*a*). *Peacemaking in Early Modern Europe: Cardinal Mazarin and the Congress of Westphalia*. Selinsgrove, NJ.

—— (1999*b*). 'The Peace of Westphalia of 1648 and the Origins of Sovereignty', *International History Review*, 21 (3).

—— and Tischer, A. (2002). *The Peace of Westphalia: A Historical Dictionary*. Westport, CT.

Dakin, D. (1979). 'The Congress of Vienna, 1814–15, and Its Antecedents', in Sked (1979*a*).

Daunton, M. and Halpern, R. (1999). *Empire and others: British Encounters with Indigenous Peoples, 1600–1850*. London.

Dennett, R. and Turner, R. K. (1948). *Documents on American Foreign Relations*, Vol. VIII. Princeton, NJ.

Donelan, M. (ed.) (1978). *The Reason of States*. London.

—— (1984). 'Spain and the Indies', in Bull and Watson (1984*a*).

Donnelly, J. (1993). *International Human Rights*. Boulder, CO.

—— (1998). 'Human rights: a new standard of civilization?', *International Affairs*, 74 (1).

—— (1999). 'The Social Construction of International Human Rights', in Dunne and Wheeler (1999).

—— (2002). 'Ancient Greece and international relations Theory' (Paper presented at BISA annual conference, London).

Doran, C. (1971). *The Politics of Assimilation: Hegemony and its Aftermath*. Baltimore, MD.

Doyle, W. (1978). *The Old European Order, 1660–1800*. Oxford.

Drayton, R. (2000). *Nature's Government: Science: Imperial Britain, and the 'Improvement' of the World*. New Haven, CT.

Duffield, M. (2001). *Global Governance and the New Wars: The Merging of Development and Security*. London.

Dunne, M. (2003). 'The United States, the United Nations and Iraq: "Multilateralism of a Kind"', *International Affairs*, 79 (2).

Dunne, T. (1998). *Inventing International Society: A History of the English School*. Basingstoke.

—— (2001). 'Sociological Investigations: Instrumental, Legitimist and Coercive Interpretations of International Society', *Millennium*, 30 (1).

—— (2003). 'Society and Hierarchy in International Relations', *International Relations*, 17 (3).

—— and Wheeler, N. J. (eds.) (1999). *Human Rights in Global Politics*. Cambridge.

Dyzenhaus, D. (1997). *Legality and Legitimacy: Carl Schmitt, Hans Kelsen and Hermann Heller in Weimar*. Oxford.

Elcock, H. (1972). *Portrait of a Decision: The Council of Four and the Treaty of Versailles*. London.

Elliott, J. H. (1970). *The Old World and the New, 1492–1650*. London.

—— (1992), 'A Europe of Composite Monarchies', *Past and Present*, 137.

—— (1998). 'War and Peace in Europe, 1618–1648', in Bussmann and Schilling (1998).

Evans, G. (2004). 'When is it Right to Fight? Legality, Legitimacy and the Use of Military Force'. Cyril Foster Lecture, 10 May, Oxford.

Falk, R. (1999). *Predatory Globalization: A Critique*. Cambridge.

—— (2003). *The Great Terror War*. Moreton-on-Marsh.

Farer, T. J. (2003a). 'Humanitarian Intervention Before and After 9/11: Legality and Legitimacy', in Holzgrefe and Keohane (2003).

—— (2003b). 'The Prospect for International Law and Order in the Wake of Iraq', *American Journal of International Law*, 97 (3).

Feinstein, L. and Slaughter, A-M. (2004). 'A Duty to Prevent', *Foreign Affairs*, 83 (1).

Ferrero, G. (1942). *The Principles of Power: The Great Political Crises of History*. New York.

Fierlbeck, K. (1998). *Globalizing Democracy: Power, Legitimacy, and the Interpretation of Democratic Ideas*. Manchester.

Filitov, A. M. (1996). 'Problems of Post-War Construction in Soviet Foreign Policy Conceptions during World War II', in Gori and Pons (1996).

Finnemore, M. (1996). *National Interests in International Society*. New York.

Foot, R. (2003). 'Introduction', in Foot, Gaddis, and Hurrell (2003).

—— , Gaddis, J. L., and Hurrell, A. (eds.) (2003). *Order and Justice in International Relations*. Oxford.

Forbes, I. and Hoffman, M. (eds.) (1993). *Political Theory, International Relations and the Ethics of Intervention*. Basingstoke.

Fox, G. H. and Roth, B. R. (2001). 'Democracy and International Law', *Review of International Studies*, 27 (3).

Franck, T. M., (1988). 'Legitimacy in the International System', *American Journal of International Law*, 82.

—— (1990). *The Power of Legitimacy Among Nations*. Oxford.

—— (1995). *Fairness in International Law and Institutions*. Oxford.

—— (2002). *Recourse to Force: State Action against Threats and Armed Attacks*. Cambridge.

Freedman, L. and Karsh, E. (1993). *The Gulf Conflict*. London.

Fry, G. and O'Hagan, J. (eds.) (2000). *Contending Images of World Politics*. Basingstoke.

Gaddis, J. L. (1997). *We Now Know: Rethinking Cold War History*. Oxford.

—— (1998). 'History, Grand Strategy and NATO Enlargement', *Survival* 40 (1).

George, D. Lloyd (1938). *The Truth about the Peace Treaties*. London.

Gelpi, C. (2003). *The Power of Legitimacy: Assessing the Role of Norms in Crisis Bargaining*. Princeton, NJ.

Gerhardt, V. (1998). 'On the Historical Significance of the Peace of Westphalia: Twelve Theses', in Bussmann and Schilling (1998).

Gilpin, R. (1981). *War and Change in World Politics*. Cambridge.

—— (2000). *The Challenge of Global Capitalism: The World Economy in the 21st Century*. Princeton, NJ.

Giry-Deloison, C. (2000). 'Westphalie 1648: l'Angleterre en marge de l'Europe', in Bély and Richefort (2000).

Goemans, H. E. (2000). *War and Punishment: The Causes of War Termination and the First World War*. Princeton, NJ.

Goldstein, J. and Keohane, R. (eds.) (1993). *Ideas and Foreign Policy: Beliefs, Institutions, and Political Change*. Ithaca, NY.

Gong, G. W. (1984a). *The Standard of 'Civilization' in International Society*. Oxford.

—— (1984b). 'China's Entry into International Society', in Bull and Watson (1984a).

Goodrich, L. M. and Carroll, M. J. (eds.) (1947). *Documents on American Foreign Relations*, Vol. VII. Princeton, NJ.

Gori, F. and Pons, S. (eds) (1996). *The Soviet Union and Europe in the Cold War 1945–53*. Basingstoke.

Grafstein, R. (1981). 'The Failure of Weber's Conception of Legitimacy', *Journal of Politics*, 43.

Grenville, J. A. S. (1974). *The Major International Treaties 1914–1973: A History and Guide with Texts*. London.

Grewe, W. G. (ed.) (1988). *Fontes Historiae Iuris Gentium*, Vol. 2: *1493–1815*. Berlin.

Gross, L. (1948). 'The Peace of Westphalia, 1648–1948', *American Journal of International Law*, 42.

Grotius, H. (1918). *On the Law of War and Peace*. Washington, DC.

Gulick, E. V. (1967). *Europe's Classical Balance of Power*. New York.

Guyatt, N. (2000). *Another American Century? The United States and the World after 2000*. London.

Guzzini, S. (2002). 'Foreign Policy without Diplomacy: The Bush Administration at a Crossroads', *International Relations*, 16 (2).

Haas, R. (1997). *The Reluctant Sheriff: The United States after the Cold War*. New York.

Habermas, J. (1976). *Legitimation Crisis*. London.

Hall, J. A. (1996). *International Orders*. Cambridge.

Hall, R. B. (1999). *National Collective Identity: Social Constructs and International Systems*. New York.

Halliday, F. (1999). *Revolution and World Politics: The Rise and Fall of the Sixth Great Power*. Basingstoke.

Hampson, F. O. (2002). *Madness in the Multitude: Human Security and World Disorder*. Don Mills, ON.

Hanke, L. (1965). *The Spanish Struggle for Justice in the Conquest of America*. Boston.

Hankey, Lord (1963). *The Supreme Control at the Paris Peace Conference 1919*. London.

Hardt, M. and Negri, A. (2001). *Empire*. Cambridge, MA

Hargreaves-Mawdsley, W. N. (1979). *Eighteenth-Century Spain 1700–1788: A Political, Diplomatic and Institutional History*. London.

Haslam, J. (2002). *No Virtue Like Necessity: Realist Thought in International Relations since Machiavelli*. New Haven, CT.

Hassner, P. (1993). 'Beyond Nationalism and Internationalism', *Survival*, 35 (2).

—— (2002), 'Definitions, Doctrines and Divergences', *The National Interest*, 69.

Hatton, R. (ed.) (1976). *Louis XIV and Europe*. London.

Headlam-Morley, J. (1972). *A Memoir of the Paris Peace Conference*. London.

Heeren, A. H. L. (1834). *A Manual of the History of the Political System of Europe and its Colonies*, 2 vols. Oxford.

Held, D. and McGrew, A. (eds.) (2002). *Governing Globalization*. Cambridge.

Helms, J. (2000/2001). 'American Sovereignty and the UN', *The National Interest*, 62.

Hendrickson, D. C. (2002). 'Toward Universal Empire: The Dangerous Quest for Absolute Security', *World Policy Journal*, 19 (3).

Henrikson, A. K. (2000). 'The Constraint of Legitimacy: The Legal and Institutional Framework of Euro-Atlantic Security', in Martin and Brawley (2000).

Hertslet, E. (ed.) (1875). *The Map of Europe by Treaty*, Vol. 1: *1814–1827*. London.

Higgins, R. (1994). *Problems and Process: International Law and How we Use It*. Oxford.

Hinsley, F. H. (1967). *Power and the Pursuit of Peace*. London.

Hirsh, M. (2003), *At War with Ourselves: Why America is Squandering its Chance to Build a Better World*. Oxford.

Hobden, S. and Hobson, J. M. (eds.) (2002). *Historical Sociology of International Relations*. Cambridge.

Hobson, J. M. and Seabrooke, L. (2001). 'Reimagining Weber: Constructing International Society and the Social Balance of Power', *European Journal of International Relations*, 7 (2).

Hoffmann, S. (1978). *Primacy or World Order: American Foreign Policy since the Cold War*. New York.

—— (1990). 'International Society', in Miller and Vincent (1990).

—— (2003). 'US-European Relations: Past and Future', *International Affairs*, 79 (5).

Holbraad, C. (1970). *The Concert of Europe: A Study in German and British International Theory, 1815–1914*. London.

Holden, B. (ed.) (1996). *The Ethical Dimensions of Global Change*. Basingstoke.

Holmes, S. (1982). 'Two Concepts of Legitimacy: France after the Revolution', *Political Theory*, 10 (2).

Holsti, K. J. (1991). *Peace and War: Armed Conflicts and International Order*. Cambridge.

Holzgrefe, J. L. and Keohane, R. (eds.) (2003). *Humanitarian Intervention: Ethical, Legal, and Political Dilemmas*. Cambridge.

House, E. M. (1926). *The Intimate Papers of Colonel House*, C. Seymour ed., 4 vols. London.

Howorth, J. (2003/4). 'France, Britain and the Euro-Atlantic Crisis', *Survival*, 45 (4).

Hurd, I. (1999). 'Legitimacy and Authority in International Politics', *International Organization*, 53 (2).

Hurrell, A. (1999). 'Security and Inequality', in Hurrell and Woods (1999).

—— (2002). ' "There are no Rules" (George W. Bush): International order after September 11', *International Relations*, 16 (2).

—— (2003). 'Order and Justice in International Relations: What is at Stake?', in Foot, Gaddis, and Hurrell (2003).

—— and Woods, N. (eds.) (1999). *Inequality, Globalization, and World Politics*. Oxford.

Ignatieff, M. (2003). *Empire Lite: Nation-Building in Bosnia, Kosovo and Afghanistan*. London.

Ikenberry, G. John (2001). *After Victory: Institutions, Strategic Restraint, and the Rebuilding of Order after Major Wars*. Princeton, NJ.

—— (2004). 'The End of the Neo-Conservative Moment', *Survival*, 46 (1).

Independent International Commission on Kosovo (2000). *The Kosovo Report: Conflict, International Response, Lessons Learned*. New York.

International Commission on Intervention and State Sovereignty (2001). *The Responsibility to Protect: Report*. Ottawa.

Ischinger, W. (2004). 'Transatlantic Power, Legitimacy, and Credibility', speech at Aspen Conference, 30 January, Lyon, at www.germany-info.org. (visited 19 May 2004).

Israel, F. L. (ed.) (1967). *Major Peace Treaties of Modern History: 1648–1967*, Vol. 1. New York.

Jackson, R. H. (2000). *The Global Covenant: Human Conduct in a World of States.* Oxford.

Jacobson, J. (1998). 'The Soviet Union and Versailles', in Boemeke, Feldman, and Glaser (1998).

Jervis, R. (2002). 'Correspondence: Institutionalized Disagreement', *International Security*, 27 (1).

Jones, J. R. (1980). *Britain and the World, 1649–1815.* Brighton.

Kagan, R. (2003). *Paradise and Power: America and Europe in the New World Order.* London.

—— (2004). 'America's Crisis of Legitimacy', *Foreign Affairs*, 83 (2).

—— and Kristol, W. (2000). 'The Present Danger', *The National Interest*, 59.

Kaiser, D. (1990). *Politics and War: European Conflict from Philip II to Hitler.* Cambridge, MA.

Kamen, H. (1969). *The War of Succession in Spain, 1700–15.* London.

Keal, P. (2000). 'An "International Society" ', in Fry and O'Hagan (2000).

—— (2003). *European Conquest and the Rights of Indigenous Peoples: The Moral Backwardness of International Society.* Cambridge.

Keene, E. (2002). *Beyond the Anarchical Society: Grotius, Colonialism and Order in World Politics.* Cambridge.

Kegley, C. W. and Raymond, G. A. (1999). *How Nations Make Peace.* Basingstoke.

Kennedy, P. (1988). *The Rise and Fall of the Great Powers: Economic Change and Military Competition from 1500 to 2000.* London.

Kennedy-Pipe, C. (1995). *Stalin's Cold War: Soviet Strategies in Europe, 1943 to 1956.* Manchester.

Kertesz, G. A. (ed.) (1968). *Documents in the Political History of the European Continent, 1815–1939.* Oxford.

Keylor, W. R. (1998). 'Versailles and International Diplomacy', in Boemeke, Feldman, and Glaser (1998).

Kingsbury, B. and Roberts, A. (1990). 'Introduction: Grotian Thought in International Relations', in Bull, Kingsbury, and Roberts (1990).

Kissinger, H. A. (1977). *A World Restored.* London.

—— (1995). *Diplomacy.* New York.

—— (2001). 'America at the Apex', *The National Interest*, 64.

Kitromilides, P. (1986). 'Enlightenment and Legitimacy', in Moulakis (1986).

Knutsen, T. L. (1999). *The Rise and Fall of World Orders.* Manchester.

Koskenniemi, M. (2002). *The Gentle Civilizer of Nations: The Rise and Fall of International Law.* Cambridge.

Kraehe, E. E. (1983). *Metternich's German Policy*, Vol. II: *The Congress of Vienna, 1814–1815.* Princeton, NJ.

Krasner, S. D. (1993). 'Westphalia and All That', in Goldstein and Keohane (1993).

—— (1995/6). 'Compromising Westphalia', *International Security*, 20 (3).

—— (1999). *Sovereignty: Organized Hypocrisy.* Princeton, NJ.

—— (2001). 'Rethinking the sovereign state model', *Review of International Studies*, 27 (special issue).

Krauthammer, C. (2003). 'The Unipolar Moment Revisited: America, the Benevolent Empire', in Sifry and Cerf (2003).

Kuhn, T. S. (1970). *The Structure of Scientific Revolutions*, 2nd edn. Chicago.

Lake, A. (1994). 'Confronting Backlash States', *Foreign Affairs*, 73 (2).

Lansing, R. (1921). *The Peace Negotiations: A Personal Narrative*. Boston.

Leffler, M. (2003). '9/11 and the Past and Future of American Foreign Policy', *International Affairs*, 79 (5).

Legg, L. G. (1925). *British Diplomatic Instructions, 1689–1789*, Vol. II: *France 1689–1721*. London.

Lentin, A. (1985). *Guilt at Versailles: Lloyd George and the Pre-History of Appeasement*. London.

Lesaffer, R. (ed.) (2004). *Peace Treaties and International Law in European History: From the Late Middle Ages to World War One*. Cambridge.

Linklater, A. (1999). 'The Evolving Spheres of International Justice', *International Affairs*, 75 (3).

—— (2000). 'The Good International Citizen and the Crisis in Kosovo', in Schnabel and Thakur (2000).

Little, R. (1996). 'Friedrich Gentz, Rationalism and the Balance of Power', in Clark and Neumann (1996).

Litwak, R. (2000). *Rogue States and US Foreign Policy: Containment after the Cold War*. Washington, DC.

Loth, W. (1996). 'Stalin's Plans for Post-War Germany', in Gori and Pons (1996).

Luard, E. (1992). *The Balance of Power: The System of International Relations, 1648–1815*. New York.

Lundestad, G. (1986). 'Empire by Invitation? The United States and Western Europe, 1945–1952', *Journal of Peace Research*, 23.

—— (1998). *'Empire' by Integration: The United States and European Integration*. Oxford.

Lyons, G. M. and Mastanduno, M. (eds.) (1995). *Beyond Westphalia? State Sovereignty and International Intervention*. Baltimore, MD.

MacFarlane, S. N. (2002). *Intervention in Contemporary World Politics*. IISS, Adelphi Paper 350. Oxford.

Maier, C. S. (1996). 'The Social and Political Premises of Peacemaking after 1919 and 1945'. Unpublished paper, Symposium on 'Altered Strategic Landscapes in the Twentieth Century', Yale University.

McKay, D. and Scott, H. M. (1983). *The Rise of the Great Powers, 1648–1815*. London.

Macmillan, M. (2001). *Peacemakers: The Paris Conference of 1919 and Its Attempt to End War*. London.

Malettke, K. (2000). 'Le concept de sécurité collective de Richelieu et les traités de paix de Westphalie', in Bély and Richefort (2000).

Mann, G. (1946). *Secretary of Europe: The Life of Friedrich Gentz, Enemy of Napoleon*. New Haven, CT.

Mantoux, P. (1955). *Les Délibérations du Conseil Des Quatre, 24 mars-28 juin 1919*, 2 vols. Paris.

—— (1964). *Paris Peace Conference 1919: Proceedings of the Council of Four*. Geneva.

Mapel, D. R. and Nardin, T. (eds.) (1998a). *International Society: Diverse Ethical Perspectives*. Princeton, NJ.

—— (1998b), 'Introduction', in Mapel and Nardin (1998a).

Marks, S. (2002). *The Ebbing of European Ascendancy: An International History of the World 1914–1945*. London.

Marston, F. S. (1944). *The Peace Conference of 1919: Organization and Procedure.* London.

Martel, G. (1998). 'A Comment', in Boemeke, Feldman, and Glaser (1998a).

Martin, P. and Brawley, M. R. (eds.) (2000). *Alliance Politics, Kosovo, and NATO's War: Allied Force or Forced Allies?* Basingstoke.

Mastny, V. (1996). *The Cold War and Soviet Insecurity: The Stalin Years.* New York.

Mattingley, G. (1955). *Renaissance Diplomacy.* Boston.

Mayall, J. (1990). *Nationalism and International Society.* Cambridge.

—— (2000). 'Democracy and International Society', *International Affairs*, 76 (1).

Mazarr, M. J. (2003). 'George W. Bush, Idealist', *International Affairs*, 79 (3).

Metternich, Prince de (1881). *Mémoires, Documents et L'Ecrits Divers*, 3rd edn. Paris.

Miller, J. D. B. and Vincent, J. (eds.) (1990). *Order and Violence: Hedley Bull and International Relations.* Oxford.

Minchev, O. (2000). 'The Kosovo Crisis and the International System: Issues of Legitimacy and Actors' Motivation'. Paper presented at ISA 41st annual convention, 14–18 March, Los Angeles, at www.ciaonet.org/isa/m1001 (visited 7 February 2003).

Mommsen, W. J. (1998). 'Max Weber and the Peace Treaty of Versailles', in Boemeke, Feldman, and Glaser (1998).

Morgenthau, H. J. (1973). *Politics Among Nations*, 5th edn. New York.

Moulakis, A. (ed.) (1986a). *Legitimacy/Legitimé.* Berlin.

—— (1986b). 'Introduction', in Moulakis (1986a).

Mowat, R. B. (1928). *A History of European Diplomacy, 1451–1789.* London.

Mueller, C. (1973). *The Politics of Communication: A Study in the Political Sociology of Language, Socialization and Legitimation.* New York.

Muldoon, J. (1994). *The Americas in the Spanish World Order: The Justification for Conquest in the Seventeenth Century.* Philadelphia.

Murphy, C. N. (2000). 'Global Governance: Poorly Done and Poorly Understood', *International Affairs*, 76 (4).

Murphy, S. (1994). 'The Security Council, Legitimacy and the Concept of Collective Security after the Cold War', *Columbia Journal of Transnational Law*, 32.

—— (1999). 'Democratic Legitimacy and the Recognition of States and Governments', *International and Comparative Law Quarterly*, 48.

Namier, L. B. (1958). *Vanished Supremacies: Essays on European History, 1812–1918.* London.

Nardin, T., (1993). *Law, Morality and the Relations of States.* Princeton, NJ.

—— (1998). 'Legal Positivism as a Theory of International Society', in Mapel and Nardin (1998a).

Nau, H. R. (2002). 'Correspondence: Institutionalized Disagreements', *International Security*, 27 (1).

Neumann, I. B. and Welsh, J. M. (1991). 'The Other in European self-definition: an addendum to the literature on international society', *Review of International Studies*, 17 (4).

Nichols, I. C. (1971). *The European Pentarchy and the Congress of Verona, 1822.* The Hague.

Nicolson, H. (1946). *The Congress of Vienna: A Study in Allied Unity, 1812–1822.* London.

Nye, J. S. (2002). *The Paradox of American Power: Why the World's Only Superpower Can't Go it Alone.* Oxford.

—— and Donohue, J. D. (eds.) (2000). *Governance in a Globalizing World.* Washington, DC.

Onuf, N. G. (1998). *The Republican Legacy in International Thought.* Cambridge.

Organization of American States (2001). *Inter-American Democratic Charter,* 11 September, at www.oas.org.

Osiander, A. (1994). *The States System of Europe 1640–1990: Peacemaking and the Condition of International Stability.* Oxford.

—— (2001). 'Sovereignty, International Relations, and the Westphalian Myth', *International Organization,* 55 (2).

Owen, J. M. (2001/2). 'Transnational Liberalism and U.S. primacy', *International Security,* 26 (3).

Pagden, A., (1993). *European Encounters with the New World from Renaissance to Romanticism.* New Haven, CT.

—— (1995). *Lords of All the World: Ideologies of Empire in Spain, Britain and France, c1500–c1800.* New Haven, CT.

—— (ed.) (2002a). *The Idea of Europe: from antiquity to the European Union.* Cambridge.

—— (2002b), 'Introduction', in Pagden (2002a).

Palmer, A. (1983). *The Chancelleries of Europe.* London.

Paris, R. (2002). 'International Peacebuilding and the "Mission Civilisatrice" ', *Review of International Studies,* 28 (4).

Parker, G. (1987). *The Thirty Years' War.* London.

Parrott, D. (2001). 'War and International Relations', in Bergin (2001).

Parry, C. (1969). *Consolidated Treaty Series.* Dobbs Ferry, NY.

Partridge, P. H. (1971). *Consent and Consensus.* London.

Patrick, S. (2001). 'Don't Fence Me In: The Perils of Going it Alone', *World Policy Journal,* 18 (3).

—— (2002). 'More Power to You: Strategic Restraint, Democracy Promotion, and American Primacy', *International Studies Review,* 4 (1).

Petrie, C. (1946). *Diplomatic History, 1713–1933.* London.

—— (1949). *Earlier Diplomatic History, 1492–1713.* London.

Pfaff, W. (2001). 'The Question of Hegemony', *Foreign Affairs,* 80 (1).

Philipps, W. A. (1914). *The Confederation of Europe.* London.

Philpott, D. (2001). *Revolutions in Sovereignty: How Ideas Shape Modern International Relations.* Princeton, NJ.

Pitt, H. G. (1971). 'The Pacification of Utrecht', in Bromley (1971).

Pocock, J. G. A. (2002). 'Some Europes in Their History', in Pagden (2002a).

Polisensky, J. V. (1971). *The Thirty Years War.* London.

Pomerance, M. (2002). 'US Multilateralism, Left and Right', *Orbis,* 46 (2).

Preece, J. J. (1998). *National Minorities and the European Nation-States System.* Oxford.

Pugh, M. (2002). 'Maintaining Peace and Security', in Held and McGrew (2002).

Raack, R. C. (1995). *Stalin's Drive to the West, 1938–1945: The Origins of the Cold War.* Stanford, CA.

Rabb, T. K. (1975). *The Struggle for Stability in Early Modern Europe.* New York.

Randle, R. F. (1973). *Origins of Peace: A Study of Peacemaking and the Structure of Peace Settlements.* New York.

Rescher, N. (1993). *Pluralism: Against the Demand for Consensus*. Oxford.

Reus-Smit, C. (1997). 'The Constitutional Structure of International Society and the Nature of Fundamental Institutions', *International Organization*, 51 (4).

—— (1999). *Moral Purpose of the State*. Princeton, NJ.

—— (2001). 'Human Rights and the Social Construction of Sovereignty', *Review of International Studies*, 27 (4).

—— (2002), 'The Idea of History and History with Ideas', in Hobden and Hobson (2002).

—— (2003). 'Politics and International Legal Obligation', *European Journal of International Relations*, 9 (4).

—— (2004*a*), *American Power and World Order*. Cambridge.

—— (2004*b*) (ed.), *The Politics of International Law*. Cambridge.

—— (2004*c*), 'Introduction', in Reus-Smit (2004*b*).

—— (2004*d*), 'Society, power, and ethics', in Reus-Smit (2004*b*).

Rice, C. (2000). 'Promoting the National Interest', *Foreign Affairs*, 79 (1).

Richardson, J. L. (1994). *Crisis Diplomacy: The Great Powers since the Mid-Nineteenth Century*. Cambridge.

Roberts, A. (1999). 'NATO's "Humanitarian War" over Kosovo', *Survival*, 41 (3).

—— (2003). 'Law and the Use of Force after Iraq', *Survival*, 45 (2).

Roberts, B. (ed.). (1995). *Order and Disorder after the Cold War: A Washington Quarterly Reader*. Cambridge, MA.

Roberts, P. (1947). *The Quest for Security, 1715–1740*. New York.

Robinson, F. (1999). 'Globalising Liberalism? Morality and Legitimacy in a Liberal Global Order', in Shaw (1999).

Rodman, P. W. (2000). 'The World's Resentment: Anti-Americanism as a Global Phenomenon', *The National Interest*, 60.

Rölling, B. V. A. (1990). 'Are Grotius' Ideas Obsolete in an Expanded World?', in Bull, Kingsbury, and Roberts (1990).

Rosecrance, R. (2002). 'International security and the virtual state', *Review of International Studies*, 28 (3).

Rosenau, J. and Czempiel, E-O. (eds.). (1992) *Governance without Government: Order and Change in World Politics*. Cambridge.

Rosenberg, J. (1994). *The Empire of Civil Society: A Critique of the Realist Theory of International Relations*. London.

Ruggie, J. G. (1998). *Constructing the World Polity: Essays on International Instutionalization*. London.

Rule, J. C. (1976). 'Colbert de Torcy, an Emergent Bureaucracy, and the Formulation of French Foreign Policy 1698–1715', in Hatton (1976).

Sadeniemi, P. (1995). *Principles of Legitimacy and International Relations*. Helsinki.

Sato, T. (2001). 'The Legitimacy of Security Council activities under Chapter VII of the UN Charter Since the End of the Cold War', in Coicaud and Heiskenen (2001).

Sauvigny, G. de (1962). *Metternich and His Times*. London.

Schabert, T. (1986). 'Power, Legitimacy and Truth: Reflections on the Impossibility to Legitimise Legitimations of Political Order', in Moulakis (1986).

Schenk, H. G. (1947), *The Aftermath of the Napoleonic Wars: The Concert of Europe— An Experiment*. London.

Schilling, H. (1998). 'War and Peace at the Emergence of Modernity—Europe between State belligerence, religious wars, and the desire for peace', in Bussmann and Schilling (1998).

Schmidt, G. (1998). 'The Peace of Westphalia as the Fundamental Law of the Complementary Empire-State', in Bussmann and Schilling (1998).

Schnabel, A. and Thakur, R. (eds.). (2000) *Kosovo and the Challenge of Humanitarian Intervention*. Tokyo.

Schroeder, P. W. (1989). 'Nineteenth century System: balance of Power or Political Equilibrium', *Review of International Studies*, 15 (2).

—— (1992). 'Did the Vienna settlement rest on a balance of power?', *American Historical Review*, 97.

—— (1994). *The Transformation of European Politics, 1763–1848*. Oxford.

—— (1995). 'A New World Order: A Historical Perspective', in Roberts (1995).

Schulzinger, R. D. (1994). *American Diplomacy in the Twentieth Century*, 3rd edn. New York.

Schwabe, K. (1998). 'Germany's Peace Aims: Domestic and International Constraints', in Boemeke, Feldman, and Glaser (1998).

Scott, J. B. (1934). *The Spanish Origin of International Law: Francisco de Vitoria and his Law of Nations*. Oxford.

Sharp, A. (1991). *The Versailles Settlement: Peacemaking in Paris, 1919*. Basingstoke.

Shaw, M. (ed.). (1999) *Politics and Globalization: Knowledge, Etics and Agency*. London.

—— (2000), *Theory of the Global State: Globality as an Unfinished Revolution*. Cambridge.

—— (2002), 'Post-Imperial and Quasi-Imperial', *Millennium*, 31 (2).

Shennan, J. H. (1995). *International Relations in Europe, 1689–1789*. London.

Sifry, M. L. and Cerf, C. (eds.) (2003). *The Iraq War Reader: History, Documents, Opinions*. New York.

Simpson, G. J. (2004). *Great Powers and Outlaw States: Unequal Sovereigns in the International Legal Order*. New York.

Sked, A. (ed.). (1979a) *Europe's Balance of Power*. London.

—— (1979b). 'Introduction', in Sked (1979a).

Slocombe, W. B. (2003). 'Force, Pre-emption and Legitimacy', *Survival*, 45 (1).

Smith, M. J. (2003). 'Sovereignty, Human Rights and Legitimacy in the Post-Cold War World', at www.faculty.virginia.edu/irandhumanrights (visited 7 February 2003).

Soutou, G-H (2001). 'L'ordre européen de Versailles à Locarno', in Carlier and Soutou (2001).

Spencer, M. E. (1970), 'Weber on Legitimate Norms and Authority', *British Journal of Sociology*, 21 (2).

Spruyt, H. (1994). *The Sovereign State and its Competitors: An Analysis of Systems Change*. Princeton, NJ.

Steiger, H. (1998). 'Concrete Peace and General Order: The Legal Meaning of the Treaties of 24 October 1648', in Bussmann and Schilling (1998).

Sternberg, D. (1968). 'Legitimacy', *International Encyclopaedia of the Social Sciences*. New York.

Stevenson, D. (1998). 'French War Aims and Peace Planning', in Boemeke, Feldman, and Glaser (1998).

Sturdy, D. J. (2002). *Fractured Europe, 1600–1721*. Oxford.

Suganami, H. (1990). 'International Equality', in Bull, Kingsbury, and Roberts (1990).

Symcox, G. (ed.) (1974). *War, Diplomacy, and Imperialism, 1618–1763*. London.

Talbott, S. (2003). 'War in Iraq, Revolution in America', *International Affairs*, 79 (5).

Talleyrand, Prince de (1891). *Mémoires* (Le Duc de Broglie, 5 vols). Paris.

—— (1996). *Mémoires: L'époque napoléonienne* (J. Tulard ed.). Paris.

Tardieu, A. (1921). *The Truth about the Treaty*. London.

Temperley, H. W. V. (ed.). (1920–4) *A History of the Peace Conference of Paris* (reproduced 1969). London.

Teschke, B. (2003). *The Myth of 1648: Class, Geopolitics, and the Making of Modern International Relations*. London.

Thakur, R. and Schnabel, A. (2000). 'Unbridled Humanitarianism: Between Justice, Power, and Authority', in Schnabel and Thakur (2000).

Todorov, T. (1984). *The Conquest of America: The Question of the Other*. New York.

Torcy, Marquis de (1757). *Mémoires de Torcy pour server à l'histoire des négociations, Depuis le Traité de Ryswyck jusqu'à la Paix d'Utrecht*, 3 vol. London.

Towle, P. (1997). *Enforced Disarmament: From the Napoleonic Campaigns to the Gulf War*. Oxford.

Trachtenberg, M. (1999). *A Constructed Peace: The Making of the European Settlement 1945–1963*. Princeton, NJ.

United Nations Department of Public Information (UNDPI) (1995). *Yearbook of the United Nations Special Edition: UN Fiftieth Anniversary 1945–1995*. The Hague.

United Nations Information Organizations (UNIO) (1945). *United Nations Conference on International Organization: Documents, VIII Dumbarton Oaks*. New York.

United States National Security Council (USNSC) (2002). 'The National Security Strategy of the United States of America', at www.whitehouse.gov/nsc(visited 24 October 2003).

Vattel, E. de (1916). *The Law of Nations or the Principles of Natural Law*. Washington, DC.

Victoria, F. de (1918), *De Indis et de Iure Belli Rectiones*. Washington, DC.

Vincent, R. J. (1984a), 'Edmund Burke and the Theory of International Relations', *Review of International Studies*, 10 (3).

—— (1984b), 'Racial Equality', in Bull and Watson (1984a).

—— and Wilson, P. (1993), 'Beyond Non-Intervention', in Forbes and Hoffman (1993).

Von Laue, T. H. (1987). *The World Revolution of Westernization: The Twentieth Century in Global Perspective*. New York.

Walker, M. (ed.). (1968) *Metternich's Europe*. London.

Walker, R. B. J. (1993). *Inside/Outside: International Relations as Political Theory*. Cambridge.

Waltz, K. (1979), *Theory of International Politics*. London.

Watson, A. (1984). 'European International Society and its Expansion', in Bull and Watson (1984a).

—— (1992). *The Evolution of International Society*. London.

Weber, M. (1968a). *Economy and Society: An Outline of Interpretive Sociology*. Berkeley, CA.

—— (1968b). *On Charisma and Institution Building* (S. N. Eisenstadt ed.). Chicago.

Webster, C. K. (ed.) (1921). *British Diplomacy 1813–15: Select Documents Dealing with the Reconstruction of Europe*. London.

—— (1929). *The European Alliance, 1815–1825*. Calcutta.

—— (1931). *The Foreign Policy of Castlereagh 1812–1815: Britain and the Reconstruction of Europe*. London.

Webster, C. K. (ed.). (1945). *The Congress of Vienna, 1814–15*, 2nd edn. London.

Weller, M. (1999/2000). 'The US, Iraq, and the Use of Force in a Unipolar World', *Survival*, 41 (4).

Welsh, J. M. (1996). 'Edmund Burke and the Commonwealth of Europe: The Cultural Bases of International Order', in Clark and Neumann (1996).

—— (1999). *Social Theory of International Politics*. Cambridge.

Wendt, A. (1995). 'Constructing International Politics', *International Security*, 20 (1).

Weston, B. H. (1991). 'Security Council Resolution 678 and Persian Gulf Decision Making: Precarious Legitimacy', *American Journal of International Law*, 85.

Wheeler, N. J. (1992). 'Pluralist or Solidarist Conceptions of International Society: Bull and Vincent on Humanitarian Intervention', *Millennium*, 17 (2).

—— (2000). *Saving Strangers: Humanitarian Intervention in International Society*. Oxford.

—— (2001*a*). 'Humanitarian intervention after Kosovo: Emergent Norm, Moral Duty or the Coming Anarchy?', *International Affairs*, 77 (1).

—— (2001*b*). 'Reflections on the Legality and Legitimacy of NATO's Intervention in Kosovo', in Booth (2001).

—— (2003). 'The Bush Doctrine: The Dangers of American Exceptionalism in a Revolutionary Age', *Asian Perspective*, 27 (4).

—— and Dunne, T. (1996). 'Hedley Bull's Pluralism of the Intellect and Solidarism of the Will', *International Affairs*, 72 (1).

Wight, M. (1972). 'International Legitimacy', *International Relations*, 4 (1).

—— (1977). *Systems of States* (H. Bull ed.). Leicester.

—— (1991). *International Theory: The Three Traditions* (Wight and Porter eds.). Leicester.

Willhoite, F. (1963). 'Political Order and Consensus: A Continuing Problem', *Western Political Quarterly*, 16 (2).

Williams, A. (1998). *Failed Imagination? New World Orders of the Twentieth Century*. Manchester.

Williams, J. (1996). 'Nothing Succeeds Like Success? Legitimacy in International Relations', in Holden (1996).

—— (1998). *Legitimacy in International Relations and the Rise and Fall of Yugoslavia*. London.

Wolf, J. B. (1962). *The Emergence of the Great Powers, 1685–1715*. New York.

Wolfowitz, P. (2000). 'Remembering the Future', *The National Interest*, 59.

Wyduckel, D. (1998). 'The Imperial Constitution and the Imperial Doctrine of Public Law: Facing the institutional challenge of the peace of Westphalia', in Bussmann and Schilling (1998).

Youngs, R. (2001). *The European Union and the Promotion of Democracy*. Oxford.

Zacher, M. (1992). 'The Decaying Pillars of the Westphalian Temple: Implications for International Order and Governance', in Rosenau and Czempiel (1992).

Zakaria, F. (2002). 'Our Way: The Trouble with Being the World's Only Superpower', *New Yorker*, 14 & 21 October.

Index

Printed in Great Britain
by Amazon.co.uk, Ltd.,
Marston Gate.